Exercises for AS Level
Psychology

Grahame Hill

OXFORD

UNIVERSITY PRESS

OXFORD

UNIVERSITY PRESS

Great Clarendon Street, Oxford OX2 6DP

Oxford University Press is a department of the University of Oxford.
It furthers the University's objective of excellence in research, scholarship,
and education by publishing worldwide in

Oxford New York

Auckland Bangkok Buenos Aires Cape Town Chennai
Dar es Salaam Delhi Hong Kong Istanbul Karachi Kolkata
Kuala Lumpur Madrid Melbourne Mexico City Mumbai Nairobi
São Paulo Shanghai Taipei Tokyo Toronto

Oxford is a registered trade mark of Oxford University Press
in the UK and in certain other countries

British Library Cataloguing in Publication Data

Data available

ISBN 0 19 832822 2

10 9 8 7 6 5 4 3 2 1

Illustrated by Oxford Illustrators, Angela Lumley and Stephen Preedy

Typeset by Blenheim Colour Ltd, Eynsham, Oxford

Printed in Great Britain by Ebenezer Baylis, Worcester

For mum and dad
Love and thanks for all the support and encouragement to:
Valerie, The Hills, Hillwoods and Férecs, Don, David, and the local people.

Contents

How to use this book

The exercises in this book typically consist of stimulus material on a psychological topic, together with questions to elicit the analysis and evaluation of that material. The questions are designed so that readers who are new to psychology can use their own knowledge and evaluative skills, with the clues in the text, to answer them.

Some questions are straightforward and easy to answer, while others are more challenging or discursive and may require an educated guess or opinion. Do not be put off by the questions; although some do have specific or 'correct' answers, others may have more than one answer – indeed, psychologists are often divided in their opinions on certain topics or issues.

The stimulus material and questions are followed (usually on turning the page) by a 'teacher's answer' which will introduce the evaluative points that psychologists have made on the topics. Do not be tempted to peek at the answers before having a go at the questions yourself! That way you can develop your own evaluative skills, and the psychologists' answers will have more meaning for you (thus helping you remember the material, as you will see in the exercises on 'memory').

The stimulus material in the exercises, therefore, provides factual knowledge on psychological concepts, issues, theories and studies, while the questions serve to encourage the evaluation or discussion of them – both important factors for learning AS and A level psychology. Also provided are activities such as crosswords, anagrams and summary charts to help consolidate and revise your knowledge (and spelling) of the subject matter. The answers for these review activities are at the back of the book.

Although each exercise can be considered separately, the book is ordered so that the earlier exercises provide certain background information which may help you to answer the questions in the later exercises.

A note on the role of the teacher

Exercises for AS level psychology is suitable for the independent reader and for use as a class text. Although 'teacher's answers' are provided to inform you of how psychologists analyse, evaluate and apply psychological concepts, issues, theories and findings, you will gain more from this book by using it in class with your own teacher. Your teacher will, of course, be familiar with the knowledge and evaluation contained in this book, but may want to introduce you to alternative theories, studies, applications or issues that there was not room to cover in this book. In addition, your teacher may want to provide more detail, evaluation or other points of view, and will help you get the most out of class discussions (especially with a few hints for the more difficult questions!).

One of the most important functions of your teacher, however, is to help you to prepare for any examinations you might want to take. This book helps you to acquire psychological knowledge and skills, but you must also be able to apply these to the specific demands of the examination papers set by whichever examination board specification you are following. If you are an independent reader without a teacher and want to take an examination, you should get an examination board specification with example examination papers to practise and to see how you will be tested and marked.

A note on the different examination board specifications (syllabuses)

The topics covered by this book are mostly those tested at AS level in psychology. However, because of the degree of variation between the specifications offered by the different examination boards, you will find that the material covered by an exercise in this book may be tested in the AS examination of one specification and in the A level (second year) of another. Also, it might not be tested directly at all, or might represent only good background reading, in some specifications. Overall, however, you will find that the exercises in this book cover material relevant to the AQA Specification A, Edexcel and OCR AS level specifications in psychology. Some content may also apply to the AQA Specification B.

1 | What is psychology?

Definitions

The word 'psychology' is derived from two Greek roots: 'psyche', meaning 'mind' or 'soul', and 'logos', meaning 'study of'. Psychology, therefore, literally means 'study of the mind', though a more recent definition by Atkinson et al (1991) suggests that it is:

'the scientific study of behaviour and mental processes'

Essentially, psychology investigates how, when and why we think, feel and behave as we do. It is an extremely wide-ranging subject, since psychologists investigate all sorts of topics and have asked questions concerning many aspects of human nature.

> ### Just a few examples of questions that psychologists have asked
>
> - How far can people be influenced by the social power of others?
> - Why do we forget and how accurate are our memories?
> - Can hypnosis be used to improve memory?
> - How do people become intelligent?
> - How important is it for infants to form warm attachments to others?
> - Why do we spend one third of our lives asleep?
> - What are the causes and effects of stress?
> - How can we distinguish a 'normal' person from an 'abnormal' one?
> - What causes mental disorders like schizophrenia?
> - How different are humans from other animals?

You may have already considered such questions yourself (it might account for why you are reading this book now), however it is important to realise how psychology as a science differs from the common sense people use every day to explain behaviour.

Common sense vs. scientific psychology

Common sense explanations are often vague and contradictory (think of the proverbs 'many hands make light work' or 'too many cooks spoil the broth'), and so are good at explaining behaviour after it has occurred, but not so good at predicting what will happen in the future.

According to Allport (1946), as a science, psychology aims for 'understanding, prediction and control above the levels achieved by unaided common sense'. It therefore strives to create coherent and precise theories and hypotheses, and to put these to the *objective* test using scientific methods in order to provide *evidence* to support, refute or decide between them.

For example, psychologists have created a number of theories to explain and predict the relationship between the number of people working on a task and the performance of it. These theories have then been investigated by precisely measuring the quantity and quality of performance in a variety of tasks, from pulling on a rope to jury decision-making, produced by adding more people.

In fact, psychologists have come up with many *counter-intuitive findings* that seem to defy common sense. Stanley Milgram, for example, in his 1963 study of obedience took the precaution of asking people to estimate the percentage of 'average' American participants who would give a potentially lethal 450-volt shock to another person just because a psychologist told them to. He found that the highest estimate of 3% was far lower than the actual percentage of 65% who gave the shocks when tested!

Additionally, psychology has shown that there are many instances when we do not or cannot know the reasons for our behaviour (Nisbet and Wilson, 1977), so our common sense ideas are usually just 'best guesses'. There is nothing wrong with making guesses – many psychological theories start off as just that – however, without the scientific approach, their validity can never be properly assessed.

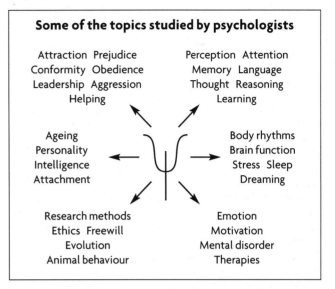

> ### Some of the topics studied by psychologists
>
> Attraction Prejudice
> Conformity Obedience
> Leadership Aggression
> Helping
>
> Perception Attention
> Memory Language
> Thought Reasoning
> Learning
>
> Ageing
> Personality
> Intelligence
> Attachment
>
> Body rhythms
> Brain function
> Stress Sleep
> Dreaming
>
> Research methods
> Ethics Freewill
> Evolution
> Animal behaviour
>
> Emotion
> Motivation
> Mental disorder
> Therapies

The uses and difficulties of psychology

As Allport's quote implies, psychological knowledge not only helps us *understand* human nature better, but can also be *used* by society to help predict and control it, thus the subject has many *practical applications*.

Such knowledge is not always easy to gain, however, since there are many problems involved in studying human thoughts, feelings and behaviour. Psychology is a relatively young science and is beset, more so than most other subjects, with many philosophical, practical and ethical problems – so do not expect to find that it has solved all the mysteries of human minds and behaviour!

> ### Exercise 1
>
> 1 The answers to the 'questions that psychologists have asked' are interesting in their own right, but can you think of how such knowledge could be *used in practice*?
>
> 2 What *difficulties* do you think there are for psychologists who study *people* as a subject matter, especially their thoughts, feelings and behaviour (as opposed, for example, to biologists studying cells or chemists studying chemical interactions)?

1 The answers to the 'questions that psychologists have asked' are interesting in their own right, but can you think of how such knowledge could be *used in practice*?

All of the knowledge gained from answering the example questions that psychologists have asked can have important practical implications.

If we know, for example, how far other people such as authority figures, peer groups and crowds can influence our behaviour, we can use this knowledge to help managers to lead their work forces, advertisers to sell the latest fashions, or the police to deal with violent mobs.

Understanding why we forget, how accurate our memories are, and whether hypnosis can improve recall, is all of use to students revising for exams, therapists discovering childhood memories, and the police who rely on the reliability of an eyewitness's memory and might seek to improve it.

Working out the causes of intelligence, stress and mental disorders will also, hopefully, lead to improvements in people's well-being.

A proper understanding of the answers to the questions that psychologists have asked has important implications for society. An infant's early attachments do seem to have lasting consequences, but psychologists have pointed out that this does not mean that it is only the mother who can provide such attachments, nor that day care by others is always bad for a child. Similarly, knowing how to distinguish the 'normal' from the 'abnormal' has important implications for classifying, diagnosing and treating individuals who may be suffering from mental disorder.

Psychologists, therefore, work in many applied areas, for example:

- **Educational psychology** – which involves testing for learning difficulties and identifying suitable teaching methods.
- **Clinical psychology** – which involves diagnosing and assessing mental disabilities or disorders and rehabilitating or treating them.
- **Criminological psychology** – which involves helping the police or prison services in matters relating to criminal behaviour and its prosecution and treatment.
- **Occupational psychology** – which involves helping employers to select, train and manage their employees, as well as sell their goods and services.

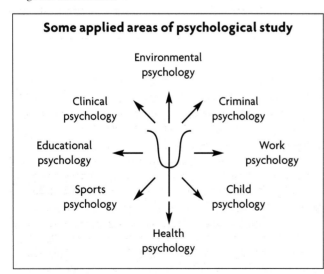

Some applied areas of psychological study

Environmental psychology

Clinical psychology

Criminal psychology

Educational psychology

Work psychology

Sports psychology

Child psychology

Health psychology

2 What difficulties do you think there are for psychologists who study *people* as a subject matter, especially their thoughts, feelings and behaviour (as opposed, for example, to biologists studying cells or chemists studying chemical interactions)?

There are many difficulties which psychologists have in studying people, for instance:

i Practical difficulties – You may have thought of a number of practical difficulties in actually conducting studies on human beings, such as:

- *Human reactivity* – humans react to being studied (cells or chemicals do not become uncomfortable or 'show off' if you stare at them!). We may be unwilling to participate in research (for reasons of self-esteem, for example) or may react differently in the artificial and controlled conditions of a laboratory.
- *Access to other people's minds* – psychology is faced with the problem that only the individual can directly observe and experience their own thoughts and feelings, psychologists can only directly and objectively study behaviour and physiology, not minds.
- *Permission to study other people* – ethically, there are moral limitations to studying human behaviour. We do not have unrestricted access to and control of our subject matter.

ii Human complexity – You might have said something along the lines of 'people are very complicated', and you would be right. Psychology aims to investigate one of the most complex topics in the universe, the human mind and the behaviour it produces. Our minds are capable of executing a huge variety of tasks – everyday tasks that we take completely for granted such as perceiving, remembering, speaking, deciding, and walking – despite the fact that many factors contribute to produce even the most simple of thoughts or behaviours.

The 'machine' we think of as 'holding' our minds and physically producing our behaviour, the brain, is one of the most sophisticated living structures we know of, containing billions of neuronal cells, each capable of connecting with thousands of other neurones (or neurons). This biological machine is constructed according to a DNA blueprint gained from the mixing of each parent's multitude of genes – structures which themselves have been evolving for millions of years.

During construction, both in the womb and after, numerous environmental factors, from nutrients and blood pressure to pollution and viruses, can shape the brain's development and abilities. On top of these factors, we also have to consider the learning influences that experience in our social and cultural environment provides. Thanks to language, humans can store information and ideas from an enormous number of sources over thousands of years, and communicate this information to their offspring. An 18-year-old, for example, would have already been exposed to around nine and a half million minutes of these environmental influences upon behaviour.

In addition to the complexity we develop and carry around with us in our heads, we must remember that human beings do not exist in a vacuum. At any one time there are a number of immediate social and environmental influences on our thinking and behaviour, from the reactions of our peer groups and the invisible pressure of social expectations, to weather conditions and the presence of psychoactive substances.

Human minds and behaviour are the victim of *so many variables* and influences that investigating and explaining them gives psychology one of the hardest challenges any science could face!

2 | Exploring psychological explanations and issues

The following exercise will help you realise how many ways there are of looking at problems in psychology, and introduce you briefly to some of the major issues, methods and approaches in the subject.

A case of aggression

Please read the rather contrived story below:

Evening of 14 June, Chicago, USA
Jake crept out of the flat, leaving behind the deafening sound of his father shouting at his mother again. Jake's father was a very violent man, both to his only son and his wife. This time his rage had been sparked off when his poor mother had tried to change the channel on the television to avoid one of the westerns or war films that always seemed to occupy the screen whenever Jake was home. Jake's father was obsessed with them and Jake even bore the name of his father's favourite gunfighter, a name that had made him the victim of many humiliating jokes from his so-called 'friends'. As the front door shut behind him, Jake felt a pang of pity for his mother, whom he loved very much, and although he hated his father enormously, Jake never ceased to marvel at the way his bullying always got him what he wanted.

Jake walked to the elevator, pressed the call button and waited. He was still waiting ten minutes later, not an unusual occurrence in his tower block, due to the huge number of people who were packed in it like sardines. He grimaced and, savagely kicking an empty can down the fire escape stairs, began the long march down them, trying to count the change in his pocket at the same time. There was not much, since he had been unemployed since leaving school, but it would be enough to buy a few drinks for himself and his new girlfriend at his local bar.

Jake eventually stepped out into the night air, which was humid and sticky, and listened to the police sirens that often wailed in the crime-ridden area. Suddenly, as Jake was crossing a dark side street, a car screamed round the corner and, just as he jumped clear, he caught a glimpse of men inside wearing masks like bank robbers on their heads. The car roared around another bend and just before it disappeared he saw one of the men throw something out of the window and into a nearby hedge. When the car was out of earshot, Jake walked over and pulled the object out of the hedge. It was a small handgun!

Surprised, Jake just stared at it in his hands and almost missed the sight of a police car swerving round the same corner that the other car had appeared from. In a panic he stuffed the gun hastily inside his jacket and turned quickly into the main road. Sweating, he glanced at his watch, and groaned. He was going to be late for his first proper date.

Jake arrived at his local bar, out of breath and looking extremely tense, to be ridiculed by his 'friends' who knew he was late for his date. 'Horse went lame did it cowboy?' came a voice, followed by an outburst of unpleasant laughter. He endured their taunting as he had for years and went, head down, to order a strong drink. Jake gulped it down in one go and, as he ordered another, he happened to see across the room his new girlfriend, Jane, talking on her own with another man. The man was unknown to Jake but reminded him oddly of his own father, albeit younger, better looking and more pleasant…and Jane certainly seemed to be enjoying his company.

She laughed aloud, which drew the attention of his friends who began their baiting again. 'Isn't that your girlfriend Jake?…and who is that stranger chatting up your girl on our patch?' Jake's knuckles whitened and he began to flush bright red. 'Oooooh, looks like Jake is getting real mad now…what are you going to do cowboy, shoot him?'

Jake looked around and saw them looking at him. Some were laughing but others seemed to be expecting him to do something. He looked over at his girlfriend. She had seen him…and she was smiling too…and so was the stranger. For a split second the room quietened and then, to everyone's amazement, Jake pulled out the gun and shot the stranger, unfortunately Jane's brother, dead.

During the police interview, Jake's mother said 'I just can't understand it, he was always so quiet and never lost his temper.' Witnesses at the scene said 'he just seemed to snap'. Jake himself said 'I kept thinking over and over that nothing was going right, and that nothing would ever go right. I don't know why I did it, it just happened.'

Exercise 2

1 How many possible explanations can you think of for Jake's aggression? Looking through the above passage for clues, write down as many contributing factors as possible to explain why he shot Jane's brother, no matter how insignificant you may think they are. (Hint: there are at least 20!)

2 Do you think that just one of the possible explanations is correct, or could there be multiple and interacting causes?

3 What is significant about Jake saying 'I don't know why I did it.'? Do you think people always know why they do things?

4 Do you think that Jake was responsible for his actions? Given all the influences upon his behaviour, did he have a choice to pull the trigger or not? Should we blame him for his aggression or were factors outside his control responsible? Should he be imprisoned, and if so, for how long?

5 If you wanted to understand why such aggression occurs, would you want to investigate just one person in in-depth detail (e.g. Jake) or would you want to test many people? Why?

6 If you wanted to provide evidence for one of the possible explanations, for example, the theory that violent television made Jake more aggressive, how would you go about gathering it? Write down two or three methods of investigating the theory.

7 For a realistic study, perhaps it would be best to experiment on Jake – perhaps by dissecting his brain to look for abnormalities. Alternatively, we could conduct an experiment on the effects of alcohol on aggression by giving people lots of alcohol and a loaded gun. If we find that aggression is caused by biological factors, psychologists could force aggressive people to take drugs, or operate on their brains. Do you agree with these suggestions?

Answers 2.1 – 2.4

1 How many possible explanations can you think of for Jake's aggression?

Here is a list of possible influences on Jake you may have thought of:

- He copied his dad's violent behaviour.
- He thought violence would get him what he wanted.
- He copied the war films/westerns on television.
- He learned that violence is a way to solve problems.
- He inherited his violence from his dad.
- He was young and male – full of testosterone!
- He had drunk a strong alcoholic drink.
- He was in an angry state.
- He may have been mentally ill.
- He was naturally jealous of the stranger.
- The stranger was on 'his territory'.
- His friends pressured him.
- He acted as he was expected to act.
- It was a violent neighbourhood.
- Violence seemed like a normal thing to do.
- He was too used to violence, it no longer shocked.
- The gun tempted him with a quick solution to his problems.
- He had many sources of frustration which made him become angry and aggressive.
- He made a mistake about who Jane's brother was because he kept thinking nothing would ever go right.
- He lost control of his behaviour.
- His thinking lacked morality.
- His life was going nowhere so it made no difference.
- He wanted to gain some self-respect.
- He wanted his friends to respect him.
- He just did it because he could.
- He took out his frustrations on the stranger.
- He bottled up all his aggression until he exploded.
- Without realising it, Jane and her brother reminded Jake of his hatred for his father and desire to protect his mother.

2 Do you think that just one of the possible explanations is correct, or could there be multiple and interacting causes?

Psychologists consider many different causes of behaviour (see approaches to psychology) at several levels of explanation, and have become ever more interested in how they interact. Some explanations involve the influence of society and the environment, others focus on purely psychological-level influences involving the mind (e.g. thought processes) and behaviour, while still others are concerned with underlying biological-level causes concerning the brain.

Some psychologists argue that higher-level (or holistic) explanations are the most suitable, while others believe in using lower-level explanations to explain phenomena at a higher level (this is known as reductionism).

An example of reductionism might involve explaining the thoughts in a person's mind in terms of the physical activity of neurones in the brain, or the behaviour of a social crowd in terms of the individual personalities of those who make it up.

Another debate relating to psychological explanations concerns the relative importance they assign to inherited versus environmental or learned influences (the nature/nurture debate)

> SOCIAL/ENVIRONMENTAL LEVEL EXPLANATIONS
>
> PSYCHOLOGICAL (BEHAVIOURAL & MENTAL) LEVEL EXPLANATIONS
>
> BIOLOGICAL (GENETIC & PHYSIOLOGICAL) LEVEL EXPLANATIONS

A hierarchy of levels of explanation

3 What is significant about Jake saying 'I don't know why I did it.'? Do you think people always know why they do things?

Jake's statement, if truthful, implies either that our behaviour has causes too complex to understand, or that we may often be unaware of what causes it. The issue of conscious awareness is one that pervades psychology and has provoked many debates over its importance. Some psychologists have completely ignored consciousness, regarding it as irrelevant, whereas others believe that much of our behaviour is caused by unconscious influences. Variations in consciousness, as produced by sleep, hypnosis, competing sources of attention, memory recall, mental disorders and drugs, have all been investigated. Some argue that human conscious experience and decision making is central to understanding human nature, that consciousness distinguishes us from animals, or even that it provides us with freewill – once we are aware of all the different things we might do, we are then free to choose from among them.

4 Do you think that Jake was responsible for his actions? Given all the influences upon his behaviour, did he have a choice to shoot or not? Should we blame him for his aggression or were factors outside his control responsible? Should he be imprisoned, and if so, for how long?

The answers to these questions depend upon the degree to which the assumption that humans have free will to choose their behaviour is correct. Those who believe completely in free will assume that influences (biological or environmental) can be rejected at will, whereas those who adopt a deterministic approach assume that every physical event is caused, and since human behaviour is a physical event it follows that it too is caused by preceding factors such as heredity or upbringing.

Determinism, with its emphasis on laws of cause and effect is a basic assumption of science, which aims to reveal those laws to provide prediction and control of the future. Most scientific approaches to psychology, therefore, have deterministic assumptions.

It is worth noting that the legal system assumes that people have freewill and are responsible for their actions, unless there are very strong reasons for diminished responsibility, or they are found insane.

5 If you wanted to understand why such aggression occurs, would you want to investigate just one person in in-depth detail (e.g. Jake) or would you want to test many people? Why?

Psychologists consider both approaches of value, but each has its own advantages and disadvantages.

The **nomothetic** approach to psychology involves investigating large groups of people to try to find general laws that apply to everyone. The advantage of this is that it allows psychologists to generalise their findings to other people with more confidence, and predictions about the way people behave in general can, therefore, be made; this idea of finding 'laws' of behaviour is the aim of science. However, testing many people usually results in a more superficial understanding of each individual person.

The **idiographic** approach involves studying individuals in personal, in-depth, detail to arrive at a unique understanding of them. The advantage of this is that it increases the psychologist's ability to understand and predict the behaviour of that individual. However, because people show many differences from each other, not just similarities, it is not always a good idea to generalise the findings from just one person to the rest of the population.

6 If you wanted to provide evidence for one of the possible explanations, for example, the theory that violent television made Jake more aggressive, how would you go about gathering it? Write down two or three methods of investigating the theory.

Psychologists use many techniques to gather evidence for their ideas, including:

Interviews / questionnaires

You might have suggested something along the lines of 'just *ask* people about their aggression', which is essentially what interviews and questionnaires do in psychological research.

An interviewer could ask a person about the motives for their own or other people's aggression, and whether they thought television was an important influence.

Alternatively, a questionnaire could be devised that listed different types of aggression and violent television programmes, to enable people to rate how many times they had been aggressive and how much violent television they had watched in the last month.

Observations

You might also have thought about *watching* how people react during or after viewing violence on television. A psychologist could conduct an observation by carefully rating people for aggression during or after viewing a boxing match or violent film. The examples of aggression would have to be precisely defined before the observation began and, ideally, two observers should separately rate the aggression and compare scores afterwards to ensure agreement.

Correlation

Another method you could have suggested might have involved *comparing* the amount of aggressive acts people show with the number of hours of violent television they watch in a fixed period of time, to see if there was a positive correlation.

From your knowledge of mathematics, you may remember that a positive correlation between two measures means that they have a similar relationship – increasing or decreasing together.

If the measures for many people are plotted on a scattergram, the results may look something like this:

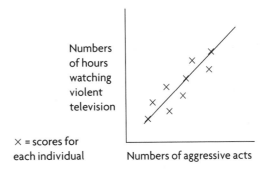

× = scores for each individual

Experiments

Finally, you may have been more ambitious and thought about *testing* the idea in an experiment. An experiment involves more than just recording or measuring data. The experimenter would have to manipulate the amount of violent television watched, letting one set of people watch a violent film and another set watch a non-violent one, for example, after first ensuring that there were similar kinds of people in each group. The aggression they then showed would have to be measured under exactly the same conditions, perhaps with the use of a specially devised test (e.g. the amount of punching on a punch bag).

7 For a realistic study, perhaps it would be best to experiment on Jake – perhaps by dissecting his brain to look for abnormalities. Alternatively, we could conduct an experiment on the effects of alcohol on aggression by giving people lots of alcohol and a loaded gun. If we find that aggression is caused by biological factors, psychologists could force aggressive people to take drugs, or operate on their brains. Do you agree with these suggestions?

I hope not. Psychological knowledge can be very useful, but to attain it, minds, bodies and behaviour have to be studied. These attributes always belong to someone, however, and humans have rights of protection and privacy that do not allow psychologists to conduct the kinds of unrestricted, realistic investigations that give the required information quickly and accurately. If we want the valuable ends of psychological research, we must ask whether we can justify our means of getting it.

The existence of ethical constraints is clearly a serious but necessary limitation on the advancement of psychology as a science and the major professional psychological organisations of many countries have published ethical guidelines for conducting research. In Britain, the British Psychological Society (1993) has published guidelines such as the *Ethical Principles for Conducting Research with Human Participants*, which deal with ethical issues such as consent, deception, debriefing, withdrawal from the investigation, confidentiality, protection of participants, observational research, and giving advice.

However, ethical obligations do not end once knowledge has been gained, since psychologists have to be careful how this knowledge is understood and used, especially where it is going to be used to control people's thoughts, feelings, and behaviour.

3   A brief history of the approaches to psychology

When did psychology start and how did it develop?

The date *1879* is usually said to be the start of psychology as a *separate scientific discipline*, since that was when Wilhelm Wundt created the first psychology laboratory in Leipzig, Germany.

Wilhelm Wundt   William James

Long before this date, however, a great many of the questions and problems that psychology went on to investigate had been outlined by philosophers, for example the Greeks Socrates, Plato and Aristotle as early as the fifth century BC. Psychology was also influenced by both the methods of other sciences (e.g. physics and chemistry) and their findings (e.g. biology).

Unlike other sciences, however, psychologists now and throughout their history seem to have shown more disagreement about *what* should be studied in the subject and *how* it should be studied. This means that many different *approaches* to the subject have developed.

First approaches – analysing the conscious mind

The first approach to investigating psychology, adopted by Wundt himself, focused on studying the *conscious mind* by the method of *introspection* – 'looking inwards' at one's own mental experiences and reporting the observations very precisely to others.

Some psychologists, known as *structuralists*, aimed to use introspection to break our conscious experiences down into their most basic elements, such as sensations (e.g. sights, sounds, smells) and feelings (e.g. love, hate, sadness) as the science of chemistry had done with chemicals. The structuralist Titchener, for example, distinguished the elements of conscious experience from each other in terms of their quality, intensity, duration and clearness, claiming to have identified 32,820 different sensory qualities in vision alone. Unfortunately, there was a lack of agreement between the observations and classifications of different introspectors and the approach was rather limited in its usefulness.

Other psychologists, such as William James, were more concerned with explaining the *function* of consciousness and mental abilities, i.e. what they were for, than merely describing the contents of conscious minds. These *functionalists* were influenced by Charles Darwin's views on evolution and argued that the workings of the mind helped humans adapt to and survive the world. Functionalists used methods other than just introspection and sought to find practical applications of psychology, but as the twentieth century progressed, functionalism soon became overshadowed by other approaches.

Freud and the psychodynamic approach – exploring the unconscious mind

The first approaches to psychology rested on the common sense assumption that, by and large, people knew what was going on in their own minds and could tell you simply by introspecting. This basic premise soon became undermined by the work of Sigmund Freud (1856–1939), an Austrian doctor who became convinced that

many of the most important influences on human thinking and behaviour were *unconscious*. Freud argued that *emotional impulses*, often associated with childhood experiences, build up in our unconscious like steam in a steam engine and influence our thoughts, feelings and behaviour without us being aware of them. Typically, these forgotten memories and hidden emotional causes were linked to our relationships with other people, particularly our parents. Freud developed '*psychoanalysis*' – a set of techniques for identifying and treating the causes of mental disorder, and in many books such as *The Interpretation of Dreams* (1900), he began describing an underlying *psychoanalytic theory* that aimed to explain how both normal personality and abnormality develop from childhood. Freud's ideas had an important (and controversial) impact on psychology, psychiatry and society, and were developed in different ways by other *psychodynamic* theorists (those influenced by psychoanalytic assumptions) such as Jung, Adler, Anna Freud (his daughter) and Erikson.

Sigmund Freud   John Watson

Behaviourism and the learning theory approach – forget minds, focus on what can be seen

In 1913, the American psychologist John Watson wrote an article entitled 'Psychology as the behaviourist views it' which set out the main principles and assumptions of a new movement in psychology; behaviourism.

The behaviourist approach was influenced by the philosophy of *empiricism* (which argues that humans are like a 'tabula rasa' or blank slate at birth and gain knowledge from the environment via the senses) and the physical sciences (which emphasise scientific and objective methods of investigation).

Behaviourists such as Watson and Skinner, therefore, attempted to make psychology more scientific by only studying *observable behaviour* and how *learning experiences* with the environment could change it. They rejected any study or even mention of minds or mental processes, whether conscious or unconscious and, by drawing on earlier work by Pavlov and Thorndike, proceeded to develop and apply theories of learning (such as classical and operant conditioning) to explain virtually *all* behaviour.

The behaviourist approach dominated experimental psychology and the study of learning until the late 1950s, when its assumptions and methods became increasingly criticised by other approaches to psychology. Other learning theories have been developed to take into account factors the behaviourists ignored, for example, by Bandura with his social learning theory. Nevertheless, behaviourism made a lasting impact on both learning theory and psychology in general.

Piaget and the cognitive developmental approach – studying changes in understanding

While behaviourism, its rejection of the mind and its ideas on learning were gaining popularity, not everyone was willing to give up on the mind. Jean Piaget, a Swiss zoologist who had been involved in the early development of intelligence tests, argued that the study of the development of knowledge and understanding (epistemology) had to take into account the *inner mental processes of thinking and reasoning, underlying mental structures, and how these change over time.*

Piaget and others interested in cognitive development (changes in understanding), such as the Russian psychologist Vygotsky, also disagreed with the behaviourist view that humans learn in an automatic and passive way, and stressed that active interaction with the environment was necessary. Unfortunately, though, cognitive developmental psychologists had more success in outlining the developmental changes than the actual mental structures and processes underlying them.

Carl Rogers   Roger Sperry

Jean Piaget   Jerome Bruner

Cognitive psychology – a science of mental processes

It was the arrival of the *computer* that gave cognitive psychology the terminology and analogy it needed to investigate mental activities such as *thought processes.* Cognitive psychologists began suggesting that human minds, like computers, are information processors – regardless of our hardware (brains or circuits) both receive, interpret and respond to information – and these processes *can be modelled* (like computer flow charts) and *tested scientifically.*

With more precise models of mental processes and experimental evidence to support them, cognitive psychologists such as Jerome Bruner have been able to explain in greater detail how our behaviour is affected by the way we perceive and attend to the world, think about it and remember it.

The cognitive approach began to revolutionise psychology in the late 1950s and early 1960s to become the dominant paradigm in the subject by the 1970s. It has influenced and integrated with many other approaches and areas of study, for example, social learning theory, cognitive neuropsychology and artificial intelligence.

The humanistic approach – back to human consciousness and freedom

The humanistic movement also developed in the early 1960s and, with its greater belief in *free will* and the need to understand people's *conscious experience* of the world, aimed to replace the two main approaches in the subject at that time (behaviourism and psychoanalysis).

The humanistic approach emphasised the need to study all the uniquely *human* aspects of experience such as love, hope and creativity, as well as the individual's interactions with and feelings towards their social environment. Humanists such as Abraham Maslow believed that every individual has many needs, including the need to *self-actualise* (reach one's full potential), while Carl Rogers outlined the importance of gaining self-respect and respect from other people.

Humanism made many valid points and criticisms of other approaches but had less of an impact on mainstream academic psychology since it deliberately adopted a less-scientific view of how people should be studied.

Social psychology – the context and influence of others

Like the humanists, social psychologists also study social relationships, but in contrast have adopted a more scientific approach. Social psychologists point out that all behaviour occurs in a social context and assume that a major influence on behaviour, thought processes and emotions are other people and the society they have created. Such influences include those of individuals (e.g. leadership and obedience), groups (e.g. conformity and crowding), societies (e.g. social expectations and norms) and culture (e.g. history, politics and language).

Social psychology has a long history within scientific psychology (Triplett was carrying out social facilitation studies in 1898), with most of the research being experimental and conducted in America. A more sociological and European approach also developed, adopting other methods and taking more account of wider cultural, historical and political contexts and shared group identities.

Biology and the physiological approach to psychology – the effects of brains, bodies and genes

The biological or physiological approach to psychology has integrated with and run parallel to the rest of psychological thought since early Greek times. The Greek physician Galen, for example, suggested that personality might be linked to the levels of body fluids such as blood and bile in the body.

Biologically orientated psychologists assume that, since the mind appears to reside in the brain, all thoughts, feelings and behaviour ultimately have a physical / biological basis. Psychology should, therefore, investigate the brain, nervous system, endocrine system, neurochemistry and genes.

In addition, since human genes have evolved over millions of years to adapt behaviour to the environment, much behaviour will have a genetic basis and it may be useful to study why human behaviour has evolved in the way it has (the subject of Charles Darwin's theory of evolution).

As knowledge of human anatomy, physiology, biochemistry and medicine developed, important insights for human behaviour and experience were gained. Roger Sperry, for example, investigated the function of the left and right sides of the brain by examining the effects of splitting the brain in two. The approach will progress still further as the technology to isolate the effects of genes and scan the living brain develops.

Exercise 3

Look at the explanations you gave for Jake's aggression in exercise 2 (or those in the answers), and try to see which ones might agree with each of the approaches above (except structuralism and functionalism).

After such a brief introduction to the approaches to psychology, this exercise was quite tricky. However, hopefully, it helped you think about the particular kinds of explanation favoured by each one.

LEARNING THEORY APPROACH

Examples of explanations that would be in line with learning theory assumptions might include:

- He thought violence would get him what he wanted.
- He learned that violence is a way to solve problems.
- He copied his dad's violent behaviour.
- He copied the war films/westerns on television.

The above could be linked with the learning theories of operant conditioning (e.g. his violent behaviour may have been previously rewarded by his society and father, or enabled ridicule to be avoided) and the imitation/observational learning of social learning theory.

PSYCHODYNAMIC APPROACH

Examples of explanations that would be in line with psychodynamic assumptions might include:

- He bottled up all his aggression until he exploded.
- He took out his frustrations on the stranger.
- Without realising it, Jane and her brother reminded Jake of his hatred for his father and desire to protect his mother.

The above could be linked with psychodynamic theories such as those relating to inner emotional impulses/drives, defence mechanisms for releasing or controlling drives, unconscious causes and the influence of family relationships.

SOCIAL PSYCHOLOGICAL APPROACH

Examples of explanations that would be in line with social psychological assumptions might include:

- His friends pressured him.
- He acted as he was expected to act.
- It was a violent neighbourhood.
- Violence seemed like a normal thing to do.
- The stranger was on 'his territory'
- He had many sources of frustration which made him become angry and aggressive.

The above could be linked with social theories such as those relating to conformity, self-fulfilling prophecy, social norms, out-group prejudice and frustration–aggression theory.

HUMANISTIC APPROACH

Examples of explanations that would be in line with humanistic psychological assumptions might include:

- His life was going nowhere so it made no difference.
- He wanted to gain some self-respect.
- He wanted his friends to respect him.
- He just did it because he could.

The above could be linked with humanist psychological theories such as those relating to the prevention of achieving basic needs, goals, ambitions or self-actualisation, self-respect, respect from others and free will choice.

COGNITIVE APPROACHES

Examples of explanations that would be in line with cognitive psychological assumptions might include:

- He made a mistake about who Jane's brother was because he kept thinking nothing would ever go right.
- He lost control of his behaviour.

The above could be linked with cognitive psychological theories such as those relating to attribution errors, negative thinking and errors in logic, bias in interpretation of events due to negative schemas/perceptual set, and locus of control

- His thinking lacked morality.

This could be linked with cognitive developmental theories such as those relating to levels of moral development.

PHYSIOLOGICAL APPROACH

Examples of explanations that would be in line with physiological assumptions might include:

- He inherited his violence from his dad.
- He was young and male – full of testosterone.
- He had drunk a strong alcoholic drink.
- He was in an angry state.
- He may have been mentally ill.
- He was naturally jealous of the stranger.
- The stranger was on 'his territory'.

The above could be linked with physiological theories such as those relating to genetics, hormones, drug effects, physiological 'fight or flight' arousal, brain damage/misfunction, and the evolution of aggression due to territoriality and mate competition.

4 | Variables

Question: When psychologists conduct research, what are they actually investigating?

Answer: Variables!

What are variables?

A variable is any object, quality or event that changes or varies in some way. Psychological variables include aggression, intelligence, attraction, memory, obedience and driving ability. Physical variables include time, height, noise, temperature, and amount of alcohol.

Psychologists propose theories and hypotheses about how variables interact with each other and, when conducting research studies, they want to measure, manipulate or control variables to see whether they confirm or refute their theories and hypotheses.

Operationalisation

Before psychologists can test their theories and hypotheses, they have to identify what variables are involved and work out how to test them physically. However, many of the variables that psychologists are interested in are *abstract concepts* such as aggression or intelligence.

Operationalisation refers to the process of making variables physically *measurable* or *testable*. This is done with psychological variables by recording or affecting some aspect of *observable behaviour* that is assumed to be indicative of the variable under consideration. For example, recording the number of punches thrown or murders committed for the variable of 'aggression' or calculating the score on an IQ test to operationalise 'intelligence'.

How are variables investigated?

This depends on the methods used by the psychologist.

In observations, case studies, interviews or questionnaires, variables are *just recorded or measured* in varying amounts of detail, but hopefully in an objective and fair way.

When using a correlation, variables are not only measured but also *compared* to see how they *co-vary* with each other (what relationship they have together).

In an experiment, however, one variable (the *independent variable*) is *altered* to see what effect it has on another variable (the *dependent variable*).

- The independent variable can, therefore, be defined as the variable that is *manipulated* in two or more conditions to see what effect it has on the dependent variable.
- The dependent variable is defined as *the main measured outcome* of the experiment, hopefully due to the manipulation of the independent variable.

For example, the independent variable (IV) of alcohol could be manipulated to see what effect it had on the dependent variable (DV) of driving ability by testing participants in two conditions, one with alcohol consumed beforehand and the other without (a sober *control condition*).

- However, many *extraneous variables* (other variables that could potentially influence the dependent variable apart from the independent variable), could spoil the experiment and so *controls* are employed to prevent extraneous variables from becoming confounding variables (those that actually affect the dependent variable).
- Extraneous variables can be either *random* (unsystematic variables that affect the dependent variable but should not affect one condition more than another) or *constant* (those that have a systematic effect on one condition more than another). While random variables may affect the DV only constant variables will usually obscure the effect of the IV on the DV enough to spoil the experiment.

How are variables recorded and measured?

Variables are either recorded quantitatively (in terms of numbers) or qualitatively (described in words) using a variety of data recording equipment, from hand-written responses and researcher notes or coding systems to audiotape or videotape recording.

Quantitative data can be recorded using *frequency grids*/tally charts to count the *number of times* something (e.g. a behaviour or event) occurs, *rating scales* to show an *assessment of the degree* to which something occurs, or *fixed unit scales* (e.g. time in seconds) to show the *precise degree* to which something occurs.

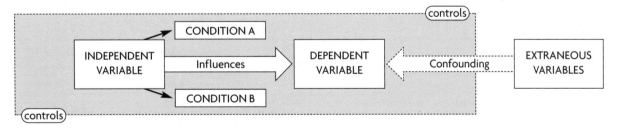

Exercise 4

1 Think of ways that the following variables could be operationalised (made physically measurable or testable):
   a memory   b attraction   c obedience
   d helping behaviour   e driving ability   f age
   g alcohol intake   h gender

2 Identify any two variables, that can be measured on a scale, which it might be interesting to correlate together.

3 Identify the independent variable (with two experimental conditions) and dependent variable in the following research ideas:
   a Are attractive people helped more?
   b Do teenagers or pensioners have worse memories?
   c Are men or women better drivers?

4 If you were to investigate the effect of alcohol on driving ability, what extraneous variables would you have to control to make sure that nothing else affected the test of driving ability apart from the amount of alcohol consumed? Which of these extraneous variables might be regarded as random and which might be constant?

5 What are the advantages and disadvantages of
   a direct hand-written recording of behaviour?
   b videotape recording of behaviour?
   c frequency grids (tally charts)?
   d assessment rating scales?
   e fixed unit measurement scales?

Answers 4.1 – 4.5

1 Think of ways that the following variables could be operationalised (made physically measurable or testable):

a **Memory** – e.g. the number of previously presented items of information recalled or recognised after a time delay.

b **Attraction** – e.g. the rating out of ten for attractiveness given by one person to another.

c **Obedience** – e.g. whether or not people obey an unreasonable command (for an action they would not otherwise perform) from another person.

d **Helping behaviour** – e.g. how quickly in seconds (if at all) help is given to a person obviously in need of it.

e **Driving ability** – e.g. the number of errors made in a standard driving test.

f **Age** – number of days, months and years since birth.

g **Alcohol intake** – e.g. the number of units of alcohol consumed.

h **Gender** – male or female.

2 Identify any two variables, that can be measured on a scale, which it might be interesting to correlate together.

One could correlate together alcohol intake and driving ability to see whether the time it took to manoeuvre through an obstacle course of traffic cones (with time penalties for each one knocked over) increased with the number of units of alcohol consumed. Alternatively, one could correlate together age and obedience or the attractiveness of brides compared with their grooms.

3 Identify the independent variable (with two experimental conditions) and dependent variable in the following research ideas:

a **Are attractive people helped more?**
The independent variable could be the attractiveness of a victim in a staged accident, manipulated by operationalising it into two conditions, one with an attractive victim the other with an unattractive victim. The dependent variable would be helping behaviour (as operationalised above).

b **Do teenagers or pensioners have worse memories?**
The independent variable would be age, which could be manipulated by selecting participants of between 13 to 19 years of age, and of pensionable age (for example, between 65 and 71). The dependent variable would be memory retrieval (as operationalised above).

c **Are men or women better drivers?**
The independent variable would be gender, which could be manipulated by selecting male and female participants of similar age and experience. The dependent variable would be driving ability (as operationalised above).

4 If you were to investigate the effect of alcohol on driving ability, what extraneous variables would you have to control to make sure that nothing else affected the test of driving ability apart from the amount of alcohol consumed? Which of these extraneous variables might be regarded as random and which might be constant?

Extraneous variables might include:
- the existing driving ability, age, eyesight and alcohol tolerance of the participants in each condition
- the car used in each condition
- the driving conditions, e.g. the weather in each condition.
- the order of conditions (sober followed by drunk or drunk followed by sober?) if the same participants do both tests.

Variables such as the driving experience, age, eyesight and alcohol tolerance of the participants will vary randomly between individuals. If the same participants are used in each condition or if different participants are randomly allocated to each condition then such random differences are usually equally divided and should not affect one condition more than the other of the independent variable.

Variables such as the car used and the driving conditions, e.g. the weather, should not affect one condition more than another and confound the experiment *if* they remain the same. If, however, a different type of car is used in the two conditions, then differences such as the car's size and steering could become constant confounding variables. A drunk driver using a better car might perform in the same way as a sober driver using a worse car for the test, and the effect of the independent variable (alcohol intake) will be obscured.

Similarly, if it rains during the first condition but not during the second, the weather may become a constant confounding variable. The experimenter should, therefore, take care to ensure similar driving/weather conditions are experienced by the participants in each condition.

The order of the conditions if the same participants do both tests will become a constant confounding variable unless it is controlled for (see p. 19 experimental design and control). For example, if all participants are tested using the same driving test in the sober condition followed by the drunken condition, then although their driving performance may worsen with alcohol, it may also improve due to practice and knowing what to expect in the test in the second condition. The net result may indicate no difference in performance due to alcohol.

5 What are the advantages and disadvantages of

a **direct hand-written recording of behaviour?**
The straightforward taking of notes by hand is quick and easy to do, but has the disadvantage that data may be missed (by looking down at the note pad rather than at what is to be recorded). Also, if the notes of a single observer are the only record, then it is difficult for others to check whether the data was accurately or subjectively recorded.

b **videotape recording of behaviour?**
Videotaping accurately records all data in view for later analysis, which increases objectivity, and does not omit important gestures and non-verbal communication accompanying speech (as do audiotapes).

However, participants may feel ill at ease knowing they are being videotaped which can produce participant reactivity and unnatural behaviour.

c **frequency grids (tally charts)?**
These allow a larger variety of behaviours to be recorded at a time and are fairly simple and accurate to use. Just noting whether something occurred on a tally chart is not very informative, however, since it cannot say how long or intensely something occurred for.

d **assessment rating scales?**
Rating scales provide more information than frequency grids by showing the degree to which something occurred (e.g. how aggressive someone was rather than just whether they were aggressive or not). Nevertheless, using opinion assessment rather than fixed scales (such as timing) to measure introduces more subjectivity into the recording of data.

e **fixed unit measurement scales?**
These provide higher objectivity, precision and standardisation of data, but can sometimes lack descriptive detail, e.g. just recording how long someone was aggressive for does not include what kind or intensity of aggression was shown.

5 | Scientific theories, hypotheses and methodology

Psychology claims to be a science and psychologists wish to investigate their variables 'scientifically', but what does this scientific approach actually involve? Three important aspects of the scientific process are theories, hypotheses and methodology.

Scientific theories

To be 'scientific', psychological theories should be *orderly*, *internally consistent*, *parsimonious* and, of course, *true*. In other words, they should impose order upon the world by describing, in a clear, precise and coherent (non-contradictory) manner, the smallest number of concepts, principles and laws necessary to accurately explain the greatest amount of reality.

However, theories that claim to be scientific should not only provide explanations, but also make *predictions* about the future – this makes them *testable*. The ability to test theories to provide evidence for or against them is the hallmark of science. According to Popper (1959) scientific theories have to be *refutable* (capable of being shown to be wrong).

Hypotheses

Hypotheses are *precise, testable statements*. They are based upon the predictions made by theories and are stated *before* they are investigated.

A hypothesis describes what is expected to happen to variables and can be observational (a certain measurement of a variable is expected under certain conditions), correlational (one variable will increase or decrease at the same time as another variable) or experimental (one variable will cause a change in another variable).

In order to function as precise, testable statements that can be properly investigated to provide good evidence for or against a theory, hypotheses should be bold, precise and refutable.

Two-tailed and one-tailed hypotheses

Bold and precise hypotheses are ones that are very specific and detailed about what is predicted or expected, so the results of an investigation will clearly either support the hypothesis or not. Precise hypotheses should contain fully operationalised variables and the words 'statistically significant' if inferential statistics are to be conducted on the results.

For instance, a **two-tailed hypothesis** simply *predicts an effect* will occur, such as a difference or correlation.

Thus an *experimental two-tailed hypothesis* predicts a significant difference in the dependent variable [DV] between the various conditions of the independent variable [IV] and might be phrased something like:
'There will be a significant *difference* in [the DV] *between* [condition A of the IV] *and* [condition B of the IV].'
For example:
'There will be a statistically significant difference in IQ scores between male participants and female participants.'

On the other hand, a *correlational two-tailed hypothesis* predicts significant patterns of relationship between two variables and might be phrased something like:
'There will be a significant *correlation between* [variable 1] *and* [variable 2].'
For example:
'There will be a statistically significant correlation between hours of psychology revision conducted and marks gained in a psychology test.'

A bolder, **one-tailed hypothesis**, however, predicts a *particular direction in the effect* that is expected, e.g. that a certain condition will do better than another, or that a positive rather than negative kind of correlation will occur.

Thus an *experimental one-tailed hypothesis* might be phrased:
'There will be a significant *increase in* [the DV] in [condition A of the IV] *compared to* [condition B of the IV].'
For example:
'There will be a statistically significant increase in IQ scores in male participants compared to female participants.'

Whereas a *correlational one-tailed hypothesis* might be phrased:
'There will be a significant *positive* correlation between [variable 1] and [variable 2].'
For example:
'There will be a statistically significant positive correlation between hours of psychology revision conducted and marks gained in a psychology test.'

(Of course, the above one-tailed hypotheses could be phrased in the opposite direction, e.g. a *decrease in* or *negative correlation*).

Null hypotheses

To be scientific, every hypothesis should be refutable – capable of being shown to be wrong. For this reason, a **null hypothesis** can be proposed which states that there will be *no significant effect* (either difference or correlation). For example:
An *experimental two-tailed null hypothesis*:
'There will be no statistically significant *difference* in IQ scores between male participants and female participants.'
A *correlational two-tailed null hypothesis*:
'There will be no statistically significant *correlation* between hours of psychology revision conducted and A level grade gained in psychology.'

So, if the results of an investigation do not find a significant difference or relationship, the null hypothesis is supported and the alternative hypothesis is rejected. Note, however, that sometimes it is the null hypothesis that a theory predicts (no significant difference or correlation is expected) – so if the results *do* reveal a significant effect, the null hypothesis is rejected and the alternative hypothesis supported.

Scientific methodology

Regardless of the particular method used (experiment, observation, correlation, interview, etc.) psychologists should investigate their theories and hypotheses with techniques that are both valid and reliable. Scientific methodology is ideally thought to be objective (without personal bias), standardised (the same for each participant), controlled (to exclude extraneous variables) and replicable (able to be repeated again for confirmation).

Exercise 5

1 Why are hypotheses stated before they are tested?

2 Write out suitable experimental and correlational hypotheses, with null versions of each, for an experimental study and a correlational study on the variables of 'units of alcohol consumed' and 'number of errors made in a driving test'. Try the same with the variables of 'hours of violent TV viewed' and 'number of aggressive acts committed'.

3 If a hypothesis is refuted do you think the whole theory it was based on should be refuted/rejected?

4 What do you think is meant by the 'validity' and 'reliability' of a method?

5 Do you think that it is possible for a scientist to be truly objective? Given, for example, that the majority of psychological investigations used to be conducted by *male* psychologists from *Western* industrialised countries, what *biases* might have crept into psychology?

1 Why are hypotheses stated before they are tested?

Hypotheses are stated before they are tested so they can function as real predictive tests of the theory. This makes theories refutable and avoids researchers trying to use them to explain any combination of results that might be found. Some theories are regarded as unscientific because they are very good at explaining the results of studies after they have been conducted but are not very good at predicting them beforehand.

2 Write out suitable experimental and correlational hypotheses, with null versions of each, for an experimental study and a correlational study on the variables of 'units of alcohol consumed' and 'number of errors made in a driving test'. Try the same with the variables of 'hours of violent TV viewed' and 'number of aggressive acts committed'.

A one-tailed hypothesis would probably be expected based on current theories of the negative effects of alcohol on driving ability, for example:

> 'There will be a statistically significant increase in the number of errors made in a driving test in participants who have consumed five units of alcohol compared to participants who have consumed no alcohol.'

The null hypothesis could be stated by simply adding a 'no':

> 'There will be no statistically significant increase in the number of errors made in a driving test in participants who have consumed five units of alcohol compared to participants who have consumed no alcohol.'

A correlational study would also use a one-tailed hypothesis:

> 'There will be a statistically significant positive correlation between the number of errors made in a driving test and the number of units of alcohol consumed.'

Again, the null hypothesis could be stated by simply adding a 'no':

> 'There will be no statistically significant positive correlation between the number of errors made in a driving test and the number of units of alcohol consumed.'

A one-tailed hypothesis would also probably be expected based on theories of the negative effects of violent TV viewing on aggression, for example:

> 'There will be a statistically significant increase in the number of aggressive acts committed by participants who have watched 10 hours of violent TV compared to participants who have watched no violent TV.'

The null hypothesis adds a 'no':

> 'There will be no statistically significant increase in the number of aggressive acts committed by participants who have watched 10 hours of violent TV compared to participants who have watched no violent TV.'

A correlational study would also use a one-tailed hypothesis:

> 'There will be a statistically significant positive correlation between the number of hours spent watching violent TV and the number of aggressive acts committed.'

Again, the null hypothesis could be stated by simply adding a 'no':

> 'There will be no statistically significant positive correlation between the number of hours spent watching violent TV and the number of aggressive acts committed.'

3 If a hypothesis is refuted do you think the whole theory it was based on should be refuted/rejected?

Although science tends to advance, according to the philosopher of science Karl Popper, more through refutation than confirmation, we should not necessarily be too hasty in completely rejecting a theory based upon one rejected hypothesis. The possibility exists that the methods used to conduct the falsifying study were at fault somehow or that the results may have been a fluke. This is why studies need to be replicated, ideally by other researchers, to confirm findings. Alternatively, the theory may actually be partly correct so it may provide other hypotheses that will be confirmed by studies. Imre Lakatos, for example, argues that theories often have a protective belt of auxiliary hypotheses that can be rejected without too much harm to the theory, but also a hard core of central assumptions that cannot be refuted without rejecting the whole theory.

4 What do you think is meant by the 'validity' and 'reliability' of a method?

The validity of a method of measurement (whether it be an experimental test, questionnaire or observational procedure) refers to whether it *measures what it is supposed to measure* – how realistically or truly variables have been operationalised.

For example, people have questioned whether IQ tests really measure intelligence and how well a formal driving test reflects real driving ability.

The 'reliability' of a method, on the other hand, refers to how *consistently* it measures – whether its procedures are sufficiently standardised and objective.

For example, a test that keeps providing wildly different results when carried out on the same unchanged person might lack reliability, perhaps because of variations in the way it is conducted.

5 Do you think that it is possible for a scientist to be truly objective? Given, for example, that the majority of psychological investigations used to be conducted by *male* psychologists from *Western* industrialised countries, what *biases* might have crept into psychology?

People sometimes tend to think of scientists as impartial and objective machines, and forget that they are human beings with certain background experiences, expectations, beliefs, and ambitions like everyone else. Such factors may well influence the topics they choose to investigate, the people they study, how they go about studying them and even the way they phrase their hypotheses and conclusions. For example, male, western psychologists:

- may have neglected to study topics that are relevant to women and those from other cultures
- have sometimes only studied male, American participants and have just generalised the results to women and other cultures without bothering to test them
- have sometimes conducted research with tests or procedures that are biased towards participants from their own culture
- have sometimes aimed to investigate and emphasise differences rather than similarities between men and women, or different cultures, often with biased one-tailed hypotheses and conclusions, e.g. reporting that women are lacking in self-confidence or dominance rather than concluding that men are over-confident or domineering.

6 | Gould (1982) – 'A nation of morons'

This article is an edited extract from Gould's (1981) book *The Mismeasure of Man* in which he describes one part of the early history of intelligence testing in order to illustrate a number of problematic issues in psychology.

The history of Yerkes's testing of intelligence

Yerkes was a psychologist who wanted to show that psychology could prove itself as a respectable science by using intelligence testing to *aid recruitment* (by helping to select between different people for different jobs), and to find support for the *hereditarian* view of intelligence (that intellectual ability is inherited through the genes).

Yerkes became involved in testing 1.75 million army recruits in the USA during the First World War, using three intelligence tests that were designed to measure *innate* intellectual ability regardless of education and experience, even for new immigrants to the USA.

The Army Alpha test was a written exam for literate (those who could read and write) recruits. They were given a number of written test items, for example 'The number of Kaffir's legs is – 2, 4, 6 or 8?' and 'Washington is to Adams as first is to…?'.

The Army Beta test was a pictorial exam for illiterate recruits and those who failed the Alpha. The Army Beta, for example, asked participants to spot errors in pictures such as a tennis match without a net or a phonograph without its horn, and then write their answers. An individual exam was also included for those who failed the Beta.

Every individual was given a grade from A to E (with plus and minus signs), for example 'C–' indicated a low average intelligence, suitable for the position of ordinary private in the army, while 'D' indicated a person rarely suited for tasks requiring special skill, forethought, resourcefulness or sustained alertness.

Unfortunately, given the huge numbers tested, the standardised procedures were not always followed and recruits were often rushed, given the wrong test and not given the appropriate re-tests. This was especially the case with the testing of black participants.

Nevertheless, Yerkes and his fellow researchers reported that, although white American adults only had an average mental age of 13 (just above the level of moronity), other nations scored lower

and could be accurately graded on their innate intelligence based on immigrants' intelligence test scores. People from Nordic countries scored higher than those from Latin or Slavic countries, with American 'Negroes' at the bottom of the scale.

From these results, Yerkes and others concluded that intelligence *can* be *objectively* measured, that intelligence is *inherited*, and that IQ tests can *predict* future performance and thus be used for *selection* purposes. Racists and eugenicists (those who support the idea that human breeding should be controlled to improve the genetic stock) particularly welcomed the intelligence test results and conclusions, and argued that interbreeding with 'inferior races' should be restricted.

Gould's analysis

Gould was highly critical of Yerkes's research methodology and the conclusions he drew. In describing the testing, Gould drew attention to the problematic nature of psychometric (mental measurement) testing in general and the measurement of intelligence in particular. He also demonstrated how theoretical bias can influence research in psychology, in particular how the psychological theories on the inherited nature of intelligence and the prejudice of a society can dramatically distort the objectivity of intelligence testing.

Importantly, Gould also discussed the political and ethical implications of research in psychology – in this case the use of biased data to discriminate between people. The questions below should help you understand in greater detail the methodological problems and negative implications of Yerkes's research into intelligence that Gould described.

Exercise 6

1 The validity of a psychological test refers to whether it truly measures what it is supposed to measure, i.e. general intellectual ability rather than other factors such as specific areas of general knowledge. Why do the questions above from the Army Alpha and Beta tests seem to lack validity as measures of *innate* intelligence as Yerkes claimed?

2 The reliability of a psychological test refers to whether it measures in a consistent and fair way each time it is used. How did Yerkes's intelligence testing lack reliability?

3 If you had been a psychologist back then, how could you have demonstrated that the IQ test results of the immigrants were due to lack of American general knowledge rather than innate intelligence?

4 Given that Yerkes's research findings and conclusions on innate differences in intelligence between individuals and races were accepted and especially welcomed by supporters of eugenics, what do you think the implications might have been for army recruits, educators who wanted to help improve intelligence, and new immigrants into the USA?

5 If you devised a new IQ test of your own, how could you go about demonstrating
   a its validity as a test of intelligence?
   b its reliability?

1 The validity of a psychological test refers to whether it truly measures what it is supposed to measure, i.e. general intellectual ability rather than other factors such as specific areas of general knowledge. Why do the questions above from the Army Alpha and Beta tests seem to lack validity as measures of *innate* intelligence as Yerkes claimed?

The Army Alpha test may not have measured innate intelligence since the questions were often based on *American* general knowledge that recent immigrants would be unlikely to know, e.g. historical facts about past American presidents. (Washington and Adams were the first and second presidents of the USA, but this question is biased towards existing residents of America). The Army Beta also asked often poor and illiterate immigrants to spot errors in pictures of things they had probably *never seen* before, e.g. a tennis court, and then *write* their answer.

2 The reliability of a psychological test refers to whether it measures in a consistent and fair way each time it is used. How did Yerkes's intelligence testing lack reliability?

Unstandardised procedures were followed with individuals being given the wrong test, being rushed and not given the appropriate re-tests – especially during the testing of black subjects. This means that the intelligence test scores for the same participants would vary each time they were tested.

3 If you had been a psychologist back then, how could you have demonstrated that the IQ test results of the immigrants were due to lack of American general knowledge rather than innate intelligence?

You could have investigated to see if immigrants scored higher the longer they stayed in America – whether there was a positive correlation between the intelligence test score and the number of years of residence in America. In fact, Yerkes *did* find such a positive correlation, but was so determined to explain differences in intelligence in terms of innate factors to support his hereditarian views that he ignored or rejected the role of experience and education. For example, Gould points out in the original *The Mismeasure of Man* that Yerkes found a strong positive correlation of .75 between the number of years in education and IQ test scores but interpreted causation from this by arguing that intelligent people chose to stay longer in education.

4 Given that Yerkes's research findings and conclusions on innate differences in intelligence between individuals and races were accepted and especially welcomed by supporters of eugenics, what do you think the implications might have been for army recruits, educators who wanted to help improve intelligence, and new immigrants into the USA?

Gould pointed out many undesirable implications of Yerkes's results and conclusions, especially given how doubtful they were. Firstly, the scores for army recruits could have had implications for how they were assigned military positions and tasks – the biased results could be used to justify the prejudiced allocation of menial jobs to recruits of certain 'races'. Secondly, Yerkes's false conclusion that IQ is the result of fixed genetic causes provided support for the argument that special educational measures for those who achieved low scores (mostly poor immigrants and black participants) were a waste of time and money. Finally, the results and conclusions provided illegitimate evidence for those who advocated eugenics, racist politics, and immigration restriction to prevent damaging interbreeding with 'inferior races'.

Gould suggested that this may have been influential in denying the immigration into America of up to 6 million people from southern, central and eastern Europe, many seeking political refuge, between 1924 and 1939.

5 If you devised a new IQ test of your own, how could you go about demonstrating

a its validity as a test of intelligence?

The validity of a new intelligence test could be demonstrated in a number of ways. Carefully examining (especially by impartial experts) the test items to see if they *appear* to measure what they claim to measure (psychologists call this *face* or *content validity*) should eliminate obviously irrelevant items. Unfortunately, this is not a very rigorous method (many beginners in psychology, for example, have spotted the lack of face validity in some of Yerkes's IQ test questions). Alternatively, one could give the same people both the new IQ test and an older established one and then correlate the results of the two tests to see if a high positive correlation is gained (the higher the correlation, the more likely it is that they measure the same thing). This test of *concurrent validity* (comparing a new method or test with an already well-established one that claims to measure the same variable) suffers from the problem that although both tests may be measuring the same thing, there is still no guarantee that that 'thing' is intelligence. Also if there is not a strong positive correlation, how do we know which test is wrong?

Fortunately, psychologists have other methods of demonstrating the validity of their tests. *Construct validity* refers to whether the test or method can be used to support the underlying theoretical constructs concerning the variable that it is supposed to be measuring. For example, if psychological theory suggests the offspring of two highly intelligent parents raised in a stimulating environment should be intelligent, an IQ test should confirm this. *Predictive validity* refers to whether the test will predict future performance indicated by its results. For example, those who score high on an IQ test at a young age should be predicted to later perform better in studies or jobs requiring intelligence.

b its reliability?

The reliability could be checked for IQ test items by the *test–re-test method* – correlating the results of the test conducted on one occasion with the results of the test conducted on a later occasion (with the same participants) and gaining a high positive correlation coefficient. Psychologists regard this method as a test of *external reliability* – how consistently a method measures over time when repeated. Methods of measurement have low external reliability if they give different scores when repeated on the same people under similar conditions, for example if an IQ test scored the same person a genius one day but just average a week later.

In contrast to this, *internal reliability* refers to how consistently a method measures within itself, for example if an IQ test was made up of half ridiculously easy questions and half ridiculously difficult questions virtually everyone would score half marks and be equally intelligent. Internal reliability could be checked for test items by the *split half method* – correlating the results of half the items with the other half (e.g. the odd numbers with the even numbers of the test) and gaining a high positive correlation coefficient.

7 | Experimental methods, design and control in psychology

Experiments

Unlike non-experimental methods such as observations, interviews and correlation, an experiment involves the manipulation of one variable, known as the independent variable, to see what effect it has on another variable, the dependent variable, while attempting to control the influence of all other extraneous variables. This enables inferences about cause and effect relationships to be made with greater certainty.

There can be differences, however, in where these manipulations occur and the experimenter's degree of control over the independent variable.

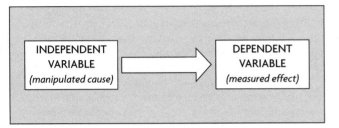

- *Laboratory experiments*
  Experiments can be conducted in the laboratory where the researcher can deliberately manipulate the independent variable while maintaining strict control over all extraneous variables through standardised procedures in a controlled environment.

  Bandura (1961), for example, manipulated the independent variable of 'exposure to aggression' to see what effect it had on the dependent variable of 'imitation of aggression in children' by allocating similar kinds of children to conditions where they watched an adult in a playroom for ten minutes a) being violent towards an inflatable Bobo doll, or b) showing no violence. Each child was tested individually and the type and number of aggressive acts they showed over a 20-minute time period was later measured in the laboratory through a one-way mirror.

- *Field experiments*
  In a field experiment the researcher also deliberately manipulates the independent variable, but does so in the participants' own natural environment.

  Feshbach and Singer (1971), for example, manipulated the independent variable of 'exposure to aggression' to see what effect it had on the dependent variable of 'imitation of aggression in children' by showing boys in a residential school either a) aggressive television or b) non-aggressive television. This field study was conducted over 6 weeks, during which the boys' aggression was rated by the school staff.

- *Natural or quasi experiments*
  Quasi experiments are those where the researcher lacks direct control over the independent variable and/or the allocation of participants to the conditions (often making use of naturally allocated or pre-existing groups of participants). In natural experiments, for instance, the independent variable is changed by natural occurrence; the researcher just records the effect on the dependent variable in each condition.

  Joy et al (1977) investigated the independent variable of 'exposure to aggression' to see what effect it had on the dependent variable of 'imitation of aggression in children' by measuring levels of aggression in children of a small Canadian town a) before television was introduced to the town, and b) after television was introduced to the town.

Design and control in experiments

In order to test the cause and effect relationship between the independent and dependent variable in an experiment clearly, extraneous variables need to be controlled. The control can take the form of removing the influence of other variables on the dependent variable completely, or balancing their effect so that they do not influence one condition more than another.

Sources of extraneous influence and bias that need to be controlled by suitable experimental design include situational variables, participant variables and experimenter influence.

Controlling situational variables

These are usually eliminated or balanced between conditions by limiting distractions during testing, e.g. by testing in a quiet, isolated room, using simple, clearly explained and standardised instructions and procedures so each participant receives equal information and opportunities.

Controlling participant variables

Since participants need to be used in each condition but differ from each other in many ways, individual differences in their characteristics, abilities, attitudes, motivation, past experience, etc. could become a source of extraneous variables.

A *repeated measures design* involves using *the same participants in each condition* of an experiment, e.g. giving a group of participants a driving test with no alcohol, followed at a later time by the same test after consuming alcohol.

An *independent measures design* involves using *different participants in each condition* of the experiment, e.g. giving one group of participants a driving test with no alcohol, and a different group the same test after consuming alcohol.

A *matched pairs* design involves using different but similar participants in each condition of an experiment. An effort is made to match the participants in each condition in any important characteristics that might affect performance, e.g. in terms of existing driving ability, alcohol tolerance, etc.

Experimenter influence

An experimenter has to be careful in the way they design and conduct the experiment to avoid demand characteristics and experimenter expectancy effects.

Demand characteristics are those aspects of a study that enable the participants to work out the aim of the investigation and so may cause them to behave differently than they otherwise would, e.g. trying to please the researcher or spoil the study.

Experimenter expectancy effects are where the expectations of the researcher influence the results either by consciously or unconsciously revealing the desired outcome (causing demand characteristics) or through procedural or recording bias.

Exercise 7

1 State one similarity and one difference
   a between a laboratory and a field experiment.
   b between a field experiment and a natural experiment.

2 Using the example aggression experiments to help you, what do you think are the main advantages and disadvantages of
   a laboratory experiments?
   b field experiments?
   c natural experiments?

3 Using the example alcohol experiments to help you, what do you think are the advantages and disadvantages of
   a repeated measures designs?
   b independent measures designs?
   c matched pairs designs?

4 How do you think demand characteristics and experimenter expectancy effects could be controlled?

1 State one similarity and one difference

a between a laboratory and a field experiment.
Both involve the researcher deliberately manipulating the independent variable, but they differ in the location or environment where this manipulation occurs.

b between a field experiment and a natural experiment.
Both involve a larger number of uncontrolled variables than in a laboratory experiment, but whereas researchers can deliberately manipulate the independent variable in a field experiment, they lack this control over it in natural experiments.

2 Using the example aggression experiments to help you, what do you think are the main advantages and disadvantages of

a laboratory experiments?
The laboratory experiment is regarded as the most scientific method for a number of reasons. Firstly, the direct manipulation of the independent variable while controlling the effects of other variables provides the best evidence for any *cause* and *effect relationships*. Secondly, the laboratory increases control and accurate measurement of dependent variables, thus increasing the *objectivity* of the investigation. Thirdly, the laboratory standardisation means greater ability to *replicate* (repeat again) the study to verify its results.

Unfortunately, laboratory experiments have certain disadvantages. *Artificial* laboratory manipulation and controlled conditions may produce unnatural behaviour that *lacks ecological validity* (results do not generalise to real life). Laboratory results are also more likely to be *biased* by *sampling problems* (e.g. volunteers) and demand characteristics.

b field experiments?
Field experiments have *greater ecological validity* than laboratory experiments since behaviour occurs in its own natural environment. There is also *less bias* from sampling (participants do not have to be brought into the laboratory) and demand characteristics (if participants are unaware of being tested).

However, there is *greater difficulty controlling* extraneous variables and recording accurate results outside the laboratory. They are also more *difficult* to *replicate* exactly.

c natural experiments?
Natural experiments have *great ecological validity* since a 'natural' change (not induced directly by the experimenter) occurs in a natural environment. There is also *very little bias from sampling* or *demand characteristics* (if the participants are unaware of being observed by the experimenters).

It is, however, *hard to infer cause and effect* due to *little control* over extraneous variables and no direct manipulation of the independent variable. Natural experiments are also *virtually impossible to replicate* exactly.

3 Using the example alcohol experiments to help you, what do you think are the advantages and disadvantages of

a repeated measures designs?
One advantage is that *participant variables* (individual differences between participants, e.g. their driving ability and alcohol tolerance) *are kept constant between conditions*. Another is that fewer participants are required (because each is used more than once) therefore the design is more economical.

Negatively, however, *order effects* such as learning, fatigue or boredom may become constant errors when one condition is done after another, e.g. a participant given the same test may do better the second time due to practice or worse because they are tired. *Different tests* may therefore be needed, but then these might differ between conditions, e.g. in terms of their difficulty. *Demand characteristics* can also become a problem as the subject does both conditions of the experiment, may guess the aim of the study and act differently.

Order effects can be *counterbalanced* between conditions by testing half the participants in condition 'A' followed by condition 'B', and the other half with 'B' followed by 'A'.

b independent measures designs?
On the positive side, *no order* effects such as learning, fatigue or boredom influence a second condition since the participants are only tested in one condition. *Demand characteristics are also less of a problem* as the participants are only tested in one condition so are naive to the test, and are less likely to guess the aim of the study and act differently. In addition, the same test can be used for all participants in all conditions.

The disadvantages, of course, are that *participant variables differ between conditions*, which could become confounding variables unless controlled for by randomly allocating participants to each condition in the hope that random chance will balance the differences fairly equally between them. *More participants* are also required (because each is used only once) and, therefore, the design is less economical.

c matched pairs designs?
This design has many advantages. *Participant variables are kept more constant between conditions. Order effects do not occur and demand characteristics are less of a problem* since the participant is only tested in one condition, and the *same test* can be used.

The weaknesses of the design are that matching participants is *time consuming and difficult*, participant variables can *never be perfectly matched* in every respect anyway and *more participants* are required (because each is used only once).

4 How do you think demand characteristics and experimenter expectancy effects could be controlled?

Demand characteristics could be controlled by using an independent measures design to stop exposure to both conditions of the experiment and, therefore, reducing the chances of participants guessing the research aim, or by using deception to hide it (but there are ethical problems with this).

A *single blind method* could be used, whereby the participant does not know which condition of the experiment they are in. For example, when testing a new drug, the participant is not told whether they have been given real pills or a placebo (fake pills that resemble the real medicine but have no active ingredients). However, the researcher assessing the effects *does* know which condition the participants are in and may act in a biased way towards them.

Experimenter expectancy effects can be controlled by using a *double blind method*, whereby neither the subject nor the researcher carrying out the procedure and recording the results knows the hypothesis or which condition the subjects are in. For example, when testing a new drug, neither the participant nor the researcher assessing the effects is told the research aim or who has been given real pills or placebos.

8 Non-experimental methods in psychology

Non-experimental methods are those that do not involve the manipulation of an independent variable to investigate its effect on a dependent variable. These methods collect data on variables that can be analysed and interpreted to support or refute theories and hypotheses, but cannot legitimately be used to infer cause and effect relationships between variables.

Observation
Observations involve the precise measurement of spontaneously occurring behaviour in an objective way. The variables to be observed and recorded should be carefully and exactly pre-defined and their measurement agreed upon so that different researchers can show inter-observer reliability (measure variables in the same way).

There are various types of observation that differ according to the degree of interaction the observer has with those observed and where they take place.

- *Undisclosed observations* – These involve the observation of participants without their knowledge. This may be because the observer is hidden from view or is visible to the participants but has not revealed that data is being recorded.

  Undisclosed observations can be accomplished, e.g. by using one-way mirrors, observing from a distant or camouflaged position, and using hidden recording devices.

- *Participant observations* – These involve the researcher becoming involved in the everyday life of the participants to be observed (either with or without their knowledge).

  Rosenhan (1973), for example, used eight 'normal' undisclosed participant observers to gain admittance to psychiatric hospitals through faking symptoms and then recording their experience of being a psychiatric in-patient.

- *Naturalistic observations* – These involve the recording of spontaneously occurring behaviour in the subject's own natural environment.

  Fagot (1973), for example, conducted a naturalistic observation of parent–child interaction in the participants' own home to record what gender behaviour the parents encouraged or discouraged in their male and female children.

- *Laboratory observations* – These controlled observations also involve the recording of spontaneously occurring behaviour, but under conditions contrived by the researcher.

  Laboratory observations of sleep, for example, involve participants sleeping in a research room with recording electrodes attached to their eyes and scalp to measure eye movement and brain activity over a night's sleep.

- *Content analysis* – Rather than observing people themselves, content analysis involves observing, measuring and analysing the *communication* of people, groups or organisations, e.g. records of their conversations or media productions (i.e. television emissions, literature, etc.).

  The researcher first decides what media they are going to sample and then devises the *coding units* they are interested in measuring, e.g. the frequency of, or amount of time and space devoted to, certain words or themes.

Interviews and questionnaires
Interviews and questionnaires both collect people's *self-reports* about their behaviour, but do so in either an oral, face-to-face (interview) or written (questionnaire) way.

- *Interviews* – All interviews involve direct verbal questioning of participants by the researcher, but differ in how structured the questions are.

  Structured interviews contain fixed, predetermined questions and ways of replying (e.g. yes/no answers), whereas at the opposite extreme an *unstructured interview* may involve a general topic area for discussion but no fixed questions or ways of answering them – the interviewer just helps and clarifies.

  Between these two extremes, are *semi-structured interviews* and *clinical interviews*. Semi-structured interviews contain guidelines for the questions to be asked but the phrasing and timing is left up to the interviewer and answers may be open-ended. Clinical interviews, on the other hand, have semi-structured guidelines but allow further questioning to elaborate upon or probe more deeply into the answers that are given.

- *Questionnaires* – Questionnaires are written methods of gaining self-report data from participants, which do not necessarily require the presence of a researcher to fill them out. The questions can be closed (e.g. a yes/no, multiple-choice or rating on a scale response) or open-ended (involving a freely chosen, individually expressed written response), and should be designed to be precise, clearly understandable and easy to answer.

  Questionnaires are often used to gather data on attitudes and opinions or for psychometric tests (those that measure psychological variables such as personality or intelligence). If questionnaires are to function as true psychometric measures and allow a proper comparison of scores between different individuals in a population, they should not only show reliability and validity but also discriminatory power.

Correlation
A correlation is actually a method of analysis that compares two (or more) variables, which have been measured on a scale, to find the pattern of relationship they have with each other. The correlation between the variables can be positive (both increase at the same time), negative (one variable increases as another one decreases) or there may be no correlation (for example, no overall significant relationship or pattern). Correlations can use data gathered from observations, interviews or questionnaires.

Exercise 8
1 How could different observers test their inter-observer reliability to ensure their observations are objective (not biased by personal opinion)?
2 What are the advantages and disadvantages of
  a undisclosed observations?
  b participant observations?
  c laboratory observations compared to naturalistic ones?
3 How might you go about conducting a content analysis of gender stereotyping in television commercials?
4 What are the advantages and disadvantages of
  a information gained from self-report methods?
  b structured compared to unstructured interviews?
  c questionnaires compared to interviews?
5 What is wrong with the open-ended question: 'Why is today's media so bad for you?'

1 How could different observers test their inter-observer reliability to ensure their observations are objective (not biased by personal opinion)?

After carefully and precisely defining the behaviour to be observed and the method of recording it, *different observers using the same criteria should separately watch and record the same examples of behaviour.* Afterwards they should *compare* their *data* and if they *rate identically* or *very similarly* then they are showing good inter-observer (or inter-rater) reliability. (If their ratings are correlated together they should show a strong positive correlation). Of course the possibility exists that both could be showing similar kinds of bias!

2 What are the advantages and disadvantages of

a undisclosed observations?

If the participant is aware of being observed, *participant reactivity* may distort the data – they may behave in a more nervous or inhibited manner, or even 'show off'. If the subjects are told that they are going to be observed, they are more likely to work out the research aim and show *demand characteristics*. Undisclosed observations avoid these problems, but also produce a number of *ethical problems* of deception, lack of consent, invasion of privacy and confidentiality of data.

b participant observations?

Participant observations can produce extremely *detailed* and *in-depth knowledge* about participants and their environments, not gained from any other method. The data recorded is often of very *high ecological validity* if the observer is undisclosed, although somewhat less if they are disclosed – depending upon the level of integration with the participants.

The disadvantages are that it is often *difficult* to *record data promptly* and *objectively* (the close interaction with those observed may produce feelings that bias the observation) and a participant observer is more likely to *influence* the behaviour of those observed than a non-participant observer. Participant observations are also difficult to *replicate* exactly.

c laboratory observations compared to naturalistic ones?

Laboratory conditions provide more control over the environment than naturalistic ones, which leads to more *standardised* and *accurate* observations (it is easier to record and score data in the laboratory, especially if specialist equipment is needed, as with the sleep study example). In addition, the greater control also leads to *easier replication* (conducting again) of the observation under the same conditions to verify the findings. Inviting participants into the laboratory also usually avoids the ethical problems of lack of consent (unless the research purpose and observer are hidden).

Unfortunately, the greater control of environmental conditions in laboratory observations may cause the participants to behave differently than they would otherwise, e.g. in a more *constrained*, unnatural manner. The artificial conditions are also more likely to make the participants realise that they are being watched, causing *participant reactivity*, or enable them to work out the aim of the study, causing demand characteristics (although the use of one-way mirrors helps to avoid this). These factors all reduce what is often referred to as the ecological validity (realism) of the observed behaviour, e.g. abnormal sleep patterns may be produced in the unnatural conditions of the laboratory.

Naturalistic observations, on the other hand, usually have higher ecological validity (realism), especially if the observer is hidden, since participants go about their normal behaviour in their everyday environments. However, lack of control over conditions can make accurate observations and replication more difficult.

3 How might you go about conducting a content analysis of gender stereotyping in television commercials?

Firstly, you might have suggested sampling a large number of television commercials for certain products (e.g. washing-up liquid, baby nappies, sports cars), from a variety of channels and times during the day, over a period of a week, to gain a reasonably representative sample.

Secondly, you might have suggested measuring coding units such as the frequency of male and female actors appearing as the main user of each product in the commercials, or the amount of time male and female actors are seen using them for.

4 What are the advantages and disadvantages of

a information gained from self-report methods?

Asking people for information enables you to gain data on their inner mental world of experiences, knowledge, mental states, motivations, beliefs, attitudes and opinions, which may not be gained from other methods.

However, information from self-reports may be invalid because the respondents may lie, not know or be mistaken about their inner mental world. Respondents may want to present a certain image of themselves and give socially desirable or expected answers, which is why interviewers and questionnaire designers may want to obscure the true nature of the questions from the respondent (e.g. by asking irrelevant distracting questions mixed in with the real ones).

b structured compared to unstructured interviews?

Structured interviews, because of their high degree of standardisation and use of closed questions, are more reliable, replicable and easier to compare between respondents. They are also easier to score, quantify and analyse.

Unfortunately, their rigid framework and restricted answers may make them insensitive and so reduce their validity by ignoring the data respondents could potentially give, or distorting it.

Unstructured interviews, by comparison, can gain highly detailed and valid data due to their extremely flexible and un-constrained style of questioning and use of open-ended answers. However, these factors also mean that unstructured interviews are less replicable, reliable and comparable, because each can take a very different direction, and the answers are more difficult to quantify and analyse.

c questionnaires compared to interviews?

Questionnaires enable large amounts of standardised data to be collected more quickly and conveniently than interviews since they do not require the presence of the researcher to be filled out. They are also more replicable and standardised because each participant receives the same information, without variation in intonation, clarity or appearance of the interviewer.

Generally, however, questionnaires lack the flexibility and sensitivity of interviews, and highly reliable and valid psychometric questionnaires are difficult to construct.

5 What is wrong with the open-ended question: 'Why is today's media so bad for you?'

The open-ended question is ambiguous, a little too imprecise and leading. Does the question mean for you personally or people in general? Bad in quality or its effects? There are perhaps too many kinds of media (books, newspapers, TV, radio, Internet sites) to consider. The question also assumes the media is bad and so leads the respondent to only consider the negative aspects.

9 | Sampling

In order to conduct their research to gain evidence for or against their hypotheses and theories, psychologists need participants. Obviously not everyone can be studied and there will usually be limited access to the population of humankind, so psychologists can only legitimately claim to investigate a certain *target population* (a specified section of humankind)

Sampling is the process of selecting participants to study from the target population.

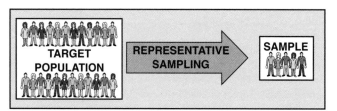

Since the results of the study on the sample will be *generalised* back to the target population (through inference), samples should be as *representative* (typical) of the target population as possible. Samples should be of a *sufficient size* (e.g. 30) to represent the variety of individuals in a target population but not so large as to make the study uneconomical in terms of time and resources.

Types of sampling
There are a number of methods that psychologists use to select their participants, including:

■ *Random sampling* – Truly random sampling only occurs when every member of a target population has an equal chance of being selected. For example, putting the names of every member of the target population in a hat and pulling a sample out (without looking!). A *quasi-random* method is *systematic sampling*, which involves a selection system that approximates random choice, e.g. picking every tenth name from a list.

■ *Stratified or quota sampling* – Involves dividing the target population into important subcategories (or strata) that need to be represented and then selecting members of these subcategories in the proportion that they occur in the target population. For example, if a target population consisted of 75% women and 25% men, a sample of 20 should include 15 women and 5 men.

■ *Opportunity sampling* – Simply involves selecting those participants that are around and available at the time. For example, university psychologists may sample from their students.

■ *Self-selecting sampling* – Self-selecting samples consist of those individuals who have determined their own involvement in a study, for example volunteers who respond to advertisements for studies.

Selecting target populations
In the same way that a psychologist has to be careful in drawing conclusions about the representativeness of his sample to his target population, the same applies when selecting a target population to study from the whole population of humankind.

The timing and location of investigations (when and where psychologists select their target populations) may affect the overall generalisability of the results to humankind.

■ *Cross-sectional studies* – cross-sectional studies investigate participants at *one particular point in time*. They are often used as a form of independent measures design to compare participants of different ages at the same time (rather than waiting for the same subjects to grow older) or different participants at different points in history.

Kohlberg, for example, compared the moral development of three groups of boys aged 10, 13 and 16 in 1981. Asch found an average rate of conformity of 32% in 1951, but later replication studies on different subjects in the 1970s and 1980s found varying rates.

■ *Longitudinal studies* – In longitudinal studies the same participants are investigated *over a long period of time*. It is a form of repeated measures design. Developmental psychologists, in particular, concentrate on how abilities and behaviour may vary over time, from infancy to adulthood, and so may find that studying the same participants over a long period of time is the most accurate way of discovering the principles and processes of development. With mental illness a longitudinal study may be the only way of reliably determining how a disorder progresses.

Kohlberg also conducted a longitudinal study of moral reasoning on the same participants over a twenty-year period, while Hodges and Tizard studied a group of children who had been in institutional care at ages 4, 8 and 16.

■ *Cross-cultural studies* – In cross-cultural studies, participants from *different cultures* are given the same test and their results are compared. Cross-cultural studies have investigated whether variation occurs across different countries in many psychological phenomena, such as perception, attachment, conformity, obedience and intelligence.

Deregowski (1972), for example, described perception tests conducted on African participants, while Mead (1935) studied three different tribes in New Guinea and compared their gender role behaviours.

Case studies
Case studies involve the *in-depth* and *detailed* study of a *single* particular individual, group or event. The case study method is often used with unusual, rare and valuable examples of behaviour that might provide important insights into psychological functioning, e.g. certain kinds of naturally occurring brain damage. It is also the favoured method when a good deal of time or resources are needed to study a psychological phenomenon. For example, Freud used the case study method in his patients' therapy to discover and deal with their problems, and Piaget studied his own children's cognitive development as they grew up.

Exercise 9
1 What are the advantages and disadvantages of
  a random compared to stratified/quota sampling?
  b opportunity compared to self-selecting sampling?
2 What are the advantages and disadvantages of
  a cross-sectional compared to longitudinal studies?
  b cross-cultural studies?
3 What are the advantages and disadvantages of case studies?

1 What are the advantages and disadvantages of

a random compared to stratified/quota sampling?

Random sampling (in large numbers) provides the best chance of a representative sample of a target population. However, small samples may not allow the laws of chance to create a sufficiently random sample, and the larger the target population the more difficult it is to sample randomly, since compiling a selection list of everyone becomes more impractical. True random sampling is therefore very rare, systematic sampling is usually more practical.

With stratified/quota sampling a deliberate effort is made to identify those characteristics of a sample which are most important for it to be representative of the target population. With small samples this can lead to a more representative spread of participants and with large target populations there is no need to create a list of every person. However, stratified sampling can still be very time consuming since the subcategories have to be identified and their proportions of the target population calculated.

b opportunity compared to self-selecting sampling?

Opportunity sampling is quick, convenient and often the most economical method of sampling. It has, therefore, been the most common type of sampling. Unfortunately, it gives rather unrepresentative samples *biased on the part of the researcher*, who may only choose certain kinds of people (those who seem easy to test, or even, perhaps unintentionally, those participants who might be more likely to behave as expected).

Self-selecting samples are also relatively convenient and, if volunteering is made on the basis of informed consent, ethical.

Nevertheless, self-selecting samples are also often unrepresentative, being *biased on the part of the subject* since volunteers are unlike non-volunteers in many ways (e.g. they can be more helpful and thus more likely to follow demand characteristics and behave as desired).

2 What are the advantages and disadvantages of

a cross-sectional compared to longitudinal studies?

With cross-sectional studies, immediate results can be gained which often makes the study more convenient, less time-consuming and cheaper than longitudinal studies. There is also less likelihood of losing participants between conditions.

However, cross-sectional studies may be overly influenced by the social environment of the time, and therefore need to be regularly replicated. Asch's findings on conformity, for example, were not always replicated when his experimental procedures were carried out years later, indicating that his results may have been influenced by factors present in his society *at that particular time*. In addition, if groups or studies are being compared, there are the disadvantages of an independent measures design to consider, e.g. subject confounding variables.

By contrast, longitudinal studies have less bias from subject variables since the same participants are used in all tests and conditions over time. This allows comparisons between conditions to be made with greater certainty.

Unfortunately, longitudinal studies are often more time-consuming, expensive and have a high likelihood of losing participants between conditions. They are also extremely difficult or impossible to replicate. Longitudinal studies can be carried out retrospectively by examining the history of participants, but this has many disadvantages, such as memory distortion and lack of objectivity.

b cross-cultural studies?

Cross-cultural studies help to combat an ethnocentric, culturally biased view of human psychology. They help to test how far the results of a study conducted in one culture can be generalised to other cultures. Such studies also provide data on cultural differences or similarities that may contribute to an understanding of psychological development. For example, with the nature/nurture debate, similarities across cultures may be attributed to shared inherited traits common to all humans, while differences may be caused by environmental/cultural variations between societies.

On the negative side, cross-cultural studies can be more time consuming, difficult to conduct (due to language barriers, etc.) and expensive. The behaviour observed may be open to ethnocentric misinterpretation and procedural bias when a researcher from one culture investigates participants from another culture, and subject reactivity may increase with a cross-cultural observer. For example, some researchers have argued that Mead did not spend enough time getting to know the tribes she was interviewing and may have been misled by some of the participants (whose occasionally joking answers she took seriously).

3 What are the advantages and disadvantages of case studies?

Case studies provide highly detailed and in-depth data which more superficial methods might miss or ignore. The method often allows the opportunity for many types of investigation (e.g. interview, observation and experiment) to be conducted.

The main problems, however, concern the lack of generalisability of the results to a wider population due to single cases being too small and unrepresentative a sample. For example, Piaget's children may have been different in some ways to other children and findings related to Freud's patients may not generalise to non-patients.

The objectivity of the researcher and reactivity of the participants can also become a problem when the researcher spends so much time dealing with a particular case, for example due to forming a closer relationship and investing so much effort. Case studies are often difficult or impossible to replicate exactly.

SAMPLING WORDSEARCH

G	R	D	E	I	F	I	T	A	R	T	S	U	M
O	T	C	U	F	E	X	S	A	M	P	L	E	L
U	K	E	M	L	V	O	E	S	I	F	A	A	E
N	V	I	G	A	I	U	P	C	P	P	N	R	O
I	O	P	P	R	T	B	J	H	O	O	I	S	P
M	L	R	E	U	A	O	E	G	I	P	D	N	P
Y	U	G	H	T	T	T	U	T	M	U	U	R	O
D	N	R	E	L	N	P	C	Q	I	L	T	P	R
U	T	E	L	U	E	E	O	X	D	A	I	I	T
T	E	B	C	C	S	R	T	A	I	T	G	A	U
S	E	L	F	S	E	L	E	C	T	I	N	G	N
E	R	H	S	S	R	M	W	Y	A	O	O	E	I
S	S	O	M	O	P	E	U	N	R	N	L	T	T
A	R	K	F	R	E	U	D	A	T	Q	E	V	Y
C	E	Z	U	C	R	S	M	O	D	N	A	R	E

Find 17 sampling terms or names in the grid. They can be found horizontally, vertically and diagonally (backwards or forwards). The answers are at the back of the book.

Deregowski's article summarises a number of cross-cultural studies of pictorial perception conducted by different researchers (e.g. William Hudson) on a variety of cross-cultural groups. Deregowski claims that such studies show that people from one culture may perceive pictures differently from those of another. This provides an insight into how perception works (indicating the role played by learning in perception) and implies that pictures do not necessarily provide a universal cross-cultural means of communication (a 'lingua franca').

Deregowski presents evidence from two main kinds of investigation to support his claims.

Pictorial object recognition studies

Anecdotal reports from missionaries and anthropologists living among remote cultures have shown these cultures to have difficulty recognising objects from pictures, especially from accurate perspective drawings which do not represent all aspects of an object. For example, some studies have shown that African subjects from remote villages can pick out the correct toy from pictures of familiar animals (e.g. lions) but not unfamiliar ones (e.g. kangaroos).

Hudson showed that African children and adults prefer split drawings (those that show all the essential features of an object, even if they cannot usually be seen from one viewpoint or perspective) to correct perspective drawings.

Deregowski briefly discusses theories that attempt to account for split-drawing preferences, including Boas's idea that it developed from turning sculptures into flat pictures, Levi-Strauss's social view that it symbolically reflects the split personality of mask-wearing cultures, and his own postulation. Deregowski suggests that perhaps children from all cultures have an aesthetic preference for the split style of drawing but some cultures learn to suppress it because the split style does not communicate information about objects as accurately as perspective drawing.

Pictorial depth recognition studies

Hudson tested black South African workers to see whether they could interpret combinations of pictorial depth cues as three-dimensional representations. The three main pictorial depth cues used were familiar size (where the larger of two objects is drawn further away), overlap (where nearer parts of a picture obscure farther away parts) and linear perspective (where lines known to be parallel converge at the horizon).

The subjects were asked questions about the relationship between objects in the picture to see whether they had two- or three-dimensional vision, e.g. Which is closer? What is the man doing?

What is the man doing?

Hudson found mostly two-dimensional perception in African tribal participants across all ages, educational and social levels, and this finding was confirmed by pictorial depth measuring apparatus developed by Gregory.

Hudson showed Zambian participants a drawing of two squares (arranged so that western subjects perceive them as a three dimensional cube) and asked them to build a model of it out of modelling clay and sticks. Most of the Zambians built two-dimensional models, whereas the few who showed three-dimensional perception built a three-dimensional cube. This confirmed the validity of Hudson's pictorial depth perception test.

2-dimensional picture   3-dimensional model   2-dimensional model

Exercise 10

1 Which of the elephants opposite represents the split drawing and which the perspective drawing?

2 Which of the elephants, according to Hudson, would his black African subjects have preferred?

3 In the pictorial depth recognition diagram above, what would a supposedly two-dimensional viewer say the man was throwing his spear at and why?

4 A group of Zambian school children having been divided into two- and three-dimensional perceivers were shown pictures of an illusory trident and a normal three-pronged trident (the control picture). The amount of time each group spent looking at each picture when asked to draw a copy of it themselves was recorded. One group spent longer looking at the illusory trident than the control trident when trying to copy them, the other group showed no significant difference between the two tridents. Which group do you think took longer with the illusory trident and why?

5 What are the independent variables in the above studies?

6 What is wrong with using western materials and styles of picture drawing to test pictorial depth perception in non-western participants?

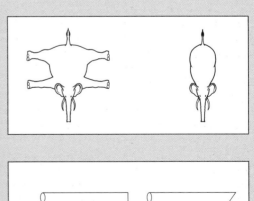

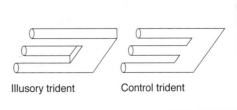

Illusory trident   Control trident

1 Which of the elephants opposite represents the split drawing and which the perspective drawing?

The one on the left shows all the features regardless of viewpoint. The perspective drawing on the right only shows those features visible from a certain viewpoint (in this case, viewed from above).

2 Which of the elephants, according to Hudson, would his black African subjects have preferred?

The split drawing on the left. When Hudson showed African children and adults the two elephants, all preferred the split drawing except one (who thought the elephant looked like it was jumping around dangerously).

3 In the pictorial depth recognition diagram above, what would a supposedly two-dimensional viewer say the man was throwing his spear at and why?

A three-dimensional viewer would say that the man is about to throw his spear at the antelope, a two-dimensional perceiver would say that the man is about to throw his spear at the elephant. The two-dimensional perceiver does not make use of the two depth cues in the picture – familiar size (the elephant is drawn smaller than its known size relative to the man and antelope to represent its further distance away) and overlap (the lines of the nearer hills obscure the lines of the hill behind).

4 A group of Zambian school children having been divided into two- and three-dimensional perceivers were shown pictures of an illusory trident and a normal three-pronged trident (the control picture). The amount of time each group spent looking at each picture when asked to draw a copy of it themselves was recorded. One group spent longer looking at the illusory trident than the control trident when trying to copy them, the other group showed no significant difference between the two tridents. Which group do you think took longer with the illusory trident and why?

The three-dimensional perceivers spent longer looking at the illusory trident than the normal control trident, whereas the two-dimensional perceivers showed no significant difference in viewing the two. Three-dimensional perceivers become confused by the ambiguous illusory trident since they attempt to see it as a three-dimensional picture of a trident (which is physically impossible to realise). They thus spend longer looking at it than the two-dimensional perceivers – who merely copy the lines as they are drawn on both pictures without being misled by depth perception.

5 What are the independent variables in the above studies?

The independent variables are either the culture of the participants (e.g. Western vs. African) or ability to perceive depth (e.g. two-dimensional vs. three-dimensional perceivers, as identified by Hudson's pictorial depth perception test). Note, however, that the researcher does not directly manipulate these independent variables, so the method represents a quasi-experimental or natural experimental design.

6 What is wrong with using western materials and styles of picture drawing to test pictorial depth perception in non-western participants?

Care has to be taken that the methodology is not biased towards one culture rather than another so that the results only reflect the independent variable under consideration. For example, even presenting pictures on paper rather than ecologically natural materials, or focusing more on some depth cues rather than others (e.g. the more realistic texture gradient cue) may lead to inaccurate or over-generalised conclusions about cultural differences being drawn from the results. Care also has to be taken that not only are the results fair and accurate, but that they are reported in an unbiased way. Reporting should avoid statements that imply that one culture is superior or inferior to another, based on one culture's norms and values, when they are merely different. Overall, Deregowski seems to avoid this kind of value-laden reporting style, although some critics have argued that there is an ethnocentric assumption that western methods of pictorially representing objects especially involving depth cues are more correct than others and should be universally recognised.

DEREGOWSKI CROSSWORD

1 The kind of study that compares people from different societies (5/8).
2 A kind of assumption that only considers one's own cultural viewpoint and beliefs (12).
3 A pictorial depth cue where nearer parts obscure farther away parts of a picture (7).
4 Scientists who study mainly preliterate human societies (15).
5 The pictorial depth perception shown by the majority of African tribal participants (3/11).
6 Abilities shown across all cultures and societies are _____ (9).
7 The type of report based on informal or unsystematic observation (9).
8 A researcher who tested cultural differences in South African pictorial depth perception (6).
9 The kind of object drawing preferred by most African children and adults (5).
10 The animal that three-dimensional perceivers thought the hunter was throwing his spear at (8).
11 The term for a means of communication understood across all societies (6/6).
12 The picture that two- and three-dimensional perceivers had to copy in two versions (7).
13 The nationality of those who had to build models out of sticks and modelling clay (7).
14 The kind of animals that African participants from remote villages could identify from pictures (8).

11 Data analysis in psychology

Once the results of a study have been gained, psychologists analyse the data to pick out trends and patterns to help them draw conclusions. The data can be analysed quantitatively (in terms of numbers) by using descriptive and inferential statistics or qualitatively (described in words).

Qualitative data analysis

The analysis of qualitative data in its own right, without reducing it to quantitative numbers, can be very useful.

Qualitative data can be gained from a variety of methods, such as observations, interviews, case studies and even experiments, for example in terms of describing *how* the subject *behaved* during testing and what they *said* (rather than how many times they did or said things).

It can be analysed by firstly extracting samples of relevant, important and/or typical behavioural reactions or quotes from the data obtained, and then summarising and grouping them into categories to illustrate the trends or themes in the data.

Quantitative data analysis

Types of quantitative data

The data gained from measuring variables differs in its detail and quality. Before psychologists can properly analyse it, they have to identify what *level of data* they have.

- *Nominal data* is a simple *frequency headcount* (the number of times something occurred) found in *discrete categories* (something can only belong to one category), e.g. the number of people who pass or fail a test, recorded on a tally chart or frequency grid. Nominal data is the simplest data.

- *Ordinal data* concerns measurements that can be put in an order, rank or position, e.g. ratings or scores on unstandardised psychological scales (such as attractiveness out of 10) or who came 1st, 2nd, 3rd, etc. in a test. However, the *intervals* between each score, rating or rank are *unknown* or *unequal*, i.e. we do not know how far ahead the 1st was from the 2nd.

- *Interval* and *ratio data* are both measurements on a *scale*, the *intervals* of which are *known and equal*. Ratio data has a true zero point, however, whereas interval data can go into negative values, e.g. temperature for interval data (degrees centigrade can be minus), length or time for ratio data (no seconds is no time at all). These are the most precise types of data.

Descriptive statistics

Descriptive statistics involve summarising and presenting data, and the trends in it, in a numerical or graphical manner.

Numerical descriptive statistics

Numerical descriptive statistics summarise the data by calculating measures of central tendency and dispersion.

Measures of central tendency estimate the most typical or representative value or trend in the data, and include:

- *The mode* – this is simply the value or event that occurs the most frequently. The mode is the most suitable measure of central tendency for nominal data. For example, for the values: 12, 4, 7, 8, 3, 9, 7, 14, 17, 18, 17 there are two modes 7 and 17 (the data is bimodal).

- *The median* – this is the middle value when all the scores are placed in rank order. The median is the most suitable measure of central tendency for ordinal data. For example, for the values: 3, 4, 7, 7, 8, 9, 12, 14, 17, 17, 18 the median is 9.
  If there had been two 'middle numbers', for example, 3, 4, 7, 7, 8, 9, 12, 14, 17, 17, 18, 82, the average of the two is taken, which would be $9 + 12 = 21 \div 2 = 10.5$.

- *The mean* – this is the average value of all scores (all values are added up and the total is divided by the number of values). The mean is the most suitable measure of central tendency for interval or ratio data. For example, for the values 12, 4, 7, 8, 3, 9, 7, 14, 17, 18, 17 the mean would be 10.54 (total of $116 \div 11$ values).
  Alternatively, for the values 3, 4, 7, 7, 8, 9, 12, 14, 17, 17, 18, 82, the mean would be 16.5 (total of $198 \div 12$).

Measures of dispersion, however, describe the variation in the values or scores under consideration, and include:

- *The range* – this is the difference between the smallest and largest value, plus 1. For example, for the values 12, 4, 7, 8, 3, 9, 7, 14, 17, 18, 17 the range = 16 $(18 - 3) + 1$. Alternatively, for the values 12, 4, 7, 8, 3, 9, 7, 14, 17, 18, 17, 82 the range = 80 $(82 - 3) + 1$.

- *The semi-interquartile range* – when data is put in order, find the first quartile (Q1) and third quartile (Q3) of the sample, subtract the Q1 value from the Q3 value and divide the result by two. For example, for the values

3,	4,	7,	7	8,	9,	12,	14,	17,	17,	18
		Q1			Q2			Q3		
		7						17		

  $17 - 7 = 10$ $10 \div 2 = $ semi-interquartile range of 5
  Note that if the 18 was replaced with an 82, the semi-interquartile range would remain the same (5).

- *The standard deviation* – this is the average amount that all scores deviate from the mean. The difference (deviation) between each score and the mean of those scores is calculated and then squared (to remove minus values). These squared deviations are then added up and their mean calculated to give a value known as the variance. The square root of the variance gives the standard deviation of the scores. For example, for the values 6, 8, 10, 12, 14 (let's keep this one simple!) the variance would be 8 and the standard deviation would be 2.8 (see below).

score		mean		d	d squared
6	–	10	=	–4	16
8	–	10	=	–2	4
10	–	10	=	0	0
12	–	10	=	+2	4
14	–	10	=	+4	16
					40

The mean of 40 = 8 = variance
The square root of the variance
= the standard deviation = 2.8

Exercise 11 (the answers are on page 30)

1 What advantage does quantitative data have over qualitative data?

2 From looking at the operationalised variables on page 14, what level of data would be recorded in each case?

3 What are the advantages and disadvantages of
   a the mode, median and mean?
   b the range, inter-quartile range and standard deviation?

Graphical descriptive statistics

Graphical descriptive statistics represent, summarise and display trends in data in a pictorial manner. For example:

- *Pie charts* – show the proportions of all scores gained by various categories. The proportions of the pie chart are calculated by the formula:

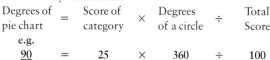

e.g.

$$\underline{90} = 25 \times 360 \div 100$$

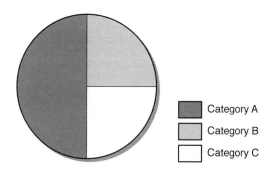

	Category A
	Category B
	Category C

- *Scattergrams* – plot pairs of scores against each other to show their correlational relationship. Correlations between variables can be positive (both increase at the same time), negative (one variable increases as another one decreases), or there may be no correlation (for example, no overall significant relationship or pattern). A line of best fit can be drawn to show patterns or trends in the data.

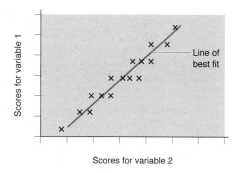

- *Bar charts* – show data only for those categories that the researcher is interested in comparing, e.g. two or more conditions in an experiment.

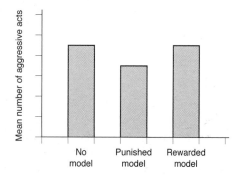

- *Histograms* – show data for all categories, even those with zero values. The column width for each category interval is equal so the area of the column is proportional to the number of cases it contains of the sample.

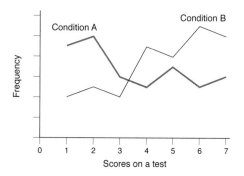

- *Frequency polygon* – also known as a line graph, the frequency polygon is similar to the histogram except it allows two or more sets of data to be shown on the same graph.

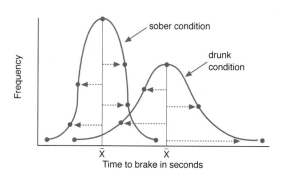

Variance in graphical statistics

The two conditions below differ in variance, perhaps because people vary more in their tolerance to alcohol.

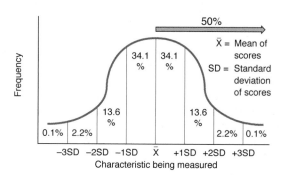

Normal distribution curves occur in the populations of many continuous psychological variables and are involved in parametric statistics. They are bell shaped and symmetrical at the midpoint where the mode, median and mean all fall.

The percentage of scores covered by the areas between the standard deviations of the curve are known.

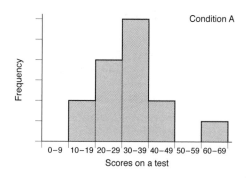

Inferential statistical tests

Significance

Inferential statistical tests tell psychologists how significant their results are. A significant result is one where there is a *low probability that chance factors* were responsible for any observed difference, correlation or association in the variables.

Does the difference between these two sets of data look large enough to be **significant** (not down to chance)?

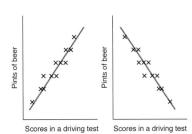

Do the points of data on these scattergrams look **significantly like** positive or negative correlations?

Levels of significance

How large an effect (difference or relationship) is required for psychologists to conclude that a result is significant (probably *not* due to chance factors)? Well, significance levels are expressed as a decimal in the form *P < 0.00* (where '*P*' stands for probability that chance factors are responsible for results), and psychologists have concluded that, for most purposes in psychology, the 5% *level of significance (P < 0.05)* is appropriate. A result that is significant at this level can be said *to be less than 5% likely to be due to chance factors* (a 1 in 20 chance it was a 'fluke' result). There are other possible levels of significance/probability but the P < 0.05 level seems reasonable for most psychological evidence.

How do inferential statistics work?

There are many different types of inferential statistical test (there is not room here to explain exactly how each is conducted) but basically each provides a '*calculated value*' based on the results of the investigation. This value can then be *compared* to a '*critical value*' (a value that statisticians have estimated to represent a significant effect) to determine whether the results are significant. The critical value depends upon the level of significance required (e.g. P < 0.05, P < 0.01 etc.) and other factors such as the number of subjects used in the test and whether the hypothesis is one or two tailed.

In the Chi squared, Sign test, Spearman's Rho, Pearson's product and Related or Unrelated T – tests the calculated value has to exceed the critical value for a significant result. In the Wilcoxon and Mann Whitney U tests the calculated value has to be equal or less than the critical value for a significant result.

The calculated value of correlation statistics is known as the correlation coefficient, and describes the relationship between the variables as a precise number ranging from minus 1 (a perfect negative correlation) through 0 (no significant relationship), to plus 1 (a perfect positive correlation).

Inferential statistics allow us to infer that the effect gained from the results on a sample of subjects is probably typical of the target population the sample was derived from.

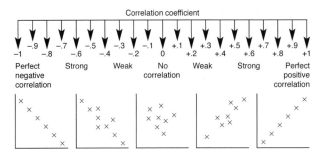

Which test to use?

If there are only two conditions in an experiment, or two variables in a correlation, then the tests in the decision table below will usually suffice. To decide which test is the appropriate one, the following decisions have to be made:

1 Is a test of difference (for an experiment) or relationship (for a correlation or test of association) required?
2 If a test of difference is required, what experimental design has been used (an independent measures or repeated measures/matched pairs design)?
3 Is the data used nominal, ordinal, interval or ratio data?
4 If interval or ratio data is used, then it may be possible to conduct a more statistically powerful (or sensitive) parametric test (these are the tests highlighted in grey in the table). However, to conduct such a test two other conditions should ideally be met, namely that:
   a both sets of data should be normally distributed or from normally distributed populations
   b both sets of data have similar variance.

	Tests of difference		Tests of relationship
	Independent measures design	Repeated measures or matched pairs design	Association or correlation
Nominal data	Chi Squared Test	Sign Test	Chi Squared Test
Ordinal data	Mann Whitney U Test	Wilcoxon Signed Ranks Test	Spearman's Rho Correlation
Interval or Ratio data	Unrelated T-Test	Related T-Test	Pearson's Product Moment Correlation Coefficient

Exercise 11 (continued)

4 What do the values P < 0.01 and P < 0.5 stand for in terms of chance?

5 Why do you think psychologists would prefer to use their P < 0.05 level of significance rather than the two above?

6 Why should one always plot out a correlation's scattergram rather than just look at the correlation co-efficient?

7 What test would be appropriate if a study had
   a ordinal data and a repeated measures design?
   b nominal data and an independent measures design?
   c two sets of normally distributed ratio data with different variance and a matched pairs design?

1 What advantage does quantitative data have over qualitative data?

Quantitative data, being based on numbers, can be more *precisely* and *objectively* analysed using descriptive and inferential statistics. However, qualitative data is useful to describe information lost in the quantified and narrowed analysis of figures. Interviews with participants after experiments can often reveal the causes of their behaviour and provide ideas for future research. Qualitative analysis is often attacked for its lack of objectivity. However,

- techniques exist to check its reliability and validity, e.g. triangulation (using more than one method of investigation) and repetition of the research cycle (to check previous data);
- subjective opinion and participant consultation is regarded as a strength by many researchers, e.g. feminist psychologists.

2 From looking at the operationalised variables on page 14, what level of data would be recorded in each case?

Memory – for example, the number of previously presented items of information recalled or recognised after a time delay. Ratio data is scored out of the total number of items to be remembered (no items = no recall), *if* the items are equally easy to remember.

Attraction – for example, the rating out of ten for attractiveness given by one person to another. Ordinal data is scored, but note that rating using opinion rather than fixed unit scales, such as timing, introduces subjectivity.

Obedience – for example, whether or not people obey an unreasonable command (for an action they would not otherwise perform) from another person. Nominal data, the number of people who obey or do not obey, is scored. Note that nominal data provides little information, e.g. it cannot say how long or intensely a behaviour was shown.

Helping behaviour – for example, how quickly in seconds (if at all) help is given to a person obviously in need of it. Ratio data is scored, a precise and standardised rating.

3 What are the advantages and disadvantages of

a the mode, median and mean?
The mode is useful to show most the popular value and is easy to calculate, but it is a crude measure of central tendency and is not useful if there are many equal modes.
The median is not distorted by extreme freak values, e.g. the '42' in the set of data 2, 3, 3, 4, 4, 4, 4, 4, 5, 5, 6, 42. However, it can be distorted by small samples and is less sensitive as a measure of central tendency than the mean.
The mean is the most sensitive measure of central tendency. However, it can be distorted by extreme freak values, e.g. the '42' in the data 2, 3, 3, 4, 4, 4, 4, 4, 5, 5, 6, 42.

b the range, inter-quartile range and standard deviation?
The range is quick and easy to calculate but distorted by extreme 'freak' values. The inter-quartile range overcomes this problem, but can neglect important data. The standard deviation is the most sensitive measure of dispersion, using all the data available. It can be used to relate the sample to the population's parameters.

4 What do the values P < 0.01 and P < 0.5 stand for in terms of chance?

The significance level of **P < 0.01** stands for a 1% or 1 in a 100 probability that chance factors were responsible for the results observed.

The significance level of **P < 0.5** stands for a 50% or 50:50 probability that chance factors were responsible for the results observed.

5 Why do you think psychologists would prefer to use their P < 0.05 level of significance rather than the two above?

There are many other possible levels of probability but the P < 0.05 seems reasonable since
- significance levels of **P < 0.5** or **P < 0.3** are regarded as *too lenient* – the effect (difference or correlation) is too likely to have happened by chance and a *type-one error* is more likely to be made (the *null hypothesis may be falsely rejected* – the researcher may falsely claim an effect exists).
- significance levels of **P < 0.01** or **P < 0.001** (a 0.1% or 1 in a 1000 probability that chance factors were responsible) are regarded as *too strict or stringent* – a strong effect (difference or correlation) is too likely to be ignored because the level is overly demanding and a *type-two error* is more likely to be made (the *null hypothesis may be falsely accepted* – the researcher may falsely claim an effect does not exist).
N.B. – Stringent levels are required when greater certainty of significance is needed, e.g. during safety tests.

6 Why should one always plot out a correlation's scattergram rather than just look at the correlation co-efficient?

A correlation coefficient of 0 may not necessarily mean a random distribution of scores – a pattern may still exist. For example, each of the following patterns would give no overall correlation.

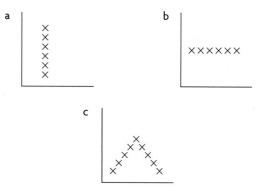

No overall positive or negative correlation is shown by the scattergrams above (in 'c' they cancel each other out).

7 What test would be appropriate if a study had

a ordinal data and a repeated measures design?
The Wilcoxon Signed Ranks Test would be appropriate.

b nominal data and an independent measures design?
The Chi Squared Test would be appropriate.

c two sets of normally distributed ratio data with different variance and a matched pairs design?
The Related T-Test would be appropriate *if* both sets of data had similar variance. However, because all the criteria for a parametric test are not met, the data can be ranked and an appropriate ordinal level test conducted – in this case the Wilcoxon Signed Ranks Test.

RESEARCH METHODS CROSSWORD

1. The aspects of a study that give away its purpose or encourage certain behaviour (6/15)
2. A participant design where an effort is made to use similar people in each condition (7/5)
3. The term for learning, boredom or fatigue in the second condition of an experiment (5/7)
4. A participant design using the same subjects in each condition (8/8)
5. A hypothesis that states a direction in the outcome of the results (3/6)
6. A sample where every member of a target population has an equal chance of selection (6)
7. The measured variable of an experiment (9)
8. Observations where the researcher is involved in the everyday life of the subjects (11)
9. A graph that only shows data for categories the researcher wants to compare (3/5)
10. Unwanted variables that could influence the dependent variable of an experiment (10)
11. A graph that plots correlational scores (11)
12. The average amount all scores vary from their mean is the standard _____ (9)
13. A diagram showing the proportions of all scores gained by various categories (3/5)
14. Data that does not consist of numbers (11)
15. A control where neither the subject nor the experimenter conducting the procedure knows which condition the subjects are in (6/5)
16. Methods like questionnaires and interviews where the subjects provide the data (4/6)
17. The middle score when all scores are placed in order of magnitude (6)
18. A sampling method where subjects determine their own involvement in the study (4/9)
19. A study of the same subjects over time (12)
20. Data that ranks measurements (7)
21. P<0.05 is a level of _____ (12)
22. An in-depth study of a particular person, group or event (4/5)

RESEARCH METHODS ANAGRAMS

1. D O E M
2. D Y I L T I V A
3. M A N L I N O
4. L I A I T Y R E B I L
5. T R A M O G I S H
6. L A T O O R I N R E C
7. D I S A D A R S T A N T I O N
8. E I S A T I O N O P A L R A T I O N
9. P O T N I T O P R U Y   S P L E A M
10. M A L N O R   I B U T D I S T R I O N

Ethical guidelines for conducting research

Ethical guidelines for the use of animals in research

The Experimental Psychology Society (1986) has issued guidelines to control animal experimentation based on the legislation of the Animals (Scientific Procedures) Act (1986). In general all researchers should:

- Avoid or minimise stress and suffering for all living animals.
- Always consider the possibility of other options to animal research.
- Be as economical as possible in the numbers of animals tested.

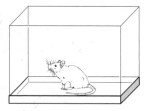

However, before any animal is tested, a Home Office Licence to conduct animal research has to be acquired. The Home Office provides legislation for and monitors

- **the conditions under which animals are kept** – cage sizes, food, lighting, temperature, care routine, etc. all have to be suitable for the species and its habit.

- **the researchers conducting the research** – all involved have to demonstrate they have the necessary skills and experience to work with the particular species they wish to study in order to acquire their personal licences.

- **the research projects allowed** – applications must be submitted outlining the project's aims and possible benefits as well as the procedures involved (including the number of animals and the degree of distress they might experience). Projects are only approved if the three requirements above are met and the level of distress caused to the animals is justified by the benefits of the research. The conditions of the licence have to be strictly adhered to regarding the numbers, species and procedures (e.g. limits on the maximum level of electric shock) allowed. Research on endangered species is prohibited unless the research has direct benefits for the species itself, e.g. conservation.

Bateson (1986) has specified some of the factors involved in deciding on the viability of animal research. Often the decision will involve a trade off between

a the certainty of benefit from the research
b the quality of the research
c the amount of suffering involved for the animals.

Home Office licences are most likely to be awarded if factors 'a' and 'b' are high, and factor 'c' is low.

Ethical issues in human research

The aim of psychology is to provide us with a greater understanding of ourselves and, if required, to enable us to use that understanding to predict and control our behaviour for *human betterment*. To achieve this understanding psychologists often have no other choice but to investigate human subjects for valid results to be obtained. Humans, however, not only experience physical pain and anxiety but can also be affected mentally – in terms of embarrassment or loss of self-esteem, for example. Humans also have rights of protection and privacy above the levels granted to other animals, and so this leads us to ethical dilemmas:

- How far should psychologists be allowed to go in pursuing their knowledge?
- Should humankind aim to improve itself by allowing people to be dehumanised in the process?
- Do the *ends* of psychological research justify the *means*?
- Can we ever know whether a piece of research will justify abusing the rights of individuals before we conduct it?

The existence of ethical constraints is clearly a serious but necessary limitation on the advancement of psychology as a science and the major professional psychological bodies of many countries have published ethical guidelines for conducting research. In Britain, the British Psychological Society (1993) has published the *Ethical Principles for Conducting Research with Human Participants*, which guides psychologists to consider the implications of their research (e.g. by asking members of the target population if they would take offence to the research) and deals with a number of methodological ethical issues such as

- *consent* – researchers are obliged, whenever possible, to obtain the participants' *informed* consent – *all* aspects of the research that might affect their willingness to give consent should be revealed. Consent is especially an issue when testing involves children or those unable to give it themselves, e.g. people with serious brain damage. Authority or payment must not be used to pressure participants into consent.

- *deception* – the BPS Ethical Principles (1993) states that 'Participants should never be deliberately misled without extremely strong scientific or medical justification. Even then there should be strict controls and the disinterested approval of independent advisors'. Many psychology studies would not achieve valid results due to demand characteristics if deception was not employed, and so a cost–benefit analysis of the gains vs. the discomfort of the participant must be considered.

- *debriefing* – this involves clarifying the participants' understanding of the research afterwards and discussing or rectifying any consequences of the study to ensure that they leave the study in as similar a state as possible to when they entered it. This is especially important if deception has been employed and the procedures could cause long-term upset.

- *withdrawal from the investigation* – any participant in a psychological study should be informed of their right to withdraw from testing whenever they wish.

- *confidentiality* – under the Data Protection Act (1984) participants and the data they provide should be kept anonymous unless they have given their full consent to make their data public. If participants are dissatisfied after debriefing they can demand that their data is destroyed.

- *protection of participants* – participants should leave psychological studies in roughly the same condition in which they arrived, without suffering physical or psychological harm. The risk of harm should not be greater than that found in everyday life.

- *observational research* – hidden observational studies produce the most ecologically valid data but inevitably raise the ethical issue of invasion of privacy.

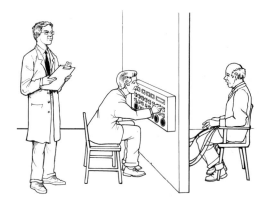

Human studies in psychology with ethical implications

Milgram (1963)

In Milgram's study of obedience, subjects were falsely led to believe that they were giving real electric shocks to another participant (in fact a confederate of the experimenter) in an experiment on learning. If they indicated they wanted to stop giving the shocks, they were told by an experimenter (the authority figure in the study) 'you have no other choice, you must go on' to see if they would continue to obey.

Milgram reported that 'In a large number of cases the degree of tension reached extremes that are rarely seen in sociopsychological laboratory studies. Subjects were observed to sweat, tremble, stutter, bite their lips, groan and dig their fingers into their flesh…Full-blown, uncontrollable seizures were observed for 3 subjects.' Milgram was surprised at both the degree of obedience and the reactions his participants showed, since nobody he asked before the experiment estimated they would be so influenced by the authority figure. After the experiment all subjects were told what the experiment was really about and were reassured that the learner was unharmed and had not received any shocks.

Haney, Banks and Zimbardo (1973)

In this prison simulation experiment, the participants signed a formal statement agreeing to a temporary loss of some civil rights such as the invasion of privacy. However, the prison simulation procedures were more stressful than the volunteer students playing the prisoner role expected; a surprise arrest by city police outside their homes and a humiliating prison induction procedure were followed by brutal treatment from the students playing the role of the guards. The simulation had to be stopped after just six days instead of the two weeks it was meant to run because of the extreme reactions shown by the participants, for example, crying, rage, depression, and even the development of a psychosomatic rash.

Rosenhan (1973)

In the study 'On Being Sane in Insane Places' eight 'normal' people gained admission to psychiatric hospitals merely by pretending to hear voices and faking their name and occupation to test the ability of mental health professionals to diagnose mental illness.

Case studies

In many case studies, especially involving data gained as part of a client–patient relationship, pseudonyms are used to maintain anonymity, for example, Genie, H.M., Anna O, etc.

Watson and Rayner (1920)

Watson and Rayner conditioned a phobia of rats into an emotionally stable 11-month-old infant, 'Little Albert', by repeatedly startling the child with a loud noise every time a white rat was presented. The fear response generalised to other objects including rabbits, fur coats and even facial hair (including that on a Santa Claus mask!) but was never removed from the subject by the researchers.

Craik and Tulving (1975)

Craik and Tulving tested levels of processing ideas by using incidental learning – participants were given some words to examine but were not told they would be tested on their memory of them.

Drug-testing studies

These studies often involve the use of placebo control groups. Patients may be given either the real drug or pills that have no effect (placebos), but are not told which they have be given so their expectations do not influence the effects of the drugs.

Areas of psychological research that have used animals as participants

Learning

Pavlov used dogs as participants in his classical conditioning experiments, while Skinner used rats and pigeons in his studies on operant conditioning. Some learning studies use food and water to reinforce behaviour, others use electric shocks as punishing stimuli. Seligman and Maier (1967), for example, found a 'failure to escape traumatic shock' in dogs by repeatedly administering unavoidable electric shocks. One of the dogs died.

Obedience

Sheridan and King's (1972) later variation of Milgram's obedience study involved subjects being instructed to give real electric shocks to a puppy. High levels of obedience were shown.

Brain function

Many studies have investigated the function of brain areas by removing them or stimulating them in animals and recording the difference in behaviour. Lashley (1929), for example, removed parts of rats' brains in order to find the location of memory, while Delgado (1969) implanted electrodes into monkeys' brains to stimulate aggressive behaviour.

Attachment deprivation

Harlow raised rhesus monkeys in complete social deprivation. Their later behaviour was extremely maladaptive, being unable to properly interact with other monkeys or look after their young.

Language acquisition

Studies involving the long-term captivity of chimpanzees and gorillas have been conducted to teach them language.

Exercise 12

1 Using the studies on humans above, find examples of the ethics of consent, deception, debriefing, right to withdraw from testing, confidentiality and protection of participants.

2 By considering some of the studies using animals as participants above, do you think the 'benefits' of the findings justify the 'costs' involved in animal suffering?

3 Why do you think some psychologists think they should use animals to investigate human psychological issues, while others object to it?

1 Using the studies on humans above, find examples of the ethics of consent, deception, debriefing, right to withdraw from testing, confidentiality and protection of participants.

Consent

- Milgram (1963) – the subjects had volunteered to participate in a study of learning, not obedience. Having not been told of the researcher's objectives their informed consent was not given.
- Haney, Banks and Zimbardo (1973) – the subjects in the prison simulation experiment signed a formal 'consent' statement specifying there would be a loss of some civil rights, although one might argue that they were not, and could not have been, completely informed about what they were letting themselves in for.

Deception

- Milgram (1963) – the subjects were led to believe they were giving real electric shocks to another in an experiment on learning rather than obedience. However, Orne and Holland (1968) suggested that the subjects were involved in a 'pact of ignorance' with the experimenter – they did not really believe they were harming anyone.
- Rosenhan (1973) – the eight 'normal' people gained admission to psychiatric hospitals by pretending to hear voices and faking their name and occupation. One might argue that this case of deception was one that the victims were able to avoid.
- Drug testing – perhaps a necessary case of deception but what about the patients' rights to receive the best care?
- Craik and Tulving (1975) – a minor case of deception.

Debriefing

- Milgram (1963) – all subjects were fully debriefed and reassured after the experiment.

Confidentiality

- Case studies – pseudonyms are used to maintain anonymity, and thus confidentiality of data.

Right to withdraw

- Milgram (1963) – abused the right of subjects to withdraw from a psychology study; those wishing to leave were told 'you have no other choice, you *must* go on'. However subjects could have left, they were not physically restrained, and indeed some did disobey.
- Haney, Banks and Zimbardo (1973) – the imprisonment, by definition, prevented withdrawal, however the study was stopped after just six days instead of the intended two weeks because of the extreme reactions shown by the participants.

Protection of participants

- Milgram (1963) – the procedure caused distress and anguish to the subjects at the time and could have caused long-term psychological damage. However, the results obtained were completely unexpected (Milgram asked for estimates beforehand), and although the subjects appeared uncomfortable with their obedience, Milgram concluded that 'momentary excitement is not the same as harm'. The subjects were examined one year after the experiment by a psychiatrist who found no signs of harm. Milgram argued that it was the shocking nature of his findings that provoked a moral outrage. A follow-up opinion survey found that the majority of the participants were positive about the study.
- Haney, Banks and Zimbardo (1973) – the prison simulation procedures were more stressful than expected.
- Watson and Rayner (1920) – the conditioning process involved fear and the child was left with a phobia of rats.

2 By considering some of the studies using animals as participants above, do you think the 'benefits' of the findings justify the 'costs' involved in animal suffering?

As far as benefits are concerned, animal studies have contributed to our understanding of many topics in psychology, which in turn have led to many useful applications. For example, the principles of operant and classical conditioning and the behavioural treatments and therapies developed from them were derived from learning studies on animals. Brain studies and drug testing on animals have also been important in helping humans. However, some studies using animals (e.g. Sheridan and King's) seem to have relatively trivial implications.

The costs to the animals in these studies range from captivity and/or a quick death (which one can compared to pets, zoos and farm animals), to mild food and water deprivation or a painful and tortured existence (which is less comparable).

Ultimately one's consideration of the value of these studies depends upon the relative value one assigns to the interests of humans versus other animals (see below).

3 Why do you think some psychologists think they should use animals to investigate human psychological issues, while others object to it?

Reasons for conducting animal research in psychology

- Evolutionary continuum – psychologists such as the behaviourists claimed that animal research was justified because humans have evolved from other animals and so the difference between them is only quantitative. Since humans are just more complex animals, it makes sense to study more simple organisms first, and then generalise to humans.
- Convenience – animals are 'good subjects', they do not try to understand the purpose of the experiment, are more controllable, and their faster breeding cycles allow tests to be conducted on the influence of heredity and environment.
- Ethical reasons – many experiments that psychologists want to conduct are deemed unethical for human testing, but important enough to be justified for animal testing, e.g. controlled interbreeding, deprivation studies, brain surgery or the trial testing of drugs. Some psychologists suggest that humans have a moral obligation to help humans first and the alternatives to animal research are often practically undesirable (using less reliable methods such as non-experimental observations or computer simulations).
- The legislation of the Animals (Scientific Procedures) Act (1986) provides safeguards to prevent the unnecessary use of animal research in psychology.

Reasons for not conducting animal research in psychology

- The animals tested often suffer. There is little doubt that a number of objective and behavioural measures indicate that animals can be said to suffer stress, pain and anxiety. Inflicting suffering upon another creature is morally objectionable. In many cases the suffering of animals (the means) has not been justified by the knowledge gained from the studies (the ends).
- Humans are physically qualitatively different to other animals, for example in terms of brain structure, complexity and specialisation (e.g. the human areas for language) and may react differently to drugs.
- Humans are mentally qualitatively different to other animals, for example the humanists would regard human consciousness as a key difference. The projection of human-like traits onto animals (anthropomorphism) may lead to an exaggeration of similarity.
- Laboratory studies on animals are often even more likely to lack ecological validity than those conducted on humans, and so these invalid findings are even less useful for generalisation to human behaviour.

13 | The psychodynamic approach to psychology

What made Freud and others think that hidden emotional causes and early experience were so important, and how did they go about investigating the unconscious mind?

Sigmund Freud

Assumptions

The importance of the unconscious mind and motivation

Freud's ideas and the key assumptions of the psychodynamic approach were strongly influenced by his study of patients suffering from '*hysteria*'. In broad terms, hysteria, as it was understood then, was a medical term applied to patients who seemed to be suffering symptoms of disorder to the nervous system such as pain, disturbed actions or speech, and even temporary paralysis or blindness, for which no physical neurological cause could be found. As a neurologist himself, Freud reasoned that if no physical cause could be found, and the patients were not consciously faking the symptoms, then the cause of the symptoms may well be psychological and stem from a part of the mind that the patient was not aware of – *the unconscious*.

Freud came to believe that his patients, and indeed all humans, were strongly motivated by unconscious emotional drives, and their attempts to control them. Freud emphasised mainly sexual drives, although not all psychodynamic theorists agreed with him and proposed other causes of unconscious motivation.

The importance of early experience

From studying his patients, Freud became convinced that *events in the past*, often experiences from early childhood involving emotional impulses that had become trapped in the unconscious, could create lasting impressions upon personality and even symptoms of mental disorder. Typically, these forgotten memories and their hidden emotional causes were linked to relationships with other people, particularly parents (who are mostly closely associated with satisfying or controlling our desires when young). Psychodynamic theorists, while all accepting the importance of early experience, differ in their views on how it affects later behaviour.

The case of Anna O

These ideas of a person's behaviour being influenced by memories that they were unaware of, was illustrated by one of the first and most important patients involved in the development of psychoanalysis, 'Anna O', who was treated by a close associate of Freud's, Josef Breuer.

Anna O, according to Breuer, suffered from a range of hysterical symptoms, including paralysis of the right arm and leg, disturbances of speech, hearing and vision, and even a fear of drinking water (she lived only on fruit such as melons for six weeks!). Breuer found that by tracing back each symptom to its first occurrence Anna would eventually recall an event that seemed to have caused it, since once she had described the previously forgotten memory the symptom would disappear.

For example, her fear of drinking vanished the moment she recalled an unpleasant memory concerning a dog drinking from a glass, and the majority of her symptoms, including her apparent inability to speak her native German language (she would only speak English), disappeared after recalling a traumatic incident she experienced while looking after her ill father. Anna had fallen asleep at her father's bedside with her arm over the back of her chair and, due to her anxiety over his health, had awoken and hallucinated that a black snake was crawling towards her father to bite him. Anna could not move her arm to beat the snake away (since it had gone to sleep) and in her terror found she could not speak until some words of English came to mind. 'The whole illness was brought to a close', Breuer concluded, when she recalled the 'terrifying hallucination…which constituted the root of her whole illness'.

Methods

Case studies

The detailed, in-depth investigation of Anna O is an example of the *case study* method – an important source of evidence used by psychodynamic psychologists. Freud's psychoanalysis was often a lengthy, time-consuming process, typically requiring five, hour-long sessions per week for months or even years in order to understand and treat patients. Freud wrote up his notes at the end of each day and often published his patients' case histories (using pseudonyms) when they had finished therapy.

Clinical interviews

In general terms Freud, like many later psychodynamic researchers, used the *clinical interview* method to gather his data – asking open-ended questions to each patient and following up upon the answers they gave with further questions. Importantly, this method not only allowed him to deeply analyse and interpret all that his patients said, but also how they said it and every aspect of their behaviour from the moment they entered the room. Even accidents and slips of the tongue, were thought to provide clues or links to the memories that were disturbing them. 'He that has eyes to see and ears to hear', Freud wrote, 'may convince himself that no mortal can keep a secret. If the lips are silent, he chatters with his fingertips: betrayal oozes out of him at every pore.'

The analysis of symbolism

When interpreting his patients' behaviour, Freud discovered that the link to its unconscious cause was usually '*symbolic*' (where one thing stands for or represents another). For example, Anna O's paralysis of the arm was a physical symbol of her traumatic memory of being unable to use it to defend her father from the hallucinated snake. Freud extended his interpretation of symbolism to the analysis of dreams, cultural traditions and literature, and later psychodynamic researchers also saw the value of looking for the related meanings of objects, events and behaviour.

Exercise 13

1 What problems are there with suggesting causes of behaviour that come from the unconscious mind?

2 What problems might there be in investigating the past causes of behaviour?

3 What do you think are the strengths and weaknesses of case studies, clinical interviews and the analysis of symbolism for psychodynamic researchers?

1 What problems are there with suggesting causes of behaviour that come from the unconscious mind?

Nobody can directly observe the unconscious mind
The main problem is that it is difficult to discover and verify what those causes are, since not only is the researcher unable to directly observe them in another person's mind, but even the owner of the mind cannot.

Of course, theories and models of unconscious causes can be proposed, as both psychodynamic and cognitive psychologists have done, but even if the theories and models are very precise and make testable predictions which are scientifically verified, it is still difficult to know if they are true.

In relation to this, critics have pointed out that psychodynamic concepts, theories and predictions are sometimes a little too vague and the methods a little too unscientific to be easily established as valid.

In comparison, the cognitive psychological approach with its more precise and testable theories, computer flow chart-like models, and experimental evidence has often provided better-supported explanations for some of the issues investigated by psychodynamic psychologists, e.g. forgetting.

What is meant by the term 'unconscious'?
Another problem is with the term 'unconscious' itself. Researchers not only have to rely on the honesty of the reports from those investigated, but have problems knowing how *deeply* unconscious a cause really is. Psychodynamic researchers have proposed different levels of consciousness and unconsciousness but if, for example, a certain event cannot be recalled, how do we know whether it is just awaiting a memory jog and may become conscious later, if it is still there exerting an influence but will remain forever inaccessible, or if it has disappeared from memory altogether?

2 What problems might there be in investigating the past causes of behaviour?

Problems getting accurate data
An important problem is getting reliable first-hand data since the researcher is relying on retrospective data – the individual's reports of their memories of past events. Naturally these memories may not be complete or may be distorted – and there will be a lot of them, making it difficult to find the most relevant ones.

OK, you may be thinking, why not study younger individuals, record what happens to them and wait to see the effects on their behaviour. Unfortunately this long-term (longitudinal) method would require an enormous amount of data collection and perhaps a long wait for the effects to show. Even then it would be difficult to show that certain past events were the cause of later behaviour (see non-experimental methods).

3 What do you think are the strengths and weaknesses of case studies, clinical interviews and the analysis of symbolism for psychodynamic researchers?

Strengths – a richer understanding of individuals
All three techniques are suited to the original therapeutic purpose of psychodynamic psychology – to identify and resolve the *particular* set of problems an *individual* is experiencing.

Case studies are very in-depth and detailed investigations of an individual person or event that can provide greater understanding than more superficial studies of larger numbers. This depth of understanding and gathering of unique details is also gained from the use of the clinical interview method, which allows increased exploration and discovery of information that might otherwise have been missed. Many psychologists, not just psychodynamically orientated ones, acknowledge that the human mind works in a symbolic way – the written words you are reading now are symbolic of both linguistic sounds and meanings, for example. Indeed a single word can have more than one meaning and can conjure up different memories relating to it in different people (think of the word 'nuts'). By exploring these associations, psychodynamic researchers gain important insights into the mental lives of those they investigate.

Weaknesses – problems with reliability and objectivity
Unfortunately, these methods are not always so good as sources of scientific evidence for psychodynamic theories. Science typically requires large numbers of representative people to be tested using experimental procedures under standardised conditions (to isolate cause and effect) before a study's conclusions can be said to apply to everyone.

Case studies, however, often provide non-experimental and unstandardised information gained under variable conditions from individuals who may not necessarily be typical of the general population. The patients from whom Freud first developed his ideas for example, were typically Viennese, Jewish, hysterical, middle-to-upper-class women – hardly a representative sample. It must also be remembered that the case studies of psychodynamic researchers are not primarily conducted for research purposes but for treatment. Although Freud did use his case studies to support his theories, he admitted that 'a psychoanalysis is not an impartial scientific investigation, but a therapeutic measure. Its essence is not to prove anything, but merely to alter something.'

Clinical interviews can be standardised by asking the same initial questions to each individual, however the flexibility of using follow-up questions based on the answers given means the standardisation may soon become reduced. A related danger of these flexible questions is that the interviewer may lead the interviewee into only giving information that supports rather than contradicts their theories. This interviewer bias could also creep into the interpretation of the interviewee's answers which, being based on self-report information, may not be honest or accurate anyway.

The problems of subjective (based on one's own views) rather than objective (publicly accepted) interpretation in psychodynamic methods is most obvious in the analysis of symbolism. Because one word, action or event can have a variety of meanings, how can either the researchers or their participants demonstrate which meaning is the most relevant or important in explaining behaviour? Many psychodynamic theorists have suggested that they are better qualified and able to interpret symbolism than their participants, but of course their interpretations may be biased by their theoretical beliefs and preconceptions.

Freud, for example, was convinced that sexual causes were responsible for the symptoms of his own hysterical patients (he even thought Anna O's symptoms had a sexual basis). This could have led to him interpreting many symbols in a sexual manner to support his theories. Indeed Freud managed to find sexual symbolism in a huge variety of objects and behaviours, from ticking clocks (throbbing excitement) and dreams of 'going upstairs' (intercourse) to playing with small containers (masturbation) and nervous coughs or speech impediments (I am not even going to tell you what he said those could symbolise!).

14 | Psychoanalytic theory

Freud and the unconscious mind

According to Freud, the most important processes that influence the development of behaviour take place in the unconscious – that part of the mind of which we have no direct awareness. It follows, therefore, that although we may think we know why we do things, this may often not be the case. We are not masters of our own minds. Freud distinguished the unconscious, with its complete lack of access, from the pre-conscious, which contains material that we can bring into conscious awareness once our attention is directed to it.

Freud and unconscious motivation

The idea that unconscious psychological factors, such as bottled-up emotions, could influence behaviour and create mental problems was not new; Freud had been very influenced by the famous Parisian physiologist Charcot, who had used the psychological technique of hypnotic suggestion to remove or even create hysterical symptoms in his patients. What was new, however, was Freud's emphasis on the cause of these symptoms since, by studying a number of his own patients whom he had diagnosed as hysterical, he became convinced that the unconscious cause in every case was a hidden impulse or memory that was *sexual* in nature. From psychoanalysing patients, friends, society and himself, Freud developed a theory to explain why sexual causes were so important, why they became trapped in the unconscious and how they influenced the development of both normal and abnormal behaviour.

Freud proposed that we are driven or motivated by our *instinctual* drives, which come from two basic instincts. Thanatos, the death instinct, is responsible for aggressive drives, whereas Eros, the life instinct, is responsible for the sex drive or libido. The instinctual drives create *psychic energy* which will build up hydraulically in the mind (rather like steam in a steam engine) and create tension if it can not be released in some form. Freud saw the life instinct and sex drive as exerting the most influence in the early years of life and thus childhood is a time of key importance in personality development.

Freud's psychosexual stages of development

Freud proposed a stage theory of infantile psychosexual development, suggesting children are polymorphously perverse (able to derive sexual pleasure from any part of their bodies), but as they grow older the sexual drive becomes focused upon (and seeks expression and satisfaction from) different parts of the body.

The stages are governed by biological maturation and begin with the oral stage where pleasure is gained first from passively and dependently sucking and swallowing (the oral receptive sub-stage) and later, as the teeth emerge, from biting and chewing (the oral aggressive sub-stage).

At the anal stage, gratification shifts to the anus where pleasure is gained first from expelling and playing with faeces (the expulsive sub-stage) and then, during toilet training, from holding on to and controlling bowel movements (the retentive sub-stage).

From around 3 to 5 or 6 years of age the child experiences the phallic stage, where the libido becomes focused upon curiosity and pleasure involving the genitals, which becomes directed towards the opposite sex parent. Both boys and girls at this age unconsciously desire the opposite sex parent, but differ slightly in the way they deal with this situation, which Freud termed the Oedipus complex.

The Oedipus complex for a boy involves sexual attraction towards his mother and wishing his rival for his mother's affection, his father, out of the way (ideally dead). However, the boy fears that the more powerful father will discover his illicit desires and will punish him by depriving the boy of what he currently holds most dear – his phallus. This 'castration complex' is resolved when, out of fear of castration, the boy identifies with the father figure, introjecting all his values, attitudes and behaviour, so that in becoming like his father the boy can indirectly have the mother in his fantasies and later grow up to have mother-like figures in the same way as his father. As a result we acquire our gender behaviour and some aspects of morality.

The Oedipus complex for girls (sometimes referred to as the Electra complex) involves the girl's desire for the father. The girl believes that she has already been castrated, and out of penis envy she turns to her father to provide her with a symbolic penis substitute – a baby. However, out of fear of losing her mother's love, the girl identifies with her mother and, by becoming like her, she too can indirectly satisfy her sexual desires.

After the turmoil of the phallic stage, the child enters a period of latency where the child's desires diminish somewhat, before the genital stage occurs at puberty and the reawakened libido is directed to love objects outside the family.

Id, ego and superego

Freud also proposed that by the end of the phallic stage, the three main aspects of the mind would have developed – the id, ego and superego. Babies begin life dominated by the id, which Freud referred to as 'a cauldron full of seething excitations'. The id (the 'Es' or 'it' was Freud's original German term) is the primitive, biological part of the mind that is the source of the psychic energy associated with both the sexual and aggressive instinctual drives, and hidden memories. The id has impulses to release this psychic energy and, since it is unsocialised and has no sense of time or logic, it will seek such satisfaction without any regard for social appropriateness (it works on the pleasure principle). The ego (the 'Ich' or 'I') is the part of the mind that has been modified by contact with the external world with all its restraints on behaviour; thus toilet training during the anal stage is a particularly important time for its development. The ego aims to gratify the id's impulses in line with what is possible (it works on the reality principle) and is free from any moral constraint until the superego develops in the phallic stage. The superego (the 'Uber-ich' or 'above I' in German) is one product of the Oedipus complex, since it represents the internalised inner parent who rewards us with pride (the ego-ideal) or punishes us with guilt (the conscience) when we do good or bad things.

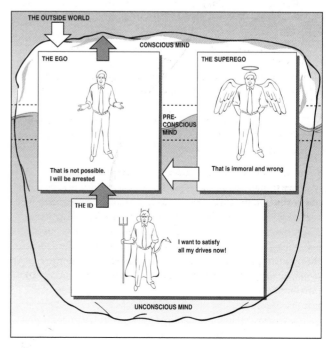

Theory of personality

Freud therefore believed that the experiences of childhood are of utmost importance, since they shape the structure of the unconscious mind and the majority of human personality. Freud suggested that too much or too little pleasure at a stage might lead to *fixation* at it, causing the individual in later life to still want to indulge in its sexual pleasures. For example, fixation at the oral receptive stage due to over-indulgence (the slightest whimper brought food and oral gratification), may lead to an optimistic personality that gains pleasure from being dependent and passive. Any traumatic events, especially of a sexual nature, in earlier life might also become hidden in the unconscious and influence later behaviour.

However, Freud also argued that the extent to which behaviour and personality would be affected depended upon the overall balance between the id, ego and superego (a strong superego, for example, would result in a very moral person) and the outcome of the constant *dynamic conflict* between them.

The ego cannot allow many of the id's aggressive and sexual impulses to reach respectable, adult, conscious life and so uses many methods to control, alter, deny or redirect the impulses whenever they may occur. These methods include defence mechanisms and dreams.

Oral stage	Oral receptive
	Oral aggressive
Anal stage	Anal expulsive
	Anal retentive
Phallic stage	Oedipus complex and identification
Latency stage	Libido diminishes infantile amnesia
Genital stage	Libido reawakens non-family love objects

Stages of development

Defence mechanisms

There are many defence mechanisms employed by the ego. The most successful is usually *sublimation*, which allows the expression of id impulses through behaviour that is a socially acceptable symbolic alternative. For example, fixation at the oral stage may later lead to seeking oral pleasure, not from sucking the mother's breast in public, but from sucking at one's thumb, pen or cigarette. The desire to expose one's genitals due to fixation at the phallic stage may well lead to a later sublimated choice of a career as a fireman, who can happily drive large hoses and extending ladders with much attention through the streets, after first sliding down the pole back at the fire station (Kline, 1984).

In contrast, *repression* is not a very successful defence mechanism since it just involves forcing disturbing wishes, ideas or memories into the unconscious where, although hidden, they will create psychic pressure or anxiety and constantly seek expression. Thus, someone may repress homosexual feelings and become a latent (hidden) homosexual who consciously reports attraction to the opposite sex, but has to use other defence mechanisms, such as *denial* (a complete refusal of acknowledgement) or *projection* (attributing aspects of oneself to others), to control their unconscious urges.

If unconscious impulses become too powerful, then sometimes the ego is forced to make the individual consciously feel and act in exactly the opposite way to that unconsciously desired – a defence called *reaction formation*. Thus latent homosexuals may themselves declare not just dislike, but a hatred of overt homosexuals, while those with an 'anal character' such as an exaggerated concern for orderliness, cleanliness, control and routine may be showing reaction formations against their anal expulsive desire to mess.

If while reading this you are getting a little too angry in your objection to some of Freud's ideas, then your ego is probably helping you react against your anxiety provoking unconscious recognition of their truth!

There are many other defence mechanisms, such as *regression* (returning to child-like strategies or states such as crying or helplessness when we feel unable to cope) and *displacement* where feelings are expressed by redirecting them onto something or somebody harmless and convenient rather than the original cause (we do not slam a door because we hate it!).

Between them they make humans and their society the way they are; indeed without the restraints that defence mechanisms impose, civilisation would not be possible.

Dreams

Freud suggested that dreams represent *unfulfilled wishes* from the id, which try to break into consciousness and seek satisfaction while we are 'off guard'. Dreams are the way these id wishes are *disguised* by the dream censor using defensive measures such as *symbolism* (using a dream image or event to stand for an id wish), *condensation* (the merging of many unconscious meanings into one dream image) and *displacement* (where emotions are separated from their true source and attached to trivial sources in the dream). Freud believed many symbols are personal but others might have universal meanings, e.g. phallic symbols such as guns and knives.

Thus the *manifest content* of a dream (what is consciously remembered) reflects the 'dreamwork' carried out on the *latent content* (the hidden id impulses or meaning). Despite displaying many aspects of id 'thinking' however, often being disjointed and generally showing little respect for time and reality, dreams act as the 'guardians of sleep' to protect us from our own unconscious while asleep.

Exercise 14

1 What do you think people dominated by their id or ego may be like?

2 Name the defence mechanisms that might be involved in the following behaviour:
   a A child, who has been told off by a parent, smacks her doll and tells it not to be so naughty.
   b An employee rushes to bring his hated boss a cup of coffee but accidentally spills it on him.
   c A student faced with a vital exam goes out partying the night before, forgets his pen on the day of the exam and throws a tantrum on realising.

3 What stage fixations might be involved in pencil biting, pottery, greediness or pornography?

4 How far do you agree with Freud that
   ■ we are unaware of many causes of our behaviour?
   ■ we are motivated by sexual and aggressive urges?
   ■ pleasure from body parts influences later behaviour?
   ■ girls have 'penis envy'?
   ■ interactions with parents influence later behaviour?
   ■ we have an id, ego and superego influencing us?
   ■ defence mechanisms can explain behaviour?
   ■ dreams are disguised unconscious wishes?

1 What do you think people dominated by their id or ego may be like?

Those dominated by their id would be very impulsive and irresponsible individuals whose sexual and aggressive urges might lead them to commit related crimes in an unplanned manner and without regard for the consequences. Their thinking may also be rather disorganised and illogical.

Those dominated by their ego, however, would be expected to be rational, logical and controlled. With a strong superego as well, they would be able to keep their impulses under close control – perhaps even too much control, leading to frustration and anxiety. With a weak superego and strong id, on the other hand, the result may be a manipulative psychopath.

2 Name the defence mechanisms that might be involved in the following behaviour:

a A child, who has been told off by a parent, smacks her doll and tells it not to be so naughty.

Displacement of aggression towards the parent and *projection* of her own characteristics onto the doll.

b An employee rushes to bring his hated boss a cup of coffee but accidentally spills it on him.

Reaction formation against the hate by showing over-compensation in eagerness to please and *sublimation* of aggression by spilling the coffee (to Freud an accident is not necessarily an accident!).

c A student faced with a vital exam goes out partying the night before, forgets his pen on the day of the exam and throws a tantrum on realising.

Denial of the exam's importance by partying, *repression* of the need to bring a pen (Freud believed in motivated forgetting – we often forget for a reason) and *regression* to childlike behaviour with the tantrum.

3 What stage fixations might be involved in pencil biting, pottery, greediness or pornography?

Pencil biting – oral aggressive stage fixation
Pottery – anal expulsive stage fixation (modelling clay symbolises playing with faeces)
Greediness – oral receptive stage fixation
Pornography – phallic stage (exhibition, curiosity and pleasure relating to the genitals)

4 How far do you agree with Freud that

- we are unaware of many causes of our behaviour?
- we are motivated by sexual and aggressive urges?
- pleasure from body parts influences later behaviour?
- girls have 'penis envy'?
- interactions with parents influence later behaviour?
- we have an id, ego and superego influencing us?
- defence mechanisms can explain behaviour?
- dreams are disguised unconscious wishes?

From considering the above points you probably agreed with each to differing extents. Some seem likely, others appear partly true and some seem just plain wrong.

Yes, we probably are unaware of many causes of our behaviour, but you may be unsure how important unconscious causes are compared to conscious ones. Yes, interactions with parents probably do have important influences on later behaviour, but Freud seems to have overemphasised the sexual aspects of them and ignored interactions with people other than the parents. Yes, dreams may have hidden meanings, but are they always so disguised?

You may have rejected, or even been offended by, the ideas that your character was so influenced by pleasure from your genitals or that you had sexual desires towards your parents.

Psychoanalytic theory is probably best regarded as a collection of ideas or hypotheses (Farrell, 1961). Many psychologists have tended to completely reject psychoanalytic theory as a whole because they find aspects of it unlikely, bizarre and disturbing, and/or argue that it was constructed based upon methods regarded as unscientific (see pages 36 and 42). This approach has led to 'throwing the baby out with the bath water' and, as Freud often pointed out, such an absolute rejection appears to reflect unconscious resistance. Even if Freud's methods were unscientific, that does not mean to say that all psychoanalytic ideas are wrong or that others cannot scientifically test them.

However, reviews of research that have attempted to scientifically validate psychoanalytic concepts are largely negative in their conclusions, because it is difficult to show that the unconscious mechanisms which Freud proposed are responsible. Freud emphasised the importance of the Oedipus complex, calling it the 'kernel of neurosis' yet while social learning theory research has found imitation of same sex parents does occur, there has been no conclusive evidence that unconscious motives like castration fear are responsible.

Freud regarded repression as 'the cornerstone on which the whole of psychoanalysis rests', yet although research has linked trauma to amnesia, the degree to which repressed events are truly unconscious has been questioned and other causes of forgetting have been suggested as more likely by cognitive psychologists (see pages 84 to 87).

While Kline and Storey (1977) found evidence for oral and anal personality traits by using personality questionnaires, it has not been demonstrated that these traits have been caused by Freudian fixation at a stage.

Many of Freud's closest colleagues in psychoanalysis, including Breuer, Jung and Adler, disagreed with Freud's insistence on sexual causes, Breuer even commented that Freud was prone to 'excessive generalisation'. However a more general bias in Freud's theory stems from his cultural background with, for example, its sexist male viewpoint (as illustrated by his views on female moral inferiority and penis envy) and its focus on traditional family environments.

In evaluating Freud's contribution, critics have argued that philosophers and writers had long considered the importance of the unconscious, dream interpretation, defence mechanisms, etc. whereas Freud's more original ideas concerning them have been criticised. This has led psychologists such as Eysenck (1985) to agree with Ebbinghaus that 'what is new in these theories is not true, and what is true is not new'.

More negatively, Freud's emphasis on sexuality may have actually put psychologists off studying many important concepts, while his Oedipus complex may have led to genuine cases of child abuse being dismissed as childhood sexual fantasies.

Nevertheless, one could also argue that Freud has served to popularise and draw attention to important ideas. He developed his theory throughout his life and proposed explanations for a huge variety of phenomena, from humour and forgetting, to crowd behaviour, customs and warfare. Many psychologists and psychoanalysts, although often disagreeing with some of them, have been inspired by his theories to develop their own. Psychoanalytic terms and concepts have become ingrained into western psychology and society, and psychoanalysis is still practised today.

FREUD CROSSWORD

1 Methods used by the ego to control the id (7/10)
2 The instinctual part of the mind containing the psychic energy of the drives (2)
3 Many of Freud's early patients were thought to suffer from this (8)
4 The dream content that is remembered (8)
5 The part of the mind that works according to the reality principle (3)
6 Toilet training is important at this stage (4)
7 As a result of this we acquire our gender behaviour (7/7)
8 The life instinct providing the sex drive (4)
9 How the ego expresses id impulses in a symbolic but socially acceptable way (11)
10 The moral part of the mind (8)
11 Where many of the important influences on behaviour are to be found (11)
12 The stage where pleasure-seeking first becomes focused on the genitals (7)
13 Fixation at this stage may result in an optimistic or dependent personality (4)
14 An important patient for the development of psychoanalytic theory (4/1)
15 Too much or too little pleasure at a stage can lead to this (8)
16 Forcing id impulses or unpleasant experiences into the unconscious (10)
17 A very important source of information on unconscious impulses (6)
18 The id works according to the _____ principle (8)

FREUD ANAGRAMS

1 C Y T E N L A
2 R E A C T E L
3 G O E - L A I D E
4 H A N T O A S T
5 M O B S L I M S Y
6 R A T I N C O A S T
7 O G R E S I N R E S
8 C L E M E N T I S P A D
9 N O P R E S S C I O U C
10 A C O R N E I T   F A I N T R O O M

Key application – Freud, mental health and psychoanalysis

Freud and the causes of mental health problems

A key application of psychoanalytic theory is, of course, to help explain and treat the causes of mental health problems. Mental health problems develop, according to Freud, when sexual or aggressive psychic energy associated with memories of earlier experiences or id impulses becomes trapped in the unconscious. This occurs when the ego has used *defence mechanisms* that block the energy or release it in an unhelpful form.

Repression of traumatic experiences, for example, especially from childhood, can create later unconscious anxiety. Freud concluded that neurotics (e.g. those with anxiety disorders) suffer from reminiscences (memories). This unconscious anxiety could be *displaced* onto external symbolic objects and situations, resulting in phobias (see the case of Little Hans), or *sublimated* by being symbolically expressed as physical symptoms, as in hysteria (see the case of Anna O).

Worse still, such inner turmoil could lead to major *regression* to earlier states. Freud suggested that the disorganised and delusional thinking of schizophrenia may result from regression to a self-absorbed state of 'narcissism' in the early oral stage where the irrational id dominates and there is no well-developed ego to make contact with reality. Depression may also result from regression to an early state of dependency and helplessness due to a loss in later life triggering the emotional effects of a more serious childhood loss.

Freud and the treatment of mental health problems

Freudian psychoanalysis consisted of a number of techniques that aimed to first *identify* the unconscious source of disorder and then try to *relieve* it by making the unconscious causes conscious.

To identify the early experiences and id impulses that he assumed caused behavioural problems, Freud questioned his patients about their past in search of memories of events that might be associated with them. He assured his patients that something must have happened to them to trigger their problems and would continue probing their memories until they remembered something that seemed to be associated with an improvement in their condition. He stated 'I accustomed myself to regarding as incomplete any story that brought about no therapeutic improvement'. Freud suspected, however, that some of the memories his patients reported were not real but reflected unconscious wishes or fantasies.

Freud looked for hidden symbolic meanings in what his patients said and did (both spontaneously and in response to his questions) and interpreted their free associations and dreams. In free association he had his patients lie on a couch and encouraged them to report whatever came into their mind without inhibition, no matter how strange, unimportant or embarrassing it may seem. The links between the associations were thought to provide clues to the hidden causes of their behaviour, while pauses in or drying up of associations indicated closeness to the source of unconscious anxiety.

Freud regarded dream analysis as the 'royal road' to the unconscious since, by undoing the 'dreamwork' of the *manifest content* of the dream (what is consciously remembered), he believed the *latent content* (the hidden id impulses or meaning) could be discovered. This was achieved by free associating to each element of the manifest content to trace it back to the latent content, decoding the symbolism of the manifest content and identifying the event within the previous 24 hours that had acted as the trigger for the dream.

Finally, the process of transference, whereby unconscious feelings of love and hate are projected onto the analyst, was also thought important in identifying the causes of problems, and in helping the patient accept and discuss the analyst's interpretation of the problem.

Once the unconscious causes have been identified, improvement is achieved by bringing them out into the open for discussion 'to enable the patient to obtain a conscious grasp of his unconscious wishes'. Freud originally thought that catharsis (discharging the emotional or psychic energy associated with repressed impulses or traumatic memories) brought about improvement, but concluded that the *insight* provided by the analyst was the crucial therapeutic element. Insight increases ego control over the revealed unconscious causes – 'where id was, there shall ego be' (Freud, 1933). Freud (1909) stated that 'Analysis replaces the process of repression, which is an automatic and excessive one, by a temperate and purposeful control on the part of the highest agencies of the mind.'

However, Freud found that his patients would often show '*resistance*' to his questions and interpretations; they tried to digress or avoid the topic when he thought he was getting close to the unconscious causes or would deny that the causes he was identifying were true. He suggested that this was because the hidden memories and fantasies were often traumatic or embarrassing so the ego tries to maintain its defences and keep its secrets hidden.

Since his patients lacked insight and objectivity regarding their unconscious and would even report fake memories, Freud decided that the psychoanalyst was 'obliged to *reconstruct* the unconscious complexes and wishes' and what had really happened in the patient's past. By 'working upon the basis of the hints he [the patient] throws out' and psychoanalytic theory, Freud believed 'it is of use if we can guess the ways in which things are connected up and tell the patient before we have uncovered it'.

The patient then had to be persuaded to accept and come to terms with the analyst's interpretation of the cause of their problems, no matter how much they may disagree with it. For these reasons, psychoanalysis was frequently an intimate, lengthy and sometimes upsetting process.

Freud's notion of a cure, however, was fairly modest – to 'turn neurotic misery into common unhappiness' – since he regarded all humans as neurotic to some extent (including himself!). Freud emphasised that merely eradicating symptoms was not enough, the analyst had to identify and deal with the deeper, underlying unconscious mental causes.

Studies of the effectiveness of Freudian psychoanalysis have not always reached positive conclusions. For example, the famous critic of psychoanalysis, Eysenck (1952), found that psychoanalytic therapy had lower success rates (44%) than alternative psychotherapies (64%) or spontaneous remission (72%).

Exercise 15

1 What do you think is meant by the 'spontaneous remission' of a mental disorder and what do Eysenck's percentages imply about psychoanalysis?

2 What is wrong with Freud waiting until his patients remembered something that seemed to be associated with an improvement in their condition and then assuming that this memory was linked to the cause?

3 What is wrong with Freud *assuming* that something *must* have happened to his patients in their past to create the *psychological* causes of their problems and that he could guess the cause before it had been revealed?

1 What do you think is meant by the 'spontaneous remission' of a mental disorder and what do Eysenck's percentages imply about psychoanalysis?

Spontaneous remission is where symptoms disappear on their own – some people will recover from their mental disorder without any particular treatment at all. Eysenck's figures, therefore, imply that not only is psychoanalysis less effective than other psychotherapies (psychologically based treatments), but that people get better more often without *any* treatment than with psychoanalysis!

Eysenck's findings have been hotly disputed because of the very high spontaneous remission rate (some research suggests only 30%) and criteria used to assess the effectiveness of psychoanalysis. Eysenck regarded those who left psychoanalysis early as failures; if these people are omitted the success rate for psychoanalytic therapy increases to 66%. A meta-analysis (an assessment of many studies) of the therapeutic success rates of different therapies by Smith and Glass (1977) found that psychoanalysis is more effective than no therapy at all for most people, but has slightly lower success rates than other therapies. Sloane et al (1975) found psychoanalysis was most effective for clients with less-severe problems.

Freud applied psychoanalysis to a range of disorders, such as hysteria, phobias and obsessive compulsive disorder (e.g. the 'Rat Man'), yet it seems more appropriate for minor neuroses and anxiety disorders, with more intelligent and articulate clients. Freud himself argued *psychotic* patients could not be treated by psychoanalysis because they lacked insight and the ability to form transference attachments to the therapist (although psychoanalysis with schizophrenics has been attempted in combination with drug therapy). In addition, free-association may be inappropriate for obsessive–compulsive patients and transference may encourage further dependency in depressed patients. Given that psychoanalysis often requires a good deal of time (and money) it has been suggested that other forms of therapy may be more time and cost effective, although shorter versions have been developed e.g. Malan's brief focal therapy.

As you may also have gathered, Freud's view of therapeutic success makes it difficult to say when someone is cured (when they are unhappy rather than miserable). Rather than just removing the symptoms of disturbed behaviour, psychoanalysis aims to change the underlying unconscious processes that cause them. However, any unconscious progress made may not always produce immediate observable changes in behaviour and it is not possible to measure these unconscious changes or even guarantee that they were responsible for any improvements in behaviour.

Psychoanalysis offers a therapy distinct from most other therapies and, using certain criteria, can produce progress and self-reports of improvement (although the latter, as with all therapies, may just reflect the patient's and therapist's justification of the time and effort they have committed). Ethically speaking, psychoanalytic therapy can be distressing for the patient (some say it can be counter-productive for schizophrenics because of its emotional stress) but it is not the only therapy with negative side effects. In terms of therapist–patient power and control, the therapy involves complete trust in the interpretations of the analyst. Due to the concept of unconscious resistance, the therapist may directly or indirectly discourage the patient's right to withdraw from therapy, since refusing or leaving therapy could indicate ego defence to progress in uncovering hidden truths.

2 What is wrong with Freud waiting until his patients remembered something that seemed to be associated with an improvement in their condition and then assuming that this memory was linked to the cause?

Since psychoanalysis took so long, the symptoms may have spontaneously recovered (disappeared on their own) and the memory being recalled at the time could just have been coincidental.

3 What is wrong with Freud *assuming* that something *must* have happened to his patients in their past to create the *psychological* causes of their problems and that he could guess the cause before it had been revealed?

Such an approach could lead to *ignoring other causes* of disorder that might be unrelated to his patients' pasts or their unconscious, such as present experiences or biological causes.

Critics of psychoanalysis, such as Webster (1995), have suggested, for example, that Breuer and Freud may have misdiagnosed their patients. Many of them may have been classified as suffering from organic, physical disorders today, such as forms of epilepsy (Anna O), Tourette's Syndrome (Emmy von N, Freud's first hysterical patient treated by psychoanalysis) or even tumours (M-l, who died from a tumour of the stomach, had her stomach pains diagnosed as hysterical by Freud). This possibility of misdiagnosis seems to be supported by the fact that many patients supposedly cured through psychoanalysis, including Anna O, continued to show their symptoms after treatment by it.

There is also evidence that Freud repeatedly ignored important information or alternative explanations of behaviour that did not fit his theory (see the case of Little Hans, for example).

By not trusting a patient's reports and memories and guessing the causes based on psychoanalytic theory before they have been uncovered, there is a danger that the psychoanalyst will only search for and interpret information from the patient in a way that fits in with their ideas.

When another patient, Elisabeth von R, showed signs of pain on rising from Freud's couch after hearing her brother-in-law arrive outside, Freud concluded that it was due to painful inadmissible feelings of love for the brother-in-law, rather than just the movement aggravating the severe rheumatism he thought was hysterical (Webster, 1995).

This theoretical bias is aggravated by Freud's lack of accurate and objective data upon which to base his theory. Not only did Freud write up his case notes at the end of the day, thus relying on his memory (unbiased?) of what all his patients had said, but his data was based on their adult memories of childhood events that had happened many years ago. However, because of his belief in patient fantasy and resistance, Freud often did not even rely on this actual data but guessed at what the real hidden memories might be (based on psychoanalytic theory).

In the case of the Wolf Man, for example, Freud assumed that the Wolf Man's first reported anxiety dream (of wolves sitting in a tree outside his window) at the age of four must have been caused by an earlier memory of seeing his parents having intercourse when he was just 18 months old. Only Little Hans could be observed directly, however Freud conducted the analysis through the boy's father.

Freud (1909) – 'Analysis of a phobia in a five-year-old boy'

The following represents a summary of the only detailed case study Freud reported on a child. The child was called Hans and Freud states that the parents were 'among my closest adherents' and had agreed to bring up their first child using 'no more coercion than might be absolutely necessary for maintaining good behaviour'.

The child developed into 'a cheerful, good-natured and lively little boy' and 'the experiment of letting him grow up and express himself without being intimidated went on satisfactorily'. Hans started to experience some problems at the age of four, however, which, according to Freud, required psychoanalysis. Freud only saw Hans once during the analysis, which was conducted by the father under Freud's advice.

Try covering the shaded right hand side of each page and reading the key elements of the case study on the left before reading the interpretation (see if you reach the same conclusions!)

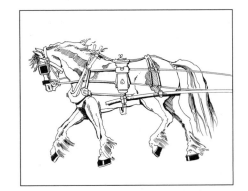

Some key elements of the case-study report

Introduction

April 1906 – Jan 1907 (3–3¾ years old)
'The first reports of Hans date from a period when he was not quite three years old. At that time, by means of various remarks and questions, he was showing a quite peculiarly lively interest in that portion of his body which he used to describe as his "widdler".'

He showed interest in the widdlers of farmyard animals and those at the zoo, began classifying animate and inanimate objects based on whether they had widdlers and asked his mother and father if they had one, even adding to his mother 'I thought you were so big you'd have a widdler like a horse'.

Freud continues '…his interest in widdlers was by no means a purely theoretical one; as might have been expected, it also impelled him to touch his member. When he was three and a half his mother found him with his hand on his penis. She threatened him in these words: "If you do that, I shall send for Doctor A to cut off your widdler. And then what'll you widdle with?" Hans: "With my bottom".'

Hanna was born when Hans was three and a half. He had been told that babies are delivered by the stork and was excluded from his parents' bedroom during the later part of the pregnancy and after the birth.

He was jealous of the new arrival, criticising her for her lack of teeth and small widdler and when taken ill with a fever was heard saying 'But I don't want a baby sister!'. The father reported, however, that 'Some six months later he had got over his jealousy'.

Hans's father and mother still allowed him to come into their bed, though only occasionally. Hans was very fond of his playmates and was especially attracted to the daughters of his neighbours and landlord, one of which (Mariedl) he wanted to sleep with him.

Summer 1907 (4¼ years old)
After a bath one day, as his mother was drying and powdering round his penis and taking care not to touch it, the following conversation took place. Hans said: 'Why don't you put your finger there?'

    Mother: 'Because that'd be piggish.'
    Hans: 'What's that? Piggish? Why?'
    Mother: 'Because it's not proper.'
    Hans (laughing): 'But it's great fun.'

Psychoanalytic interpretation/action

According to the psychoanalytic theory of psychosexual development, little Hans was in the phallic stage, where he would be expected to discover the pleasure to be gained from his phallus and show curiosity about this organ in others.

The theory suggests that, for boys at this stage, sexual gratification will soon be sought from an external source or 'object', the mother, since she also provided the pleasure associated with care at the oral and anal stages. This leads to the Oedipus complex.

The threat from the mother according to Freud '…was the occasion of his acquiring the " complex", the presence of which we are so often obliged to infer in analysing neurotics, though they one and all struggle violently against recognising it.' This threat of castration did not have an immediate effect, however.

According to Freud, 'The most important influence upon the course of Hans's psychosexual development was the birth of a baby sister.' The arrival not only deprived him of his mother's attention and caused his exile from his parents' bedroom, but also stimulated his curiosity about where babies came from and what the role of his father (another competitor for his mother's attention) was in the process.

Freud suggested 'Lying in bed with his father and mother was a source of erotic feelings in Hans just as it is in every other child' so 'there can be no doubt that lying beside them had aroused erotic feelings in him; so that his wish to sleep with Mariedl had an erotic sense as well'. Freud continued, 'The sexual aim which he pursued with his playmates, of *sleeping* with them, had originated in relation to his mother. It was expressed in words which might be retained in maturity, though they would then bear a richer connotation.'

The powdering incident was seen as further confirmation that Hans wished to 'seduce' his mother.

The Oedipus complex predicts, however, that Hans will soon realise that such wishes are forbidden and will fear that his father will punish him for them.

Exercise 16 (the answers are on page 46)

1 What advantages and problems might there be in conducting psychoanalysis on so young a child?

2 What advantages and problems might there be in having the father conduct the psychoanalysis?

Some key elements of the case-study report

January & February 1908 (4¾ years old)

Hans's father wrote to Freud '…I am sending you a little more about Hans – but this time, I am sorry to say, material for a case history. As you will see, during the last few days he has developed a nervous disorder…No doubt the ground was prepared by sexual over-excitation due to his mother's tenderness; but I am not able to specify the actual exciting cause. *He is afraid a horse will bite him in the street…*'

Hans woke up in tears and said to his mother 'When I was asleep I thought you were gone and I had no mummy to coax with' ('coax' was Hans's expression for 'to caress'). The previous summer he had expressed similar anxiety about losing his mother. On a walk with his nursemaid he began to cry and wanted to go home to 'coax' with his mother. Even out with his mother he expressed fright that 'a horse would bite me'. On the very same day Hans admitted that he put his hand to his widdler every evening in bed.

Hans was first informed about the meaning of his anxiety (but not about women's lack of widdlers) and seemed to show some improvement, but after a period of illness the phobia increased and he would not go out.

March 1908

Hans's father tried to persuade him that horses do not bite but Hans replied 'But white horses bite' and explained how the previous summer he had seen a cart with a white horse and heard a father warn his daughter *'Don't put your finger to the white horse or it'll bite you'.*

On 15 March, Hans was told that women have no widdlers. He did not seem to accept this, since he later had a fantasy of seeing his mother's widdler. He still showed his phobia and on a trip to the zoo seemed to fear all large animals. Hans's father suggested that perhaps Hans was afraid of large animals because he had been frightened by their large widdlers, adding 'But there's no need for you to be frightened of it. Big animals have big widdlers, and little animals have little widdlers'. Hans replied '…And my widdler will get bigger as I get bigger; it's fixed in of course.'

Towards the end of the month, Hans reported a strange fantasy he had thought of, saying 'In the night there was a big giraffe in the room and a crumpled one; and the big one called out because I took the crumpled one away from it. Then it stopped calling out; and then I sat down on top of the crumpled one.' The father explained to Hans that he (the father) was the large giraffe and that its long neck had probably reminded Hans of a widdler, to which Hans replied 'Mummy has a neck like a giraffe, too. I saw when she was washing her white neck.'

Hans also started imagining doing naughty things with his father as an accomplice, such as crawling into a forbidden area of the zoo and smashing a window.

On 30 March, Hans and his father paid a short visit to Freud. He was told that Hans was 'particularly bothered by what horses wear in front of their eyes and by the black round their mouths' and as Freud saw the two of them before him he suddenly realised that these must represent the father's eyeglasses and moustache.

Freud then told Hans 'that he was afraid of his father, precisely because he was so fond of his mother. It must be, I told him, that he thought his father was angry with him on that account; but this was not so, his father was fond of him in spite of it, and he must admit everything to him without any fear. Long before he was in the world, I went on, I had known that a little Hans would come who would be so fond of his mother that he would be bound to feel afraid of his father because of it.'

Psychoanalytic interpretation/action

This combined with the 'seduction attempt' of last summer was interpreted as meaning Hans wanted to be with his mother. The gain from the illness was to enable him to stay and coax with his mother. Freud advised the father 'that he should tell the boy that all this business about horses was a piece of nonsense and nothing more. The truth was, his father was to say, that he was very fond of his mother and wanted to be taken into her bed. The reason he was afraid of horses now was that he had taken so much interest in their widdlers.' Freud further suggested that the father should, '…assuming that his libido was attached to a wish to see his mother's widdler…take away this aim from Hans by informing him that his mother and all other female beings (as he could see from Hanna) had no widdler at all.'

Freud and the father did not yet realise that there was more to Hans's fear of horses than just guilt over masturbating and his 'fondness' for his mother.

The father suggested 'I say, it strikes me that it isn't a horse you mean, but a widdler, that one mustn't put one's hand to', to which Hans replied 'But a widdler doesn't bite.'

Freud interpreted the statement '…And my widdler will get bigger as I get bigger' as due to Hans's unconscious anxiety about the size of his penis, and the 'it's fixed in of course' as reflecting his fear of losing it – the delayed effect of the castration threat made a year and a quarter ago and triggered by the news that women have no widdlers (so perhaps they could be taken away). However, Freudian theory also suggests that there is a deeper reason for fear of castration.

This was interpreted by the father as representing a scene that had occurred for the last few mornings when Hans had come into their bedroom and been taken into their bed for a cuddle by the mother despite the protests of the father. Symbolically, Hans was sexually taking possession of (sitting down upon) the crumpled giraffe (the mother) despite the big giraffe (the father) who was calling out (protesting).

Freud interpreted this as Hans suspecting his father of doing 'that enigmatic forbidden something with his mother which he replaced by an act of violence such as smashing a window-pane or forcing a way into an enclosed space.'

Freud suddenly realised that in all senses 'Hans really was a little Oedipus who wanted to have his father "out of the way", to get rid of him, so that he might be alone with his beautiful mother and sleep with her.' Little Hans's fear of white horses was in fact symbolic of his fear of punishment from his father because of the forbidden desires towards his mother and his death wish against the father.

Freud suggested that the information he gave Hans now offered him the possibility of 'bringing forward his unconscious productions and of unfolding his phobia'. Hans was clearly impressed and asked his father 'Does the Professor talk to God as he can tell all that beforehand?'

Some key elements of the case-study report

April 1908
On 2 April the *'first real improvement'* was noted, and this improvement increased throughout the month.

The next day Hans provided his own explanation for his morning visits to his parents bedroom – he only came when he was frightened, adding 'Why did you tell me I'm fond of *Mummy* and that's why I'm frightened, when I'm fond of *you?*' Hans said he was afraid that his father would go away and not come home (something his mother had threatened).

Hans also began revealing more details about his phobia. He was particularly afraid of horses falling down, especially the bigger ones that pulled heavily loaded carts and were moving quickly or about to turn. Hans then reported that he gained his 'nonsense' (phobia) after he had seen a horse pulling a bus fall down and kick about noisily with its feet, saying 'When the horse in the bus fell down, it gave me such a fright, really! That was when I got the nonsense.' This, and the fact that the anxiety broke out immediately afterwards, was confirmed by his mother.
    The father asked 'When the horse fell down, did you think of your daddy?', to which Hans replied 'Perhaps. Yes. It's possible.'

During the month of April Hans's father investigated many other aspects of Hans's behaviour and thinking, including his dislike of heavily loaded carts, his lingering feelings of dislike towards his sister, his disgust at things that reminded him of 'lumf' (his term for faeces) and evacuating his bowels, his ideas on where babies came from, and his own imaginary children including his favourite 'Lodi'.
    Regarding his attitude towards his sister, when asked 'Are you fond of Hanna?' Hans replied 'Oh yes, very fond', but when the father added 'Would you rather that Hanna weren't alive or that she were?' Hans admitted 'I'd rather she weren't alive' adding 'I can't bear her screaming'. He was very fond of his imaginary children, however, and pretended he was their mummy. His favourite was a girl with black eyes and hair called 'Lodi' because it reminded him of a word he used ('Saffalodi') for the type of sausage he liked.

Hans had also developed a fear that his mother would let him fall in the big bath.

On 30 April, Hans's father asked 'are your children still alive? You know quite well a boy can't have any children.'
    Hans: 'I know. I was their Mummy before, *now I'm their Daddy.*'
    Father: 'And who's the children's Mummy?'
    Hans: 'Why, Mummy, and you're their *Granddaddy.*'
    Father: 'So then you'd like to be as big as me, and be married to Mummy, and then you'd like her to have children.'
    Hans: 'Yes, that's what I'd like, and…Grandmummy will be their Grannie.'

May 1908   (5 years old)
On 2 May Hans had a fantasy about a plumber who *'took away my behind with a pair of pincers, and then gave me another, and then the same with my widdler.'*
    Father: 'He gave you a *bigger* widdler and a *bigger* behind.'
    Hans: 'Yes.'
    Father: 'Like Daddy's; because you'd like to be Daddy.'
    Hans: 'Yes, and I'd like to have a moustache…and hairs like yours.'

Psychoanalytic interpretation/action

Hans was extensively and laboriously questioned to find support for Freud's interpretation.

This was interpreted as Hans's affection for his father being exaggerated as a compensation for the hostile wish that his father would go away permanently and leave him alone with his mother.

Freud and the father, however, argued that this event was 'insignificant in itself' and 'carried no "traumatic force"' apart from to remind Hans of his death wish against his father. It was the father that Hans wished to 'fall down' or die so he could be alone with his mother.
    Freud and Hans's father saw this interpretation confirmed by Hans saying things like 'Daddy, don't trot away from me!' or 'Daddy, you are lovely! You're so white' and by a toy horse he was playing with falling over when he had just been asked 'Are you fond of Daddy?'

All these things were actually found to be linked by a shared symbolism. According to Freud children believe in anal birth – that babies 'grow inside their Mummy, and are then brought into the world by being pressed out of her like a "lumf"' (something Hans's parents actually told Hans). Since the 'father went into the lumf symbolism, and recognised that there was an analogy between a heavily loaded cart and a body loaded with faeces' and that to Hans 'Hanna was a lumf herself', they learnt that Hans was actually afraid of his mother becoming pregnant again and being deprived of her attentions once more. That Lodi was Hans's own faecal child was confirmed by Hans's father on asking 'I say, doesn't a Saffalodi look like a lumf?', to which Hans replied 'Yes.'

The fear of falling in the bath was interpreted as a fear of being punished for his wanting Hanna to fall in the bath.

Freud suggests this shows 'Things were moving towards a satisfactory conclusion. The little Oedipus had found a happier solution than that prescribed by destiny. Instead of putting his father out of the way, he had granted him the same happiness that he desired himself: he made him a grandfather and married him to his own mother too.'

Freud comments: 'Hans's father grasped the nature of this wishful fantasy, and did not hesitate a moment as to the only interpretation it could bear.' Hans wanted to become like his father. The plumber might take away his penis but he would gain a bigger one. According to psychoanalytic theory identification with the father resolves the Oedipus complex. The illness was regarded as cured.

Exercise 16 (continued)

3 Freud says 'we will suspend our judgement and give our impartial attention to everything that there is to observe'. However, some of Freud's and the father's interpretations might seem a little biased by psychoanalytic theoretical expectations. From looking at the symbolic interpretations given to Hans's fantasies, speech and behaviour (such as the giraffe fantasy and the fear of horses), can you think of any alternative interpretations or reasons for Hans's anxieties?

4 What problems are there with drawing general conclusions from this case study?

1 What advantages and problems might there be in conducting psychoanalysis on so young a child?

Freud himself points out the advantages of conducting a psychoanalysis on a child as being able to directly study the 'sexual impulses and wishes which we dig out so laboriously in adults from amongst their own debris' rather than relying on adult memories of childhood.

However, children may well be more prone to giving

a answers that are untrue because of their imaginations – Hans was a very imaginative child and himself admitted at times 'I say, what I'm telling you isn't a bit true'.

b answers that they think their questioners want to hear (demand characteristics) – for example, agreeing with an adult's explanation because they think they know better.

Regarding 'a', Freud argues 'I do not share the view…that assertions made by children are invariably arbitrary and untrustworthy. The arbitrary has no existence in mental life.' He adds that although 'The untrustworthiness of the assertions of children is due to the predominance of their imagination…even children do not lie without a reason.' This shows that Freud believes in determinism – that there is always a cause (often unconscious) to behaviour.

Regarding 'b' Freud says 'It is true that during the analysis Hans had to be told many things that he could not say himself, that he had to be presented with thoughts which he had so far shown no signs of possessing, and that his attention had to be turned in the direction from which his father was expecting something to come. This detracts from the evidential value of the analysis; but the procedure is the same in every case. For a psychoanalysis is not an impartial scientific investigation, but a therapeutic measure. Its essence is not to prove anything, but merely to alter something. In a psychoanalysis the physician always gives his patient (sometimes to a greater and sometimes to a lesser extent) the conscious anticipatory ideas by the help of which he is put in a position to recognise and to grasp the unconscious material.' Freud adds 'It is true that a child, on account of the small development of his intellectual systems, requires especially energetic assistance', but thinks 'And yet, even during the analysis, the small patient gave evidence of enough independence to acquit him upon the charge of "suggestion".'

2 What advantages and problems might there be in having the father conduct the psychoanalysis?

Freud points out that the analysis of a child through the father helped overcome 'the technical difficulties in the way of conducting a psychoanalysis upon so young a child'. For example, Hans's father had the opportunity to see and question Hans about all he spontaneously said and did, in his home environment, over a long period of time.

However, the father conducting the analysis meant that Freud received the information second hand and according to psychoanalytic theory Hans may not have admitted forbidden feelings that he feared his father would punish him for.

Also, because the father was a strong believer in psychoanalysis, his questioning and interpretations may not have been objective and 'impartial' (of course the same applies to Freud!). Biased questioning will obviously produce biased confirmation from a child that may be prone, as pointed out above, to demand characteristics. Indeed, the father's questioning often seems like an inquisition, for instance:

I: 'Did you often get into bed with Mummy at Gmunden?' (this was on holiday while the father was often away)
Hans: '*Yes.*'

I: 'And you used to think to yourself you were Daddy?'
Hans: 'Yes.'
I: 'And then you felt afraid of Daddy?'
Hans: '*You know everything; I didn't know anything.*'
I: 'When Fritzl fell down you thought: "If only Daddy would fall down like that!" And when the lamb butted you you thought: "If only it would butt Daddy!" Can you remember the funeral at Gmunden?'
Hans: 'Yes. What about it?'
I: 'You thought then that if only Daddy were to die you'd be Daddy.'
Hans: 'Yes.'

3 Freud says 'we will suspend our judgement and give our impartial attention to everything that there is to observe'. However, some of Freud and the father's interpretations might seem a little biased by psychoanalytic theoretical expectations. From looking at the symbolic interpretations given to Hans's fantasies, speech and behaviour (such as the giraffe fantasy and the fear of horses), can you think of any alternative interpretations or reasons for Hans's anxieties?

There does not seem much doubt that Hans was showing a good deal of interest in 'widdlers', where children came from and parenthood, and may have been jealous of his sister and father for the attention they received from the mother. However, Hans's sexual focus on the mother, his supposed death wish towards, and fear of, his father, as well as the interpretations of his fear of horses and heavily loaded carriages, are probably more the result of psychoanalytic theoretical expectation and bias.

Hans seemed equally fond of both parents and showed more 'romantic' interest in girls closer to his own age.

The 'giraffe fantasy' could be interpreted in different ways – for example it could represent Hans taking away and punishing Hanna (the crumpled giraffe he sat on) from the mother (the big giraffe who called out in protest). This interpretation is supported by a test the father conducted by calling the mother 'big giraffe' to which Hans replied 'Oh yes. And Hanna's the crumpled giraffe, isn't she?'

That Hans's fear of white horses was the result of his fear of the father (punishing him for his desires towards the mother) being displaced onto white horses, also has alternative explanations. The fear could have been of the mother, who had actually threatened castration, had been thought to have a widdler like a horse, and had also been described as white. When Hans was first asked if the black around the horses mouth resembled a moustache he laughed, and said 'Oh no!' and later replied 'only by its colour'.

A more straightforward explanation of his phobia was provided by Hans himself, who noted that it began after he had been frightened by the cart horse collapsing and making such a noise and also by hearing that white horses could bite. According to learning theorists the former incident could have classically conditioned a fear into Hans, which may also explain why he was afraid of heavily loaded carts that seemed unstable and likely to collapse.

4 What problems are there with drawing general conclusions from this case study?

Since this psychoanalytic case study was the only one Freud conducted on a child, it may not be legitimate to generalise since Hans may not have been a 'normal' child. Freud mostly disagrees with this assessment of Hans saying that similar processes and experiences occur in everyone, and adding anyway that 'no sharp line can be drawn between "neurotic" and "normal" people'.

17 | Jung's analytical psychology

Jung and analytical psychology

Carl Gustav Jung (1875–1961) was a Swiss psychiatrist who worked in a Zurich mental hospital before moving on to his own private practice. He was, at first, a favourite disciple of Freud's but increasingly developed his own 'analytical psychology' theories on personality and mental disorder that differed from Freud's psychoanalysis, and the two men parted company on bad terms in 1913.

Exercise 17

Read some of Jung's main ideas below, then compare and contrast them with Freud's ideas.

Jung's theory	Freud's theory
Theory of the unconscious Jung proposed three levels of consciousness: *The conscious* – all we are directly aware of. *The personal unconscious* – the unconscious of each individual, it contains temporarily forgotten as well as truly repressed material and 'complexes' resulting from personal experience. *Collective unconscious* – a level of consciousness shared with other members of our species that contains common archetypes. INDIVIDUAL CONSCIOUSNESS / INDIVIDUAL PERSONAL UNCONSCIOUS / SHARED COLLECTIVE UNCONSCIOUS	
Different aspects of the mind and personality – Jung's analytical psychology suggests there are many aspects to the unconscious psyche (mind), such as complexes and archetypes, which can influence an individual's personality. *Complexes* are clusters of linked emotions, memories and attitudes in the personal unconscious that result from personal experience and can form mini sub-personalities in themselves. *Archetypes* are inherited predispositions to feel, act and experience the world in certain ways. Thus people may behave in similar ways to their ancestors and people from other cultures they have never met. Important archetypes include The Persona (our social mask), The Shadow (our animal urges) and The Anima/Animus (our female or male sides).	
Motivation of behaviour – Jung believed that our thoughts, emotions and behaviour result from a *self-regulating* psyche – our minds constantly *seek balance* and integration between the conscious and unconscious, and between different aspects of our personality. Imbalance will cause *compensations* – behaviour, personality characteristics, dreams or even symptoms of mental disorder that try to redress the balance. For example, an introverted personality may have dreams of doing extraverted things. Jung regarded the goal of development as *individuation* – the self-actualisation of one's potential and the achievement of psychic balance and integration.	
Word association tests – involve replying with the first word that comes to mind that is associated with another word. Jung composed lists of words and measured the exact time it took for an association to be made to each as well as the physiological response to it (recorded by skin conductance using a polygraph or 'lie-detector' apparatus). He thought collections of words that produced variations from normal responses indicated a common emotional link or 'complex'.	
Analysis and interpretation of symbolism – Jung focused on the cross-cultural study of symbolism in mythology. He frequently found important similarities in the myths and symbols of cultures that did not seem to have had any contact with each other, especially mystical 'mandala' symbols, such as circular shapes, crosses or other divisions of four, that represent psychic balance and harmony. He interpreted this as evidence for a collective unconscious.	
Dream interpretation – Jung suggested that dreams reflect current preoccupations and may be compensations for conscious attitudes and behaviour that are causing imbalance. Dreams are a symbolic language, difficult to always understand in verbal linguistic terms, but not deliberately disguised. Dreams come from everyday emotional problems in the personal unconscious (and may suggest ways of solving such problems in the future) or from images and symbols from the deeper collective unconscious.	
Therapy – Jung initially applied psychoanalytic concepts to the study of schizophrenics but his therapy became increasingly focused on middle-aged clients with high levels of insight, time and money, and with relatively minor problems or just those seeking more meaning in their lives. Lacking objective therapeutic outcomes, it is unclear when full individuation is reached.	

Read some of Jung's main ideas below, then compare and contrast them with Freud's ideas.

Jung's theory	Freud's theory
Theory of the unconscious Jung proposed three levels of consciousness: *The conscious* – all we are directly aware of. *The personal unconscious* – the unconscious of each individual, it contains temporarily forgotten as well as truly repressed material and 'complexes' resulting from personal experience. *Collective unconscious* – a level of consciousness shared with other members of our species that contains common archetypes. 	Freud also proposed three levels of consciousness, the conscious, the preconscious and the unconscious – the latter two together roughly correspond to Jung's personal unconscious, but Freud did not propose a collective unconscious.
Different aspects of the mind and personality – Jung's analytical psychology suggests there are many aspects to the unconscious psyche (mind), such as complexes and archetypes, which can influence an individual's personality. *Complexes* are clusters of linked emotions, memories and attitudes in the personal unconscious that result from personal experience and can form mini sub-personalities in themselves. *Archetypes* are inherited predispositions to feel, act and experience the world in certain ways. Thus people may behave in similar ways to their ancestors and people from other cultures they have never met. Important archetypes include The Persona (our social mask), The Shadow (our animal urges) and The Anima/Animus (our female or male sides).	Freud suggested fewer aspects of the psyche (the id, ego and superego). Jung was more inclined to personify different behaviours or characteristics. The Shadow, with its animal urges, is similar to the id but more positive in its influence.
Motivation of behaviour – Jung believed that our thoughts, emotions and behaviour result from a *self-regulating* psyche – our minds constantly *seek balance* and integration between the conscious and unconscious, and between different aspects of our personality. Imbalance will cause *compensations* – behaviour, personality characteristics, dreams or even symptoms of mental disorder that try to redress the balance. For example, an introverted personality may have dreams of doing extraverted things. Jung regarded the goal of development as *individuation* – the self-actualisation of one's potential and the achievement of psychic balance and integration.	Freud's view of development was a little more pessimistic and based on controlling innate sexual urges than Jung's. However, the ego also strives to balance the demands of id, superego and reality using defence mechanisms.
Word association tests – involve replying with the first word that comes to mind that is associated with another word. Jung composed lists of words and measured the exact time it took for an association to be made to each as well as the physiological response to it (recorded by skin conductance using a polygraph or 'lie-detector' apparatus). He thought collections of words that produced variations from normal responses indicated a common emotional link or 'complex'.	Similar to free association, but carried out in a more scientific way, not just recording the associated word but also measuring the exact response time and physical reaction.
Analysis and interpretation of symbolism – Jung focused on the cross-cultural study of symbolism in mythology. He frequently found important similarities in the myths and symbols of cultures that did not seem to have had any contact with each other, especially mystical 'mandala' symbols, such as circular shapes, crosses or other divisions of four, that represent psychic balance and harmony. He interpreted this as evidence for a collective unconscious.	Freud focused more on personal symbolic meanings but accepted that some symbols could have universal meanings, and he also studied different cultures and symbolism in mythology.
Dream interpretation – Jung suggested that dreams reflect *current* preoccupations and may be compensations for conscious attitudes and behaviour that are causing imbalance. Dreams are a symbolic language, difficult to always understand in verbal linguistic terms, but not deliberately disguised. Dreams come from everyday emotional problems in the personal unconscious (and may suggest ways of solving such problems in the future) or from images and symbols from the deeper collective unconscious.	Jung disagreed with Freud that dreams are always disguised wish fulfilment resulting from *past* circumstances and sexual or aggressive urges. Jung also saw dreams as more constructive.
Therapy – Jung initially applied psychoanalytic concepts to the study of schizophrenics but his therapy became increasingly focused on middle-aged clients with high levels of insight, time and money, and with relatively minor problems or just those seeking more meaning in their lives. Lacking objective therapeutic outcomes, it is unclear when full individuation is reached.	Freud had different ideas on the causes of schizophrenia but also tended to treat the same kind of limited sample of patients.
Contribution to psychology and society – Jung's theory focuses very much on the development of the *individual* and their inner life, and tends to ignore human relationships, the past and childhood experiences. Also, the cross-cultural similarities in myth and symbolism Jung found could just have resulted from similar *experiences* shared by different cultures rather than a shared unconscious. However, some of Jung's ideas influenced humanist psychology and Eysenck used introversion and extraversion as the basis for his personality tests.	Jung's ideas have not been as popular as Freud's, perhaps because they were a little more mystical and obscure, and less clearly explained.

18 | The learning theory approach to psychology

As we have seen, the learning theory approach to psychology was probably most strongly influenced (and advocated) by *behaviourism* – the movement formally started by John Watson in 1913. Later learning theorists tended to reject the extremity of the behaviourists' views, but were still influenced by their assumptions, principles and methods.

John Watson

Assumptions

The importance of the environment

The behaviourist approach was influenced by the philosophy of empiricism which, in very simple terms, argues that knowledge comes from the environment via the senses and that humans are like a 'tabula rasa' or blank slate at birth. This means the behaviourists believed that the majority of all behaviour is learned from the *environment* after birth (behaviourism takes the nurture side of the nature – nurture debate). Where a person is raised and what they learn from those surroundings is therefore thought to be more important than the abilities a person has inherited. The optimism created by this view of human flexibility and potential is reflected by Watson's (1930) famous quote:

'Give me a dozen healthy infants, well-formed, and my own specified world to bring them up in and I'll guarantee to take any one at random and train him to become any type of specialist I might select – doctor, lawyer, artist, merchant-chief and, yes, even beggarman and thief, regardless of his talents, penchants, tendencies, abilities, vocations, and race of his ancestors.'

Later learning theory also emphasised the importance of the environment on the development of behaviour, but began to accept that inherited factors could influence how easily such influences were acquired.

The importance of the processes of learning

Because of the importance of the environment and learning, the behaviourists strongly believed that psychology should aim to investigate and discover the *laws* of learning and the extent to which behaviour could be shaped by the environment. Understanding *how* the processes of learning occur is important to increase the efficiency of learning, to encourage the development of useful/adaptive behaviour and also, on a more philosophical level, to explain the role of the organism in the whole process.

The behaviourists, for instance, believed that the laws of learning were *universal* across species and that the process was a fairly *automatic* and passive one. The implication of this is that behaviour is *determined* by the environment and, since we are merely the total of all our past learning experiences, freewill is an illusion. Humans, like other animals, were regarded as puppets at the mercy of environmental experience.

This strict view of automatic and passive environmental determinism was criticised by other approaches to psychology and later learning theorists did introduce a more active view of the organism in the learning process. For example, Bandura's social learning theory suggests that factors like a person's attention, memory and beliefs can influence learning.

Methods

The behaviourists were extremely critical of all the approaches that concerned themselves with 'minds' of any sort (whether conscious or unconscious), and proposed that psychology should only investigate *observable behaviour* if it wanted to be an objective science. Behaviourism became known as 'stimulus and response psychology' since only observable phenomenon, the stimuli coming from the environment and the behavioural responses made to those stimuli, were considered.

Animal studies

This emphasis on stimulus and response, with no need to involve minds or physiology within the organism between the two, implies that differences in minds and brains were of little importance to the behaviourists. In fact, because they believed that the laws of learning were universal and that there was only a quantitative difference between animals and humans, behaviourist learning studies were usually conducted on *animals* such as cats, dogs, rats and pigeons.

Laboratory studies

This desire to follow the objectivity of other sciences also helps to explain why the behaviourists adopted strictly controlled laboratory conditions in which to conduct their studies of learning. Pavlov, the physiologist whose work on conditioning had such an important influence on behaviourism and learning theory, insisted on highly controlled laboratory conditions, even going so far as to construct a 'tower of silence' – a research building designed to minimise external sounds, drafts, odours and temperature extremes. Skinner constructed standardised and automated learning cages for his research animals, which became known (despite his dislike of the term) as 'Skinner boxes'.

Even when learning theorists began to consider other factors between stimulus and response, the tradition of laboratory studies of learning using animals continued and was influential in encouraging the use of scientific methodology in psychology.

Exercise 18

1 On reading Watson's quote, do you think that he could really have guaranteed to produce any type of specialist? If so, do you think that if he attempted to train all twelve to be artists, giving them all exactly the same experiences, that they would all be equally good? If not, what would make one infant better than another?

2 If Watson's 'own specified world to bring them up in' involved isolation in a laboratory with psychologists for ten years, and if you believed he could do what he said, would you give him one of your own 'well-formed infants'?

3 Why did the behaviourists not want to study minds?

4 What are the advantages and disadvantages of conducting investigations in the controlled conditions of a laboratory?

5 What are the advantages and disadvantages of using animals as research participants in learning studies?

1 On reading Watson's quote, do you think that he could really have guaranteed to produce any type of specialist? If so, do you think that if he attempted to train all twelve to be artists, giving them all exactly the same experiences, that they would all be equally good? If not, what would make one infant better than another?

Your opinion on these questions probably depends, in turn, upon your views on the nature vs. nurture and freewill vs. determinism debates.

If you think that certain abilities and behaviour, such as artistic, musical or intellectual abilities, are strongly influenced by inherited factors, you may not believe that Watson could create a specialist artist, musician or scientific genius. Even if Watson did succeed in creating a dozen specialists, and such innate factors had only a small effect, then this would still probably create differences between them in how good a specialist they became.

In addition, you might have thought that his infants may, at some point, have used their freewill and rejected Watson's training or decided to become a different type of specialist instead. However, if they had never been exposed to or taught information relevant to other specialities, and the knowledge was not inherited, how could they make such a decision? Where would the freewill come from?

Of course, Watson's quote also assumes that he had discovered the laws and techniques of learning that would enable him to shape human behaviour to such an extent (see the applications of classical and operant conditioning). In fact, no one gave him a dozen healthy infants to test his claim and he later admitted that in making it he was going beyond the facts (Schultz and Schultz, 1987).

2 If Watson's 'own specified world to bring them up in' involved isolation in a laboratory with psychologists for ten years, and if you believed he could do what he said, would you give him one of your own 'well-formed infants'?

This is a question that relates to the ethics of behavioural control and change in society.

The behaviourist, Skinner, argued that since freewill is an illusion and all behaviour is controlled by the environment (including other people) anyway, it makes sense to have experts (psychologists!) doing the controlling. Skinner firmly believed that behaviour should be socially engineered and controlled by expert state psychologists, and he wrote books such as *Beyond Freedom and Dignity* and *Walden Two* that offered many suggestions regarding the large scale manipulation of behaviour in society.

Although Skinner's views represent an extreme view of social control, and ten years of isolation from other distractions in a laboratory may seem a little harsh, if effective learning techniques existed perhaps it would be more efficient than many more years of conventional schooling and university with less certain results.

Such an approach has other problems, however. What about the ethics of denying choice to the infant about its future profession? Well, parents already make choices that affect their children's future, some even send them to specialist boarding schools or intensively educate them in certain subjects (known as 'hothousing') at home. Such a selective bias could be rejected by the child at some point, especially with an awareness of alternative possibilities, but this would present certain difficulties. A narrow specialist education may ignore and deprive the child of abilities and skills (particularly social ones) necessary to succeed in other areas – many a youthful prodigy has been found to lack important skills that are unrelated to their talent.

3 Why did the behaviourists not want to study minds?

The behaviourists only wanted to study observable behaviour and not minds to make psychology an objective science. Since we cannot see into other people's minds, and if we ask them about their thoughts they may lie, not know or just be mistaken, the behaviourists believed it was best to eliminate any reference to mental activity or concepts from psychology altogether.

Other psychological approaches disagreed with this rejection of the mind, suggesting that behaviourist explanations are incomplete without some consideration of all the important and interesting things that go on in our heads – even in the area of learning. Cognitive psychologists, for example, thought that behaviourism ignored important mental processes involved in learning.

4 What are the advantages and disadvantages of conducting investigations in the controlled conditions of a laboratory?

The controlled conditions of the laboratory enable psychologists to not only limit outside influences and distractions in their studies that might interfere with their reliability, but also helps standardise (make the same) the conditions for each participant or study. Such standardisation helps psychologists to generalise their results and enables others to replicate (repeat again) their studies to see if they achieve the same findings.

Unfortunately, controlled laboratory conditions are often not very typical environments and may make participants act in artificial ways (e.g. making them nervous and aware they are being tested), thus reducing the (ecological) validity of generalising the results to other environments.

5 What are the advantages and disadvantages of using animals as research participants in learning studies?

There are many advantages to be gained from using animals as research participants in learning studies.

Practically, animals are 'good subjects' and convenient. They do not try to understand the purpose of the study and they are more controllable in that they can be bred, raised and kept under certain conditions. Their faster breeding cycles allow tests to be conducted on the influence of heredity and environment on behaviour. They are more economical to produce, feed and care for.

Ethically, many studies that psychologists want to conduct are deemed unethical for human testing, but important enough to be justified for animal testing. We do not find it acceptable to breed human infants for research purposes nor raise them under controlled conditions in cages.

There are, however, also problems and disadvantages in using animals as research participants in learning studies.

The behaviourists claimed that animal research was justified because humans have evolved from other animals and so the difference between them is only quantitative. Since humans are just more complex animals, it makes sense to study more simple organisms first, and then generalise to humans by 'scaling up' the results. Many psychologists disagree with this claim and suggest that humans are physically and mentally *qualitatively* different to other animals. For example, biologically orientated psychologists argue that the behaviourists ignored innate, built-in biases in learning abilities between different species.

In addition, laboratory studies on animals are often even more likely to lack ecological validity than those conducted on humans, and so the findings may be even less useful for generalisation to human behaviour.

19 Classical conditioning

Classical conditioning is concerned with learning by association and refers to the conditioning of *reflexes – how animals learn to associate new stimuli with innate bodily reflexes*. The principles of classical conditioning were first outlined by *Pavlov*, and were then adopted by behaviourists such as Watson, who attempted to use them to explain how virtually all of human behaviour is acquired.

Pavlov was a physiologist who, while studying the salivation reflex, found that the dogs he was using in his experiments would sometimes start salivating before the food had reached their mouths, often at the sight of the food bucket. Clearly the dogs had learnt to associate new external stimuli (such as sights and sounds), with the original stimulus (food) that caused the salivation reflex.

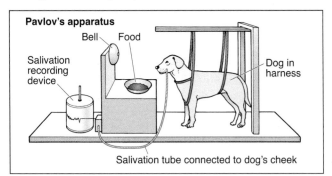

Pavlov's apparatus

Bell · Food · Salivation recording device · Dog in harness · Salivation tube connected to dog's cheek

The terminology of classical conditioning

In a series of thorough and well-controlled experiments, Pavlov found many new stimuli could be associated with reflexes and went on to introduce special terms for, and investigated many aspects of, the conditioning process.

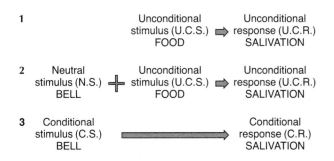

1. Unconditional stimulus (U.C.S.) FOOD ⇒ Unconditional response (U.C.R.) SALIVATION

2. Neutral stimulus (N.S.) BELL + Unconditional stimulus (U.C.S.) FOOD ⇒ Unconditional response (U.C.R.) SALIVATION

3. Conditional stimulus (C.S.) BELL ⟶ Conditional response (C.R.) SALIVATION

Variations in stimulus pairing and learning

Pavlov found that for learning associations to be made, the two stimuli had to be presented close together in time. If the time between the presentation of the N.S. (e.g. bell) and the presentation of the U.C.S. (e.g. food) was too great, then learning would not occur. This became known as the law of *temporal contiguity*.

However, Pavlov also found that the order in which the N.S. and U.C.S. were presented affected how easily learning occurred. For example, *forward conditioning* involves presenting the N.S. (e.g. bell) just before and during presentation of the U.C.S. (e.g. food) and produces the strongest learning, while *backward conditioning*, involves presenting the N.S. after the U.C.S. and produces very little learning.

Other ways of presenting the stimuli include *simultaneous conditioning*, where the N.S. (bell) and U.C.S. (food) are presented at the same time, and *trace conditioning*, which involves presenting and removing the N.S. before the U.C.S.

Extinction and spontaneous recovery

Pavlov demonstrated that the learning link would last as long as the U.C.S. (e.g. food) is occasionally re-presented with the C.S. (e.g. bell) – it is the reflex-based U.C.S. that strengthens the learning link. If, on the other hand, the C.S. (bell) is continually presented without the U.C.S. (food) then the C.R. (e.g. salivation) will gradually die out or *extinguish*.

This does not necessarily mean that the learning link is completely lost, however, since it was also shown that, if a period of time was left after the C.R. had extinguished, the C.R. would be exhibited again (albeit to a weaker degree) if the C.S. was re-presented. The fact that the C.R. shows this *spontaneous recovery* after extinction has occurred shows that the learning link does not disappear, but has been actively *inhibited* by the non-presentation of the U.C.S.

Generalisation and discrimination

Another interesting discovery in classical conditioning was stimulus generalisation – the finding that the C.R. could be triggered by stimuli that resembled the original C.S. – the closer the resemblance the greater the C.R. For example, if the original C.S. bell had a tone of C, then the dogs would also salivate to a lesser degree to tones of B and A. This stimulus *generalisation* could be prevented by only presenting the U.C.S. with the original C.S., which produces *discrimination*. For example, only presenting food with the original C bell causes the salivation response for the other tones to undergo extinction.

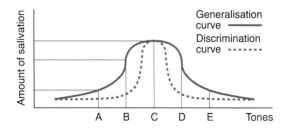

Generalisation curve ——
Discrimination curve ······

Amount of salivation / A B C D E Tones

Higher order conditioning

Once the C.S. is reliably producing the C.R., the C.S. acquires some conditioning properties itself – a new N.S. can be associated with the original C.S. until the new C.S. also produces the C.R. (without the need for the C.S. or U.C.S.). For example, once the bell is reliably producing salivation, the bell can be associated with a flashing light which will itself come to produce salivation, without the presence of the food or bell.

Little Albert and learning phobias

Classical conditioning has also been demonstrated with human participants. For example, Watson and Rayner (1920) showed how an infant called 'Little Albert' could be conditioned to fear a white rat, that he had originally been completely unafraid of, by making a sudden loud noise (which naturally provokes a fear response) while presenting the rat to the infant.

Exercise 19

1. Using classical conditioning terminology, describe how Watson and Rayner conditioned Little Albert to fear the rat.

2. After the conditioning, Little Albert also showed signs of the fear response towards a rabbit, cotton wool, Watson's hair and a Santa Claus mask, but played happily with his blocks and the hair of other people. What does this show?

3. Based on Watson and Rayner's Little Albert study, do you think that all phobias are learned by classical conditioning?

4. Watson and Rayner did not remove or de-condition Little Albert's rat fear. Suggest how this could have been done.

5. How ethical do you think Watson and Rayner's study was?

1 Using classical conditioning terminology, describe how Watson and Rayner conditioned Little Albert to fear the rat.

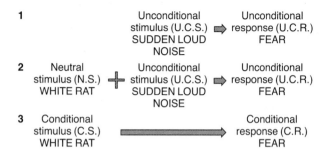

2 After the conditioning, Little Albert also showed signs of the fear response towards a rabbit, cotton wool and a Santa Claus mask (with beard) but played happily with his blocks and the hair of other people. What does this show?

Little Albert was showing stimulus generalisation when he showed signs of the fear response towards the rabbit, cotton wool, Watson's hair and Santa Claus mask (with beard). Presumably he played happily with his blocks and the hair of other people because these stimuli were not sufficiently similar to the furry white rat.

3 Based on Watson and Rayner's Little Albert study, do you think that all phobias are learned by classical conditioning?

Firstly, it would not be prudent to draw such a conclusion from the results of a single case study. As a sample of one, Little Albert may not have been representative of other people and of course there may have been methodological problems with the study which would need to be replicated. For example, Albert was described by Watson and Rayner as a 'stolid and unemotional' young infant who in fact showed a good deal of resistance to the conditioning process and did not display a fear reaction if he was allowed to suck his thumb.

Secondly, the idea that all phobias are learned by classical conditioning implies that at some point in the life of all phobic people a frightening experience with the phobic stimuli must have occurred. While this may often be the case, it is not always so.

Thirdly, the classical conditioning theory that all phobias are learned ignores the role of biological factors such as the natural 'built-in' biases in learning ability that have evolved in many animals to better adapt them to their environment. Species tend to evolve the ability to learn with greater ease those associations with stimuli that help them to survive. Seligman (1970), for example, proposed the concept of *biological preparedness* and argued that humans have evolved selective learning associations for survival reasons, in the form of *phobias*, for example. The most frequently occurring phobias of heights, snakes, spiders, etc., all share the evolutionary characteristic of being dangerous to us, and these sorts of stimuli have been experimentally shown to be more easily classically conditioned with fear than non-dangerous stimuli such as flowers and grass, which are far more rarely found as phobias. Also of interest is the finding that modern-day dangerous objects such as guns and cars are also rare phobias, since evolution has not had time to prepare us for these stimuli.

4 Watson and Rayner did not remove or de-condition Little Albert's rat fear. Suggest how this could have been done.

Albert was removed from the hospital by his mother and so Watson and Rayner stated that 'the opportunity to build up an experimental technique by means of which we could remove the conditioned emotional responses was denied us'. They suggested

they might have tried continually presenting the fearful stimuli to encourage fatigue of the fear response, associating the fearful stimuli with pleasant stimuli, e.g. stimulation of the erogenous zones or food, and encouraging imitation of non-fearful responses. The first technique is known today as flooding or implosion therapy and the second as systematic desensitisation therapy – both behavioural treatments based on classical conditioning principles. The third technique is known as modelling and is based on social learning theory.

Flooding and implosion therapy are both methods of forced reality testing that aim to produce the *extinction* of a phobic's fear by the *continual* and dramatic presentation of the phobic object or situation. In implosion therapy the phobic individual is asked to continually *imagine* the worst possible situation involving their phobia, whereas in flooding therapy the worst possible situation is actually *physically* and continuously presented. For example, Wolpe (1960) forced a girl with a fear of cars into the back of a car and drove her around for 4 hours until her fear completely disappeared. The key to the therapy is that the dramatic presentation is continuous and *cannot be escaped from or avoided*, therefore the patients anxiety is maintained at such a high level that eventually some process of stimulus exhaustion takes place (you cannot scream forever!) and the conditioned fear response extinguishes.

Systematic desensitisation aims to *extinguish* the fear response of a phobia and *substitute* a relaxation response to the conditional stimulus gradually, step by step. This is done by

1 forming a hierarchy of fear, a list of fearful situations, real or imagined, involving the CS that are ranked by the subject from least fearful to most fearful
2 giving training in deep muscle relaxation techniques
3 getting the subject to relax at each stage of the hierarchy, starting with the least fearful situation, and only progressing to the next stage when the subject feels sufficiently relaxed.

Mary Cover Jones applied systematic desensitisation to infants with phobias, such as the case of 'Little Peter'. Little Peter was a three-year-old child who had a strong phobia of rats and rabbits, and initially 'fell flat on his back in a paroxysm of fear when a white rat was dropped into his playpen' (Walker, 1984). Peter's treatment began by being presented with a rabbit in a cage at the same time as he ate his lunch, and ended 40 sessions later with him stroking the rabbit on his lap with one hand and eating his lunch with the other!

5 How ethical do you think Watson and Rayner's study was?

The study has serious ethical problems. Watson and Rayner reported that they hesitated about proceeding with the experiment but comforted themselves that Albert would encounter such traumatic associations when he left the sheltered environment of the nursery anyway. This is not a very good ethical defence, especially since they believed such associations might persist indefinitely and did not leave sufficient time to remove them afterwards, despite knowing Albert was due to leave the hospital where they were testing him.

The procedure obviously involved participant distress. Watson and Rayner reported how the sudden noise was made by striking a steel bar with a hammer behind Albert's head, which caused him to whimper, burst into tears, jump violently, fall forward and bury his face in the mattress. After conditioning, the sight of the rat alone caused him to instantly begin to cry, fall over, and then crawl away so fast that he was caught with difficulty before reaching the edge of the table.

20 | Operant conditioning

Operant conditioning involves *learning through the consequences of behavioural responses*. The principles of operant conditioning were first investigated by Thorndike, and were then thoroughly developed by the behaviourist Skinner, who used them to explain many aspects of human behaviour.

Thorndike studied the way cats would learn to escape from his puzzle box by *trial and error* – his cats did not immediately acquire the desirable escape behaviour but gradually increased in their ability to show it over time. Nevertheless, Thorndike found that any response that led to desirable consequences was more likely to occur again, whereas any response that led to undesirable consequences was less likely to be repeated – a principle which became known as the *Law of Effect*.

However, as with classical conditioning, the law of contiguity applies – associations between responses and consequences have to be made close together in time for learning to occur.

Thorndike's puzzle box
Cats had to emit the response of pulling the string inside the box to release the catch on the door to provide escape (a pleasant consequence). Time to escape decreased with each trial (the number of times the cat was put back in the box).

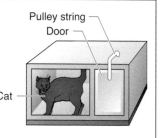

Types of consequence and their effects
There are two types of consequence for a behaviour that will increase the likelihood of it being repeated in the future.

Positive reinforcement increases the likelihood of a behavioural response occurring again by providing pleasant consequences for it, e.g. the behaviour leads to food.

Negative reinforcement also *increases* the likelihood of a response occurring but does so because it involves the removal of, or escape from, unpleasant consequences, e.g. the behaviour leads to stopping or avoiding an electric shock.

Punishment, on the other hand, *decreases* the likelihood of a behavioural response being repeated because it is followed by an inescapable unpleasant consequence, e.g. the behaviour leads to an electric shock.

Skinner box
A Skinner box typically contains a food delivery opening for dispensing food pellets, a metal grid floor for administering electric shocks, and levers.

The levers can be made to activate food delivery or to give or stop electric shocks. Rats or pigeons are often used.

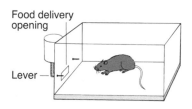

Most operant-conditioning studies use naturally occurring primary reinforcers such as food, water and warmth. However, *secondary reinforcers* (those that are associated with primary reinforcers through classical conditioning), such as money, tokens or parents, can also be used to change behaviour in some animals, particularly humans.

Generalisation and discrimination
Skinner found that animals would make responses which resembled the originally reinforced response. For example, a pigeon reinforced with food for pecking a warning button when it saw the orange colour of a lifejacket, would *generalise* and also peck (although less frequently) when it saw yellow or red colours, unless it was taught to *discriminate* by presenting all colours but only reinforced for pecking at orange. If a response is not reinforced it will usually gradually undergo *extinction*.

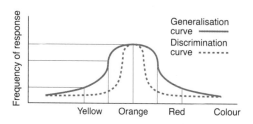

Schedules of reinforcement
Continuous schedules involve reinforcing every response made, whereas partial schedules involve reinforcing responses in varying frequencies to affect response and extinction rates.

A *fixed ratio schedule*, for example, involves reinforcing a fixed number of responses (e.g. a food pellet for every ten lever presses in a Skinner box), while a *fixed interval schedule* involves reinforcing after a fixed amount of time (e.g. a food pellet for lever pressing each minute in a Skinner box).

Variable schedules, by comparison, are less predictable. A *variable ratio schedule* reinforces an average number of responses (e.g. a food pellet on average every ten lever presses, i.e. sometimes after 8 sometimes after 12 presses), whereas a *variable interval schedule* reinforces after an average amount of time (e.g. a food pellet on average each minute, i.e. sometimes after 50 seconds sometimes after 70).

Behaviour shaping and language learning
By reinforcing successive approximations – selectively rewarding behavioural responses that increasingly resemble a desired end behaviour in a step-by-step manner – very complex behaviour can be built up from simple units. The first responses are reinforced until perfected and then reinforcement is withheld until the behaviour is refined to the next desired behaviour.

For example, the behaviourist Skinner argued that human language is learned through operant-conditioning principles, as parents selectively reinforce and shape their infant's babbling into the correct units of sound (phonemes) for their language, then into units of meaning (morphemes), which are in turn further shaped into proper words, phrases and sentences.

Exercise 20

1 Identify one similarity and one difference between
   a positive reinforcement and negative reinforcement.
   b negative reinforcement and punishment.

2 State two ways of using a Skinner box to increase a rat's lever-pressing behaviour and one way to decrease it.

3 Pigeons have been trained to guide missiles towards targets like enemy ships. Why is it important to teach them stimulus discrimination and how could this be done?

4 How many apples would you pick and how soon would you stop working after I ran out of money if I came to pay you after a each hour, b each box filled, c about each hour, but sometimes sooner, sometimes later?

5 What do you think parents reinforce their children's speech *with* and how do you think they selectively shape *correct* language in their children?

Answers 20.1 – 20.5

1 Identify one similarity and one difference between

a positive reinforcement and negative reinforcement.

Positive reinforcement and negative reinforcement both *increase* the likelihood that a behavioural response will be repeated in the future, however positive reinforcement involves *providing pleasant* stimuli to the animal, whereas negative reinforcement involves the *removal or avoidance of negative stimuli.*

b negative reinforcement and punishment.

Negative reinforcement and punishment both involve the use of *negative stimuli*, however in negative reinforcement the negative stimuli can be *removed or avoided to increase* the likelihood that a behavioural response will be repeated in the future, whereas with punishment the negative stimuli are *administered to decrease* the likelihood that a behavioural response will be repeated in the future.

2 State two ways of using a Skinner box to increase a rat's lever-pressing behaviour and one way to decrease it.

The lever-pressing behaviour of a rat could be increased by either giving a food pellet reward as a consequence of pressing the lever (positive reinforcement), or by enabling the lever pressing to stop or avoid an electric shock (negative reinforcement). It could be decreased by giving an electric shock as a result of pressing the lever.

3 Pigeons have been trained to guide missiles towards targets like enemy ships. Why is it important to teach them stimulus discrimination and how could this be done?

'Project Pigeon' involved reinforcing pigeons with food for correct guidance towards a target. In such a project it would be important to prevent inappropriate generalisation – to ensure that the pigeon did not guide a missile towards targets (e.g. non-enemy ships!) that *resembled* the training target. To produce discrimination, a variety of different (but similar) targets should also be presented to the pigeon but only showing the guidance response behaviour to the original target should be reinforced with food. Generalised responses which are not reinforced should undergo extinction (punishing them might help prevent nasty accidents too) until the pigeon shows precise discrimination.

4 How many apples would you pick and how soon would you stop working after I ran out of money if I came to pay you after a) each hour, b) each box filled, c) about each hour, but sometimes sooner, sometimes later?

Different partial reinforcement schedules lead to different types of response rate (how often the response is made) and extinction rate (how quickly the response disappears after the reinforcement for it ceases).

Paying you for picking apples at the end of each hour of work resembles a *fixed interval* reinforcement schedule. The overall response rate for this schedule is relatively low and the extinction rate is relatively quick. For example, you would probably not pick that many apples (payment depends on time rather than productivity) and if I ran out of money you would soon realise and stop picking (given the past predictability).

Paying you for picking apples at the end of each box filled resembles a *fixed ratio* reinforcement schedule. The overall response rate for this schedule is high and again the extinction rate is relatively quick. For example, you would probably pick lots of apples (the more you pick, the more you are paid) and if I ran out of money you would soon realise and stop picking (given the past predictability).

Paying you for picking apples at, on average, the end of each hour of work but sometimes sooner, sometimes later, resembles a *variable interval* reinforcement schedule. The overall response rate for this schedule is fairly high and steady, and the extinction rate is relatively slow. For example, you would probably steadily pick apples to make sure you are paid and if I ran out of money you would probably keep picking for some time (given the past unpredictability).

It is important to remember that, according to Skinner, no mental reasoning or calculation is needed, these reinforcement schedules have an automatic effect on behavioural responses.

5 What do you think parents reinforce their children's speech *with* and how do you think they selectively shape *correct* language in their children?

According to the behaviourist learning theorist Skinner, in his book *Verbal Behaviour* (1957), words are merely behavioural responses emitted because they have been reinforced by the environment. In the case of language, he argues that positive reinforcement is provided by the parents' smiles, attention and approval which are pleasant to the child (parents are *secondary reinforcers* because they are associated with the primary rewards of food, warmth, etc.).

Babies utter many different phonemes (basic units of sound, e.g. 'm' or 'ah') while babbling and as echoic responses (imitations). Parents respond by *reinforcing familiar* phonemes from their own language by smiling or paying increased attention, thereby making them more likely to be repeated, and *ignore unfamiliar* sounds thereby extinguishing them as responses. By *selective reinforcement* the child therefore produces more and more suitable phonemes for their language.

During babbling, different phonemes will, by trial and error, combine to form morphemes (basic units of meaning, e.g. 'mah / mah' or 'dah /dah'). Since these sound even more like a language that the parents recognise they draw even more attention and reinforcement for the baby and are, therefore, more likely to be repeated. Those *trial* and *error* combinations that are not recognised (e.g. 'ah / ba' or 'ge / ge') are not paid attention to and so are likely to be extinguished as responses.

Morphemes become refined into words by behaviour shaping. Parents want their children to produce more accurate words for communication and gradually reinforce morpheme combinations that sound more and more like proper words. Step by step, correct words will be spoken more frequently while 'baby' pronunciation will be extinguished.

Through the processes of trial and error, selective reinforcement and behaviour shaping words are then shaped into telegraphic two-word utterances, then into phrases and then into sentences until the full language has been acquired.

Producing words in the right context is also reinforced, as words gain their 'meaning' (not a word favoured by the behaviourists) through their associations with objects, events or activities. Skinner distinguished between two different types of verbal behaviour that parents reinforce in different ways. A '*mand*' is verbal behaviour that is reinforced by the child receiving something it wants, e.g. the word 'chocolate' is reinforced by receiving some. A '*tact*' is verbal behaviour caused by imitating others in the correct context and is reinforced by approval, e.g. the word 'tree' may be imitated from the parent's speech and reinforced by a smile or approval.

While operant conditioning is certainly a more flexible form of learning than classical conditioning (which is limited to reflexive behaviour), it has been argued that in-built differences in learning abilities, particularly between species, impose limitations upon learning. A *species-specific, evolved human potential* for language (a Language Acquisition Device according to Noam Chomsky) would account for the ease with which young children learn complex grammar as well as the failure to teach human language to apes to the same standard.

21 | Gardner & Gardner (1969) – 'Teaching sign language to a chimpanzee'

This study describes the first phase of a project designed to teach a chimpanzee a human language. Chimpanzees, being regarded as intelligent and sociable animals (although strong and occasionally difficult to handle), are regarded as good subjects for this kind of study.

Past attempts at teaching chimps vocal language, e.g. Hayes and Hayes (1951) with the chimp Vicky, failed because of the chimps' inappropriate vocal apparatus. Since chimpanzees employ a variety of gestures in their natural environment, the aim of the study was to see if a chimp could be taught American Sign Language (ASL) – a gestural language used by the deaf. Although some ASL gestures are symbolically arbitrary, others are quite representational or iconic (they resemble what they stand for). Since humans currently use ASL, comparisons of young chimp and human performance could be made.

Method
The researchers used a wild caught female chimpanzee called Washoe, named after the county where the University of Nevada was situated. Although Washoe was at first very young and dependent (aged between 8 and 14 months in June 1966 when the study began), it was decided to work with a chimp so young in case there was a critical time period for language acquisition.

Washoe was raised by, and during her waking hours was always in the company of, trainers able to communicate in American Sign Language – all of whom used ASL in their games and activities with her. A slightly modified form of ASL was used with finger spelling avoided as far as possible and with some variation in the gestures used to form the signs.

In training Washoe to use sign language, the researchers made use of *imitation* and *instrumental (operant) conditioning* – especially *behaviour shaping* of her babbling.

Past researchers noted that chimpanzees naturally imitated visual behaviour, so the researchers repeatedly signed in Washoe's presence. Washoe would readily imitate gestures but not always on command or in appropriate situations at first, so correct and exaggerated gestures were repeatedly made as prompts until she emitted the correct sign. Routine activities such as bathing, feeding and tooth-brushing also helped produce (delayed) imitation.

Washoe's spontaneously emitted gestures (babbling) were encouraged and shaped into signs by indulging in appropriate behaviour and providing positive reinforcement. Tickling was particularly effective as a reinforcer to shape more accurate signs by withholding it until a clearer version of the sign was shown.

Results
Detailed records of daily signing behaviour were kept until 16 months when their increasing frequency made such record keeping difficult. From 16 months, new signs were recorded on a checklist when three different observers noted a sign occurring in the correct situation without specific prompting. A sign was said to have been acquired when it was correctly used without prompting at least once a day for 15 consecutive days.

- *Vocabulary* – Thirty signs met the above criteria by the end of the 22nd month, plus four more which occurred on more than half the days of a 30-day consecutive period. Four new signs were shown in the 1st seven months, nine signs during the next seven months and 21 during the following seven months.

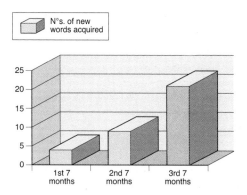

- *Differentiation* – Washoe's signing became more context and object *specific* over time, even showing the ability to distinguish between the use of 'flower' (originally used for all smells) and 'smell'.

- *Transfer* – Washoe spontaneously *generalised* signs acquired in one context to other contexts, e.g. 'picture' to all pictures, 'dog' to unknown dogs, etc.

- *Combinations* – Washoe used signs in combination once she had 8 to 10 signs at her disposal. Some combinations, e.g. 'gimme tickle' or 'listen dog' were shown spontaneously, before the researchers had used them.

The Gardners conclude that it is difficult to say whether Washoe has acquired language because there is no distinct defining point for determining when 'communication' becomes 'language' and because Washoe is young and still progressing. Also the researchers suggest that the training conditions for Washoe were not optimal and that new methods need to be developed to objectively test Washoe's use of sign language.

Nevertheless, they point out that they have shown that sign language is an appropriate form of two-way communication for chimps, and because of Washoe's achievements with spontaneous transfer and combination (which may be exceeded by other chimps), they argue that we should be cautious about identifying aspects of language as exclusively human.

Exercise 21

1 What method does this study employ and what are the advantages and disadvantages of using it?

2 What practical problems do you think there are with trying to teach language to chimpanzees?

3 The researcher Terrace argued that Washoe was merely responding to cues from her trainer rather than spontaneously using and 'understanding' the signs she was using. How could this claim be tested?

4 How far do you think Washoe could be said to have acquired language based on the Gardners' report? What differences are there between Washoe's and a 3- to 4-year-old human child's language?

5 What implications does this study have for Skinner's learning theory of language acquisition?

6 If apes can talk, do you think they should be given the same rights and privileges as humans?

1 What method does this study employ and what are the advantages and disadvantages of using it?

The study is a longitudinal case study of one chimp. The advantages of this method are that it provides the necessary amount of time and resources to be dedicated to such a long-term and demanding project, and provides a great deal of in-depth and detailed information.

The disadvantages are that with only one subject the ability to generalise to other apes is reduced. The longitudinal nature of the study also makes it expensive.

2 What practical problems do you think there are with trying to teach language to chimpanzees?

As the Gardners point out, chimpanzees are very strong animals, which can make close interaction difficult and dangerous. They can also become easily distracted, run away from the trainer or even throw a tantrum and bite.

3 The researcher Terrace argued that Washoe was merely responding to cues from her trainer rather than spontaneously using and 'understanding' the signs she was using. How could this claim be tested?

The Gardners were developing methods whereby Washoe had to communicate information to a trainer who had no previous knowledge of it. For example, Washoe would have to name what she could see in a box for someone who did not know (and who therefore could not prompt her).

4 How far do you think Washoe could be said to have acquired language based on the Gardners' report? What differences are there between Washoe's and a 3- to 4-year-old human child's language?

There are many problems involved in deciding whether Washoe was acquiring language, especially because there is no distinct defining point for determining when 'communication' becomes 'language'. Researchers have identified many criteria that human languages possess, including:

- Semanticity – using symbols to stand for/refer to objects, actions, etc.
- Displacement – using language to communicate about things not physically present here or now.
- Productivity (creativity) – combining symbols to produce and understand new meanings.
- Grammar (structure dependence) – the rules for combining symbols to provide meaning, e.g. word order.
- Cultural transmission – others can acquire the language.
- Spontaneity – the language can be used to initiate communication at will.

Washoe clearly acquired sign gestures from her trainers and her use of them appeared to show semanticity, displacement, productivity and spontaneity at times. Her signing did not show much evidence of consistent grammar, but the researchers did not necessarily reinforce this.

However, Washoe never acquired the large number of symbols nor the sophisticated grammar to consistently and precisely communicate new meanings that the vast majority of 3- to 4-year-old human children show. Even though the learning conditions were not the same as most human children experience, there seems to be a quantitative and qualitative difference in the ease and extent to which Washoe and human children acquire language. This is not to say that Washoe does not have language, only not to the same extent as humans.

5 What implications does this study have for Skinner's learning theory of language acquisition?

The methods used to teach Washoe were a mixture of imitation (social learning theory) and reinforcement with behaviour shaping (operant conditioning), so Washoe was not a pure test of Skinner's ideas. Nevertheless, given the answer in question 4 above, it seems likely that human children may have a genetic predisposition to acquire human language that chimpanzees do not, so Skinner's learning theory cannot be a complete explanation.

6 If apes can talk do you think they should be given the same rights and privileges as humans?

The research has implications for the rights of apes; if they can talk and ask, for example, not to be tested should they not be given human rights?

GARDNER AND GARDNER CROSSWORD

1 The language taught in this study (8/4)
2 The name of the chimpanzee used (6)
3 The kind of conditioning (another term for operant) used to encourage signing (12)
4 The number of consecutive days a sign had to be correctly used without prompting to say that it had been acquired (7)
5 The number of signs acquired by the end of the twenty-second month (6)
6 The copying of behaviour (9)
7 The language criteria met by the spontaneous and creative combination of signs (12)
8 The term for the first, spontaneously emitted gestures made by the infant (8)
9 The term for using different signs in more specific ways (15)
10 The term for correctly generalising a sign acquired in one context to other contexts (8)
11 A stimuli found pleasant by the chimpanzee which was used to reinforce language (8)
12 The method of withholding reinforcement until a clearer sign is emitted (7)
13 The kind of activities that helped the acquisition of signs (7)

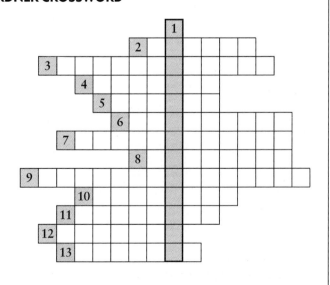

22 | Social learning theory

Social learning theory (later re-named social cognitive theory by Bandura) was developed to create a learning theory that went beyond the behaviourist learning theories (e.g. of operant conditioning) to incorporate the important *cognitive processes* that humans seem to possess between the environmental stimuli they receive and the behavioural responses they make.

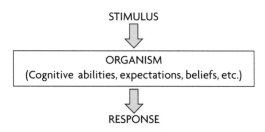

Social learning theorists such as Bandura and Walters suggest that behaviour is not only learnt from the environment by direct reinforcement, but through the process of *modelling*. Modelling involves learning through the *observation* of other people (models), which may lead to *imitation* if the behaviour to be imitated *leads to desirable consequences*.

Models
According to social learning theory, people from our social environment not only provide us with reinforcement for our behaviour but also act as models. Models provide *information* about *behaviour* (through their actions, statements, skills, etc.) and its *consequences* (whether it leads to positive or negative outcomes). Important sources of models are the family, peer group and the media.

Observational learning
Observational learning ability involves being able to *automatically learn* behaviour *from just being exposed to models, without the need for reinforcement*.

Observational learning depends upon cognitive processes such as *attention* and *memory*, abilities that allow the observer to

- focus on relevant models and behaviour, e.g. based on past memories of who and what is most useful and appropriate to imitate in a given environment
- store a memory representation of how to reproduce what was said or done
- remember information concerning the past consequences of the behaviour, e.g. whether they saw it rewarded in others, whether they were rewarded for it themselves or if they felt good about it last time (self-reinforcement).

Imitation
Imitation involves copying whole units of behaviour; the observer can duplicate what they have seen even if it consists of a quite complex series of actions.

However, social learning theory distinguishes between the learning of behaviour and the performance of it. Behaviour may be learnt from models through observation but the likelihood of it being imitated depends on a number of factors.

Assuming that proper attention was paid to the model, the behaviour was effectively stored and the person is physically capable of imitating the model, many cognitive factors are involved, such as

- *expectations* – behaviour is likely to be imitated if desirable consequences are expected for the behaviour (or at least unfavourable ones are not expected). If a child sees a model's behaviour being rewarded, this acts as *vicarious* (indirect) *reinforcement* for the child who may proceed to imitate it. If the

child sees another person's behaviour punished then, although the behaviour is learnt, it is less likely to be imitated – *vicarious punishment* is experienced.

- *cognitive beliefs* – such as *self-efficacy* (a person's belief in their ability to effectively achieve their goals) or the morality of behaviour (conscience). If the observer *believes* they are unable to successfully imitate the model (a lack of self-efficacy) and that it is morally wrong to do so (inner self-punishment) then they will be less likely to imitate the behaviour.

Social learning theory and aggression
Social learning theory has been used to explain the acquisition of many different kinds of behaviour, from personality characteristics to gender and moral behaviour. Many of the earliest investigations of the theory, however, concerned the acquisition of aggressive behaviour. Theorists like Bandura and Walters suggested that aggression is learnt from the environment mainly through observational learning and imitation, rather than being an inner biological drive (as Freud proposed) or the result of direct reinforcement of aggressive behaviour (as the behaviourists argued).

Acts of aggression are particularly noticeable and memorable behaviours that many important social models display (particularly media characters on television and at the cinema) and which may be seen to lead to rewards (desired consequences) and thus be imitated. This theory, therefore, has important implications for the portrayal of violence on television in terms of the negative effects it might produce in those who observe it. Bandura and others conducted many laboratory experiments to demonstrate that aggression could be learnt and imitated from live, filmed or even cartoon models.

Bandura et al (1961, 1963) allowed one group of children to watch an adult model perform certain aggressive acts with an inflatable 'Bobo doll' which were unlikely to occur normally, such as throwing the doll up in the air, hitting it with a hammer and punching it while saying things like 'pow' and 'boom'. When these children were left in a playroom with the inflatable doll, they frequently imitated the same acts of aggression, compared to a control group who had not seen the model and showed none of these particular behaviours.

Bandura (1965) used a similar experimental set-up, but showed different consequences for the model's aggression to three groups of children. One group saw the model's aggression being rewarded, one group saw the model being punished for the aggression, and another group saw no specific consequences. When allowed to enter the playroom the children who had seen the model punished showed less imitative aggression than the other two groups. However, if all the children were offered rewards for doing what the model had done, all groups showed high levels of imitation. The children in the model-punished group had clearly learnt the aggression by observation, but had not initially shown their potential to imitate it because they expected negative consequences (they thought they would be punished themselves if they showed the aggressive behaviour).

Exercise 22

1. What are the main differences between social learning theory and operant conditioning in how learning occurs?

2. Do you think that all children will imitate media aggression to the same extent? Why or why not?

3. Do you think that the effects of media violence are invariably negative?

1 What are the main differences between social learning theory and operant conditioning in how learning occurs?

Although both theories involve learning from environmental experience, social learning theory involves

- learning through the observation of other people's behaviour and its consequences rather than one's own individual behaviour and experience, as operant conditioning suggests
- imitation – immediately copying whole units of behaviour rather than learning gradually through trial and error, as operant conditioning proposes
- cognitive influences on learning (e.g. expectancies about future consequences) that can increase or decrease the likelihood of behaviour being shown rather than the automatic effect of experience on behaviour, as operant conditioning theorists like Skinner argued.

Unlike behaviourist learning theorists, who saw people as being passively programmed by their environment, Bandura saw humans as *actively influencing their environment* through their cognitive abilities, acquired beliefs and the effects of their behaviour.

2 Do you think that all children will imitate media aggression to the same extent? Why or why not?

The effects of media violence often depend on what the child brings to the screen. Social learning theory neglects the role of innate, biological factors upon behaviour, e.g. the genetic inheritance of aggressive predispositions.

3 Do you think that the effects of media violence are invariably negative?

Observational learning and imitation of violence is only one way in which media violence could have a negative effect on those who watch it. Other mechanisms that could lead to increased violence are

- desensitisation – watching aggression may lead to an increased acceptance or tolerance of it in society
- arousal – aggressive emotional arousal or excitement from watching aggression may lead to real violence
- disinhibition – watching aggression could reduce inhibitions about behaving aggressively as it is seen as socially legitimate.

Much of the experimental (both under laboratory and field conditions), quasi-experimental and correlational research on the effects of media violence supports its negative influence on aggression levels.

- *Laboratory experiments* – Bandura's experiments showed that aggression could be learnt and imitated from live, filmed or cartoon models. Liebert and Baron (1972) found that children who had watched a violent programme were more likely to hurt another child.

- *Field experiments* – Parke et al. (1977) showed juvenile delinquents in the USA and Belgium either violent or non-violent television for a week. Aggression was greater for the violent TV group especially in those children who had previously shown higher levels.

- *Natural experiments* – Joy et al. (1986) measured children's levels of aggression in a Canadian town one year before and after television was introduced, and found a significant increase compared to the non-significant increases in towns that already had television.

- *Correlations* – Eron (1987) found a significant positive correlation between the amount of aggression viewed at age 8 and later aggression at age 30. Phillips (1986) has found

correlations between highly publicised incidents of aggression, such as murder cases or boxing matches, and the number of corresponding incidents in society at large.

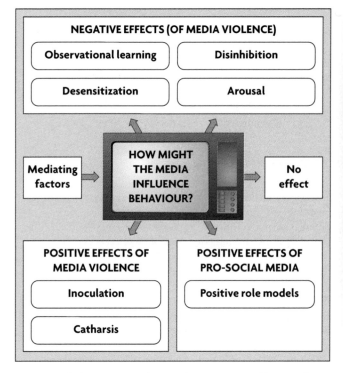

Alternatively, however, watching violence may actually 'inoculate' the watcher against showing aggression themselves. Remember that social learning theory argues that the likelihood of imitation depends on the perceived consequences of the model's aggression. If a child sees a model's aggression being punished then, although the aggressive behaviour is learnt, this acts as vicarious (indirect) punishment for the child who will be less likely to imitate it. Watching antisocial violence could provide the opportunity to see it come to no good (the 'baddie' loses) or illustrate its immorality. Instead of aggressive arousal, media violence may sicken or produce fear in the observers.

A more controversial idea relating to the positive effects of observing media aggression is catharsis – according to some psychodynamic theorists watching violence could provide a relief from pent-up aggression as it is released through emotional sympathy.

Feshbach and Singer (1971) claimed that children shown aggressive programmes over a 6-week period showed less aggressive behaviour than those who saw non-violent TV. However this study has been accused of methodological flaws and more recent studies have not replicated it or have found the opposite.

It should not be forgotten, though, that the media also show pro-social models, that there are many methodological problems involved in these studies, and that the effects are sometimes small or inconclusive.

Sprafkin et al. (1975) found over 90% of children chose to help a puppy instead of personal gain after watching a programme that involved helping ('Lassie'), while Baron et al. (1979) found children were more co-operative after watching 'The Waltons'. Hearold (1986) analysed approximately 200 studies and concluded that pro-social television has around twice the effect on children's behaviour than anti-social television.

Howitt and Cumberbatch (1974) analysed 300 studies concluding that TV violence has no direct effect on children's behaviour. Freedman (1984, 1986) argues that although there is a small correlation between levels of viewing and behaving aggressively, the causal connection is very weak.

23 | Bandura, Ross & Ross (1961) – 'Transmission of aggression through imitation of aggressive models'

Bandura et al. conducted this study to demonstrate that *learning* can occur through *mere observation* of a model and that *imitation* can occur in the absence of that model. More specifically they hypothesised that:

- Children shown aggressive models would show significantly more imitative aggressive behaviour than those shown non-aggressive or no models.
- Children shown non-aggressive, subdued models would show significantly less aggressive behaviour than those shown aggressive or no models.
- Children would show significantly more imitation of same-sex than opposite-sex models.
- Boys would show significantly more imitative aggression than girls, especially with the male rather than female aggressive model.

Method

The participants were 72 children, 36 boys and 36 girls, aged 37–69 months (with a mean age of 52 months).

The children were individually shown into a room containing toys and played with some potato prints and pictures in a corner for 10 minutes while either

- a *non-aggressive* adult model (either male or female) played in a quiet and subdued manner for 10 minutes.
- an *aggressive* adult model (either male or female) distinctively attacked a 5 foot inflated Bobo doll by sitting on it and repeatedly punching it on the nose, striking it on the head with a mallet, and throwing it up in the air and kicking it around the room. The aggressive model also uttered verbally aggressive statements such as 'sock him in the nose', 'throw him in the air' and 'pow', as well as two non-aggressive statements – 'he keeps coming back for more' and 'he sure is a tough fella'.
- *no* adult model was present (this was the control condition).

Twenty-four children (12 boys and 12 girls) were assigned to each condition, with an effort made to match subjects according to pre-existing levels of aggression.

In addition to the above manipulations, in the experimental conditions half the subjects observed a same-sex model while the other half observed opposite-sex models.

Conditions tested	Participants		
Aggressive male model	6 boys		
Aggressive female model	6 girls		
Aggressive male model	6 girls	24	
Aggressive female model	6 boys		
Non-aggressive male model	6 boys		
Non-aggressive female model	6 girls	24	72
Non-aggressive male model	6 girls		
Non-aggressive female model	6 boys		
No model	12 boys, 12 girls	24	

All children (including those in the control group) were then individually taken to a different experimental location and subjected to mild aggression arousal by being stopped from playing with some very attractive toys.

Each child was then individually shown into another room which contained both aggressive toys (e.g. a 3-foot-high Bobo doll, a mallet, dartguns and a tether ball) and non-aggressive toys (e.g. a tea set, dolls and colouring paper), and were observed through a one-way mirror for 20 minutes.

Observers recorded (with an inter-scorer reliability of 0.90 correlation coefficient) behaviour in the following categories:

1 *Imitation* behaviour of the aggressive model:
   a physical aggression, e.g. sitting on the doll and repeatedly punching it on the nose.
   b Verbal aggression, e.g. 'sock him' or 'pow'.
   c Non-aggressive speech, e.g. 'he sure is a tough fella'.
2 *Partial imitation* behaviour of the aggressive model, e.g. mallet aggression against other objects or sitting on the Bobo doll without punching it.
3 *Non-imitative* physical and verbal aggression, e.g. just punching the Bobo doll, physical aggression with other objects and verbal non-imitative remarks like 'shoot the Bobo' or 'horses fighting, biting'.
4 *Non-aggressive behaviour*, e.g. non-aggressive play or sitting quietly.

Results

- Children in the aggressive model condition showed significantly more imitation of the model's physical and verbal aggression and non-aggressive verbal responses than children who saw the non-aggressive model or no model.
- Children in the aggressive model condition usually showed more partial imitation and non-imitative physical and verbal aggression than those who saw the non-aggressive model or no model, but not always to a significant degree.
- Children in the non-aggressive model condition showed very little aggression although not always significantly less than the no model group.
- Children who saw the same-sex model were only likely to significantly imitate behaviour in some of the categories. For example, boys would imitate male models significantly more than girls for physical and verbal imitative aggression, non-imitative aggression and gun play.
- Girls would imitate female models more than boys for verbal imitative aggression and non-imitative aggression only, but not significantly.

Exercise 23

1 What kind of method was used in this study?
2 What was the independent variable and how was it manipulated?
3 What was the dependent variable?
4 What type of participant design was used and why?
5 Why were all the children subjected to mild aggression arousal before being observed?
6 How could the standardisation of the model's behaviour be improved for each child?
7 How well do you think the results supported the hypotheses?
8 How realistic do you think the study was?
9 How ethical do you think the study was?

1 What kind of method was used in this study?

A laboratory experiment.

2 What was the independent variable and how was it manipulated?

The independent variable was the 'type of model' manipulated in three main conditions: aggressive model shown, non-aggressive (subdued) model shown, and no model shown (in the control condition). The gender of the model was also manipulated in two conditions (same sex and opposite sex).

3 What was the dependent variable?

The dependent variable was 'behaviour of the children in the playroom' with a particular interest in the amount of imitative behaviour and aggression shown by the children.

4 What type of participant design was used and why?

A matched pairs design was used with an effort made to match subjects according to their pre-existing levels of aggression so that any differences found in aggressive behaviour between the conditions was more likely to reflect the experimental manipulation of the independent variable.

5 Why were all the children subjected to mild aggression arousal before being observed?

This arousal took place in order to give all groups an equal chance of showing aggression and also to allow the group shown the non-aggressive model to demonstrate an inhibition of aggressive behaviour.

6 How could the standardisation of the model's behaviour be improved for each child?

The standardisation of the model's behaviour could be improved by videotaping the model once and showing the same video so that each child sees exactly the same performance. In later experiments Bandura adopted this procedure.

7 How well do you think the results supported the hypotheses?

The research provides reasonable support for the social learning theory idea that behaviour can be acquired through observation rather than direct personal experience and that reinforcement is not required for learning to occur.

However, the lack of significant support for some of the hypotheses or some aspects of them, combined with the relatively small sample sizes used in some of the experimental conditions, means that it would be a good idea to replicate the study and treat the results with caution.

8 How realistic do you think the study was?

The findings may not generalise very well to the observational learning and imitation of aggression in everyday life. The acts of aggression witnessed were rather unusual if not bizarre and were committed and imitated against a Bobo doll, not a real person (who may fight back!).

9 How ethical do you think the study was?

The experiment may have had some harmful effects upon the children, for example, aggression was taught to the children and the exposure to the adult stranger's aggression may have been frightening for the children.

BANDURA et al. CROSSWORD

1 This was used to record the children's behaviour without their knowledge (3-3/6)
2 The inflatable victim of aggression (4/4)
3 The number of minutes of exposure to the model (3)
4 The design used to allocate participants to conditions (7/5)
5 The number of minutes the children's behaviour was observed (6)
6 The kind of imitation where, for example, the mallet was used, but against objects that the model had not hit (7)
7 The number of children tested (7/3)
8 The kind of model seen by half the children in the experimental conditions (4/3)
9 The inter-scorer _____ correlation coefficient was .9 (11)
10 The model which caused very little aggression (3-10)
11 Girls imitated this kind of aggression in female models more than the boys (6)
12 The kind of experiment conducted (10)
13 The condition where no model was shown (7)

Theories of learning

Exercise 24

Match the following names, terms, etc. on the left with their explanations on the right, then put them in the appropriate theory boxes below (see Pavlov as an example). Some may apply to more than one theory.

Pavlov —————————→ (wrote *Psychology as the Behaviourist Views it* in 1913)
Skinner (investigated the conditioning of the salivation reflex in dogs)
Watson (introduced important cognitive influences on learning)
Bandura (used a box with a lever that could deliver food or an electric shock)

Reflex conditioning (presenting a neutral stimulus before and during a reflexive one)
Unconditional stimuli (feelings that have been associated with an originally neutral stimulus)
Conditioned emotional responses (using a conditioned stimulus to condition a new neutral stimulus)
Forward conditioning (something that inherently produces a reflexive response)
Higher order conditioning (learning to associate new stimuli with reflexive stimuli)

The law of contiguity (the later appearance of a conditioned response after it has died out)
Extinction (learning effects that occur only in a precise situation)
Spontaneous recovery (learning effects that spontaneously transfer to similar situations)
Generalisation (the dying out of responses)
Discrimination (associations have to be made close together in time for learning to occur)

Trial and error learning (increases the likelihood of a response by providing pleasant consequences for it)
The law of effect (reinforcing successive approximations to a desired end behaviour)
Positive reinforcement (decreases the likelihood of a response by providing negative consequences for it)
Negative reinforcement (patterns of consequences for behavioural responses)
Punishment (behaviour is affected by its consequences)
Secondary reinforcement (randomly and gradually discovering the consequences of responses)
Schedules of reinforcement (that associated with naturally occurring primary reinforcers)
Behaviour shaping (increases the likelihood of a response by providing escape from unpleasant consequences)

Observational learning (indirectly experiencing the consequences others receive from their actions)
Modelling (the copying of whole sequences of behaviour)
Imitation (acquiring behaviour by seeing it in others, without personal reinforcement)
Vicarious reinforcement (predictions about the future consequences of behaviour)
Expectancies (how others show us behaviour and its consequences)

Bobo doll experiments (conditioned by Watson and Rayner to fear white rats)
Language acquisition (explained as a learned conditioned emotional response)
Little Albert (a practical consideration of observational learning and imitation)
Phobia acquisition (demonstrate the imitation of model's aggression)
Media influences (explained by trial and error learning and behaviour shaping according to Skinner)

CLASSICAL CONDITIONING	**OPERANT CONDITIONING**	**SOCIAL LEARNING THEORY**
Pavlov		

LEARNING THEORIES

CLASSICAL CONDITIONING

Pavlov
(investigated the conditioning of the salivation reflex in dogs)

Watson
(wrote *Psychology as the Behaviourist Views it* in 1913)

Reflex conditioning
(learning to associate new stimuli with reflexive stimuli)

Unconditional stimuli
(something that inherently produces a reflexive response)

Conditioned emotional responses
(feelings that have been associated with an originally neutral stimulus)

The law of contiguity
(associations have to be made close together in time for learning to occur – for classical conditioning stimuli have to be presented close together in time to be associated)

Forward conditioning
(presenting a neutral stimulus before and during a reflexive unconditional one)

Extinction
(the dying out of responses – for classical conditioning after the conditional stimulus is continually presented without the unconditional stimulus)

Spontaneous recovery
(the later appearance of a conditioned response after it has died out)

Higher order conditioning
(using a conditioned stimulus to condition a new neutral stimulus)

Generalisation
(learning effects that spontaneously transfer to similar situations – for classical conditioning when the conditional response is triggered by stimuli that resemble the conditioned stimulus)

Discrimination
(learning effects that occur only in a precise situation – for classical conditioning when the conditioned response is only made to the original conditioned stimulus)

Little Albert
(conditioned by Watson and Rayner to fear white rats)

Phobia acquisition
(explained as a learned conditioned emotional response)

OPERANT CONDITIONING

Skinner
(used a box with a lever that could deliver food or an electric shock)

Trial and error learning
(randomly and gradually discovering the consequences of responses)

The law of effect
Behaviour is affected by its consequences

The law of contiguity
(associations have to be made close together in time for learning to occur – for operant conditioning responses and their consequences have to be made close together in time to be associated)

Positive reinforcement
(increases the likelihood of a response by providing pleasant consequences for it)

Negative reinforcement
(increases the likelihood of a response by providing escape from unpleasant consequences)

Extinction
(the dying out of responses – for operant conditioning after the response ceases to be reinforced)

Spontaneous recovery
(the later appearance of a conditioned response after it has died out)

Generalisation
(learning effects that spontaneously transfer to similar situations – for operant conditioning when responses are made that resemble a reinforced response)

Discrimination
(learning effects that occur only in a precise situation – for operant conditioning when only responses that have been reinforced are made)

Punishment
(decreases the likelihood of a response by providing negative consequences for it)

Secondary reinforcement
(that associated with naturally occurring primary reinforcers)

Schedules of reinforcement
(patterns of consequences for behavioural responses)

Behaviour shaping
(reinforcing successive approximations to a desired end behaviour)

Language acquisition
(explained by trial and error learning and behaviour shaping according to Skinner)

SOCIAL LEARNING THEORY

Bandura
(introduced important cognitive influences on learning)

Observational learning
(acquiring behaviour by seeing it in others, without personal reinforcement)

Modelling
(how others show us behaviour and its consequences)

Imitation
(the copying of whole sequences of behaviour)

Vicarious reinforcement
(indirectly experiencing the consequences others receive from their actions)

Expectancies
(predictions about the future consequences of behaviour)

Bobo doll experiments
(demonstrate the imitation of model's aggression)

Media influences
(a practical consideration of observational learning and imitation)

25 The cognitive developmental approach to psychology

Cognitive developmental researchers not only focus their research on inner mental processes of thinking and reasoning (as do cognitive psychologists in general) but are also interested in how these *change over time*. They seek to apply their theories to explain the behaviour shown at different ages (e.g. educational performance or gender and moral behaviour) and to identify ways of improving or facilitating intellectual development (e.g. teaching methods).

Piaget is probably the best-known cognitive developmental researcher and the assumptions of the approach will, therefore, be illustrated by referring to examples of his theory.

Jean Piaget

Assumptions

The importance of cognitive abilities

Cognitive developmental psychologists assume that it is necessary to refer to inner mental concepts such as thoughts, beliefs and cognitive structures in order to understand behaviour, especially differences in behaviour shown by people at different ages. The sophistication of these inner mental structures or capabilities are assumed to govern how we interact with the world and place limitations upon the thinking and behaviour of individuals – not only in intellectual or educational performance, but also in areas such as moral reasoning and gender identity.

Piaget, for example, argued that human children do not passively receive their knowledge but are curious and *self-motivated* and *actively explore*, interact with and understand the world in terms of the *schemata* they possess.

A schema is a mental concept that consists of an internal representation of a specific physical or mental action. It is a basic building block or unit of intelligent behaviour that enables the individual to interact with and understand the world. The infant is born with certain reflexive action schemata such as sucking or gripping, and later acquires symbolic mental schemata that represent objects, people, activities, events and other concepts they encounter around them (e.g. toys, parents, bath time, school, etc.).

When a child, or indeed a person of any age, encounters a new object, idea or situation they first try to understand it in terms of the schemata they already possess – a process Piaget called *assimilation*. The world is 'fitted in' to what the person already knows. If the existing schemata are not sufficient to understand or cope with the new situations, objects or information, then they will have to be modified to incorporate them by expanding the schemata or creating new ones – a process Piaget called *accommodation*.

Through interaction with the world around them each individual *builds* their own mental framework for understanding and dealing with their environment. In this way, the schemata continue to develop and increase in their complexity and ability to adapt to and deal with the world.

Piaget outlined other, higher-order mental structures called *operations*, which enable more complex rules about how the environment works to be understood. Operations are acquired in middle childhood and are logical manipulations dealing with the relationships between schemata.

The importance of mental development over time

Just as vital as emphasising cognitive structures and capabilities, however, is the assumption of cognitive developmental psychologists that these change in important ways over time. As Owen Flanagan (1984) clearly stated:

'What makes their theories 'developmental' is the belief that the ways in which we process experience – be it physical, mathematical, or moral experience – normally change in an orderly, increasingly adaptive, species-specific fashion.'

Study of how and why such changes occur is needed, therefore, if we are to predict intellectual performance and its effects, and facilitate its improvement in human beings at different ages.

Piaget, for example, believed that children of different ages think in qualitatively different ways from each other because of their underlying level of mental development. He suggested that thinking progressed through four stages of cognitive development that occur in a sequence dictated by biological maturation. The four stages are the sensorimotor (0–2 years), pre-operational (2–7 years), concrete operational (7–11 years) and formal operational (from 11 years). At the beginning of the sensorimotor stage an infant only possesses very crude and basic schemata and has little or no inner understanding of the external world. By the formal operational stage, a person has a sophisticated inner mental structure capable of considering problems that are not immediately present and an intelligence far better adapted to surviving in the world.

Methods

Observation

Piaget gained much of the data for his theories from carefully observing and recording children's (particularly his own) everyday behaviour and speech in their normal home environments, for example when playing. This method represents a naturalistic observation, which he also supplemented by asking the children questions using the clinical interview method and by manipulating some aspect of their environment in fairly informal experiments upon their behaviour, in order to investigate their thinking further.

Longitudinal study

In addition to cross-sectional studies on different age groups at the same point in time, cognitive developmental psychologists also put great value upon studying the same individuals over an extended period of time (often years). Examples include Piaget's study of changes in his own children's abilities and thinking over the course of their childhood, and Kohlberg's study of moral reasoning in a group of adults over many years.

> ### Exercise 25
> 1 Try to think of examples of assimilation and accommodation that you may have seen in children or adults.
> 2 Piaget focused on children building up their understanding themselves, based on their *own* self-motivation, individual exploration and biological maturation. What does this view seem to neglect?
> 3 Based on Piaget's ideas on self-motivation, pre-existing schemata, assimilation and accommodation, and stages, what implications can you think of for teaching?
> 4 What are the advantages and disadvantages of observation and longitudinal study?

1 Try to think of examples of assimilation and accommodation that you may have seen in children or adults.

When an infant sucks its thumb or dummy it is assimilating these objects into its feeding schema. When given baby food by spoon for the first time, however, the feeding schema will not be adequate for the task and will have to be adjusted (accommodation).

In terms of mental schemata, a child will often over-generalise concepts by assimilating similar-looking objects into the same schema, e.g. calling all flying things 'birds', including butterflies and aeroplanes. The child has to accommodate by creating new and separate mental schemata for these objects.

2 Piaget focused on children building up their understanding themselves, based on their *own* self-motivation, individual exploration and biological maturation. What does this view seem to neglect?

This view seems to neglect the role of other people in society, from parents and siblings to peers and teachers, who help a child's cognitive development. Other researchers have disagreed with Piaget, for example Vygotsky and Bruner believe society plays a more important role in constructing a child's understanding of the world.

Vygotsky was a Russian psychologist who focused on the importance of *social interaction* and *language* as major influences on children's development of understanding. Vygotsky saw the whole process of cognitive development as being social in nature – 'we become ourselves through others'.

At first the child responds to the world only through its actions, but society provides the *meaning* of those actions through social interaction. Vygotsky illustrated this with the example of learning to point – the child may reach towards an object and fail to grasp it, but the parent will *interpret* this as a pointing gesture. Cognitive development therefore proceeds, according to Vygotsky, as the child gradually *internalises* the meanings provided by these social interactions.

Jerome Bruner

Jerome Bruner was a cognitive scientist whose ideas on cognitive development were very similar to Vygotsky's. He agreed with Piaget that active interaction with the world could increase a child's underlying cognitive capacity to understand the world in more complex ways, but emphasised the importance of *social* factors in cognitive development. In particular, he believed that language and social interaction and experience could pull the child towards better understanding. Cognitive growth depends upon the mastery of 'skills transmitted with varying efficiency and success by the culture' and occurs 'from the outside in as well as from the inside out' Bruner (1971).

3 Based on Piaget's ideas on self-motivation, pre-existing schemata, assimilation and accommodation, and stages, what implications can you think of for teaching?

- Self-motivation – because of Piaget's emphasis on the child's individual self-construction of its cognitive development, education should be *student centred* and accomplished through *active discovery learning*.
- Schemata – new knowledge should be *built on pre-existing schemata*, which should be expanded and refined through accommodation. In fact new information can only be properly understood in terms of the concepts one already knows.
- Assimilation and accommodation – there should be a *balance* between accommodation (learning new concepts) and assimilation (practising and utilising those concepts). Children need a chance to practise and apply their schemata instead of constantly adjusting them.
- Stages – because of Piaget's ideas on stages of development, the notion of *'readiness'* is important. Children show qualitatively different kinds of thinking at different ages and should only be taught concepts suitable for their underlying level of cognitive development. Some researchers have suggested that because of the notion of readiness certain concepts should be taught before others or even in a specific order. Concrete operational children should, therefore, start with concrete examples before progressing onto more abstract tasks (suitable for formal operational children).

Piaget, in fact, proposed that cognitive development should *not* be speeded up because of its dependence on biological maturation. Teaching children a concept before they are biologically ready prevents them from discovering it for themselves – resulting in incomplete understanding.

The role of the teacher in the Piagetian classroom is, therefore, one of a facilitator. Teachers should
- choose tasks that are self-motivating for the child, to engage its interest and further its own development
- set tasks that are challenging enough to put the child into disequilibrium so it can accommodate and create new schemas
- introduce abstract or formal operational tasks through concrete examples
- encourage active interaction not just with task materials but with other children
- assess the level of the child's development so suitable tasks can be set.

4 What are the advantages and disadvantages of observation and longitudinal study?

The advantages of the observational method – carefully and objectively observing and recording behaviour – are many. Much data, both quantitative and qualitative, can be gathered which can provide the basis of many theoretical ideas. These can then be further investigated using other methods. In addition, the behaviour recorded may be spontaneous and natural, especially if observed in the subject's own normal environment.

The disadvantages, however, are that observations alone cannot establish cause-and-effect relationships between the data observed, which might itself be affected by the very presence of an observer.

The advantage of a longitudinal study is that since the same individuals can be studied over time changes in their behaviour can be noted and compared with greater certainty (subject variables are kept more constant)

The disadvantages, however, are that such studies are time-consuming and because they take a long time to conduct participants may drop out of the study.

Jean Piaget thought that we develop our intelligence in *stages* and was interested in the kind of mistakes that children make at different ages, thinking that these would reflect the cognitive progress they had made.

The sensorimotor stage (0 to 2 years)

According to Piaget, when an infant is first born it only knows the world via its immediate senses and the (motor) actions it performs upon it. To begin with, the infant *lacks internal mental schemata* to represent the things it senses and manipulates – even a mental concept of itself as separate from everything else. This initial inability of a baby to distinguish between itself and its environment has been termed *profound egocentrism*.

Without mental schemata Piaget suggests that young infants show a lack of *object permanence* – when the infant cannot see or act on objects, they cease to exist for the child. Piaget investigated his children's lack of object permanence during this stage by hiding an object from them under a cover. At 0 – 5 months an object visibly hidden will not be searched for, even if the child was reaching for it. At 8 months the child will search for a completely hidden object, but will tend to search in places it has seen the object hidden before – even if the object is visibly moved to a new hiding place. This indicates that internal representations are gradually acquired and refined throughout this stage until the *general symbolic function* of a child's schemata allows both object permanence and language to occur.

The pre-operational stage (2 to 7 years)

Throughout the pre-operational stage, the child's internal mental world continues to develop but is still dominated by its sensory information regarding the external world and is thus very influenced by the *appearance* of things.

Children at this stage *lack* the mental sophistication necessary to carry out logical *operations* (to understand the logical relationships between schemata properly) on the world and show *centration* (they only focus on one aspect of an object or situation at a time – usually the most visible or obvious aspect).

These limitations in pre-operational thought are illustrated by
- *class-inclusion problems* – difficulty in understanding the relationship between whole classes and sub-classes. The child focuses on the most visibly obvious classes and disregards less obvious ones. Piaget found that young pre-operational children often fail class-inclusion tests. If a child is shown a set of beads, most of which are brown but with a few white ones, and is asked 'are there more brown beads or more beads?', the child will say more brown beads.

- *egocentrism* – the difficulty of understanding that others do not see, think and feel things like you do (the child shows centration on its own viewpoint and experience – the most obvious to itself). Piaget and Inhelder (1956) demonstrated the egocentrism of pre-operational children with their 'Three Mountain Experiment'. Four-year-olds, when shown a mountain scene and tested to see if they could correctly describe it from different viewpoints, failed and tended to choose their own view. Six-year-olds were more aware of other viewpoints but still tended to choose the wrong one.
- *lack of conservation* – the inability to realise that some things remain constant or unchanged despite changes in visible appearance. Piaget found that pre-operational children would fail to conserve a whole host of properties such as number, liquid and substance because they only focused on the most visible aspect of the changes.

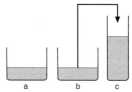

Liquid conservation

Two short, wide beakers, 'a' and 'b' are filled to the same level and the child is asked if there is the same in each or if one has more. Children usually answer that there is the same.

The liquid is poured from 'b' to 'c', and the child is asked the same question again. The pre-operational child often says there is more in 'c', failing to conserve (realise the amount of liquid remains unchanged despite the alteration in appearance).

Concrete operational stage (7 to 11 years)

At the concrete operational stage, the child's cognitive complexity allows it to carry out mental *operations* on the world and *de-centrate*, allowing it to conserve and overcome class-inclusion problems and egocentrism. Two major operations are compensation and reversibility.

For example in the conservation of liquid test above, when the liquid is poured from 'b' to 'c', a concrete operational child can compensate for increasing height with decreasing width and can mentally reverse the pouring to realise it is the same liquid, therefore, conserving liquid.

An important limitation on the child's thought at this stage, however, is that the mental operations cannot be carried out purely in the child's head – the physical (concrete) presence of the objects being manipulated is needed. Thus, although the conservation tests can be successfully completed, the child needs to see the physical transformation taking place.

Formal operational Stage (11 onwards)

At the formal operational stage, the child's mental structures are so developed and internalised that ideas can be manipulated in the head and reasoning/deductions can be carried out on verbal statements, without the aid of visual/concrete examples.

The individual can think about hypothetical problems and abstract concepts that they have never encountered before and will approach problems in a systematic and organised way.

For example, *transitive inference tasks* can be solved – the abstract form of arguments can be followed (e.g. if A>B>C, then A>C) and so problems such as 'Edith is fairer than Susan. Edith is darker than Lily. Who is the darkest?', can be answered without needing to use dolls or pictures to help.

Deductive reasoning tasks, such as the pendulum task where the child is given string and a set of weights and is asked to find out what determines the swing, are carried out logically and systematically.

Exercise 26

1 Why else might sensorimotor infants not search for a hidden object, apart from Piaget's lack of object permanence idea that it ceases to exist for the child?

2 Why else might pre-operational children find the class-inclusion bead question and the three-mountain test difficult, apart from Piaget's idea of centration?

3 Why else might pre-operational children give a different answer in conservation tests when an adult deliberately causes the change and asks the same question again, apart from Piaget's idea of lack of operations?

4 What problem may result from focusing on the *mistakes* that *all* children make?

1 Why else might sensorimotor infants not search for a hidden object, apart from Piaget's lack of object permanence idea that it ceases to exist for the child?

Some have suggested that sensorimotor infants may know that hidden objects still exist but lack, for example, schemata for knowing how to search or uncover them. Perhaps making objects disappear in a different way might produce different results.

Bower and Wishart (1972) offered an object to babies aged between 1 to 4 months and then turned off the lights as they were about to reach for it. When observed by infrared camera the babies were seen to continue reaching for the object despite not seeing it. Bower (1977) tested month-old babies who were shown a toy and then had a screen placed in front of it. The toy was secretly removed from behind the screen, and when the screen itself was taken away Bower claimed that the babies showed surprise (indicated by a physiological measure) that the toy was not there. Why would these results be obtained unless the babies had some notion that the objects still existed?

2 Why else might pre-operational children find the class-inclusion bead question and the three-mountain test difficult, apart from Piaget's idea of centration?

A criticism of some of Piaget's tests is that they are over-complicated and difficult to relate to. By clarifying the tasks and ensuring that they made what Donaldson has termed 'human sense', other researchers have improved the ability of children to show cognitive abilities that Piaget would not have expected them to possess at the age.

McGarrigle et al. modified Piaget's class-inclusion tasks to make them more understandable and appropriate. They first asked pre-operational children (with an average age of 6) a Piagetian type question – 'Are there more black cows or more cows?' They then turned all of the cows on their sides (as if asleep) and asked, 'Are there more black cows or more sleeping cows?'. The percentage of correct answers increased from 25 to 48%, presumably because the whole class and subclass were clarified.

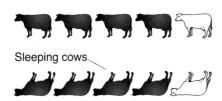

Sleeping cows

Hughes demonstrated that 3.5 to 5 year olds could de-centrate and overcome their egocentrism, if the task made more 'human sense' to them. When these children had to hide a boy doll from two policemen dolls (a task that required them to take into account the perspectives of others but had a good and understandable reason for doing so) they could do this successfully 90% of the time.

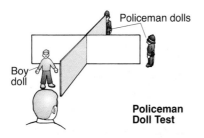

Policeman dolls

Boy doll

Policeman Doll Test

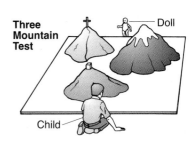

Three Mountain Test

Doll

Child

In a similar way Gladwin (1970) is one of many investigators who have questioned the appropriateness of Piagetian experimental tasks for testing the cognitive development of non-western participants. Piagetian tests are sometimes difficult for non-western participants to relate to and some studies have shown that these cultures fail the tests more frequently, or even lack formal operational thought completely. Further detailed investigation, however, has found that formal operational thought has been acquired, but in a culturally specific manner. For example, the Pulawat navigators of Polynesia show complex formal operational thought when guiding their canoes at sea, yet will tend to fail standard western tests of cognitive development.

3 Why else might pre-operational children give a different answer in conservation tests when an adult deliberately causes the change and asks the same question again, apart from Piaget's idea of lack of operations?

The children may feel they are expected to give a different answer because an adult has deliberately produced a change and asked the same question again (which might also mean the first answer was wrong). McGarrigle and Donaldson (1974) demonstrated that pre-operational children of between 4 to 6 years could successfully conserve if they were not misled by these *demand characteristics* into giving the wrong answer.

They added an 'accidental transformation' condition to a conservation of number test where a 'naughty teddy' arrives and disarranges one of the rows (for example by spreading out the counters of one row). Usually, when one of the rows is spread out pre-operational children answer that there is 'more' in it. In the 'accidental transformation' condition, however, more children (63%) could conserve number (realise there is the same number) since the transformation was not meant to have been deliberately intended and there was a good reason for asking the same question twice.

Naughty Teddy Test

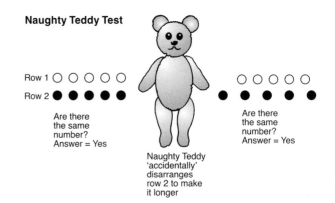

Row 1 ○ ○ ○ ○ ○   ○ ○ ○ ○ ○
Row 2 ● ● ● ● ●   ● ● ● ● ●

Are there the same number? Answer = Yes

Are there the same number? Answer = Yes

Naughty Teddy 'accidentally' disarranges row 2 to make it longer

4 What problem may result from focusing on the *mistakes* that *all* children make?

Focusing on mistakes may have caused Piaget to underestimate what children *can* do. By focusing on *common* mistakes Piaget neglected individual differences in cognitive development.

27 Samuel & Bryant (1984) – 'Asking only one question in the conservation experiment'

Samuel and Bryant aimed to support, using a more detailed procedure and a wider age range of subjects, Rose and Blank's experimental criticism of Piaget's conservation studies. Piaget and Szeminska (1952) found pre-operational children (below the age of seven) could not conserve (realise that some properties, such as number, volume and mass, remain the same despite changes in their physical appearance) by conducting experiments.

1 They showed 2 rows of counters and asked a pre-transformation question 'Are there the same number in each row?' The answer was usually 'yes'.

2 They then lengthened one of the rows and asked the (same) post-transformation question 'are there the same number in each row?' The answer given was usually 'no'.

Piaget took the 'no' answer to mean that the children thought there were now a greater number of counters in the lengthened row and that these children could not conserve. However, Rose and Blank (1974) disagreed with this conclusion. They argued that Piaget had made a methodological error by imposing *demand characteristics* – when an adult deliberately changes something and asks the same question twice, children think that a different answer is *expected*, even though they may well be able to conserve. Rose and Blank (1974) conducted a study where they only asked one question (the post-transformation one) to reduce these misleading expectations and found that more children were able to conserve when they only had to make one judgement than when they had to make two in the standard Piagetian presentation.

Samuel and Bryant (1984) wanted to replicate this study on a larger scale using
- four age groups (5, 6, 7 and 8 year olds).
- three types of conservation test (number, mass and liquid volume).

Conservation tests

Conservation of number – if the child realises that the number of counters remains the same despite one row having been spread out or pushed closer together, then the test has been passed.

Conservation of mass – if the child realises that the amount of plasticine remains the same despite one ball having been squashed over a large area or rolled into a long thin sausage, then the test has been passed.

Conservation of liquid volume – if the child realises that the volume of liquid remains the same despite being poured into a container that is taller but thinner (causing the level to rise) or shorter but wider (causing the level to fall), then the test has been passed.

- three ways of presenting the tests (standard Piagetian way, one judgement/question way and fixed array with no visible transformation).

Method

252 boys and girls were divided into 4 age groups (of 5, 6, 7 and 8 year olds). In each age group every child was tested 4 times each for conservation of number, mass and liquid volume in *one* of three ways:
1 The standard Piagetian way (asking the pre- and post-transformation questions)
2 The one judgement way (asking only the post-transformation question)
3 The fixed array way (asking only the post-transformation question, *without seeing* the transformation)

In all three methods of presentation, the 12 conservation tests each child experienced were systematically varied and two different versions of each type of conservation test were given.

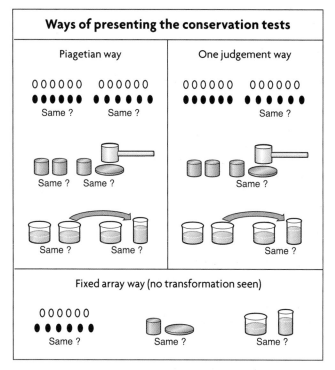

Ways of presenting the conservation tests

Results

Mixed design analysis of variance and Newman–Kreuls tests showed that
1 children were significantly more able to conserve in the one judgement task
2 older children did significantly better in conserving than younger ones
3 the conservation of number task was significantly easier than the other tasks.

	Mean errors out of 12 conservation tests		
Age	Standard Piagetian	One judgement	Fixed Array
5	8.5	7.3	8.6
6	5.7	4.3	6.4
7	3.2	2.6	4.9
8	1.7	1.3	3.3

Exercise 27

1 Which results support Piaget and which Rose and Blank?
2 Identify the three independent variables.
3 What participant designs were used and why?
4 Why was the order of the 12 conservation tests varied?

1 Which results support Piaget and which support Rose and Blank?

The finding that children were significantly more able to conserve in the one judgement task supports Rose and Blank's (1974) experiment and criticism of Piaget's methods.

That older children did significantly better than younger children in conservation supports Piaget's theory of cognitive development in general, however. The finding that the conservation of number task was significantly easier than the other tasks actually supports Piaget's notion of decalage (that not all aspects of an ability like conservation or object permanence will develop at the same time).

2 Identify the three independent variables.

The dependent variable was always 'ability to conserve' while the three independent variables were

- method of presenting the conservation tests – manipulated in three conditions (standard Piagetian way, one judgement/question way and fixed array with no visible transformation way) to see if the method of conducting conservation tests affects the ability to pass them, e.g. whether demand characteristics affect conservation.

- age – tested in four age group conditions (5, 6, 7 and 8 year olds) to see if the ability to conserve increased with age.

- type of conservation test – manipulated in three conditions (tests of number, mass and liquid volume) to check that conservation was completely achieved and to investigate whether some forms of conservation are achieved before others.

3 What participant designs were used and why?

An independent measures (or unrelated) design – different participants in each condition of the independent variable – was used with:

- The method of presenting the conservation test – to prevent the answers of one condition affecting another.

- Age – because the same people could not be different ages. In fact, this represents a cross-sectional method which is much less time-consuming than a longitudinal method of testing the same children over a four-year period.

A repeated measures (or related) design – the same participants in each condition of the independent variable – was used with:

- Type of conservation test – to check the completeness of the understanding of conservation for each child.

4 Why was the order of the 12 conservation tests varied?

The 12 conservation tests each child experienced were systematically varied to prevent order effects (to stop the answers of one conservation test affecting the answers of the next in a consistent way).

SAMUEL AND BRYANT CROSSWORD

1 The ability to realise that some qualities remain constant despite changes in visible appearance (12)
2 Piaget's term for passing some tests of an ability but not others at a certain age (8)
3 The mean number of these out of twelve tests were scored for each age group (6)
4 The kind of characteristics that may have led to children giving the wrong answer in the standard Piagetian test (6)
5 The quality tested using plasticine (4)
6 The control condition method of presentation where no transformation was seen (5/5)
7 The number of age groups tested (4)
8 The age for concrete operational thought (5)
9 This study was a replication on a larger scale of one by Rose and ____ (5)
10 The number of questions asked in the standard Piagetian method of presentation (3)
11 The quality tested using water (6/6)
12 Children at all ages were more able to pass the tests using the ____ judgement method (3)
13 The quality tested that the children found easiest to pass (6)

28 | Social influences on cognitive development

A number of cognitive developmental theorists believe that Piaget neglected the importance of society in shaping changes in mental abilities and understanding. Vygotsky and Bruner, in particular, have outlined theories on the vital role played by socially provided *language* and *education* in advancing cognitive development.

Vygotsky and language

Cognitive development proceeds, according to Vygotsky, as children gradually *internalise* the meanings provided by social interactions. However their thinking and reasoning abilities remain relatively primitive and crude until the greatest advance comes when *language* is internalised.

Speech starts off as communication behaviour that produces changes in others, but when language becomes internalised it converges with thought – 'thought becomes verbal and speech rational' (Vygotsky, 1962). Language allows us to 'turn around and reflect on our thoughts' – directing and *controlling* our thinking, as well as communicating our thoughts to others.

Eventually language splits between these two functions as we develop an abbreviated inner voice for thinking with, and a more articulate vocabulary for communicating with others. Internal language vastly increases our powers of problem solving. The use of language can be said to progress in three stages:

- Pre-intellectual social speech (0–3 years), where thinking does not occur in language and speech is used to provoke social change.

- Egocentric speech (3–7 years), where language helps the child control behaviour but is spoken out loud.

- Inner speech (7 years +), where the child uses speech silently to control their own behaviour and publicly for social communication.

Vygotsky and the zone of proximal development

Because cognitive development is achieved by the *joint* construction of knowledge between the child and society, it follows that any one child's potential intellectual ability is greater if working in conjunction with a more expert source, rather than alone. Vygotsky defines the *zone of proximal development* (ZPD) as:

'the distance between the actual developmental level as determined by individual problem solving and the level of potential development as determined through problem solving under adult guidance or in collaboration with more capable peers. The zone of proximal development defines those functions that have not yet matured but are in the process of maturation, functions that will mature tomorrow but are currently in an embryonic state. These functions could be termed the 'buds' or 'flowers' of development rather than the 'fruits' of development'.

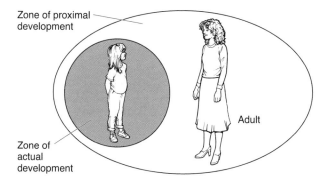

Zone of proximal development

Zone of actual development

Adult

Bruner and language

Jerome Bruner was interested in the dominant ways of representing or thinking about knowledge at different ages rather than stages. Bruner proposed three *modes of representation* (the enactive, iconic and symbolic modes) that develop in order and allow the child to think about the world in more sophisticated ways (all exist in the adult, we do not lose these modes).

The real advance in cognitive development according to Bruner comes when the dominant way of representing and thinking about knowledge is in terms of the symbolic mode (from around 7 years onwards). This mode enables children to encode the world in terms of information storing symbols such as the numbers of mathematics or the words of our language. This allows information to be categorised and summarised so that it can be more readily manipulated and considered.

Unlike Piaget, who thought that language was merely a useful tool which reflects and describes the underlying cognitive structures such as operations, Bruner suggested that language *is* symbolic/logical/operational thought – the two are inseparable. Since society provides our language and thus our symbolic thought, Bruner believed that language training could actually speed up cognitive development and so put more emphasis than Piaget upon the importance of education from others (remember that Piaget thought cognitive structures could only be developed through the child's individual maturation and interaction with the world).

Bruner and Vygotsky applied to education

Bruner and Vygotsky both disagreed with Piaget's strict notion of readiness and argued that the teacher should *actively intervene* to help the child develop its understanding – instruction *is* an important part of the learning process. The teacher, or more knowledgeable other, provides the 'tools' or 'loan of consciousness' required for the child to develop cognitively by providing structure, direction, guidance and support, not just facts. The following concepts are therefore important in education, according to the theories of both Bruner and Vygotsky:

The spiral curriculum – the spiral curriculum involves material being structured so that complex ideas can be presented at simplified levels first and then re-visited at more complex levels later on. Children should be made aware of the structure and direction of the subjects they study.

Scaffolding – scaffolding is a kind of hypothetical support structure around the child's attempt to understand new ideas and complete new tasks. The scaffolding allows the child to climb to the higher levels of development in manageable amounts by a) reducing degrees of freedom (simplifying the tasks), b) direction maintenance (motivating and encouraging the child), c) marking critical features (highlighting relevant parts or errors), d) demonstration (providing model examples for imitation).

The Zone of Proximal Development and education – Tharp and Gallimore (1988) propose the following definition of teaching according to Vygotsky's ideas: 'Teaching consists in assisting performance through the ZPD. Teaching can be said to occur when assistance is offered at points in the ZPD at which performance requires assistance' and go on to quote Vygotsky (1956) who said that teaching was only good when it 'awakens and rouses to life those functions which are in a stage of maturing, which lie in the zone of proximal development'. Teachers should assist performance by working sensitively and *contingently* within the ZPD. Bruner developed this idea of contingency (responding appropriately and flexibly to the child's individual needs only when required) in his own work, and Wood and Middleton (1975) have investigated contingency by watching mothers help their children build a puzzle. The mothers showed contingency by offering different levels of help depending on how much difficulty the child was having.

Exercise 28 – Theories of cognitive development

Match the following terms and studies on the left with their explanations on the right, then put them in the appropriate boxes below.

Operations	(an internal representation of a specific physical or mental action)
Accommodation	(children are self-motivated to explore the world and build their understanding of it)
Assimilation	(cognitive understanding changes in qualitative ways with age)
Schema	(higher-order mental structures providing more complex rules about the environment)
Stages	(understanding new objects, situations or ideas using pre-existing schemata)
Active interaction	(changing schemata in order to understand new objects, situations or ideas)
Zone of proximal development	(the representation of knowledge as information-storing symbols like words)
Language internalisation	(different methods of encoding, storing or thinking about knowledge)
Language training	(the distance between the actual level of development and potential with guidance)
Symbolic mode	(gradually using language as inner speech to aid thinking)
Egocentric speech	(language used to control one's own thinking and behaviour but spoken out loud)
Modes of representation	(believed by some to speed up cognitive development)

Concrete operational stage	(the infant only knows the world by its immediate senses and actions)
Sensorimotor stage	(from two to seven years of age)
Formal operational stage	(operations are acquired, but physical examples are still needed)
Pre-operational stage	(hypothetical ideas can be manipulated in one's head without visible examples)
Conservation acquired	(when something cannot be seen or touched it ceases to exist for the infant)
Centration	(the infant cannot, at first, distinguish between itself and its environment)
Lack of object permanence	(only focusing on one aspect of an object or situation at a time)
De-centration occurs	(difficulty in understanding that others do not see, think and feel things like you do)
Profound egocentrism	(realising that some qualities remain constant despite changes in visual appearance)
Egocentrism	(being able to focus on more than one aspect of an object or situation at a time)
Deductive reasoning	(problems like the pendulum task can be solved logically and systematically)

McGarrigle & Donaldson (1974)	(showed an infant would reach for an object it could not see, contradicting Piaget)
Transitive inference tests	(McGarrigle et al's cows helped 6-year-olds pass these, contradicting Piaget)
Piaget & Inhelder (1956)	(3 mountain study of egocentrism, contradicted by Hughes' policeman doll study)
Bower & Wishart (1972)	(showed 4 to 6-year-olds could conserve number if a Naughty Teddy was used)
Class inclusion tests	(show the abstract form of arguments, e.g. if A›B›C, then A›C, can be followed)

Spiral curriculum	(children should only be taught concepts suitable for their level of cognitive development)
Readiness	(the child's self-construction of understanding means active, student centred tasks are useful)
Contingency	(complex ideas are presented at simplified levels first, then re-visited at more complex levels)
Scaffolding	(a support structure for a child's understanding provided by more knowledgeable others)
Discovery learning	(responding appropriately and flexibly to a child's individual needs only when required)

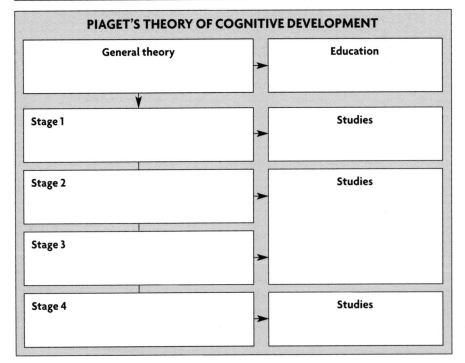

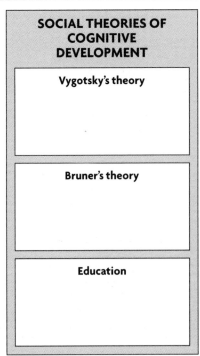

PIAGET'S THEORY OF COGNITIVE DEVELOPMENT

General theory

Schema
(an internal representation of a specific physical or mental action)

Active interaction
(children are self-motivated to explore the world and build their understanding of it)

Stages
(cognitive understanding changes in qualitative ways with age)

Operations
(higher-order mental structures providing more complex rules about the environment)

Assimilation
(understanding new objects, situations or ideas using pre-existing schemata)

Accommodation
(changing schemata in order to understand new objects, situations or ideas)

Education

Readiness
(children should only be taught concepts suitable for their level of cognitive development)

Discovery learning
(the child's self-construction of understanding means active, student centred tasks are useful)

Stage 1

Sensorimotor stage
(the infant only knows the world by its immediate senses and actions)

Lack of object permanence
(when something cannot be seen or touched it ceases to exist for the infant)

Profound egocentrism
(the infant cannot, at first, distinguish between itself and its environment)

Studies

Bower & Wishart (1972)
(showed an infant would reach for an object it could not see, contradicting Piaget)

Stage 2

Pre-operational stage
(from two to seven years of age)

Centration
(only focusing on one aspect of an object or situation at a time)

Egocentrism
(difficulty in understanding that others do not see, think and feel things like you do)

Studies

Class inclusion tests
(McGarrigle et al's cows helped 6-year-olds pass these, contradicting Piaget)

Piaget & Inhelder (1956)
(3 mountain study of egocentrism, contradicted by Hughes' policeman doll study)

McGarrigle & Donaldson (1974)
(showed 4 to 6-year-olds could conserve number if a Naughty Teddy was used)

Stage 3

Concrete operational stage
(operations are acquired, but physical examples are still needed)

Conservation acquired
(realising that some qualities remain constant despite changes in visual appearance)

De-centration occurs
(being able to focus on more than one aspect of an object or situation at a time)

Stage 4

Formal operational stage
(hypothetical ideas can be manipulated in one's head without visible examples)

Deductive reasoning
(problems like the pendulum task can be solved logically and systematically)

Studies

Transitive inference tests
(show the abstract form of arguments, e.g. if A>B>C, then A>C, can be followed)

SOCIAL THEORIES OF COGNITIVE DEVELOPMENT

Vygotsky's theory

Language internalisation
(gradually using language as inner speech to aid thinking)

Egocentric speech
(language used to control one's own thinking and behaviour but spoken out loud)

Zone of proximal development
(the distance between the actual level of development and potential with guidance)

Bruner's theory

Symbolic mode
(the representation of knowledge as information-storing symbols like words)

Modes of representation
(different methods of encoding, storing or thinking about knowledge)

Language training
(believed by some to speed up cognitive development)

Education

Spiral curriculum
(complex ideas are presented at simplified levels first, then re-visited at more complex levels)

Scaffolding
(a support structure for a child's understanding provided by more knowledgeable others)

Contingency
(responding appropriately and flexibly to a child's individual needs only when required)

Baron-Cohen et al. describe childhood autism as a severe developmental disorder affecting around 4 in 10,000 children and see the key symptom as being a profound problem in understanding and coping with the social environment – finding it unpredictable and confusing. This causes impaired verbal and non-verbal communication and a failure to develop normal social relationships – autistic children seem to treat people and objects in the same way and tend to be withdrawn or disruptive in their interactions with others.

Autistic social problems could be partly caused by other symptoms which such children show – many for example are mentally retarded. However, autistic children with normal IQs also lack social competence, while non-autistic retarded children, such as those with Down's Syndrome, are relatively socially competent. Baron-Cohen et al., therefore, suggest that autistic children lack a *specific cognitive mechanism* that is distinct from general IQ, namely a 'theory of mind'.

A theory of mind enables those who possess it to realise that 'other people know, want, feel, or believe things' and as such is vital for social skills. It is a form of *second–order representation* or metarepresentation (a representation of another person's representation of the world, or a belief about another's belief), which also accounts for the ability to pretend in play – something else autistic children are very poor at.

If a theory of mind that enables one to attribute mental states to others

- is specifically lacking in autistic children and is not related to general intelligence
- allows people to work out what others *believe* about certain situations and thus predict what they will do next

then it can be hypothesised that autistic children whose IQs are in the average range will perform significantly worse on a task that requires such belief-based prediction than non-autistic but severely retarded children with Down's Syndrome.

Method

The study tested 20 autistic children aged around 6–16 years old (average approximately 12) of higher average intelligence than the other groups. They were compared in performance to 14 Down's Syndrome children aged around 6–17 (average approximately 11) and 27 clinically 'normal' pre-school children aged around 3–5 (average approximately 4 and a half)

The following standardised procedure was used for every child, each of whom was tested individually:

- The experimenter sits at a table opposite the child with two dolls, Sally and Anne. Sally puts a marble into her basket, then leaves the scene.
- Anne transfers the marble and hides it in her box.
- Sally returns and the experimenter asks the critical *Belief Question* – 'Where will Sally look for her marble?' If the children point to the previous location of Sally's basket they pass the belief question, since they can represent the doll's false belief. If they point to the current location of Anne's basket, they fail the question since they cannot take into account Sally's false belief.
- To ensure the validity of the belief question, three control questions were also asked – the Naming Question asking which doll was which, the Reality Question 'Where is the marble really?' and the Memory Question 'Where was the marble in the beginning?'
- The scenario was repeated, but this time the marble was transferred to the experimenter's pocket.

Sally places her marble in the basket

Exit Sally

Anne transfers Sally's marble to box

Re-enter Sally
Where will Sally look for her marble?

Results
The following results were achieved for each group.

% failure on Questions	Autistic group	Down's Syndrome	'Normal' pre-schoolers
Naming Reality Memory	0%	0%	0%
Belief	80% on both trials	14% on both trials	15% on both trials

Group differences on the Belief Question were significant at the P<0.001 level. All 16 autistic children who failed pointed to the current marble location.

Since the controls rule out alternative explanations (e.g. of position preference, negativism, random pointing, misunderstanding / forgetting the task or general intellectual ability) the experimenters concluded that the autistic children specifically lacked a theory of mind to enable them to attribute belief to the doll and thus distinguish their own belief from the doll's. The *conceptual* perspective-taking tested here is distinguished from the *perceptual* perspective-taking tested by Piaget and Inhelder's 'three mountain' test.

Exercise 29

1 What method was used in the study?
2 What were the independent and dependent variables in the study?
3 What design was used to allocate participants to conditions?
4 Why were the three control questions (the naming, reality and memory questions) asked?
5 Why might this study be a little artificial regarding the way it tested the beliefs of others?
6 If the four autistic children who did not fail the Belief Question possessed a theory of mind, what might their pretend play be like?

1 What method was used in the study?

A natural or quasi experiment was used, since complete control over the independent variable was lacking (nature, not the experimenters, determined the mental ability of the children).

2 What were the independent and dependent variables in the study?

The independent variable was the type of child, naturally manipulated in three conditions: autistic, Down's Syndrome, clinically 'normal'.

The dependent variable was the ability to correctly answer the belief question of the Sally-Anne test (by pointing to the previous location of Sally's basket based on the doll's false belief).

3 What design was used to allocate participants to conditions?

An independent measures design was employed (different participants used in each condition). This was unavoidable given that the independent variable involved different types of participant.

4 Why were the three control questions (the naming, reality and memory questions) asked?

The Naming Question asking which doll was which was used to ensure knowledge of the dolls' identities. The Reality Question 'Where is the marble really?' and Memory Question 'Where was the marble in the beginning' were both used to ensure knowledge of the marble's location at each point in the scenario.

5 Why might this study be a little artificial regarding the way it tested the beliefs of others?

The scenario's use of dolls is rather artificial since dolls do not believe! More realistic tests using people instead of dolls have confirmed the results, however.

6 If the four autistic children who did not fail the Belief Question possessed a theory of mind, what might their pretend play be like?

If the four autistic children who did not fail the Belief Question possessed a theory of mind they were predicted by Baron-Cohen et al. to show differences from the other autistic children in their type of social impairment and pretend play deficiency (testing of this was not reported). They may well show *more* pretend play than the other autistic children.

BARON-COHEN et al. CROSSWORD

1 A specific cognitive mechanism that enables one to realise that other people know, want, feel or believe things (6/2/4)
2 The question that asked 'where is the marble really?' (7)
3 The percentage of autistic children who failed the belief question on both trials (6)
4 The percentage of 'normal' pre-schoolers who failed the belief question on both trials (7)
5 The question that asked 'where was the marble in the beginning?' (6)
6 The kind of experiment used in the study (7)
7 The name of the test used on the children (5/4)
8 The percentage in all groups who failed the three control questions (4)
9 The scenario and use of dolls has been criticised as being this (10)
10 The question that asked which doll was which (6)
11 The question that asked 'where will Sally look for her marble?' (6)
12 The syndrome the intellectually retarded children had (5)
13 The kind of representation that allows a belief about a belief (6-5)

Cognitive changes in old age

A Research has indicated that *longitudinal* studies of the same individuals over time reveal *less change* in cognitive abilities than *cross-sectional* studies that compare different people of different ages.

B Intelligence research has shown that older people show decreases in the *speed* of their mental processing.

The memory research of Salthouse (1990) found evidence for a decline in the *efficiency* of working memory in elderly participants.

C The amount of cognitive change in old age is likely to be falsely *exaggerated* by negative *stereotypes* in some cultures, such as older people becoming senile.

D Baltes and Willis (1982) found that *training* older adults on the aspects of IQ that usually decline over time significantly improved their performance, even in long-term follow-up studies of those adults in their early 80s.

E Some cognitive developmental researchers have suggested a *fifth*, 'post-formal' *stage* of intellectual ability in late adulthood, involving an acceptance of contradiction, ambiguity and complexity.

F Some of the changes reflect the influence of *variables other than just age* on cognitive abilities, such as those resulting from the *cohort effect*. This is when different age groups in a society at any one time will differ in other characteristics, such as the level of education or nutrition they have experienced, which may influence cognitive abilities but be unrelated to the duration of their lives.

G Performance on tests of *recall* is worse in old people than younger ones. However, there seems little or no difference in tests of *recognition*.

H Negative *cultural stereotypes* about the forgetfulness of old age or positive stereotypes about the wisdom old age bestows, may actually affect cognitive abilities by becoming *self-fulfilling prophecies*.

I The elderly may experience decreasing activity levels and *less-stimulating* environments which could adversely affect their cognitive abilities – especially in cultures where older people have less family and social contact, or are put in care homes with poor facilities, repetitive routines and limited social variability. Such environments may not present sufficient opportunity to practice and apply fluid intelligence.

J The deterioration of mental abilities can be caused by the degeneration of *neurones* resulting from either natural cell death with age or diseases such as Alzheimer's. Studies have shown that dramatic cell loss, particularly in parts of the temporal lobe and hippocampus of the brain can occur in people with Alzheimer's disease, but is not an inevitable consequence of ageing.

K Studies have found that *crystallised intelligence* (which involves the use of knowledge that has already been acquired) appears to increase with age, while *fluid intelligence* (which concerns the ability to solve problems that have not been encountered before) seems to decrease with age.

L Slower mental processing speed could result from older people having more ways of solving problems available to them. Retrieval of memory may decline with age because of interference from a greater number of memories, or a lack of cues in their present life to prompt the access to memories of the past.

M There are *large individual differences* between older people in how *much* change occurs and how *late* in the life span it occurs.

N Levy and Langer (1994) found that older American participants exposed to negative stereotypes about the effect of age on memory performed worse on memory tests than younger Americans (for whom the negative stereotype did not yet apply), older deaf Americans (who would have been less exposed to the stereotype) and older Chinese participants (who are exposed to more positive stereotypes about age bringing wisdom).

Exercise 30

From considering the information boxes, which point/s

1 describe *quantitative* changes (e.g. in amount or degree of performance) in the mental abilities of older people?

2 describe *qualitative* changes (e.g. type or kind of performance) in the mental abilities of older people?

3 suggest that the cognitive changes of old age can be caused by age-related *physiological* factors?

4 suggest that the cognitive changes of old age can be caused by age-related *social* and *environmental* factors?

5 suggest that the cognitive changes of old age can be caused by age-related *cognitive* factors?

6 argue that we should be cautious in our conclusions regarding the cognitive changes associated with old age (they may not be as bad as they seem or may not actually be due to old age)?

From considering the information boxes, which point/s:

1 describe quantitative changes (e.g. in amount or degree of performance) in the mental abilities of older people?

> **B** Intelligence research has shown that older people show decreases in the *speed* of their mental processing.
> The memory research of Salthouse (1990) found evidence for a decline in the *efficiency* of working memory in elderly participants.

2 describe qualitative changes (e.g. type or kind of performance) in the mental abilities of older people?

> **E** Some cognitive developmental researchers have suggested a *fifth*, 'post-formal' *stage* of intellectual ability in late adulthood, involving an acceptance of contradiction, ambiguity and complexity.

> **G** Performance on tests of *recall* is worse in old people than younger ones. However, there seems little or no difference in tests of *recognition*.

> **K** Studies have found that *crystallised intelligence* (which involves the use of knowledge that has already been acquired) appears to increase with age, while *fluid intelligence* (which concerns the ability to solve problems that have not been encountered before) seems to decrease with age.

3 suggest that the cognitive changes of old age can be caused by age-related physiological factors?

> **J** The deterioration of mental abilities can be caused by the degeneration of *neurones* resulting from either natural cell death with age or diseases such as Alzheimer's. Studies have shown that dramatic cell loss, particularly in parts of the temporal lobe and hippocampus of the brain can occur in people with Alzheimer's disease, but is not an inevitable consequence of ageing.

4 suggest that the cognitive changes of old age can be caused by age-related social and environmental factors?

> **D** Baltes and Willis (1982) found that *training* older adults on the aspects of IQ that usually decline over time significantly improved their performance, even in long-term follow-up studies of those adults in their early 80s.

> **H** Negative *cultural stereotypes* about the forgetfulness of old age or positive stereotypes about the wisdom old age bestows, may actually affect cognitive abilities by becoming *self-fulfilling prophecies*.

> **I** The elderly may experience decreasing activity levels and *less-stimulating* environments which could adversely affect their cognitive abilities – especially in cultures where older people have less family and social contact, or are put in care homes with poor facilities, repetitive routines and limited social variability. Such environments may not present sufficient opportunity to practice and apply fluid intelligence.

> **N** Levy and Langer (1994) found that older American participants exposed to negative stereotypes about the effect of age on memory performed worse on memory tests than younger Americans (for whom the negative stereotype did not yet apply), older deaf Americans (who would have been less exposed to the stereotype) and older Chinese participants (who are exposed to more positive stereotypes about age bringing wisdom).

5 suggest that the cognitive changes of old age can be caused by age-related cognitive factors?

> **L** Slower mental processing speed could result from older people having more ways of solving problems available to them. Retrieval of memory may decline with age because of interference from a greater number of memories, or a lack of cues in their present life to prompt the access to memories of the past.

6 argue that we should be cautious in our conclusions regarding the cognitive changes associated with old age (they may not be as bad as they seem or may not actually be due to old age)?

> **A** Research has indicated that *longitudinal* studies of the same individuals over time reveal *less change* in cognitive abilities than *cross-sectional* studies that compare different people of different ages.

> **C** The amount of cognitive change in old age is likely to be falsely *exaggerated* by negative *stereotypes* in some cultures, such as older people becoming senile.

> **F** Some of the changes reflect the influence of *variables other than just age* on cognitive abilities, such as those resulting from the *cohort effect*. This is when different age groups in a society at any one time will differ in other characteristics, such as the level of education or nutrition they have experienced, which may influence cognitive abilities but be unrelated to the duration of their lives.

> **M** There are *large individual differences* between older people in how *much* change occurs and how *late* in the life span it occurs.

Cognition means 'knowing' and cognitive psychologists study mental processes to find out *how* knowledge is gained, used and retained. They have, therefore, investigated the cognitive processes involved in areas such as perception, attention, memory, thinking, language and problem solving, and used them to explain, predict and change human behaviour.

Assumptions

The importance of mental processes

Cognitive psychologists assume that *it is vital to study the internal mental processes* which lie between the stimuli we receive and the responses we make if we are to fully understand and predict behaviour. They believe that humans do not just passively respond to their environment but that our *minds actively organise and manipulate the information we receive* in important ways. As the cognitive psychologist Ulric Neisser (1966) suggested:

'… the term 'cognition' refers to all those processes by which sensory input is transformed, reduced, elaborated, stored, recovered and used … cognition is involved in everything a human being might possibly do.'

Without these cognitive mental processes it would not be possible, for example, to make effective decisions or remember, attend to or even perceive relevant information from our environments.

Information processing and the computer analogy

Cognitive psychologists assume that humans, like computers, are *information processors* – regardless of our hardware (brains or circuits) both perform the same function of receiving, interpreting and responding to information – and these processes can be *modelled* and *tested scientifically*. Precise models of our mental processes can, therefore, be proposed (rather like computer flow charts) that will make predictions about how psychological functions are carried out, which in turn enables scientific research to be conducted to test their validity.

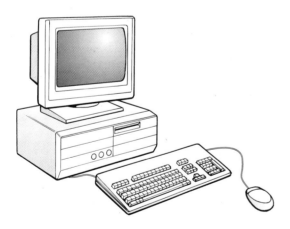

Just as computer scientists are often more interested in the *software* programming than the machinery of a computer when explaining how it performs its tasks, so cognitive psychologists also regard *functional level explanations* as important to study in their own right. Indeed, cognitive psychological models of how we process information are thought by some to be sufficient as explanations – without the need to even consider how these processes might be carried out in the brain.

While some cognitive psychologists just see the computer analogy as a useful tool to help explain and investigate human mental functions, others take the comparison further. If minds are regarded as programmes that brains run, if all human mental processes are eventually identified and modelled, and if brains and

computers are both information processing machines, then it may be possible to program a computer to duplicate human psychology in every respect. Certainly science fiction writers have long suggested such artificially intelligent machines could exist.

Methods

Experimentation

As we have seen, cognitive psychologists suggest that mental processes *can* and *should* be investigated scientifically by proposing models of how various psychological functions, such as memory, might work and then conducting research on these models to confirm, refute or modify them.

Experimentation has been regarded by cognitive psychologists as the most scientific method of finding evidence for or against their models. Typically, cognitive psychological experiments involve manipulating the type of input (e.g. information) a sample of participants receive under certain standardised conditions to see whether it affects their output (e.g. observable behaviour or conscious report) in the way predicted by the model. For example, a cognitive psychologist might develop a model of memory which suggests that we tend to keep information in our present consciousness by repeating it verbally to ourselves in our head.

If this model is true then we should find information that *sounds* similar more confusing to keep in mind than information with distinctively different sounds. This prediction from the model can be tested by showing people, for equal amounts of time (e.g. 7 seconds), equal units of information (e.g. letters) that either rhyme (e.g. **B T C P G E D**) or do not rhyme (e.g. **F T Z Q W R N**), and asking them to recall them in the *correct order* after an exact time delay (e.g. another 7 seconds). Those who saw the rhyming letters should find it harder to recall the letters properly than those who saw the non-rhyming letters if the model is correct (try it on others and see).

Case studies of brain damaged patients

As mentioned above, some cognitive psychologists argue that their models of how mental processing occurs are sufficient as explanations, and could theoretically be carried out by any information processing device, either a brain or a computer. However, others have argued that cognitive psychological models are too hypothetical and that although their predictions of performance may match the performance of people when tested, there is still no guarantee that the models and people function in the same way. There could be a huge variety of models that produce similar performances so how can we tell which is closest to human functioning?

For these reasons many cognitive psychologists have shown an interest in locating areas of the brain that may be involved in mental processes (known as cognitive neuropsychology), and have used findings from the study of brain damaged patients and brain scans to support their models.

> ## Exercise 31
>
> 1 Do you think that computer programmes will ever exactly duplicate human psychology in every respect – for example, do you think a computer-controlled robot/android could be built that would fool people into thinking it was human? Why or why not?
>
> 2 What are the advantages and disadvantages of the experimental method used in the memory study example?
>
> 3 Compare and contrast the cognitive approach with the psychodynamic and behaviourist approaches.

1 Do you think that computer programmes will ever exactly duplicate human psychology in every respect – for example, do you think a computer-controlled robot/android could be built that would fool people into thinking it was human? Why or why not?

Many objections to the idea that a computer could fool people into thinking it was human involve differences in physical appearance and action. Since, however, these depend more on achievements in mechanical robotics and synthetic materials, a more practical test of *psychological* duplication might involve removing such clues.

Such a test was suggested by Alan Turing (it became known as the Turing test) which, essentially, proposed that if a person could not tell the difference during an extended conversation conducted through written messages (no visual or audible clues) between a human and a computer correspondent, then the latter could be said to have duplicated the former. Imagine, for example, that you spent a year communicating by e-mail with someone you had never met without ever realising your correspondent was, in fact, a computer. Would that not persuade you that computers could duplicate human thinking, emotions and behaviour? To fool you so completely a computer would not only have to master language comprehension and production, but would also have to convince you that it had interests, life experiences, beliefs, opinions, emotional reactions, relationships and many other aspects of human psychology that we take for granted.

OK, you might be thinking, even if a computer could fool me in a Turing test there would still be reasons to think that the computer was not exactly duplicating human psychology. They might be behaving as if they had thoughts and emotions but surely computers are *not conscious of* the instructions they follow in their programmes and do *not feel* the emotions they might be reporting.

Such counter arguments were expressed by Searle (1980) in his Chinese room scenario, where he imagined a person with no experience of Chinese put in a room with a set of instructions to follow that changed sets of symbols that were passed into the room (unknown to the person, questions in Chinese) into other sets to be passed back out (again unknown, the correct answers in Chinese). Searle argued that this room represents a computer – the person acts as the processing hardware (microchip) carrying out the instructions (software programme) that changes the questions (input) into answers (output) – but at no point is there any understanding or meaningfulness in the room. Just as the person inside does not know what the Chinese symbols represent or what the instructions are doing, so computers can be said to lack awareness, intentions and understanding of the tasks they perform.

Of course we must also admit that humans are unaware of how they process most information; words just spring to mind but how were they selected and assembled? Additionally, you cannot directly know that other people are conscious and feel emotions like you do – how do you know that the people around you are *not* sophisticated robots short of X-raying them?

This brings us to another basis you might have had for objecting to the notion that computers will ever exactly duplicate psychological processes – perhaps there are physical differences in structure between brains and computer circuits that mean psychological functions cannot be exactly reproduced in the latter. For example, computer circuit connections typically work in a serial way – one chip connects to another, which in turn connects to yet another chip, and so on. If we break the connection between two chips, often the whole machine stops functioning. There is nothing in the hardware that does anything more than follow the rules of the software program.

Human 'hardware' is different, however, since the brain's neurones are massively interconnected with each other so a loss of some connections usually only results in a roughening of performance or loss of a particular function rather than a complete shutdown. In addition, such interconnections allow the faster *parallel* processing of many tasks at once and even the ability to guess a solution if the information given is less than complete.

Nevertheless, computer science has also attempted to model the brain's way of working and has produced parallel-distributed processing (PDP) or connectionist networks that have mimicked some of the brain's features. While there are still many differences between computers and brains, some argue that it is only a matter of time before silicon-based artificial intelligence catches up with its natural carbon-based cousin. Others argue that the brain's sheer complexity will make it practically impossible to duplicate.

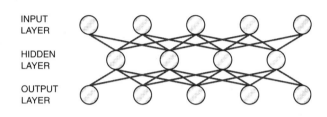

A connectionist network

2 What are the advantages and disadvantages of the experimental method used in the memory study example?

The advantage is that the experimental method manipulates the independent variable of the sound of information while controlling the influence of other variables like the difficulty of the information, the time of exposure to it and the delay before recalling it. This makes us more certain about the cause and effect relationship and thus increases the value of the study as evidence.

On the negative side, increasing control of variables can often make the test a little artificial and the results difficult to generalise, especially in laboratory conditions. In real life there are many important variables which influence memory that are not included in the study, which gives us a narrow picture of the influences involved. Information is rarely of equal difficulty, importance or relevance to us and is received under a variety of conditions which may influence its recall.

3 Compare and contrast the cognitive approach with the psychodynamic and behaviourist approaches.

Like the psychodynamic approach, the cognitive approach is concerned with underlying mental constructs and processes that influence our behaviour. However, unlike the psychodynamic approach, cognitive psychologists make their models of these constructs and process precise and testable, and use more experimentation on behaviour to confirm or refute them.

Unlike the psychodynamic and cognitive approaches, the behaviourist approach is not concerned with underlying mental constructs – only observable behaviour is of importance. With their emphasis on scientific, objective evidence and experimentation, however, behaviourists do share a similar methodological approach with cognitive scientists.

32 | Types of memory

Most of us tend to think of our memory as a single, whole 'thing' – a storage area where all information is deposited and hopefully retrieved when needed. We say, for instance, that we have a 'good' or 'bad' memory. Psychologists, on the other hand, have found it more useful to identify and investigate different types of memory. For example, they have divided memory into types based upon the kind of information stored and how long it is held for.

Encoding types of memory

The human sensory systems, such as our eyes and ears, receive many different forms of stimulation, ranging from sound waves to photons of light. Obviously the information reaching our senses is transformed in nature when it is represented in our brains (we do not store the actual photons), and encoding refers to the process of representing knowledge in different forms. Three types of encoding memory have been proposed.

Imagery memory

Some memory *representations* appear to closely resemble the raw data received from our senses, such as the fairly vivid visual images we can recall of people and places we have seen or the tunes we can hear again in our heads. Baddeley and Hitch (1974) have even suggested that we have a 'visuospatial sketchpad' for summoning up and examining visual imagery. Although extremely rare, photographic (eidetic) memory seems to be an ultra-enhanced form of imagery memory. The composer Mozart, for example, was supposed to be able to replay long extracts of music after just one hearing.

Declarative memory

Sometimes termed explicit memory, this type concerns all the factual information that we can *consciously describe or report*, and as such has been the focus of the majority of research on memory. Declarative memory includes:
Semantic memory – memory for the *meaning* of information, e.g. knowing what a word means, involving the storage of abstract, general facts regardless of when they were acquired.
Episodic memory – this is *'knowing when'* memory for specific personal experiences and linked to a particular time and place in our lives. Episodic memory can be quite precise – Lindsay and Norman (1977) asked students 'what were you doing on a Monday afternoon in the third week of September, 2 years ago?', and found many actually knew. Very vivid episodic memories have been termed 'flashbulb' memories (Brown and Kulik, 1977) which involve recalling exactly what you were doing and where you were when a particularly important, exciting or emotional event happened.

Procedural memory

Also known as implicit memory, this is the memory for *knowing how* to do things such as talk, walk, juggle, etc., even though we may not be able to consciously describe how we do these skills and abilities. Procedural knowledge is very resistant to forgetting (we can still ride a bicycle after many years) and is also resistant to brain damage which eradicates other forms of memory. Retrograde amnesiacs, who can lose all declarative memories for the last few years of their lives, do not forget how to walk, talk or ride a bike. Anterograde amnesiac patients, who lose the ability to consciously remember any new declarative information in a long-term way – forgetting simple events or verbal instructions after just a few moments, are often able to learn new procedural skills such as playing table tennis.

Duration types of memory

Cognitive psychologists have proposed *three types* of time-based memory, each with differences not only in duration, but also in capacity (how much information they can hold), encoding (what form they hold that information in) and function (what they are used for).

Sensory memory

Sensory memory (sometimes called the 'sensory store' or 'sensory register') refers to the storage of information from the senses in a fairly unprocessed way for a very short amount of time. The visual system has a fairly large capacity *iconic* memory for the shape, size, colour and location (but not meaning) of objects, that fades in less than one second. The hearing system has *echoic* memory for auditory stimuli, which lasts for up to three seconds. Coltheart et al. (1974) suggested that sensory memory allows us to hold on to environmental information just long enough to focus on what is interesting or relevant. This can then be paid attention to and thus selected and retained for further memory processing, while the irrelevant information fades away.

Short-term memory

Information selected by attention from sensory memory may pass into short-term memory (STM). STM allows us to retain information long enough to use it, e.g. looking up a telephone number and remembering it long enough to dial it. It holds what is present in our mind at any one point in time.

Peterson and Peterson (1959) demonstrated that STM lasts between 15 and 30 seconds, unless people rehearse the material, while Miller (1956) found that STM has a limited capacity, it can only hold around 7 'chunks' of information at any one time. STM appears to mostly encode memory acoustically (in terms of sound) as Conrad (1964) demonstrated, but can also retain visual images too.

Long-term memory

Long-term memory refers to the lasting retention of information and skills, from minutes to a lifetime. Brain damaged people with retrograde amnesia or anterograde amnesia show psychologists how vital our long-term memories are to help us know who, where and when we are. Long-term memory has an enormous capacity to retain information throughout our lives, and while it can store information in many forms it has the ability to encode memory semantically (in terms of meaning). For example, we can remember the gist of a conversation in the long term, if not the exact words that were used.

Exercise 32

1 If I asked you to remember how many windows you have in your house, how would you provide the answer?

2 Try to answer Lindsay and Norman's question (Do not give up too easily. Try to reconstruct where you would have been and use key events such as birthdays at that time to zero in on the actual memories).

3 What memory might be involved when
   a rapidly moving a torch around in the dark creates lines of light in the air?
   b we ask someone to repeat what they have just said but then realise what it was before they can do so?

4 How could you test the capacity of sensory memory when most information in it has faded before you can report it?

5 Why, when a teacher dictates a really long sentence in one go, do students forget the beginning or the end of it?

6 Work out how Peterson and Peterson, Miller, and Conrad might have provided evidence for the duration, capacity and acoustic encoding of short-term memory.

7 How could the semantic encoding and duration of long-term memory be demonstrated?

Answers 32.1 – 32.7

1 **If I asked you to remember how many windows you have in your house, how would you provide the answer?**

Unless you have counted them before and remember the total, it is quite likely that you would summon up a *visual mental image* of your house (no matter how vague) and 'walk round' it in your mind counting each window.

2 **Try to answer Lindsay and Norman's question (Do not give up too easily. Try to reconstruct where you would have been and use key events such as birthdays at that time to zero in on the actual memories).**

If you managed to recall the actual experiences of that particular afternoon, then you accessed your episodic memory. If you just remembered the kind of activity you were *probably* doing, then you used your semantic memory. While some brain-scanning evidence has revealed that a different area of the brain is active when thinking about personal events (the frontal cortex), rather than non-personal semantic information (the posterior areas of the cortex), these two types of memory are closely interconnected. Semantic information is the result of specific episodic experiences and you use semantic information to retrieve such particular events.

3 **What memory might be involved when**
   a **rapidly moving a torch around in the dark creates lines of light in the air?**
   b **we ask someone to repeat what they have just said but then realise what it was before they can do so?**

Sensory memory could be involved in both – *iconic* memory for **a** and *echoic* memory for **b**.

4 **How could you test the capacity of sensory memory when most information in it has faded before you can report it?**

Since sensory memory lasts less than a second, most of the material in it will have been forgotten before it can be reported. *Sperling* studied the sensory memory for vision (the iconic store) by using a *tachistoscope* – a device that can flash visual stimuli onto a blank screen for very brief instances. Using this device, Sperling asked subjects to remember as many letters as they could from a grid of 12 symbols that he displayed for just one twentieth of a second. He found that while they could only recall around *four* of the symbols before the grid faded from their sensory memory, they typically reported seeing a lot more than they had time to report.

To test the capacity of sensory memory, i.e. how much information was available in the iconic after-image, Sperling presented the 12 symbol grid for 1/20th of a second followed immediately by a high, medium or low tone which indicated which of the three rows of four symbols the subject had to attend to from their iconic memory of the grid. In this partial report condition, recall was on average just over 3 out of the 4 symbols from any row they attended to, suggesting that the iconic store can retain around 76% of all the data received.

Step 1 Show grid				Step 2 Ring tone	Step 3 Recall letters			
7	1	V	F		?	?	?	?
X	L	5	3	Medium tone	X	L	5	3
B	4	W	7		?	?	?	?

5 **Why, when a teacher dictates a really long sentence in one go, do students forget the beginning or the end of it?**

This may happen because the limited capacity of short-term memory (in this case seven, plus or minus two words) has been exceeded.

6 **Work out how Peterson and Peterson, Miller, and Conrad might have provided evidence for the duration, capacity and acoustic encoding of short-term memory.**

Peterson and Peterson (1959) investigated the duration of short-term memory by

- asking subjects to remember a single nonsense syllable of three consonants (a *trigram* of letters such as FJT or KPD). These were used so the information would be equally difficult for everyone to remember

- giving them an *interpolated task* to stop them rehearsing the trigram (such as counting backwards in threes from one hundred)

- testing their *recall after* 3, 6, 9, 12, 15 or 18 seconds (recall had to be perfect and in the correct order to count). While average recall was very good (80%) after 3 seconds, this average dropped dramatically to just 10% after 18 seconds.

Miller (1956) investigated the limited capacity of STM, referring to it as 'The magical number seven, plus or minus two', using memory span studies. These typically involve asking participants to repeat in the correct order a series of digits or random letters presented to them and gradually increasing the number of items. The memory span is the number of items a person can repeat perfectly 50% of the time. Miller found that the amount of information retained could be increased by *chunking* the information – packaging it into larger items or units, although STM can still only retain 7 + or – 2 of these chunks. Chunking is greatly improved if the chunks already have *meaning* from LTM (e.g. MP IBM ITV FBI RAF rather than MPI BMI TVF BIR AF).

Conrad (1964) demonstrated acoustic STM encoding by finding that rhyming letters (e.g. **B T C P G E D**) were significantly harder to recall properly than non rhyming letters (e.g. **F T Z Q W R N**), mostly due to acoustic confusion errors – the letters would be confused because of the similar sound.

7 **How could the semantic encoding and duration of long-term memory be demonstrated?**

Baddeley (1966) showed that LTM stores information in terms of meaning (semantic memory), by giving research participants four lists to remember.

List A – Similar sounding words, e.g. man, map, can, cap.
List B – Non similar sounding words, e.g. try, pig, hut, pen.
List C – Similar meaning words, e.g. great, big, huge, wide.
List D – Non similar meaning words, e.g. run, easy, bright.

If recall was given immediately, list A was recalled worse than list B, but there was little difference between the recall of lists C and D (indicating acoustic STM encoding).

After 20 minutes, however, it was list C that was recalled worse than D, with little difference between lists A and B (indicating semantic LTM encoding).

While it is impossible to predict the duration of any one piece of information, researchers have investigated general trends in the durability of memory. Ebbinghaus found that a large proportion of information in LTM was lost comparatively quickly (within the first hour) and thereafter stabilised to a much slower rate of loss.

Linton used a diary to record at least two 'every day' events from her life each day over 6 years, and randomly tested her later recall of them. She found a much more even and gradual loss of data over time (approximately 6 % per year).

Models of memory and memory studies

How do we go about remembering and storing information?

Multi-store model of memory

Much research was devoted to identifying the properties of sensory, short-term and long-term memory, and cognitive psychologists such as Atkinson and Shiffrin (1968) began to regard them as *stores* – hypothetical holding structures. They proposed the two-process model of memory, which showed how information flowed through the two stores of short-term and long-term memory. Like many other researchers they assumed the existence of a sensory memory that precedes the short-term memory, and so it is sometimes termed the multi-store model.

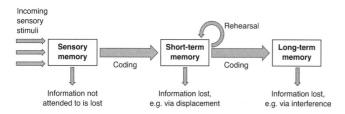

Atkinson and Shiffrin regarded the stores as the *structural components* of the model, but also proposed a number of *control processes* such as attention, coding and rehearsal which operate in conjunction with the stores. These processes effectively select and reduce the huge amount of potential information we receive from our senses to manageable and useful proportions.

Thus incoming information that is paid attention to in sensory memory passes through to the short-term memory store, otherwise it fades and is lost. Information (visual or auditory) entering short-term memory is thought to be encoded acoustically and can be maintained there and transferred to long-term memory by rehearsing it. Due to the limited capacity and duration of STM, too much material or insufficient time to rehearse it may cause it to be lost from the store. Again, information entering the long-term memory store can change in coding from an acoustic to a semantic code (from sound to meaning) to extract the overall 'gist' of the information received – further reducing the amount that needs to be stored. Information can be lost from the long-term store (become unavailable or inaccessible) in a variety of ways.

Although the multi-store model has incorporated and explained many findings in memory research, it has been criticised in a number of ways. It under-emphasises interaction between the stores, for example, the way information from LTM influences what is regarded as important and relevant to show attention to in sensory memory and helps the meaningful chunking of information in STM. Mere rehearsal is also too simple a process to account for the transfer of information from STM to LTM (the model ignores factors such as the effort and strategy subjects may use when learning and does not account for the *type* of information taken into memory). Finally, STM and LTM are more complex and less unitary than the model assumes.

Levels of processing approach to memory

Craik and Lockhart's (1972) important article countered the predominant view of fixed memory stores, arguing that it is what the person *does* with information when it is received, i.e. how much attention is paid to it or how deeply it is considered, that determines how long the memory lasts.

They suggested that information is more readily transferred to LTM if it is considered, understood and related to past memories to gain *meaning* than if it is merely repeated (maintenance rehearsal). This degree of consideration was termed the '*depth of processing*', the deeper information was processed the longer the *memory trace* would last.

Craik and Lockhart gave three examples of *levels* at which written information could be processed:

- **Structural level** – e.g. merely paying attention to what the words *look* like (very shallow processing).

- **Phonetic level** – processing the *sound* of the words.

- **Semantic level** – considering the meaning of words (deep processing).

The levels of processing approach made a good contribution to understanding the processes that take place at the time of learning and was helpful in providing an alternative explanation of memory processing that did not draw such a clear line between short- and long-term memory – allowing more of a continuum. However, the approach had problems with defining 'deep' processing and why it is effective (it described rather than explained the processes). Also, semantic processing does not always lead to better retrieval.

The working memory model

The working memory model of Baddeley and Hitch (1974, 1990) re-describes the short-term memory store as an *active* working memory store that holds and manipulates information that is currently being consciously thought about, and consists of *3 separate components*:

1 **The central executive** – a modality-free controlling attentional mechanism with a limited capacity, which monitors and co-ordinates the operation of the other two components or slave systems.

2 **The phonological loop** – which itself consists of two subsystems:
   - The *articulatory control system* or 'inner voice' which is a verbal rehearsal system with a time-based capacity. It holds information by articulating sub-vocally material we want to maintain or are preparing to speak.
   - The *phonological store* or 'inner ear' which holds speech in a phonological memory trace that lasts 1.5 to 2 seconds if it does not refresh itself via the articulatory control system. It can also receive information directly from the sensory register (echoic) or from long-term memory.

3 **The visuospatial sketchpad** – or 'inner eye' which holds visual and spatial information from either the sensory register (iconic) or from long-term memory.

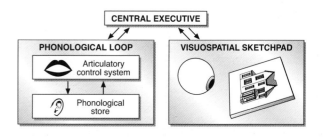

The working memory model still needs more refining in some areas (the nature and role of the central executive is still a little unclear), but it has been applied to many cognitive abilities such as reading, mental arithmetic and verbal reasoning.

Craik and Tulving's (1975) experiment

This experiment gave participants a list of words, each of which was accompanied by one of three different kinds of question. All the words were selected to be equally easy to remember, but some of the questions enquired about the case of the word, others asked whether the word rhymed with another word, and some required the participant to consider whether the word fitted appropriately into a sentence.

For example, the word '*table*' might be followed by one of the following:

- 'Is the word in capital letters?'
- 'Does it rhyme with "able"?'
- 'Does it fit in the sentence "the man sat at the _____"?'

Participants thought that they were just being tested on reaction speed to answer yes or no to each question, but they were given an unexpected test of recognition. It was found that those words that had been analysed to fit into a sentence were remembered better than the words associated with the other types of question.

Variations on the study

- Craik and Tulving (1975) found complex sentences about words, e.g. 'Does the word fit in the sentence "The great bird swooped down and carried off the struggling __"?', produced better cued recall than simple questions, e.g. 'Does the word fit in the sentence "She cooked the __"?'

- Rogers et al. (1977) found better recall for words that had questions like 'Does this word describe you?' asked about them, than questions like 'Does this mean the same as _____?' asked about them.

- Tyler et al. (1979) found that words presented as difficult anagrams, e.g. 'OCDTRO', were remembered better than words presented as simple anagrams, e.g. 'DOCTRO'.

- Eysenck and Eysenck (1980) found that participants given the rhyming kind of questions about words remembered them better if the words were unusual.

Case studies of brain-damaged patients

Anterograde amnesia is often caused by brain damage to the hippocampus, and those suffering from it are often trapped in a world of experience that only lasts for around half a minute or as long as they continually repeat the information to themselves.

Patients afflicted by anterograde amnesia such as H.M. (Milner et al., 1978) or Clive Wearing (reported in Blakemore, 1988) seem incapable of gaining new declarative memory for semantic or episodic information (e.g. new facts and when they received them) that lasts for more than half a minute. They often retain most of their memory for events up until the moment of brain damage and maintain their procedural memories (for skills and how to do things like speak and walk), and most are able to learn new procedural skills (e.g. table tennis).

If those with anterograde amnesia are given free-recall tests, they show good recency effects but extremely poor primacy effects (Baddeley and Warrington, 1970).

Free-recall experiments and the serial position curve

In free-recall experiments, subjects are given a number of words (for example 20) in succession to remember and are then asked to recall them in any order ('free recall'). The results reliably fall into a pattern known as the *serial position curve*. This curve consists of:

- a *primacy effect* – subjects tend to recall the first words of the list well
- an *asymptote* – the middle portion of the list, the items of which are remembered far less well than those at the beginning and the end
- a *recency effect* – subjects usually recall those items from the end of the list first, and tend to get more of these correct on average than all the earlier items. This effect persists even if the list is lengthened (Murdock, 1962).

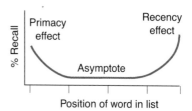

Slower rates of presentation can improve the primacy effect, but have little or no influence on the recency effect.

The recency effect disappears if the last words are not recalled straight away. Glanzer and Cunitz (1966) gave subjects an interference task immediately after the last word of the list and found a primacy but no recency effect.

Experiments using concurrent tasks

Concurrent tasks involve performing two different tasks at the same time and investigating whether one task interferes with the performance of the other.

For example, concurrent task experiments have found that the task of continually repeating a word interferes with the performance of another task that involves reading and checking a difficult text, but does not interfere with a task that involves sorting pictures.

Exercise 33

1 Identify which of the studies above support which of the models of memory opposite, and explain how they do so.

2 What multi-store model weaknesses are overcome by
  a the levels of processing approach?
  b the working memory model?

3 Which of the variations based on the Craik and Tulving (1975) experiment deal with the effect on memory of
  a distinctiveness?
  b personal relevance?
  c effort?
  d elaboration?

4 If I asked you to remember how many windows you have in your house, how would your working memory provide you with an answer (if you did not already know it)?

1 Identify which of the studies above support which of the models of memory opposite, and explain how they do so.

There are two main lines of evidence which support the *multi-store* model's assumptions about the way information flows through the system and the distinct existence of short-term and long-term memory stores – *free recall experiments* and studies of *brain-damaged patients*.

In free recall experiments, the *serial position curve* provides evidence as follows:

- The *primacy effect* – Subjects tend to recall the first words of the list well, which indicates that the first words entered short-term memory and had time to be rehearsed and passed on to long-term memory before the STM capacity was reached. The primacy effect, therefore, involves recall from long-term memory.

- The *asymptote* – The middle portion of the list, the items of which are remembered far less well than those at the beginning and the end. This is probably because the increasing number of items fills the limited capacity of the short-term memory store and these later items are unable to be properly rehearsed and transferred to LTM before they are displaced.

- The *recency effect* – Subjects usually recall those items from the end of the list first, and tend to get more of these correct on average than all the earlier items. This effect persists even if the list is lengthened (Murdock, 1962), and is thought to be due to recall from the short-term memory store – since the items at the end of the list were the last to enter STM and were not displaced by further items.

Further evidence for the primacy/recency effects comes from two other findings:

- Slower rates of presentation can improve the primacy effect, but have little or no influence on the recency effect, presumably because this allows more rehearsal time to transfer the first words into the LTM store.

- The recency effect disappears if the last words are not recalled straight away. Glanzer and Cunitz (1966) gave subjects an interference task immediately after the last word of the list and found a primacy but no recency effect. The interference task presumably displaces the words from the end of the list from the short-term memory store. The words from the beginning of the list were already in LTM so the primacy effect is unaffected.

Cases of *anterograde amnesia* such as H.M. (Milner et al., 1978) or Clive Wearing (reported in Blakemore, 1988) provide strong evidence for the distinction between STM and LTM. The brain damage to the hippocampus may mean that those suffering from it are incapable of transferring new information from STM to LTM. With this inability they are essentially trapped in a world of experience that only lasts as long as their short-term memory does.

Patients afflicted by anterograde amnesia often retain most of their long-term memory for events up until the moment of brain damage since the material was already stored in LTM. While they seem incapable of gaining new long-term declarative memory for semantic or episodic information, most maintain and are able to learn new procedural skills – which implies that the multi-store model neglects the type of information that is transferred from STM to LTM.

If those with anterograde amnesia are given free recall tests, they show good recency effects but extremely poor primacy effects. This may be because they are unable to transfer the words from the beginning of the list into their LTM but rely on their STM so much that it has a larger capacity for the last words on the list.

The Craik and Tulving (1975) experiment tested the effect of levels or depth of processing on memory by giving subjects words, e.g. 'table', with questions that required different levels of processing:

- Structural questions, like 'Is the word in capital letters?', by only considering the visual appearance of the word, encouraged a shallow level of processing.
- Phonetic questions, like 'Does it rhyme with "able"?', encouraged a little more processing in terms of sound comparisons.
- Semantic questions, like 'Does it fit in the sentence "the man sat at the ____"?', encouraged the deepest level of processing because consideration of meaning was required (involving a greater link with past knowledge).

As the levels of processing approach predicted, it was found that those words processed at the semantic level were recognised more often than those processed structurally or phonetically.

As mentioned there are problems with defining what is meant by 'deep processing' and why it is effective. The variation studies investigated the kind of factors which are involved in deep processing, namely elaboration, distinctiveness, effort and personal relevance (see answer 3 below).

The existence of separate component systems in *working memory* has been shown experimentally by using *concurrent tasks* (performing two tasks at the same time) – if one task interferes with the other then they are probably using the same component.

Thus if articulatory suppression (continually repeating a word) uses up the phonological loop, another task involving reading and checking a difficult text would be interfered with (it uses the same component), but a spatial task involving sorting pictures would not be interfered with (it uses the visuospatial sketchpad component).

2 What multi-store model weaknesses are overcome by

a the levels of processing approach?

The mere rehearsal of the multi-store model is too simple a process to account for the transfer of information from STM to LTM. The model ignores factors such as the effort and strategy subjects may use when learning (*elaborative* rehearsal leads to better recall than just maintenance rehearsal) and the model does not account for the *type* of information taken into memory (some items, e.g. distinctive ones, seem to flow into LTM far more readily than others). The multi-store model also does not explain why information changes in coding from one memory store to another.

All these criticisms are dealt with by the levels of processing approach (Craik and Lockhart, 1972).

b the working memory model?

The working memory model of Baddeley and Hitch (1974, 1990) challenged the unitary and passive view of the multi-store model's short-term memory store. Working memory is an *active* store that holds and manipulates information and consists of 3 separate components. It thus provides a more thorough explanation of function, storage and processing than the multi-store model's STM.

3 Which of the variations based on the Craik and Tulving (1975) experiment deal with the effect on memory of

a distinctiveness?

Eysenck and Eysenck (1980) found even words processed phonetically were better recalled if they were distinctive or unusual.

b personal relevance?

Rogers et al. (1977) found better recall for personally relevant questions (e.g. 'Describes you?') than general semantic ones (e.g. 'Means?').

c effort?

Tyler et al. (1979) found better recall for words presented as difficult anagrams requiring more effort (e.g. 'OCDTRO') than simple anagrams (e.g. 'DOCTRO').

d elaboration?

Craik and Tulving (1975) found complex semantic processing (e.g. 'The great bird swooped down and carried off the struggling __') produced better cued recall than simple semantic processing (e.g. 'She cooked the ___').

4 If I asked you to remember how many windows you have in your house, how would your working memory provide you with an answer (if you did not already know it)?

Unless you have counted them before and remember the total, it is quite likely that you would summon up a visual mental image of your house (no matter how vague) from your long-term memory using your visuospatial sketchpad. You could then 'walk round' in your mind looking at it with your 'inner eye' to count each window and keep the running total in your phonological loop. This would involve counting with your inner voice (articulatory control system) every time you spotted a window and repeating the tally before the 1.5 to 2 second memory trace of your inner ear (phonological store) faded away (e.g. '1…2…3….3….4….5….5…..6……6……6…..7 etc.').

Interestingly, if you paid attention to somebody speaking on the radio while completing this task you might lose the tally (the speech competes for the same component of working memory), even if you could picture what window you had reached (the image uses a different component).

MODELS OF MEMORY CROSSWORD

1 Memory researchers' favoured method of investigation (15)
2 The memory for skills or knowing how to do something (10)
3 The modality-free, controlling, attentional mechanism of the working memory model (7/9)
4 The kind of information held by the sketchpad of working memory (12)
5 The kind of study that produces the serial position curve (4/6)
6 The kind of tasks used to demonstrate that separate components exist in the working memory model (10)
7 The model that regards short-term and long-term memory as stores (5-5)
8 The effect of remembering the first words of a list well (7)
9 The kind of amnesia where new declarative memories are forgotten (11)
10 The level of processing where the meaning of material is considered (8)
11 Information is held in short-term memory and rehearsed _____ (12)
12 The complex processing of meaning (11)
13 A shallow level of processing (10)
14 Some memory experiments have been criticised as being this (10)
15 The loop that consists of the 'inner voice' and 'inner ear' (12)
16 The store that holds semantic memory (4-4)

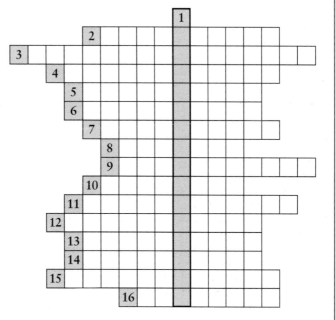

MEMORY MODEL ANAGRAMS

1 R O T E F F
2 C Y C R E E N C E T E F F
3 T I V E T I N D I S C N E S S
4 O N E T I P C H G O C E S S P R I N
5 C A L L O H O O P I N G O R E S T
6 R A T T R O Y I L U C A
  L O N C R O T M E S S Y T

Studies of forgetting

A *Peterson and Peterson* (1959) asked participants to remember a single nonsense syllable of three consonants (a trigram of letters such as FJT or KPD) and then gave them an interpolated task to stop them rehearsing the trigram (such as counting backwards in threes from one hundred).

While average recall of the trigram was very good after 3 seconds (80%), this average dropped dramatically to just 10% after 18 seconds.

B *Waugh and Norman* (1965) used the serial probe technique where 16 digits are rapidly presented to subjects who are then given one of those digits (the probe) and have to report the digit which followed it. It was found that the nearer the end of the 16-digit sequence the probe was presented, the better was the recall of the following digit.
e.g.
Order of Sequence presented
$3\ 7\ 2\ 9\ 0\ 4\ 5\ 6\ 3\ 1\ 9\ 0\ 7\ 8\ 2\ 6$
If probe = 8 then recall of digit (2) is good
If probe = 4 then recall of digit (5) is poor

C *Tulving and Pearlstone* (1966) asked subjects to memorise lists of words selected from different categories. When tested later, those participants given the category headings recalled more of the words than those who were not.

D *Smith* (1979) found more forgetting occurred a day later if subjects who had learnt 80 words in a distinctive basement room were then asked to recall them in a very differently furnished 5th floor room (12 words) compared to the original room (18 words).

Interestingly, almost as many words were recalled (17.2) by a third group who sat in the 5th floor room but were asked to remember as much as they could about the basement room before recall.

E *Godden and Baddeley* (1975) asked divers to learn word lists either on land or under water and found they recalled about 40% less in the opposite environmental context than in the same one. However this did not occur with a recognition test.

F *Bower* (1981) found that his subjects recalled more memories learnt when sad if he tested them when hypnotised to be in a sad mood than a happy one.

G *Underwood* (1957) found that the more nonsense syllable lists his students had previously learned, the greater their forgetting of new nonsense syllables was after a 24-hour delay. This was because the new nonsense syllables became increasingly confused with those from the old lists.

Wickens et al (1963) found subjects could be released from the negative influence of the old lists by changing the nature (and thus reducing the similarity) of the new items to be learned, e.g. from nonsense syllables to numbers.

H *McGeoch and Macdonald* (1931) presented participants who had learnt a list of words with various types of list to learn for ten minutes afterwards.

Recall of the original words was then tested and those students given a second list of words with similar meanings to the first list recalled on average far less (12.5%) than those given unrelated words (21.7%) or nonsense syllables (25.8%). Best recall (45%) was gained for subjects who were given no second list at all.

I *Baddeley and Hitch* (1977) found that rugby players' forgetting of the names of teams they had played depended more on the number of rugby matches played subsequently than on the passage of time.

J *Loftus and Burns* (1982) showed two groups a film of a bank robbery, but exposed one of the groups to a far more violent version which produced greater anxiety and where a young boy was shot in the face. The group that saw this violent version later showed far poorer recall of detail than the control group.

K *Levinger and Clark's* (1961) study found their subjects not only took longer to respond with free associations to emotional words (e.g. 'quarrel' and 'angry') compared to neutral words (e.g. 'cow' and 'tree') but also found their own associations to the emotional words harder to immediately recall.

L *Bartlett* (1932) asked people to reproduce stories and pictures either by remembering another person's reproduction or by testing the same person on a number of occasions. When testing English subjects with an unfamiliar North American folk story, 'The War of the Ghosts', Bartlett found their recall became shorter (indicating the gist of the story had been extracted) but also distorted by their culture (they omitted unfamiliar details and 'rationalised' the story to make it more coherent and familiar, e.g. recalling the ghosts in 'boats' not 'canoes').

M *Brewer and Treyens* (1981) tested memory for objects in an office that 30 participants had waited in individually for 35 seconds. Expected objects (e.g. a desk) that were in the room were recalled well but *unexpected* objects (e.g. a pair of pliers) were usually not. Some subjects *falsely* recalled *expected* objects that were not actually in the room (e.g. books and pens).

Theories of forgetting

Psychologists have proposed many theories of forgetting – when memory retrieval fails because received information has become unavailable (it no longer exists) or inaccessible (temporarily difficult to retrieve). Some of these theories involve forgetting from short-term memory (STM), others long-term memory (LTM), while some have been applied to both. Certain theories concern the effects of emotion on memory or the kind rather than amount of information lost or distorted.

Trace decay theory

Trace decay theory proposes that unless information in memory is regularly refreshed or used, e.g. thought about or accessed, it will spontaneously begin to *fade* or weaken over time. Memory traces are regarded as unstable with a limited life span.

Trace decay theory seems to focus on explaining STM forgetting in terms of its *limited duration*. Donald Hebb (1949) suggested that information in STM creates an active trace or *engram* in the brain in the form of a brief excitation of neurones (nerve cells) that, unless refreshed by rehearsal, will spontaneously fade away or decay after a few moments.

Others have applied trace decay to LTM, suggesting that the repeated experience of a unit of information will produce synaptic changes (physical changes where neurones connect to each other) that create a more lasting memory trace or engram. Repeatedly accessing the memory trace will strengthen it, while *disuse* will cause it to decay and be forgotten over time.

Displacement theory

Displacement theory focuses on explaining STM forgetting in terms of its *limited capacity*. Miller (1956) argued that STM capacity is approximately 7 +/– 2 items of information. Despite the fact that the capacity of these items can be increased by chunking, displacement theory suggests that there are only a fixed number of 'slots' for such information and that once they are full (capacity is reached) new information will push out or displace old material (which may be lost unless it was processed sufficiently to pass into LTM).

Cue-dependent retrieval failure

Information can be available to recall but temporarily inaccessible and so may require memory *cues* or *prompts* to access it. Much research has investigated the type of cues the presence or absence of which will determine retrieval failure.

Intrinsic cues are those meaningfully related to the material to be remembered and Tulving proposed the *encoding specificity principle* – items committed to memory are encoded with the precise semantic context present at the time of learning. If this meaningful context is missing when one wants to retrieve the information then forgetting is more likely to occur.

However, cues that are not directly semantically related to the information being memorised are also important. *Context-dependent forgetting* is caused by the absence of *external* environmental cues that were present at the time of learning, while *state-dependent forgetting* is caused by the absence of *internal* bodily cues experienced at the time of learning.

Interference theory

One explanation of LTM forgetting is that over time more and more material will be stored and become *confused* together. Interference is most likely to occur between *similar* material.

Some believe interference occurs when information is unlearned (Underwood, 1957) or over-written (Loftus, 1979) by other information. Tulving argues that interference of retrieval cues rather than the stored material is responsible.

Proactive interference is where material learnt first interferes with material learnt later. In *Retroactive interference* material learnt at a later time interferes with material learnt earlier.

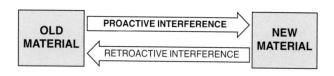

Repression

Repression is a concept from psychodynamic psychology and focuses on the role of emotion in forgetting. Freud proposed that forgetting is *motivated* by the desire to *avoid displeasure* and so embarrassing, unpleasant or anxiety-producing experiences are repressed – pushed down into the unconscious.

Repression is a protective defence mechanism that involves the ego actively blocking the conscious recall of memories, which become *inaccessible*. Direct recall attempts will either fail, lead to distorted recall or digression from the topic so psychoanalytic techniques such as dream interpretation and free association are necessary to access repressed memories.

Freud argued that repression was the most important of defence mechanisms and that it not only accounted for his patients' anxiety disorders (the result of repressing more traumatic experiences) but was a common cause of everyday forgetting.

Reconstructive memory

The pioneer of reconstructive memory research was Bartlett (1932) who argued that people do not passively record memories as exact copies of new information they receive, but *actively* try and make sense of it in terms of what they already know – a process he called 'effort after meaning'. Bartlett therefore proposed that information may be remembered in a distorted way since memories are essentially 'imaginative reconstructions' of the original information in the light of each individual's past experiences and expectations; rather than remembering what actually happened we may remember what we think should or could have occurred. Bartlett termed the mental structures that held past experiences and expectations, and could influence memory so much, *schemas*.

Information that does not quite fit our schemas, especially the minor details, may be ignored and forgotten or distorted so as to make better sense to us, while our expectations may actually cause us to guess or fill in forgotten details leading to *confabulation* (inventing memories). Schemas may thus produce inaccurate, stereotyped and prejudiced remembering.

Exercise 34

1 Use the theories above to explain the results of the studies of forgetting opposite.

2 Which of the theories of forgetting have been applied to
 a short-term memory forgetting?
 b long-term memory forgetting?
 c the role of emotion in forgetting?

3 What advantages and disadvantages are there of conducting memory experiments under controlled laboratory conditions (compare McGeoch and Macdonald's study with Baddeley and Hitch's one)?

4 Why is it difficult to study the pure degradation of a memory trace over time?

5 Do you think that information associated with negative emotions is always more likely to be forgotten?

6 Why might it be difficult to study repression forgetting?

7 Do you think that schemas only have a negative effect on memory?

8 Identify one practical application of forgetting theories.

Answers 34.1 – 34.8

1 Use the theories above to explain the results of the studies of forgetting opposite.

A Peterson and Peterson originally argued that the forgetting they found over their 3 to 18 second time delays occurred through *trace decay*. Ideally, however, no new information should be presented in the time between when the trace is acquired and when it is recalled to prevent confounding variables like displacement, yet Peterson and Peterson asked subjects to count backwards to stop them rehearsing. The increase of forgetting over time may, therefore, have been a result of the counting backwards task increasingly displacing the original trigrams.

B Waugh and Norman's (1965) serial probe technique results seem to support *displacement theory* since digits nearer the end of the sequence have fewer following digits to displace them. Thus if the order presented was: 3 7 2 9 0 4 5 6 3 1 9 0 7 8 2 6 and the probe was '8' then recall of the digit '2' was good because little displacement occurs, whereas if the probe was '4' then the recall of the digit '5' was poor due to greater displacement from the following digits.

C D E and F can all be explained through *cue-dependent retrieval failure*. In particular:

C Tulving and Pearlstone (1966) studied *intrinsic* cues since subjects given the category headings as retrieval cues (which were meaningfully related to the material to be remembered) recalled more of the words than those who were not.

D & E Godden and Baddeley (1975) and Smith (1979) studied *context-dependent forgetting* since the absence of *external* environmental cues that were present at the time of learning caused forgetting when recalling information in different surroundings.

F Bower (1981) studied *state-dependent forgetting* since the absence of *internal* bodily cues (mood) that were experienced at the time of learning caused more forgetting when recalling material in a different mood. Bower's study has not been reliably replicated by other researchers and true state-dependent memory involving mood has not always been found for emotionally neutral information. However, state-dependent effects have been found for alcohol (Goodwin et al., 1969) and other state-altering substances.

G H and I all involve *interference theory*. In particular:

G Underwood (1957) and Wickens et al (1963) studied *proactive interference* effects (the latter showing that reducing the similarity of material can release participants from the effect of proactive interference).

H & I McGeoch and Macdonald (1931) and Baddeley and Hitch (1977) studied *retroactive interference* (the former showing how the degree of similarity affects the degree of interference, the latter showing how interference may be a better explanation of forgetting over time than trace decay).

J and K could be interpreted in terms of repression.

J Freud would have explained Loftus and Burns's (1982) results in terms of anxiety-produced repression, but Loftus (1987) explained the forgetting with the *weapons focus* effect, whereby fearful or stressful aspects of a scene (e.g. the gun) channel attention towards the source of distress and away from other details. Alternatively, people may need to be in the same state (i.e. anxious) to recall properly – a *state dependent* explanation.

K Levinger and Clark's (1961) study seemed good support for repression, however other researchers found that after a longer delay the effect reversed and the emotional words were recalled better. Furthermore this occurred with associations to positive *and* negative emotional words, which supports the role of arousal rather than repression.

L and M illustrate the effects of reconstructive memory/schema theory on forgetting.

L Bartlett's (1932) study showed how the schemas of his English participants 'edited' the story, accounting for the forgetting and the distorted recall of details that they were not familiar with or thought were irrelevant.

M Brewer and Treyens (1981) showed how the expectations provided by an 'office schema' affected recall.

2 Which of the theories of forgetting have been applied to

a short-term memory forgetting?
Trace decay and displacement have most often been applied to short-term memory forgetting (although interference theory has too).

b long-term memory forgetting?
Trace decay, cue-dependent retrieval failure, interference theory, repression and reconstructive memory/schema theory.

c the role of emotion in forgetting?
Repression and state-dependent forgetting

3 What advantages and disadvantages are there of conducting memory experiments under controlled laboratory conditions (compare McGeoch and Macdonald's study with Baddeley and Hitch's one)?

The controlled laboratory conditions found in studies like McGeoch and Macdonald's (1931), allow very precise, reliable and replicable tests to be conducted. Much of the research lacks ecological validity, however, using isolated words or nonsense syllables often learned under artificially compressed laboratory conditions (rather than the more everyday distributed learning over time).

Some studies have been conducted with greater ecological validity, e.g. Baddeley and Hitch's (1977) study. In contrast to much cognitive research on memory, which focuses on quantitative tests of how many randomly selected digits, words or nonsense syllables can be remembered under strictly controlled conditions, the reconstructive memory approach has tended to concentrate more on *qualitative changes* in what is remembered, often of more *everyday material* such as stories, pictures or witnessed events under more *natural conditions*.

4 Why is it difficult to study the pure degradation of a memory trace over time?

Pure trace decay is very difficult to test without the confounding influence of other information entering memory to displace or interfere with what is there.

Reitman (1974) asked subjects to detect tones between presenting and recalling information, thinking this would hopefully prevent rehearsal without providing any new displacing material. Only about a quarter of information was forgotten after a 15-second delay, which was more likely to be due to spontaneous trace decay than the Petersons' result.

Baddeley and Scott (1971) concluded that 'something like trace decay occurs in the Peterson task, but is complete within five seconds, and is certainly not sufficiently large to explain the substantial forgetting that occurs in the standard paradigm' (quoted from Baddeley, 1997).

In some of the research it is unclear what the relative influences of displacement and trace decay are on STM forgetting. Researchers such as Shallice (1967) have found that presenting digits at faster speeds in serial probe tests increases the ability to recall the digits presented earlier in the sequence. Thus trace decay may be responsible for some of the STM forgetting, since the faster presentation means the digits nearer the beginning of the sequence have less time to decay before being tested.

It is also unclear how distinct the concepts of displacement and trace decay really are. For example, displacement in STM works on the assumption that it has a limited capacity, which is measured in terms of memory span (usually 7 +/− 2 items or chunks). However Baddeley et al. (1975) have shown that fewer words can be retained in STM if they take *longer* to pronounce. It seems STM capacity for words depends on the *duration* of pronunciation (how long it takes to say them) rather than the *number* of chunked items – in this case words.

Finally it is also unclear what is actually happening in trace decay and displacement to cause the forgetting. Is the trace really fading or, because it is so fragile, is it being degraded by other incoming information? Similarly with displacement, is the new material nudging aside, overwriting or distracting attention from the old material (or just making it harder to discriminate)? While *interference theory* has some of the same kinds of questions to answer, it has been more successful in explaining STM forgetting by showing how the *similarity* of competing information from the interpolated task used (as well as from previous trials) can affect the recall of the Petersons' trigrams (see interference theory).

5 Do you think that information associated with negative emotions is always more likely to be forgotten?

Not necessarily. Brown and Kulik (1977) suggested that people could remember some events in their lives in almost photographic detail – as if that instant had been imprinted upon their minds. They called this type of recall '*flashbulb memory*' and found it was most likely to occur when the event was not only surprising to the person but also had consequences for their own life.

Thus they found around 90% of people reported flashbulb memories associated with personal shocking events, but whether they had such memories for public shocking events like assassinations depended upon how personally relevant the event was for them – 75% of black participants in their research had a flashbulb memory for the assassination of black-rights activist Martin Luther King, compared to 33% of white participants.

Brown and Kulik (1977) argued that flashbulb memory was a *special* and *distinct* form of memory since

- the emotionally important event triggers a neural mechanism which causes it to be especially well imprinted into memory
- the memories were more detailed and accurate than most
- the structural form of the memory was very similar – people nearly always tended to recall where they were, what they were doing, who gave them the information, what they and others felt about it and what the immediate aftermath was, when they first knew of the event.

Neisser (1982), however, disagrees that flashbulb memories are distinct from other episodic memories, since

- the long-lasting nature of the memory is probably due to it being frequently rehearsed (thought about and discussed afterwards) rather than being due to any special neural activity at the time. Levels of processing theory, would explain meaningful and distinctive events lasting longer.
- the accuracy of such memories has often been shown to be no different from most other events, e.g. McCloskey et al.'s (1988) study of memory after the Challenger space shuttle explosion or Wright's (1993) of the Hillsborough football tragedy.
- the similar form of 'flashbulb memories' may just reflect the normal way people relate information about events to others.

Despite such criticisms, some research still supports the notion of flashbulb memory. Conway et al. (1994) argue that studies which use events that are really relevant to people's lives (e.g. their own on Margaret Thatcher's resignation) find more accurate flashbulb memories over time.

Cahill and McGaugh (1998) think that because it is adaptive to remember emotionally important events, animals have evolved arousing hormones that help response in the short term and aid storage of the event in the long term.

So are the effects of emotion positive or negative on memory? Research findings are mixed, but generally positive long-term effects on memory are found for slightly above average levels of arousal (perhaps supporting flashbulb memory), but negative effects for very high levels of arousal. Typical laboratory studies only produce lower arousal levels and have not provided much support for everyday repression, whereas profound amnesia, fugue states and even multiple personality might result from very traumatic or long-term negative emotional arousal, which cannot be generated in the laboratory (ethically or practically).

6 Why might it be difficult to study repression forgetting?

Experimental evidence is difficult to gather due to the ethical problems of probing for traumatic memories or creating them by exposing subjects to unpleasant, anxiety-provoking experiences. It is also difficult to tell to what extent the repressor chooses not to search their memory or is unable to.

Theoretically, forgetting more unpleasant than pleasant memories could just mean that people rehearse upsetting material less because they do not want to think, or talk to others, about it – emotion can affect memory without an ego.

Mild anxiety has been produced in the laboratory by giving false 'failure feedback', which does impair memory. However rather than causing repression, Holmes (1990) argues that it causes people to think about the failure which distracts attention away from the memory test (*interference theory*), since giving 'success feedback' also impairs recall.

7 Do you think that schemas only have a negative effect on memory?

Cohen points out five ways in which schemas may influence memory – by providing or aiding: selection and storage, abstraction, integration and interpretation, normalisation, and retrieval. These properties mean that there are both advantages and disadvantages of schemas for memory:

Advantages – schemas enable us to store the central meaning or gist of new information without necessarily remembering the precise details (abstraction, selection and storage), unless perhaps the details were particularly unusual. This saves memory resources. Schemas also help us understand new information more readily (integration and interpretation, normalisation) and fill in or guess missing aspects of it (retrieval). This makes the world more coherent and predictable. Bransford and Johnson (1972, 1973) showed how schemas help to encode and store difficult to understand or ambiguous information.

Disadvantages – information that does not quite fit our schemas, especially the minor details, may be ignored and forgotten (selection and storage) or distorted (normalisation) so as to make better sense to us, while the guesses/filling-in of memory by the default values or expectations of the schema (integration and interpretation, retrieval) may be completely wrong. This may cause inaccurate, stereotyped and prejudiced remembering.

Bartlett and other reconstructive memory researchers have been accused of over-emphasising the inaccuracy of memory and using unfamiliar material to support the reconstructive effect of schemas on memory. Even quite complex real life material can often be accurately recalled.

8 Identify one practical application of forgetting theories.

Theories of forgetting have been applied to many areas of eyewitness testimony, for example to help the police, juries and psychiatrists to assess the reliability of memory for past witnessed events.

35 The applications of memory research

Eyewitness testimony
Many studies have been conducted on the reliability and accuracy of the information retrieved from the memory of witnesses, which have strong implications for the legal system.

Witness expectations and eyewitness testimony
- Allport and Postman (1947) found that prejudice influenced the recall of whether a black or white person was holding a cut-throat razor in a picture.
- Harris (1978) found that over 60% of subjects would infer information not present in testimony based on their expectations, even when trained not to. For example, if given the testimony 'I ran up to the burglar alarm in the hall' many would later assert that it had been ringing.
- List (1986) found subjects who had watched videos of shoplifting incidents a week earlier recalled more of the actions which had a high probability of occurring during shoplifting than a low probability. They even falsely remembered high probability actions they had not witnessed on the video.

Eyewitnesses and face recognition
A Davis and Jenkins (1985) found the accuracy of face recognition is significantly reduced if subjects are shown composite photo-fit pictures of other faces beforehand. Gorenstein and Ellsworth (1980) found witnesses are more likely to identify (correctly or otherwise) a person from a line-up if they had appeared in mug shots the witnesses had searched beforehand.

B Shapiro and Penrod (1986) suggest matching witnessed faces to mug shots, photo-fits or line-ups may be difficult because mug-shots and photo-fits are only two-dimensional and without expressive movement, while line-ups involve different locations and clothing.

C Shapiro and Penrod (1986) found subjects asked to make judgements about a face rather than just look at it showed more accurate later recall. Research also shows that more distinctive faces are remembered better after long delays.

D Yarmey (1982, 1993) found people readily stereotype faces as 'good guys' and 'bad guys' and discovered that the elderly were more likely to misidentify innocents as criminals based on their stereotypes of what they thought a criminal looked like.

Post-event information and eyewitness testimony
Loftus has shown how information received after a witnessed event, especially in the form of leading questions (those that suggest a certain answer), can affect the memory of that event. Information can be

- *added to an account* – Loftus and Zanni (1975) showed subjects a film of a car accident, and got more subjects to incorrectly recall seeing a broken headlight by asking 'Did you see *the* broken headlight?' than by asking 'Did you see *a* broken headlight?'
- *distorted* – Loftus and Palmer (1974) received higher estimates of speed when asking 'How fast were the cars going when they *smashed* into each other?' than when the verb '*hit*' was used.
- *substituted* – Loftus et al. (1978) changed the recognition of a 'stop' sign to a 'yield' sign with misleading questions.

However, Yuille and Cutshall (1986) found the eyewitness testimony of a *real life* and quite traumatic event was very accurate and resistant to leading questions.

Can hypnosis recover accurate memories?
The word 'hypnotism' is derived from the Greek for sleep – 'hypnos', however there are distinct differences between the two phenomena. Hypnotised subjects give control over to the hypnotist and will respond to suggestions and obey instructions with little sign of inhibition, even if the request is unusual or seemingly impossible to do. Hypnotised subjects can apparently perform behaviours such as controlling severe pain, experiencing hallucinations and retrieving forgotten memories.

Clinical hypnosis and memory
Much debate has been generated over the accuracy of memories of childhood abuse, satanic abuse and even alien abduction retrieved using hypnosis during therapy that had not been remembered up until that point. Victims frequently find that these recovered memories help them make sense of disturbances in their behaviour, beliefs or emotions.

There may well be many genuine cases of hypnosis recovering forgotten memory, since child abuse is disturbingly common and amnesia for such traumatic events does occur – Herman and Schatzow (1987) found 28% of female incest victims reported severe childhood memory losses, especially the more violent the abuse. Hypnotic age regression is an established technique (it is item 7 on the Stanford Hypnotic Susceptibility Scale) and may work through reducing recall inhibitions, overcoming memory blocks through accessing a different level of consciousness or even aiding context recreation of the time.

Police hypnosis and memory
In contrast to the clinical use of hypnosis to recover memories the client did not know they had, forensic or investigative hypnosis is usually employed in criminal investigations to try and access forgotten information that victims or witnesses think they do, or might, possess. The information gained can be used as forensic evidence or for investigative purposes to create leads which can be corroborated. Far more objection is raised to the former use than the latter.

Police officials hope that the relaxed and focused state of hypnosis, as well as the more specific hypnotic techniques such as context recreation and the 'freeze-framing' of mental scenes to focus on detail, will greatly increase the amount and accuracy of previously inaccessible material recalled (a property termed hypermnesia).

Geiselman and Machlowitz (1987) reviewed 38 experimental studies on hypnosis; 21 found significantly more correct information recalled, 4 significantly less and 13 no difference. However, 8 experiments found an increase in errors while 10 showed no effect on error rate. Hypnosis was most effective in the studies using interactive interviews (not fixed questions), on more realistic material, after longer time delays.

Exercise 35
1 Which theory of forgetting is supported by the studies relating to witness expectations and eyewitness testimony?

2 Identify which of the studies described in eyewitnesses and face recognition (A, B, C, D) support the theories of levels of processing, cue-dependent forgetting, interference, and reconstructive memory.

3 What theories explain the effect of post-event information?

4 What criticism of most eyewitness testimony research does the Yuille and Cutshall (1986) study raise?

5 What theory explains the forgetting of recovered memories?

6 What theory explains the effectiveness of context recreation?

7 Which theories of forgetting suggest that we should be cautious about the evidence gained from hypnosis because it makes people more responsive to suggestion?

Answers 35.1 – 35.7

1 Which theory of forgetting is supported by the studies relating to witness expectations and eyewitness testimony?

Reconstructive memory, e.g. Bartlett's work on how schemas, expectations and stereotypes change memory, is supported by these studies. The prejudice, inferences and expectations of the participants distorted the recall of the information.

2 Identify which of the studies described in eyewitnesses and face recognition (A, B, C, D) support the theories of levels of processing, cue-dependent forgetting, interference, and reconstructive memory.

A Davis and Jenkins's (1985) study shows the accuracy of face recognition is significantly reduced by the *proactive interference effect* of the composite photo-fit pictures of other faces shown beforehand. Likewise, the mug-shots the witnesses had searched beforehand had a proactive interference effect on the identification of people in the line-up of Gorenstein and Ellsworth's (1980) study.

B Shapiro and Penrod's (1986) study supports *cue-dependent forgetting*. Matching witnessed faces to mug-shots, photo-fits or line-ups may be difficult because of the *different contexts* on witnessing and recall; mug-shots and photo-fits being two-dimensional and without expressive movement may provide *insufficient cues*, while line-ups involve different locations and clothing. This is why crime re-enactments may help by recreating context.

C Shapiro and Penrod's (1986) finding that greater depth of processing (making judgements about a face rather than just looking at it) leads to more accurate later recall supports the levels of processing approach, as does the research showing that more distinctive faces are remembered better after long delays.

D Yarmey's (1982, 1993) results on stereotyping leading to the misidentification of innocents as criminals supports reconstructive memory theory.

3 What theories explain the effect of post-event information?

Both *interference theory* and *reconstructive memory theory* have been applied to the effects of post-event information.

Information received after a witnessed event (especially in the form of leading questions) can have a retroactive interference effect on the memory of that event.

Loftus (1979) is convinced that post-event information replaces the original information – which cannot be recalled even if money is offered for accurate information. McCloskey and Zaragoza (1985) disagree – they showed that if subjects are given misleading information and are later offered a choice of the original or a neutral alternative, they tend to choose the original, indicating that the original material is not 'overwritten' or permanently distorted.

4 What criticism of most eyewitness testimony research does the Yuille and Cutshall (1986) study raise?

The Yuille and Cutshall (1986) finding that the eyewitness testimony of a *real life* and quite traumatic event was very accurate and resistant to leading questions indicates that much of the eyewitness testimony laboratory experimentation may be a little artificial. The effects found may depend on the kind of information witnessed, the realism and involvement of the viewing conditions and the influence of the experimental situation.

McCloskey and Zaragoza (1985), for example, suggest that subjects may just be following the *demand characteristic* expectations to recall the (misleading) information that was last given to them. However, warnings that incorrect post-event information has been given does not appear to stop incorrect information being recalled (Lindsay, 1990).

Loftus (1979) has shown that *obviously* incorrect post-event information has little or no effect on accurate recall. Interference is most likely to occur with minor details and if post-event information is given after a long time delay.

5 What theory explains the forgetting of recovered memories?

It is often assumed that recovered memories are due to the *repression* of traumatic events and that hypnotic regression was required to retrieve them.

6 What theory explains the effectiveness of context recreation?

The effectiveness of context recreation is explained by *cue-dependent memory* theory. Recreating the environmental conditions and state of mind experienced when information was witnessed adds more context and state-dependent cues to aid retrieval.

7 Which theories of forgetting suggest that we should be cautious about the evidence gained from hypnosis because it makes people more responsive to suggestion?

Many researchers think that hypnotically recovered memories should not be relied upon without objective corroborative evidence, especially given the sensitivity and implications of the claims relating to them, since hypnosis may lead to *false memory syndrome*. Therapists may give *leading suggestions* before or during hypnosis, which may distort original memories by acting as *retroactive interference* or encourage confabulation of fictitious memories by aiding *imaginative reconstruction*.

Support for this is that hypnosis increases the ability to imagine or hallucinate (hypnosis can produce experiences of future or even past existences), and very hypnotisable people may be even more imaginative and/or have a 'fantasy-prone personality' (Wilson and Barber, 1983).

Other reasons for suspicion are that certain therapists tend to retrieve certain types of recovered memory – some frequently find abuse, others alien abduction (a more recent culture-bound and less credible phenomena). Also, clients want to find causes for their problems and, being unaware of them, may readily believe they forgot others were to blame. Independent corroboration has refuted some recovered memories.

Gudjonsson (1992) agrees that the highly suggestible, compliant and imaginative state of hypnosis may lead witnesses of a crime to greater *confabulation* and vulnerability to *leading questions*, as well as overconfidence in the accuracy of their recall.

Putnam (1979) revealed that hypnotised subjects made more errors and were more likely to follow misleading information when answering questions on a videotape of an accident.

Sanders and Simmons (1983) discovered hypnotised subjects who had witnessed a pickpocket on video were less accurate in their interview answers (although just as confident) and identity parade identification (which they were more likely to be misled on) compared to non-hypnotised subjects.

Geiselman et al (1985) found American law enforcers using the cognitive interview technique (which involves context recreation and different recall perspectives) produced greater correct recall of a violent crime video (41.2 items) than a standard interview conducted under hypnosis (38 items).

36 Loftus & Palmer (1974) – 'Reconstruction of automobile destruction'

There is much support for the idea that most people, when they are witnesses to a complex event such as a traffic accident, are very inaccurate when reporting numerical details like time, distance and especially speed, even when they know that they will be questioned on them (e.g. Marshall, 1969). As a consequence, there can sometimes be large variations in estimates between witnesses and so it seems likely that such inaccurate testimony could easily be influenced by variables such as the phrasing of questions or 'leading' questions.

Loftus and Palmer, therefore, aimed to investigate the effect of leading questions on the accuracy of speed estimates in, and perceived consequences of, a car crash.

Experiment one
Forty-five students were tested in groups of different sizes in this laboratory experiment. Seven films of traffic accidents, ranging in duration from 5 to 30 seconds, were presented in a random order to each group.

After each film, the subjects had to give a general account of what they had just seen and then answer more specific questions about the accident. The critical question was, 'About how fast were the cars going when they hit each other?', since it was asked in five different ways. Nine subjects were given the sentence with the verb 'hit' in it, and then equal numbers of the remaining subjects were asked the same question but with the verb 'smashed', 'collided', 'bumped' or 'contacted' used instead of 'hit'. The estimated speed given by each participant in response to the question was recorded.

Results

Speed estimates for the verbs of experiment one		Significance of result
Verb	Mean speed estimate	Results were significant at the P< .005 level according to analysis of variance of the data.
Smashed	40.8	
Collided	39.3	
Bumped	38.1	
Hit	34.0	
Contacted	31.8	

Accuracy of subjects' speed estimates		
In 4 of the 7 films the speed of the cars was known.		
	Actual speed of collision	Mean speed estimate
Film 1	20 mph	37.7 mph
Film 2	30 mph	36.2 mph
Film 3	40 mph	39.7 mph
Film 4	40 mph	36.1 mph

Discussion
The results indicate that not only are people poor judges of speed, but they are systematically and significantly affected by the wording of a question.

However, this finding could be attributed to either response-bias (the subject remembers accurately but is pressured by the word to increase or decrease the estimate) or a genuine change in the subject's memory of the event (the word makes the subject recall the event as worse than it was). If the latter explanation is true, then the subject might be led into recalling details that did not occur. The second experiment was designed to determine which explanation of different speed estimates was correct.

Experiment two
This laboratory experiment tested 150 students.

A film lasting just less than a minute and featuring four seconds of a multiple traffic accident was presented to each group.

After the film, the subjects had to give a general account of what they had just seen and then answer more specific questions about the accident. The critical question concerned the speed of the cars. 50 subjects were asked 'About how fast were the cars going when they hit each other?', another 50 were asked 'About how fast were the cars going when they smashed into each other?' and the final 50 acted as a control group who were not asked the question at all.

One week later, without seeing the film again, all participants answered ten questions, one of which was a critical one randomly positioned in amongst the ten questions, asking 'Did you see any broken glass? Yes or no?'

Although there was no broken glass, it was expected that some might be seen if the leading question of a week ago had changed the memory of the event to seem worse than it was.

Results

Verb	mean speed estimate	Response	Smashed	Hit	Control
Smashed	10.46 mph	Saw broken glass	16	7	6
Hit	8.00 mph	Did not see broken glass	34	43	44

Probability of seeing broken glass with speed estimate				
Verb	1–5 mph	6–10 mph	11–15 mph	16–20 mph
Smashed	.09	.27	.41	.62
Hit	.06	.09	.25	.50

Discussion
The authors conclude that the results show that the verb 'smashed' not only increases the estimates of speed but also the likelihood of remembering broken glass that was not present. This indicates that information from the original memory is merged with information after the fact, producing one distorted memory. This shift in memory representations in line with verbal cues has received support from other research.

Exercise 36
1 What were the independent and dependent variables in each of the experiments?
2 What design was used to allocate participants to conditions, and why?
3 What is the methodological term for the response-bias (where the participant remembers accurately but is pressured by the word to increase or decrease the estimate) that might have occurred in experiment one?
4 What might the strengths and weaknesses be in this study of using the laboratory experiment?

1 What were the independent and dependent variables in each of the experiments?

In experiment one, the critical question 'About how fast were the cars going when they hit each other?' acted as the independent variable, since it was manipulated in five conditions. Nine subjects heard the sentence with the verb 'hit' in it, and then equal numbers of the remaining subjects were asked the same question but with the verb 'smashed', 'collided', 'bumped' or 'contacted' used instead of 'hit'. The estimated speed was the dependent variable.

In experiment two, the critical question concerning the speed of the cars was the independent variable. It was manipulated by asking 50 subjects 'About how fast were the cars going when they hit each other?', another 50 'About how fast were the cars going when they smashed into each other?' and the final 50 acted as a control group who were not asked the question at all.

One week later, the dependent variable was measured – the answer to the critical question 'Did you see any broken glass? Yes or no?' (randomly positioned amongst ten other questions).

2 What design was used to allocate participants to conditions, and why?

An independent measures (unrelated) design was used in both experiments to prevent the order effects that would have resulted from repeatedly asking the same question (with a slight change of phrasing) to the same participants; the answers of the first conditions may have affected the answers of the later conditions. Boredom or fatigue might also have affected the results of the later conditions and the participants would have been more likely to guess the aim of the study and therefore react differently.

3 What is the methodological term for the response-bias (where the participant remembers accurately but is pressured by the word to increase or decrease the estimate) that might have occurred in experiment one?

Demand characteristics (participants feel they should respond in certain ways suggested by the experiment).

4 What might the strengths and weaknesses be of using the laboratory experiment in this study?

The study was well operationalised and controlled and the experiment allows cause and effect (that leading questions can affect the recall of witnessed information) to be inferred with greater confidence. The results may be a little artificial, however, since the study lacks the ecological validity of having real, involved, witnesses experiencing the information.

LOFTUS AND PALMER CROSSWORD

1 A change of answer due to pressure of expectation rather than inaccurate memory (8/4)
2 The type of experiment used in the study (10)
3 The variable operationalised through using different verbs (11)
4 The number of traffic accident films seen in experiment one (5)
5 Estimations of this were recorded (5)
6 The authors argue that information from the original memory is merged with information after the fact to produce one _____ memory (9)
7 The group not asked the critical question in experiment two (7)
8 The type of participants tested in the study (8)
9 The time delay before subjects were asked the critical question in experiment two (3/4)
10 The critical question in experiment two asked 'Did you see any _____ glass? Yes or no?' (6)
11 The kind of question that adds post-event information by suggesting an answer (7)
12 The verb that produced the lowest estimate in experiment one (9)
13 The verb that produced the highest estimate in experiment one (7)

FORGETTING AND APPLICATIONS CROSSWORD

1 An applied area of memory research (10/9)
2 Where some information confuses or disrupts other information in memory (12)
3 Limitation of this to 7 plus or minus 2 items results in forgetting in short-term memory (8)
4 The theory that explains the short-term memory forgetting in question three (12)
5 Items of information that are commonly used in studies of forgetting (5)
6 The kind of questions that suggest a certain answer (7)
7 The memory theory that suggests that effort after meaning causes certain information to be forgotten (14)
8 Remembering information by familiarity on sensing it, even if it could not be recalled (11)
9 A psychodynamic defence mechanism thought to cause forgetting (10)
10 Information that is temporarily difficult to retrieve, although available in memory (12)
11 Memories that are remembered in particular detail (9)
12 Forgetting caused by an absence of external environmental cues present at the time of learning (7/9)
13 The type of information received after witnessing something, which may distort recall (4-5)
14 A cognitive structure that may cause information that does not fit it to be forgotten (6)
15 A famous researcher of witness forgetting (6)
16 The kind of probe test used to investigate short-term memory forgetting (6)
17 The neural representation of a memory trace (6)
18 The kind of interference where material learnt later affects material learnt earlier (11)
19 The kind of information or experience that is more likely to be forgotten according to Freud (10)
20 The fading of the memory trace with time (5)

FORGETTING AND APPLICATIONS ANAGRAMS

1 N O S H I P Y S
2 L E R T B A T T
3 E A G E R O R G E S S I N
4 B U L F A C O N A T I O N
5 C O R E D V E E R M Y R O M E
6 I N E N C G O D
   C I T Y I F I S P E C
7 S P O W E A N C U F O S
   C E T E F F
8 T R E E S P O N D A N
   P E S T O N E R
9 O P R A V E C T I
   R E F E R I N T E N C E
10 A T E S T - P E T E N D E N D
   T E T F O R G I N G

37

The social psychological approach to psychology

Researchers can be said to adopt a social psychological approach when they

- focus their research on *social behaviour* (between individuals and groups) such as attraction and aggression.
- tend to regard other people and social contexts as just as, if not more, important as *influences* upon people as their dispositions and personality characteristics.

Social psychology can be defined as 'the scientific investigation of how the thoughts, feelings and behaviours of individuals are influenced by the actual, imagined or implied presence of others' G. Allport (1935). Social psychologists study how other people and the social environment influence us (social influence) and how we process social information (social cognition).

Assumptions

The influence of other people – individuals and groups
Social psychologists assume that individuals (e.g. leadership and obedience) and groups (e.g. conformity and crowding) have social power to influence others. Social power refers to the influence a person has to change another's thoughts, feelings or behaviour. There are many different sources of power, ways in which it can work and effects it can have on those who have it or yield to it.

Raven and others have identified six different (although they can operate simultaneously) sources or *bases of power*:

- *Reward power* – this influence is based on the ability to provide what others *want* or to remove what they do not want. Many people possess this source of power but offer different types of reward (e.g. love, money, and approval). This power only works as long as the rewards can be given and are wanted.
- *Coercive power* – this involves the ability to *punish*, by inflicting some form of negative stimulus (e.g. disapproval, ridicule, pain) or by removing pleasant stimuli (e.g. affection, wages). This power base requires constant supervision since it produces negative feelings and attitudes in its victims, who only tend to comply with demands rather than really accepting them.
- *Referent power* – this is the influence a person has because they are *respected* or admired. The target wishes to identify with (be like) the influencer and is more likely to follow their wishes. Role models and idols have this power, but only maintain it as long as they are liked or respected.
- *Legitimate power* – this is where the target accepts the *norms* (probably internalised) that the influencer should have (has the right to) influence over them. The legitimacy of the power depends on the situation – we accept that a referee can tell us what to do in a football match, but not outside of that situation.
- *Expert power* – the power an influencer has because the target believes they possess *superior knowledge* in a desired area. We are thus at the mercy of doctor's advice in health matters, and the garage mechanic's when our cars need servicing.
- *Informational power* – one person or a group of people, expert or otherwise, can have power if they provide socially accepted *information*. This ties in with the social reality hypothesis and Festinger's social comparison theory (we look to others to know how to react in certain situations).

According to social impact theory (Latane, 1981), the strength of influence felt by a target is determined by three factors:

- The strength or importance of the influencer (e.g. how many and strong are their power bases).
- The number of influencers.
- The immediacy (or closeness) of the influencer/s.

Increases in each of these factors will cause the power of influence to increase. For example, you are more likely to be influenced by several very important people standing in front of you, than by one unimportant person talking over the telephone.

Social impact theory
The strength of influence or impact will increase when:

1 the strength of the influencer increases

2 the number of influencers increases

3 the immediacy of the influencer increases

Influencer/s   Target

The influence of society and culture
Social psychologists also assume that the society and culture (e.g. social roles and norms, history, politics and language) people have created strongly influences us even in the absence of other people.

Social roles are like parts in a play which we assume in different social situations, and are often complementary (e.g. father – son, teacher – student, shopkeeper – customer). Every role has norms (socially accepted ways of behaving) so social interaction is made regular and predictable. At first we may feel uncomfortable with new roles, but we soon internalise and adopt them, often without realising that we are doing so, in the appropriate situation. Importantly, role and norm theory implies an inconsistent personality across situations but not within them. Haney, Banks and Zimbardo's (1973) prison simulation experiment showed how the roles of prison guard and prisoner could be internalised to a surprising degree.

Social constructionism has taken the social psychological approach one step further by suggesting our society, culture and language affect the very way we perceive reality and are able to understand the world, even the way we define psychological concepts and the process of scientific investigation itself – making unbiased study difficult if not impossible.

Methods
Field experimentation
Field experiments are an extremely appropriate way of studying social psychological phenomena, e.g. Piliavin and others changed the type of victim requiring help in the everyday environment of a subway. Being a very scientific approach, however, many social psychological experiments have been conducted in the laboratory first and only later tested in more everyday field conditions.

Surveys
Surveys are another useful methodological tool for studying social phenomena, e.g. questionnaires have been used on many people to measure the frequency and reasons for prejudiced attitudes.

Exercise 37

1 Think of the people in your life who have the most influence over you and identify their sources or bases of social power.

2 According to social impact theory, what three factors will *reduce* or weaken the impact of social influence?

3 Do you think there is no truth but social truth?

4 What are the advantages and disadvantages of the field experiment and survey methods for social psychologists?

---

1 Think of the people in your life who have the most influence over you and identify their sources or bases of social power.

Parents/family – especially in early life these people are often the principle providers of reward power (e.g. love, money, approval), coercive power (punishing negative stimuli, e.g. shouting disapproval, or the removal of positive stimuli, e.g. pocket money), and expert/information power (and we believe what they say!). Parents also, of course, have legitimate power and, when they instil respect, referent power.

Friends – peer groups gradually gain in power bases over the course of childhood. Friends possess reward power (e.g. pleasant interactions and approval) and coercive power (e.g. ridicule and disapproval). Wanting to join certain desirable groups may provide others with referent power, while these same groups often have expert/informational power through providing certain kinds of desired knowledge.

Teachers – may sometimes possess referent power, but certainly have legitimate power in school contexts, certain kinds of reward and coercive power (good marks and praise or criticism and detention) and expert power (*if* the students want the knowledge!).

Employers – as well as legitimate power, employers possess, because of our need for them, important sources of reward (e.g. money and respect) and coercive (e.g. dismissal) power.

2 According to social impact theory, what three factors will reduce or weaken the impact of social influence?

According to social impact theory, the impact of influence will decrease or weaken when
- the strength or importance of the influencer is less than the target
- the number of targets increases (a diffusion of impact occurs)
- the remoteness of the target increases.

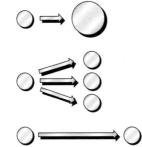

3 Do you think there is no truth but social truth?

A bit philosophical this one! Some social constructionists have argued that, because our perception of the world is so dependent upon our cultural upbringing, language, schemas, stereotypes, viewpoint, etc., our notion of 'reality' is hopelessly biased. Different cultures may, therefore, mean that there are different, and perhaps equally valid, ways of perceiving reality. This differs from the standard scientific view that there is one true reality that we can objectively investigate if we caste aside our subjective biases.

While there probably are aspects of being human that only allow us to see the world in certain ways, and so mean there may be some things that exist in the world that we may never be able to know, the extent of social and cultural influences upon our perception of reality can be investigated to a certain extent by cross-cultural study.

4 What are the advantages and disadvantages of the field experiment and survey methods for social psychologists?

Field experiments are an appropriate way of studying social psychological phenomena because they test them in more everyday conditions, which gives the studies greater ecological validity. Social situations can be very complex, which real-life conditions can reflect better than artificial laboratory environments.

Unfortunately, the greater complexity of the environment in field conditions means that it is harder to determine the influence of extraneous variables upon the dependent variable in the experiment.

Surveys in the form of questionnaires are another useful methodological tool for studying social phenomena because they allow data from many people to be considered, increasing the size and variability of the sample, and thus the ability to generalise the results. Survey methods also provide insight into people's social and cultural perceptions and views that other methods can only infer.

On the negative side, however, self-report data may be unreliable for a number of reasons, e.g. people may lack the correct insight, be unable to articulate their view clearly or may lie.

SOCIAL PSYCHOLOGICAL APPROACH ANAGRAMS

1 S L O E R

2 M O R N S

3 V E R Y U S

4 T U C R U E L

5 R E D W A R   W R O P E

6 L I F E D   M I N T R E X P E E

7 T I T L E I M A G E   W O E R P

8 I S L O C A   P I T M A C   T R Y H O E

9 L O A S C I   R U M S C O T T O N I S C I N

10 A L S O C I   C A R O O N P I M S   T O Y H E R

38

Haney, Banks & Zimbardo (1973) – 'A study of prisoners and guards in a simulated prison'

The authors of this study argue that the violence and dehumanisation produced by the prison system, as well as its failure to rehabilitate offenders, induce a respect for authority and deter future crime, is often attributed to the dispositional hypothesis. This hypothesis suggests that these negative features are a result of the 'nature' of those who run or populate prisons. Supporters of the prison system blame the deficient personality characteristics of the prisoners, while critics blame the deficient personalities of the guards.

The dispositional hypothesis, however, ignores the situational influences of the environmental conditions, social roles and norms, and procedures found in the prison system which create the feelings of power and powerlessness, control and oppression, machismo and emasculation, etc. Since it is difficult to separate out the relative influences of disposition and situation in pre-existing prisons, the researchers decided to create a mock prison with enough *functional equivalents* in terms of its structure and running to give it sufficient *mundane realism*, and populate it with 'normal-average' people to see what effects it would have on their behaviour.

The aim of the study was, therefore, to demonstrate the situational rather than the dispositional causes of negative behaviour and thought patterns found in prison settings by conducting a prison simulation with 'normal' subjects playing the roles of guard and prisoner.

Method
Twenty-two male subjects were selected (through personality assessment) from an initial pool of 75 volunteers, based on their stability, maturity and lack of involvement in anti-social behaviour. They were mostly Caucasian, middle class, college students, who were strangers to each other and were randomly allocated to either prisoner or guard roles. Prisoners signed a consent document which specified that some of their human rights would be suspended and all subjects were to receive $15 a day for up to 2 weeks.

The 'prison' was a basement corridor in Stanford University psychology department, converted into a set of 6 x 9 foot prison cells with a solitary confinement room (a tiny unlit closet), a 'yard' room and an observation screen (through which covert video and audiotape data recording could take place).

To facilitate role identification, guards were given uniforms of khaki shirts and trousers, batons and reflecting sunglasses. The prisoners wore loose fitting smocks with identification numbers, no underwear, a lock and chain around one ankle and a nylon stocking cap to cover their hair.

The procedure, as with the apparatus, was designed to establish 'functional equivalents' for the experience of prison life.

Prisoners were arrested by real police outside their houses by surprise, taken to a real police station for finger-printing and processing, and were then driven blindfolded to the mock prison (where they were stripped naked, deloused and dressed in a prisoner's uniform). Prisoners remained in the 'prison' 24 hours a day and followed a schedule of work assignments, rest periods and meal/toilet visits.

Guards worked only 8 hour shifts and were given no specific instructions apart from to 'maintain a reasonable degree of order within the prison necessary for its effective functioning' and a prohibition against the use of physical violence.

Results
The effects of imprisonment were assessed by video and audio tape observation of behaviour and dialogue, self-report questionnaires and interviews. The experiment had to be terminated after 6 days instead of the intended 14 because of the pathological (abnormal) reactions shown by both prisoners and guards.

Effects on prisoners – subjects showed what was termed the 'pathological prisoner syndrome' – disbelief was followed by rebellion which, after failure, was followed by a range of negative emotions and behaviours. All prisoners showed passivity (some becoming excessively obedient) and dependence (initiating very little activity without instruction). Half the prisoners showed signs of depression, crying, fits of rage and acute anxiety, and had to be released early (one developed a psychosomatic rash). All but two of those who remained said they would forfeit the money if they could be released early.

The experimenters proposed that these reactions were caused by a loss of personal identity, emasculation, dependency and learned helplessness brought about by the arbitrary and unpredictable control, norms and structures of the prison system.

Effects on guards – subjects showed what was termed the 'pathology of power' – huge enjoyment of the power at their disposal (some worked extra time for no pay and were disappointed when the study was over) led to guards abusing it and dehumanising the prisoners. All prisoners' rights were redefined as privileges (going to the toilet, eating and wearing eye-glasses became rewards) and punishment with little or no justification was applied with verbal insults. Although not all guards initiated aggressive action, none contradicted its use in others.

The experimenters proposed that these reactions were caused by a sense of empowerment legitimised by the role of 'guard' in the prison system. The use of power was described as self-aggrandising and self-perpetuating.

The authors of the study, while realising that there were important differences between their simulation and real prisons, suggest that the reality of the simulation was sufficient to enable the participants to go beyond the surface demands of role playing to the deep structure of the psychology of imprisonment. They point out that most of the functional equivalents of the prison system were implemented and the subjects' excessive reactions and behaviour when they thought they were not being observed went beyond the demands of the role-play. Prisoners called each other by their ID numbers and spent 90% of the time talking about prison-related matters in their private conversations. The guards showed aggression even when they thought they were not being observed.

Exercise 38
1 What were the two conditions of the independent variable in this experiment?
2 What was the dependent variable and what kind of data was recorded?
3 In what ways was the prison simulation different from real prisons?
4 What power bases did the guards operate from?
5 How ethical was this study?

1 What were the two conditions of the independent variable in this experiment?

The two conditions were guard and prisoner roles, operationalised by the different titles, uniforms, instructions and procedures adopted by each group (who were selected to be psychologically 'normal' and were allocated randomly to each condition to ensure that the differences between each group were not dispositional).

2 What was the dependent variable and what kind of data was recorded?

The dependent variable was the personal and interpersonal behaviour, thoughts and emotions of the guards and prisoners, recorded by video and audio tape observation of behaviour and dialogue, self-report questionnaires, and interviews. The data reported was mostly qualitative rather than quantitative.

3 In what ways was the prison simulation different from real prisons?

Although the uniforms, procedures and environment simulated some of the functional equivalents of the prison system, the authors of the study identify the main differences between their simulation and real prisons as being the lack of physical violence and the limited duration of the imprisonment. They also suggest that demand characteristics may have encouraged the participants to behave as expected, which is why their 'private' conversations and 'unobserved' behaviour were regarded as so important.

4 What power bases did the guards operate from?

The guards possessed legitimate power (it was their place and duty to influence others), reward power (the provision of privileges) and coercive power (insults and withdrawal of privileges).

5 How ethical was this study?

The study raises the ethical issues of consent, the right to withdraw from a study and prevention of harm to participants.

The subjects had signed an informed consent document specifying there would be a loss of some civil rights, although one might argue that they were not, and could not be, completely informed about what they were letting themselves in for. They were unaware that they would be arrested in public, since this was arranged at the last minute, which was a breach of consent. They were also unaware of exactly how traumatic their induction procedure and imprisonment would be, although the degree of distress caused was unexpected (the study had been ethically approved beforehand).

The imprisonment, by definition, prevented withdrawal, however the study was stopped after just six days instead of the two weeks because of the extreme reactions shown by the participants. Debriefing and assessment of the subjects took place weeks, months and years afterwards to ensure no lasting harm occurred to the participants.

HANEY, BANKS & ZIMBARDO CROSSWORD

1 The kind of influences the authors believe are responsible for the negative effects of the prison system (11)
2 The role which produced passivity and anguish (8)
3 The hypothesis that blames the failure of prisons on the type of people who inhabit or run them (13)
4 The equivalents the prison simulation aimed to provide (10)
5 The number of days the study was intended to last (8)
6 The role which produced empowerment and abuse of power (5)
7 The data collected was mostly this (11)
8 The number of days the study actually lasted (3)
9 The way participants were assigned to roles (8)
10 The kind of document the participants signed before the study (7)
11 The university where the prison simulation took place (8)
12 The kind of prisoner syndrome shown (12)

HANEY, BANKS & ZIMBARDO ANAGRAMS

1 F U M I N O R
2 S T E A M A U N C L I O
3 H U E I S D A M N A T I O N
4 U N D E M A N   S I R M E A L
5 B Y A R R I T A R   C O O L N T R

39

Piliavin, Rodin & Piliavin (1969) – 'Good Samaritanism: an underground phenomenon?'

Social psychologists were prompted into investigating helping behaviour by the case of Kitty Genovese (a woman stabbed to death over a period of 30 minutes in front of 38 unresponsive witnesses). Most studies were conducted under strict laboratory conditions, using non-visual emergency situations, and often found, for example, that

- bystanders would sometimes derogate rather than feel compassion for the victim's misfortune
- the more bystanders there were, the less help was given
- witnessing help being given increases the likelihood of others helping.

The main theories of helping behaviour developed to explain these findings involved diffusion of responsibility and the economic analysis of the costs and rewards involved in the situation requiring help. The former suggests that each extra witness feels less individually responsible for helping (thinking there are more other people who could do it). The latter proposes that the level of help depends upon an assessment of the relative level of costs and rewards for helping versus not helping in a situation.

Piliavin et al.'s study aimed to investigate, under real-life conditions and in an immediate, visually observed situation requiring helping, the effect on speed and frequency of helping and race of helper as a result of:

1 the type of victim (drunk or ill)
2 the race of the victim (black or white)
3 the presence of helping models (present or absent)
4 the size of the witnessing group.

Method

The study was conducted on New York subway travellers between 11am and 3pm, approximately 45% of whom were black, 55% white. The procedure was employed during a non-stop 7.5-minute journey in a subway carriage with a mean of 8.5 bystanders in the 'critical area'.

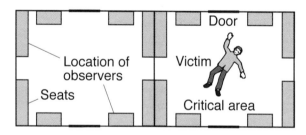

Diagram of subway carriage

Four teams of four researchers were involved, two of each team were female who recorded the reactions of the bystanders, two were male – one of whom acted as a victim, one as a model.

Of the victims, three were white and one was black, and all were aged between 26 and 35. They dressed and acted identically and were instructed to collapse after 70 seconds and remain on the floor until helped. The model was instructed to help 70 seconds after the collapse until the end of the journey if no other help was given. 103 trials were conducted in total, of which:

- 38 involved a drunk victim (the model smelt of alcohol and carried a bottle in a paper bag to encourage this perception).
- 65 involved a sober victim carrying a cane (to give the appearance of being ill).

The female observers of each team recorded the reactions of the bystanders, in particular the

- frequency of help given
- speed of help given
- race of the helper
- sex of the helper
- movement out of the area
- verbal comments

Results

1 The frequency of help in general was impressive – overall 93% helped spontaneously (before the model), 60% of which involved more than one helper. Help was so spontaneous that the model's effect could not be properly studied.
2 No diffusion of responsibility was found with group size.
3 A victim who appeared ill was more likely to receive help than one who appeared drunk. There was 100% help for the cane victim (of which 65 out of 68 trials involved spontaneous help) but 81% help for the drunk victim (of which 19 out of 38 trials involved spontaneous help). Help was also offered more quickly for the cane victim (a median of 5 seconds compared to a 109-second delay with the drunk victim).
4 There was a tendency for same-race helping to be more frequent, especially in the drunk condition.
5 Men were significantly more likely to help the victim than women.
6 The longer the emergency continued without help being given
   a the less impact the model had on the other bystanders
   b the more likely bystanders were to leave the area and/or discuss their behaviour.

Discussion of findings

The authors present a model of response to emergency situations as a possible heuristic device to explain the findings.

They suggested that a *state of emotional arousal*

- is created in a bystander when observing any emergency (and can be interpreted as fear, disgust or sympathy in different situations)
- is *higher* the
   i) more one can empathise with the victim
   ii) closer one is to the emergency
   iii) longer the emergency continues without help.
- can be *reduced* by
   i) helping directly
   ii) going to get help
   iii) leaving the scene
   iv) rejecting the victim as undeserving of help.

The response chosen depends on a *cost–reward matrix* that includes considering the

- *costs* associated with helping (e.g. effort, embarrassment, possible distasteful experiences, possible physical harm, etc.)
- *costs* associated with not helping (mainly self-blame and perceived criticism from others)
- *rewards* associated with helping (mainly self-praise and praise from victim and others)
- *rewards* associated with not helping (mainly those stemming from continuing with other activities).

Piliavin et al. point out that, according to this model, the main source of motivation is selfish (to reduce the unpleasant state of arousal) rather than altruistic (to unselfishly and positively desire to help another).

Exercise 39

1 What method was used to conduct this study and what are the advantages and disadvantages of using it?
2 What were the independent and dependent variables in the study?
3 How similar were the findings of this study compared to the previous ones mentioned?
4 By using the authors' model of response to emergency situations, try to explain the main findings of this study.
5 How ethical was this study?

1 What method was used to conduct this study and what are the advantages and disadvantages of using it?

A field experiment was used. This method has high ecological validity since it takes place under naturally occurring conditions and the participants (in this study) were unaware of being tested and so behaved normally.

Unfortunately, conditions are under less-strict control in field experiments than laboratory experiments, meaning it is difficult to rule out the influence of extraneous variables and replicate the study exactly. Insufficient trials were conducted in some conditions of the experiment to yield reliable data, e.g. fewer drunk victims and only 8 black cane carriers.

2 What were the independent and dependent variables in the study?

The four independent variables were
- type of victim (drunk or ill)
- race of victim (black or white)
- presence of helping models (present or absent)
- size of the witnessing group.

The dependent variables recorded were
- frequency of help
- speed of help
- race of helper
- sex of helper
- movement out of the area
- verbal comments

3 How similar were the findings of this study compared to the previous ones mentioned?

The previous studies mentioned were conducted under strict laboratory conditions, using non-visual emergency situations, and found, for example, that
- bystanders would sometimes derogate rather than feel compassion for the victim's misfortune
- the more bystanders there were, the less help was given
- witnessing help being given increases the likelihood of others helping.

By comparison, in the Piliavin et al. study, conducted under real-life field conditions, using a visible emergency situation
- bystanders discussed the situation (particularly when nobody helped until after 70 seconds), perhaps hoping to confirm that inaction was appropriate, but did not derogate the victim

- no diffusion of responsibility was found with group size
- the effect of a model could not be properly tested because of the degree of spontaneous help offered, but did seem to encourage help more if the model helped after 70 seconds rather than 150 seconds.

4 By using the authors' model of response to emergency situations, try to explain the main findings of this study.

- The frequency of help in general was impressive, perhaps because of the increase in arousal due to the visual and close nature of the emergency, which was difficult to escape.
- No diffusion of responsibility was found with group size, perhaps because from the visual nature of the emergency it was apparent whether anybody else was offering help and in some conditions the cost–reward matrix favoured helping.
- A victim who appeared ill was more likely to receive help than one who appeared drunk because the costs of helping the drunk are higher (greater disgust) and the costs for not helping are lower (less self-blame because he is partly responsible for his condition).
- There was a tendency for same-race helping to be more frequent, especially in the drunk condition, perhaps due to fewer costs involved in same-race helping (in terms of public censure) and more witness arousal due to greater empathy with victim.
- Men were significantly more likely to help the victim than women, probably due to the greater costs of helping (more effort) and the lower costs of not helping (less public criticism since it is not the 'woman's role')
- The longer the emergency continued without help being given; the less impact the model had on the other bystanders, the more likely bystanders were to leave the area, and the more likely it was that observers would discuss their behaviour. This may be because the arousal was not being reduced by helping directly or getting help, so they made the decision to leave the scene or rationalise their decision to themselves by rejecting the victim as undeserving of help.

5 How ethical was this study?

The deception, lack of consent and debriefing, and the anxiety and inconvenience for the bystanders are all ethically problematic.

PILIAVIN et al. CROSSWORD

1 The term for those who witness a situation requiring help (10)
2 Of the victims, only one was _____ (5)
3 The city where the subway study took place (3/4)
4 The study found no _____ of responsibility with increasing group size (9)
5 These include effort, embarrassment, possible disgusting or distasteful experiences, possible physical harm, self-blame and perceived criticism from others in our economic analysis of whether to help (5)
6 These include self-praise, praise from the victim and others and being able to continue with other activities in our economic analysis of whether to help (7)
7 This was carried by the ill model victim (4)
8 The kind of experiment used in the study (5)
9 The number of seconds journey before the model collapsed (7)
10 The model who tended to be helped least (5)
11 According to the authors, witnessing a victim needing help produces unpleasant emotional _____ (7)

40 Conformity

Crutchfield (1962) has defined conformity as 'yielding to group pressure' but, as Aronson (1976) has pointed out, this pressure can be real (involving the physical presence of others) or imagined (involving the pressure of social norms/expectations). Kelman (1958) suggests that the yielding can take three forms:

- Compliance – a change in behaviour without a change in opinion (just going along with the group).
- Internalisation – a change in both behaviour and opinion (the group's and your own opinions coincide).
- Identification – a more wholehearted change in behaviour and opinions to identify with an influencing group.

Conformity studies

A number of studies have been conducted on conformity.

Jenness (1932), for example, simply asked subjects to estimate the number of beans in a bottle first individually and then as a group. When asked individually again the subjects showed a shift towards the group's estimate rather than their own.

Sherif (1935) asked subjects to estimate how far a spot of light moved in a completely dark room. Sherif kept the point of light stable, but due to the autokinetic effect illusion (caused by small eye movements) each individual reported fairly consistent estimates of movement that often differed from other subjects. However, when subjects were put in groups, their estimates converged towards a central mean, despite not being told to arrive at a group estimate and despite denying that they had been influenced by the others in post-experimental interviews.

Asch (1951, 1952, 1956) wanted to test conformity under non-ambiguous conditions and, therefore, devised a very simple perceptual task of matching the length of a line to one of three other comparison lines. The task was so easy that control subjects made very few errors. In the experimental condition only one real (naive) subject was tested, but was surrounded by six or seven confederates of the experimenter who were also supposed to be subjects but had been told beforehand to all give the same wrong estimate on 12 out of the 18 trials. The only real subject was second to last to give their estimate, and was, therefore, faced with either giving their own opinion or conforming to the group opinion on the critical trials.

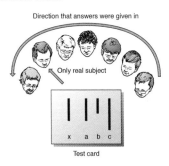

Direction that answers were given in

Only real subject

Test card

The average rate of conformity was 32% with 74% conforming at least once. Even the 26% of subjects who did not conform at all felt strong social pressure to do so. One was heard to exclaim 'I always disagree – darn it!', and on being debriefed commented, 'I do not deny that at times I had the feeling "to heck with it, I'll go along with the rest".' Asch conducted variations to identify factors influencing conformity, such as:

- increasing the group size – Asch found little increase above 3 or 4, although other studies have found that larger groups will increase conformity but at a decreasing rate.
- providing support for the subject – when Asch provided an ally who agreed with the naive subject's estimates, conformity dropped to 5.5%. It seems that the unanimity of the group is important. If the ally changed to the group's estimates, the naive subject would often follow suit.

- increasing the difficulty of the task – when the comparison lines were made closer in length, conformity increased.
- introducing privacy – when the naive subject could write down their response privately, conformity dropped.

Crutchfield (1954) tested for conformity without the physical presence of other people by placing subjects in individual cubicles with electronic display boards which supposedly let each subject know what the others had answered. In fact, he allowed each subject to believe they were the last to answer and presented them with uniformly wrong group answers on half the tasks.

Crutchfield tested over 600 subjects using a variety of stimuli such as Asch's line comparison tests, obviously incorrect factual statements and personal opinions. He found 30% conformity in Asch's line test, 46% conformity to the suggestion that a picture of a star had a larger surface area than a circle (when it was a third smaller) and 37% agreement to the statement 'I doubt that I would make a good leader' (which none agreed to when asked privately).

Abrams et al (1990) found more conformity when people were put into groups of confederates who were similar to themselves (an in-group) rather than different (an out-group).

Theories of conformity

Crutchfield's (1955) conforming personality theory – after Crutchfield had tested his subjects for conformity, he also gave them a number of personality and IQ type tests, and found, for example, that those subjects who conformed the most typically

- were less intellectually competent.
- had less ego strength.
- had less leadership ability.
- were more narrow-minded/authoritarian.

Informational social influence theory – Deutsch and Gerard (1955) suggested that when individuals are placed in ambiguous or *uncertain conditions*, they are more likely to refer to others to know how to react (Festinger called this social comparison). Under these conditions other people possess informational or expert power and individuals may show *internalisation* conformity.

Normative social influence theory – Deutsch and Gerard (1955) also proposed that when individuals are put into a potentially *embarrassing* situation, such as disagreeing with the majority, they are faced with a conflict between their own and others' opinions. Under these conditions other people have reward or coercive power which may lead individuals into *compliance*.

Referent social influence theory – Turner (1991) suggests that people have a tendency to categorise themselves as members of different groups (social identity theory) and argues that we are more likely to conform to the norms of those groups which we feel we are members of (in-groups) because we expect to agree with them. Under these conditions, members of the in-group possess informational, and perhaps also reward and referent power which may lead to *identification* conformity.

Exercise 40

1 Compare the methodologies of the studies.

2 Evaluate the methods and ethics of the studies.

3 What are the problems with conclusions about rates of conformity based on American subjects tested in the 1950s?

4 How might the characteristics of Crutchfield's conforming personality have led to a greater tendency to conform?

5 Use the theories of conformity to explain the results of the conformity studies.

1 Compare the methodologies of the studies.

By comparing the methods and procedures of Jenness (1932), Sherif (1935), Asch (1951) and Crutchfield (1954), we can see how each experiment was an improvement on the one before it.

Jenness's study was fairly simple and basic and participants probably knew that their estimates were being influenced by others, whereas Sherif's laboratory experiment was more controlled and the participants were less likely to realise the study was testing conformity. Sherif's study, however, did not investigate many influences upon conformity and only shows conformity under ambiguous conditions – to really establish the extent to which people will conform, it is better to have a test where it is clear that group pressure has caused a change in behaviour.

Asch conducted a series of experiments in the 1950s to test conformity under non-ambiguous conditions and to identify factors influencing it. Asch's experiments were highly controlled and standardised yet were very time-consuming (only one real subject could be tested at a time) and only showed the effects of group pressure when others were physically present.

Crutchfield (1954) tested for conformity without physical presence by placing subjects in individual cubicles with electronic display boards. With this more time-efficient method, Crutchfield tested over 600 subjects and used a variety of stimuli – not only Asch's line comparison tests, but also obviously incorrect factual statements and personal opinions.

2 Evaluate the methods and ethics of the studies.

The majority of conformity research has been conducted under rather artificial laboratory conditions, often with meaningless stimuli, and can, therefore, be accused of being a little artificial and lacking ecological validity. In defence of the research though, one might argue that these studies are more useful for showing the *kinds of factors* that lead to conformity rather than a valid assessment of the levels of conformity that occur in real life.

Ethically speaking, conformity studies frequently involved large amounts of deception, a lack of informed consent and even psychological stress and anxiety (e.g. in Asch's tests).

3 What are the problems with conclusions about rates of conformity based on American subjects tested in the 1950s?

There are problems with generalising the results and regarding the levels of conformity as representative of human behaviour in general. It has been argued, for example, that the high conformity rates found in the experiments of the 1950s may only have reflected the norms prevalent in the USA at that time – when non-conforming individuals may have been accused of being un-American communist spies. While replications of Asch's experiments have found similar levels of conformity more recently and cross culturally, this has not always been the case. Larsen (1974) found much lower conformity rates in American students than Asch, while Perrin and Spencer (1981) only found one conforming response out of 396 trials using British students. In the latter study, however, science students were used who are trained to be objective and accurate, which reflects a fault common to many conformity studies – the use of unrepresentative sampling – and indicates that social psychologists may have oversimplified the social causes of conformity.

4 How might the characteristics of Crutchfield's conforming personality have led to a greater tendency to conform?

Crutchfield found those subjects who conformed the most typically
- were less intellectually competent – perhaps making them more open to the expert power of others.
- had less ego strength – perhaps making them less confident in their own opinion.
- had less leadership ability – perhaps making them less able to assert their own opinion.
- were more narrow-minded/authoritarian – perhaps inclining them to stick to the majority or conventional answer.

5 Use the theories of conformity to explain the results of the conformity studies.

Informational influence probably best explains the conformity found in Jenness's and Sherif's studies, since the ambiguity produced by a lack of clear answer in each case would have led the participants to refer to each other's opinions (even if they were not aware of doing so). When changing their answers the subjects were most likely showing *internalisation*, believing their answer was more likely to be correct. Some of the conformity in Asch's tasks may have resulted from informational social influence, especially when the difficulty of the task was increased. A few of Asch's subjects seemingly experienced perceptual distortion, but the majority believed that the group's judgement was superior.

Normative influence explains some of Asch's conformity results, especially in the private answer variation. Some of his subjects reported private disagreement with the group's answers, commenting 'If I'd been the first I probably would have responded differently.' Participants may have felt embarrassed about disagreeing in front of six other people and seeming the 'odd one out', fearing ridicule. In fact studies have shown that this negative reaction from the group does occur when a *single confederate* gives obviously wrong answers in a line comparison test with a group of *real* participants. Faced with this coercive power disapproval it was probably easier for them to show public *compliance* by changing the answer they really thought was correct.

Referent social influence theory seems best illustrated by Abrams et al.'s study since those put in a group with similar people would feel more likely to belong to the group and thus more likely to expect to agree with, and conform to, the opinions of the group members. Those put into groups with different people would be less likely to *identify* with this out-group and, therefore, less likely to expect to agree with them, making the individual less susceptible to their informational, reward and coercive power.

CONFORMITY WORDSEARCH

N	U	D	L	E	I	F	H	C	T	U	R	C
O	E	W	Y	E	U	T	N	R	I	S	G	U
I	S	L	B	M	V	A	O	Z	N	H	A	K
T	L	H	A	I	J	I	I	S	F	T	M	R
A	O	D	E	C	E	P	T	I	O	N	B	E
S	S	M	E	R	T	F	A	A	R	C	I	F
I	S	H	C	S	I	U	C	R	M	A	G	E
L	E	O	N	H	O	F	I	T	A	R	U	R
A	N	P	A	X	K	E	F	I	T	L	O	E
N	N	S	I	E	K	D	I	F	I	Q	U	N
R	E	P	L	I	C	A	T	I	O	N	S	T
E	J	M	P	B	E	R	N	C	N	O	P	U
T	A	E	M	A	H	N	E	I	A	S	C	H
N	L	P	O	E	Y	I	D	A	L	M	L	K
I	C	J	C	N	U	T	I	L	F	I	G	A

Find 16 terms or names in the grid. They can be found horizontally, vertically and diagonally (backwards or forwards). Answers are at the back of the book.

Milgram (1963) – 'Behavioural study of obedience'

Milgram describes how obedience is a basic element in social life that, while often having positive consequences, can lead to terrible acts such as those seen between 1939 to 1945 in Nazi death camps, which entailed obedience to orders by a very large number of people. Milgram's study aimed to investigate how far people will go in obeying an authority figure who asks them to commit acts of aggression against others.

Method

The participants in the study were 40 males between the ages of 20 and 50 from a range of occupations and were drawn from the New Haven area. They were obtained by newspaper advertisements for participation in a study of learning at Yale University and were paid $4.50 just for turning up.

The subjects were led to believe that the experiment was investigating the effects of punishment on learning. They were tested one at a time but were introduced to an apparent co-subject who was, in reality, an actor. The actor was required to play the role of the learner in the experiment – an Irish–American, 47-year-old accountant who appeared mild-mannered and likeable. The real subject was always given the role of the teacher through a fixed lottery.

Two rooms in the Yale Interaction Laboratory were used – one for the learner containing an 'electric chair' and an answering device, the other for the teacher and experimenter with an electric shock generator. The generator did not actually give shocks to the learner, and was used to measure the dependent variable of obedience. It was a convincing machine with a row of 30 switches ranging from 15 to 450 volts in increments of 15 volts, and was marked with descriptive terms of the shock effects – ranging from 'slight shock' through to 'Danger: severe shock' and 'XXX'.

The subject was given a trial shock of 45 volts (to convince him of the reality of the shocks), saw the 'learner' strapped into a chair and have electrodes attached to him, and was told the shocks would cause no permanent tissue damage.

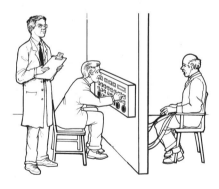

The 'teacher' (the real subject) then started the experiment in the shock generator room next door by testing the learner over an intercom, and was told by the experimenter (the authority figure) to administer an increasing level of electric shock for each wrong answer (which the actor gave often).

The experimenter was 31 years old, dressed in a grey laboratory coat, and appeared somewhat stern and impassive throughout the experiment. If at any point the subject showed reluctance to administer the shock, he would command them to continue with four standardised prompts, ranging from 'please continue' to 'the experiment requires that you continue', to 'It is absolutely essential that you continue' to 'You have no other choice, you *must* go on'.

In this basic set-up of the experiment the subject received feedback reactions from the learner he was 'electrocuting' only by a thump on the wall at 300 volts followed by no further reply. The experiment finished when either the subject refused to continue (disobeyed the experimenter's request), or had reached the maximum shock on the scale (450 volts). The subject was then fully debriefed as to the real nature of the experiment, re-introduced to the learner in a friendly way and reassured that no damage had been done since the learner had not really received any shocks at all!

Results

Psychology students and professional colleagues were asked what percentage of subjects would administer the highest degree of shock (450 volts) and the answers ranged from 1 to 3, with a mean of 1.2. In fact 65% *of subjects* continued to the maximum shock level of 450 volts and no subject stopped before 300 volts. Of those who refused to continue and disobeyed the final prompt of the experimenter, most stopped on or shortly after the 300 volt shock level (when the victim kicks on the wall and no longer answers the teacher's questions).

Number of subjects who broke off at each shock level	
Slight shock (0 – 60 volts)	0
Moderate shock (75 – 120 volts)	0
Strong shock (135 – 180 volts)	0
Very strong shock (195 – 240 volts)	0
Intense shock (255 – 300 volts)	5
Extreme intensity shock (315 – 360 volts)	8
Danger: severe shock (375 – 420 volts)	1
XXX (435 – 450 volts)	26

The subjects' realisation of shock effects was tested by asking in the post-experimental interview 'How painful to the learner were the last few shocks that you administered to him?' The mean response was 13.42 out of 14 – 'extremely painful' on the scale.

The behavioural reactions to the study were also recorded, which indicated that the subjects were not necessarily at ease with the experimental situation. In fact Milgram commented that:

'In a large number of cases the degree of tension reached extremes that are rarely seen in sociopsychological laboratory studies. Subjects were observed to sweat, tremble, stutter, bite their lips, groan and dig their fingers into their flesh. These were characteristic rather than exceptional responses to the experiment…One sign of tension was the regular occurrence of nervous laughing fits…Full-blown, uncontrollable seizures were observed for 3 subjects. On one occasion we observed a fit so violently convulsive that it was necessary to call a halt to the experiment. In the post-experimental interviews, subjects took pains to point out that they were not sadistic types, and that the laughter did not mean they enjoyed shocking the victim.'

Milgram concludes that the two surprising findings were the strength of the obedience tendencies shown and the extraordinary emotional strain generated by the procedure. He suggests that the conflict faced by the subject results from the competing demands of the experimenter (representing scientific authority and the tendency to obey those perceived as legitimate authority figures) and the victim (representing his own experience of pain and suffering and the desire not to harm others). This conflict occurs in public with little time for reflection. Milgram proposes a number of explanations to account for the obedience shown.

Exercise 41

1 How do you think the high level of obedience could be explained?

2 Evaluate the methodological strengths and weaknesses of Milgram's study.

3 How ethical do you think Milgram's study was?

1 How do you think the high level of obedience could be explained?

Milgram outlined several features in his 1963 report which could go some way to explaining the high amount of obedience shown:

i   The study takes place at respected Yale University.
ii   The learning experiment serves a worthy scientific purpose.
iii   The victim is perceived as having volunteered for the study.
iv   The subject has also volunteered and feels an obligation.
v   The pay received strengthens the sense of obligation.
vi   The subject thinks he could have drawn the learner's lot.
vii   The situation is novel and ambiguous regarding the rights of the psychologist and his subjects, with no opportunity to reduce the ambiguity through discussion with others.
viii   The subject assumes that the discomfort is momentary but the scientific gains are lasting.
ix   The victim is perceived as 'playing the game' too, until 300 volts.

Milgram (1974) later went on to develop his ***theory of agency***, which suggests that when faced with commands from legitimate authority figures we lose our sense of responsibility for our own actions. Thus the high levels of obedience found in Milgram's studies resulted from the experimenter as the authority figure *taking responsibility* for the consequences of the obedience.

According to Milgram (1974) agency involves a cognitive shift in viewpoint which results in people switching from their normal *autonomous state* (where they feel in control of, and responsible for, their actions) to the *agentic state* (where they regard themselves as 'the instrument for carrying out another person's wishes').

The purpose of the agentic state is to allow human hierarchical social systems to function properly. If people did not automatically yield to those of higher status, then society would be disorganised and unable to achieve its collective goals efficiently (or at all), and disobedient, lower-ranking individuals would constantly risk punishment from those above them in the hierarchy.

Milgram proposed the agentic state is a product of evolution and pointed out that we grow up in a society where we constantly submit to those in authority from the moment we are born, e.g. to parents, teachers and employers. The agentic state can account for the horrific acts committed in the name of obedience – for example soldiers arguing they were only following orders.

Theories of social power, roles and norms have also been applied to explain the obedience shown.

Social impact theory explains the relative impact of social influences upon the subject from the experimenter and victim.
- The impact of the *experimenter's power on the subject* was greater because the experimenter was close and important (immediacy and strength of influence was high) to the subject.
- The impact of the *learner's distress on the subject* was lower since the subject was not in close proximity to the learner (low immediacy of influence).

Role and norm theory explains the feelings of expectation, obligation and contract created by the experimental situation and the role of 'experimenter' and 'subject'.

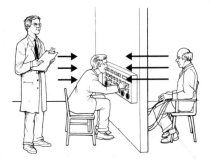

Power base theory describes the types of social influence:
- The location of respectable Yale university added *legitimate power* to the situation.
- The experimenter represented scientific authority and had *expert* and *legitimate power*, especially with his grey lab coat which represents the power uniform has in our society – see Haney, Banks and Zimbardo (1973) and Bickman (1974).

2 Evaluate the methodological strengths and weaknesses of Milgram's study.

The procedure seems to have good experimental validity – it was well standardised (the same conditions for each participant) and obedience was accurately and precisely operationalised as the amount of voltage given.

Orne and Holland (1968), however, have argued that the subjects did not really think that the learner would come to harm. They suggested that the subjects were involved in a *'pact of ignorance'* with the experimenter and obeyed in much the same way as a member of a magician's audience will comply and put their head under a guillotine which has just split a cabbage head in two! The genuine distress of the subjects, their ratings of the shock pain and their comments during debriefing count against this criticism.

Some psychologists have suggested that the experiment is an artificial test of obedience and, therefore, lacks *'mundane realism'* or ecological validity. Milgram has argued that while there are important differences between experimental and real-life obedience, there is a fundamental similarity in the psychological processes at work – especially the process of agency.

The subjects were also American, male and volunteers – an unrepresentative sample that may have already been more obedient and helpful, but later studies have found similarly high rates of obedience using other samples and more everyday tasks and contexts (see replications and field studies of obedience).

3 How ethical do you think Milgram's study was?

Baumrind (1964) criticised the study as being unethical since
- it caused distress and anguish to the subjects, including a fit so violently convulsive that it was necessary to call a halt to the experiment. The subjects could have suffered psychological damage after the study, e.g. guilt or loss of self-esteem.
- Milgram deceived the subjects about the true nature of the experiment (and, therefore, did not receive their informed consent), the reality of the lottery for who would be teacher or learner, and the reality of the shocks.
- Milgram's study abused the right of subjects to withdraw from a psychology study – those wishing to leave were told to continue (the experimenter's four prompts).

Milgram defended himself on ethical grounds by pointing out that
- the methodology was not unethical since the results obtained were completely unexpected, and although the subjects appeared uncomfortable with their obedience, Milgram concluded 'momentary excitement is not the same as harm'.
- subjects could have left, they were not physically restrained (unlike the 'learner'!). Indeed Milgram later designed many variations to increase refusal/disobedience.
- all subjects were fully debriefed and reassured. They were shown that the learner was completely unharmed.
- a follow-up opinion survey conducted a year later found that 84% were 'glad to have been in the experiment', 15% were neutral, and only 1.3% were 'sorry or very sorry to have been in the experiment'. Around 80% of the respondents said there should be more experiments like Milgram's conducted, and about 75% said they had learnt something of personal value.
- the subjects were also examined by a psychiatrist one year after the study who found no signs of harm.

42 Studies of obedience

Milgram's variations on the basic (1963) study

Milgram decided to conduct many variations of the study to determine the key factors that were responsible for the obedience (overall 636 subjects were tested during the 18 different variation studies). For example, in the basic set-up of the experiment, the subject received feedback reactions from the learner he was 'electrocuting' only by a thump on the wall at 300 volts followed by no further reply, but in a later condition vocal feedback was given. This vocal feedback was standardised by the use of a tape recording and the teacher was able to hear the learner do the following:

At **75 volts** – moan and groan.
At **150 volts** – request to be excused from the experiment.
At **195 volts** – yell 'Let me out! My heart's bothering me.'
At **285 volts** – emit an agonised scream
At **300 volts** – kick the wall and beg to be released.
At **315 volts** – emit no further responses.

The table below shows some of the different variables that were carefully manipulated to see the effect on obedience (measured by the percentage that gave the maximum 450-volt shock).

Some of Milgram's variations on his obedience study	
Condition	Obedience
■ *Remote victim condition.* The original condition, where the victim is in a separate room and no feedback is heard until a bang on the wall at 300 volts.	65%
■ *Vocal feedback condition.* With the verbal protestations, screams, wall-pounding and ominous silence after 300 volts.	
■ *Two teacher condition.* The subject was paired with another teacher (a confederate) who actually delivered the shocks while the subject only read out the words.	
■ *Shift of setting condition.* The experiment was moved to a set of run-down offices rather than the impressive Yale University.	
■ *Proximity condition.* The learner was moved into the same room so the teacher could see his agonised reactions.	
■ *Touch proximity condition.* The teacher had to force the learner's hand down onto a shock plate when he refused to participate after 150 volts.	
■ *Absent experimenter condition.* The experimenter had to leave and give instructions over the telephone.	
■ *Social support condition.* Two other subjects (confederates) were also teachers but soon refused to obey.	

Replications of Milgram's study

Many other researchers have repeated Milgram's study, with a number of variations to investigate the effect upon obedience of:

Varying the subjects

Gender – women were found to show similar levels of obedience by Milgram, but other studies have found both lower levels (when asked to electrocute another woman) and higher levels (when asked to electrocute a puppy).

Nationality – cross-cultural studies have found varying obedience levels – higher in Holland, Austria and Germany, but lower in Britain and Australia. The different procedures used in these studies make proper comparison difficult.

Varying the victim

Gender – a female victim has occasionally reduced obedience.

Species – Sheridan and King (1972) found 75% obedience when real electric shocks were used on a puppy.

Varying the setting

Field experiments – have tested obedience under more real life conditions. For example:

■ *Hofling et al (1966)* investigated obedience in American hospitals. They found that 95.5% (21 out of 22) of the nurses tested obeyed an unknown doctor's telephone instructions to administer twice the maximum allowed dose of a drug (in fact a harmless placebo) that was clearly labelled with warnings against such an action and that was not on the ward stock list for the day. This was in contrast to 21 out of 22 nurses who replied that they would not have obeyed the doctor and broken the hospital regulations for medication when asked how they would have reacted in the same situation.

■ *Bickman (1974)* investigated obedience on the streets of New York. He revealed that when an experimenter was dressed in a guard's uniform and told passers-by to pick up paper bags or give a coin to a stranger there was 80% obedience, compared to 40% when the experimenter was dressed more 'normally'. A milkman's uniform, however, did not have the same effect as the guard's on obedience.

■ *Meeus and Raaijmakers (1986)* investigated obedience in a business setting in Holland. They had an experimenter ask subjects to act as interviewers, supposedly in order to test the effects of stress on job applicants by delivering 15 increasingly distressing and insulting remarks to applicants (in fact confederates) at a time of high unemployment. 91.5% of their subjects obeyed the experimenter and made all 15 remarks despite the psychological distress shown by the applicants.

Exercise 42

1 For each of Milgram's variations listed in the table, guess whether the obedience level was higher or lower than the original condition (fill in a percentage estimation if you like!), then try to explain the reason for your guess.

2 Compare the results of the field studies with Milgram's laboratory results.

3 Are the field studies any more ethical than Milgram's laboratory study?

1 For each of Milgram's variations listed in the table, guess whether the obedience level was higher or lower than the original condition (fill in a percentage estimation if you like!), then try to explain the reason for your guess.

The *vocal feedback condition* with all the verbal protestations, screams, wall-pounding and ominous silence after 300 volts, only caused obedience to drop to **62.5%**! Only a few stopped before 300 volts. The aim was to increase the impact of the learner's plight upon the subject, but surprisingly it had little effect (out of sight, out of mind, perhaps).

The *two teacher condition*, where the subject was paired with another teacher (a confederate) who actually delivered the shocks while the subject only read out the words, caused obedience to increase to **92.5%**. The subject may have felt even less individually responsible for his actions (a diffusion of impact of the learner's plight).

The *shift of setting condition*, where the experiment was moved to a set of run-down offices, reduced obedience to **47.5%**. The new location lacked the legitimate power of the respectable Yale University.

The *proximity condition*, where the learner was moved into the same room so the teacher could see his agonised reactions, reduced obedience to **40%**. The consequences of the shocks were made more immediate and the impact of the learner's distress increased.

The *touch proximity condition*, where the teacher had to force the learner's hand down onto a shock plate when he refused to participate after 150 volts, only lowered the obedience another ten percent from the last condition to **30%**. Not only was the immediacy of the learner's plight increased, but it became increasingly difficult for the subject to shift or diffuse responsibility for his actions to the experimenter.

The *absent experimenter condition*, when the experimenter had to leave and give instructions over the telephone, lowered obedience to 20%. Many subjects also cheated and missed out shocks or gave less voltage than they were ordered to. The immediacy and thus impact of power of the experimenter decreased (relative to the learner).

The *social support condition*, involving two other subjects (confederates) who were also teachers but who soon refused to obey, produced the lowest level of obedience of 10%. Most subjects stopped very soon after the others. The subjects' obedience may have decreased as the experimenter's power and authority was spread amongst many teachers, having less impact on each one (diffusion of impact), or because of the social example set and support provided by the confederates.

2 Compare the results of the field studies with Milgram's laboratory results.

The field experiments have often found higher levels of obedience under real-life conditions. Note, however, that the Hofling et al. study was conducted under slightly unusual conditions (although in a natural environment it still lacked ecological validity), and its results have not been replicated when the procedure was changed to make it more realistic, i.e. a drug known to the nurses, with others around to consult.

3 Are the field studies any more ethical than Milgram's laboratory study?

In a similar way to Milgram's studies virtually every later study of obedience has broken some ethical guidelines. These range from deception and lack of fully informed consent over the true nature of the experiment to causing psychological distress, embarrassment and even physical harm to animals (the real electric shocks given to Sheridan and King's puppy).

OBEDIENCE CROSSWORD

1 Milgram's study was criticised as artificial and lacking in _____ / _____ (7/7)
2 Increasing this between the teacher and learner decreased obedience to 40% in Milgram's study (9)
3 Bickman (1974) tested the effect of this on obedience (7)
4 The participants in Milgram's study were falsely led to believe they were helping in a study of this (8)
5 If a study's procedure is this, then it can easily be replicated by others (12)
6 The learner in Milgram's study was really this (5)
7 Milgram's theory of obedience that involves a cognitive shift in viewpoint regarding responsibility for one's actions (6)
8 Clarifying the participant's understanding and dealing with any negative effects after a study (10)
9 The number of participants in Milgram's first (1963) study of obedience (5)
10 The number of increasingly distressing and insulting remarks made by 91.5% of participants in Meeus and Raajmakers (1986) obedience study (7)
11 The repeating of a study, sometimes with variations (11)
12 The university that gave the authority figure in Milgram's study legitimate power (4)
13 The percentage who gave the maximum shock level in Milgram's first (1963) study of obedience (5-4)
14 Hofling et al (1966) tested this type of subject (6)
15 The term for the orders given by the authority figure in Milgram's first (1963) study of obedience (7).

43

Is hypnosis

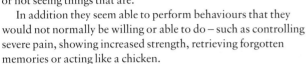

NON-HYPNOTISED VS HYPNOTISED

its still possible to have control with out hypnotising a person

Hypnosis has long fascinated both psychologists and the general public because of the dramatic changes in behaviour it produces. Hypnotised subjects can apparently experience the world in a different way – showing distortions of perception, like tasting an onion as an apple or smelling ammonia as water, and even hallucinations, such as seeing things that are not there or not seeing things that are.

In addition they seem able to perform behaviours that they would not normally be willing or able to do – such as controlling severe pain, showing increased strength, retrieving forgotten memories or acting like a chicken.

The traditional view of hypnosis

The traditional view of hypnosis is known as the *altered state or special process* approach to hypnosis, which proposes that

- hypnosis represents an altered state of consciousness, distinct from both waking and sleep states. Hilgard proposes the neo-dissociation theory, which suggests that hypnosis divides consciousness into separate channels of awareness. For example, if pain is inflicted upon a hypnotised person, one channel can be aware of it, while another channel (the conscious one!) will report not feeling any pain.
- hypnosis is a special state since phenomena can be produced during it (like pain resistance) that cannot be shown under normal conditions.

Social influence and hypnosis

In contrast to the traditional altered state view of hypnosis, some social psychologists support the **non-state** or **social psychological approach** to hypnosis, which argues that

- hypnosis is only a form of social influence, not an altered state
- all phenomena produced under hypnosis can be produced without it (by people motivated to simulate hypnosis).

It suggests that social psychological research can account for 'hypnotic' behaviour and experiences, without the need for a special state or division of consciousness:

Conformity and role playing

Social psychologists suggest that people play a variety of roles in society (e.g. son, brother, student, football supporter, shop assistant, etc.) and each role has a different set of **norms** (expected ways of behaving) that are *conformed* to in each role. We readily shift from one role to the next depending upon the social context and may thus behave very differently in various situations.

People are very aware of how those who are 'hypnotised' behave and may, therefore, deliberately or not, conform to the norms of the role of 'hypnotised subject' in situations where it is expected. One could compare such behaviour to *demand characteristics* in research situations. Pressure to conform to the hypnotic role and its norms is often increased by the presence of people other than the hypnotist, such as audiences at hypnosis stage shows – where especially dramatic behaviour may be expected.

According to social psychologists, conformity could occur for different reasons, and cause different kinds of role-playing.

- *Normative social influence* – not following suggestions in hypnotic situations is potentially very embarrassing, which may lead people to behave as expected but not believe they are really hypnotised (a kind of conformity known as *compliance*).

- *[Informat]ional social influence* – people being hypnotised want to un[der]stand or justify what happens to them when hypnotised bu[t may] be uncertain as to how else to do so other than accept the [tr]aditional and socially accepted view that being in an [alter]ed state' enables you to perform in extraordinary ways [with]out being able to refuse. This may lead them to behave as [exp]ected, even if they do not want to, and really believe they are h[yp]notised (a kind of conformity known as *internalisation*).

Obedience to authority

Studies of obedience such as Milgram's have consistently shown that we should not underestimate the ability of (non-hypnotised) people to follow the commands of an authority figure, even if reluctant to do so, especially if in close proximity to them. It can be argued that the hypnotist is essentially an authority figure whose suggestions are obeyed and who influences at close proximity.

Hypnotists who are perceived as legitimate and credible authority figures can thus produce extreme behaviour in their subjects through mere obedience since, by the very nature of the hypnotic situation, they take all responsibility for the actions produced. According to Milgram, this causes a state of 'agency' which reduces the 'hypnotised' person's inhibitions.

Studies of hypnosis

- *'Lie' detecting* – Coe and Yashinski (1985) found that people with post-hypnotic amnesia increase their recall if led to believe that a lie detector test will find out if they are lying. Pattie (1937) showed that hypnotised subjects given the suggestion that they could not feel anything in one hand reported sensations administered to the fingers of both hands if they were inter-linked (making it difficult to tell which was which). Subjects under the hypnotic suggestion of deafness have failed delayed auditory feedback tests that real deaf people pass.
- *Physiological evidence* – researchers have found differences in brain activity levels between low and highly susceptible subjects when hypnosis is attempted.
- *Task performance* – Motivated simulators have performed many tasks in the same way as hypnotised subjects, e.g. eating onions while pretending they are apples. The human plank demonstration (where it is suggested that the body is so rigid it can be placed across two chairs and sat upon) can be performed by most fit, non-hypnotised people. Barber and Hahn showed that motivated subjects could reduce their experience of cold pressor pain (caused by immersing the hand in icy water) to a similar degree to hypnotised subjects.
- *Trance logic* – Trance logic refers to the ability of hypnotised subjects to tolerate logical inconsistency. Orne showed that hypnotised subjects can hallucinate a transparent image of a person sitting in a chair, even if that person was also seen standing next to them, without being perturbed by the inconsistency. Simulators asked to fake this hypnotic situation often described their 'hallucinated' person as opaque and reported that the hallucination disappears when they turn to look at the real person next to them.

Exercise 43

1 Which of the two theories of hypnosis is supported by the studies described relating to **a** 'lie' detecting? **b** physiological evidence? **c** task performance? **d** trance logic?

2 Social influence research on conformity and obedience seems to focus on how much people yield to social pressures. What does it tell us about the amount of resistance to influence people show and why they might show it?

1 Which of the two theories of hypnosis is supported by the studies described relating to

a 'Lie' detecting?

These studies all suggest that the subjects were merely behaving *as if* they were hypnotised and did not really have these special abilities, which supports the social influence non-state theory.

b Physiological evidence?

Altered state researchers argue that the differences in brain activity levels between low and highly susceptible subjects when hypnosis is attempted support the altered state theory. Highly susceptible subjects seem to be in a different brain state – showing, for example, less activity in their frontal cortex when hypnosis is attempted. However, non-state critics suggest this may just reflect a state of relaxation rather than a special state of hypnotic trance.

c Task performance?

Social influence, non-state, psychologists provide support for their view with these studies showing that motivated people can simulate (pretend) the same phenomena without hypnosis.

However, not all studies find that simulators show exactly the same behaviour as hypnotised people. Orne et al. (1968) found that hypnotised subjects responded to a suggestion to touch their forehead (when they heard the word 'experiment' mentioned throughout a 2-day period) more often than simulators. Also, Colman argues that the fact that simulators can imitate aspects of the hypnotic state does not mean that the state does not exist.

d Trance logic?

Trance logic in particular seems to be one aspect of hypnosis that simulators do not seem to be able to reliably replicate, and so appears to support the altered state theory. Johnson et al. claimed that simulators were just as able to show trance logic, although Hilgard criticised their study.

2 Social influence research on conformity and obedience seems to focus on how much people yield to social pressures. What does it tell us about the amount of resistance to influence people show and why they might show it?

Examples of resisting social influence

Conformity and obedience studies are usually used to illustrate how people yield to the influence of others, but they can be re-examined to shed light on the amount of resistance shown.

Although disobedience in Milgram's (1963) experiment was low (35% refused to give the maximum shock), Asch's (1951) conformity experiment showed higher rates of resistance (26% did not conform at all and all 50 were resistant at least once in the original test). Resistance was significantly increased by having social support – just one ally in Asch's study lowered conformity from an average of 32% to 5%, two other teachers disobeying in Milgram's study lowered obedience to 10%.

In fact, Gamson et al. (1982) found 97% of groups showed dissent and 50% completely rebelled to unfair requests from authority figures – probably because groups provide a greater opportunity for dissent to be expressed and discussed, and social support to justify and implement rebellion. However, although resisting authority, many participants just conformed to those who rebelled.

Psychologists have distinguished between
- *independent behaviour* – which involves the true rejection of social influence to behave in accord with one's own internal attitudes, regardless of whether they coincide with the influencer's.
- *anti-conformity* – which involves resisting social influence by deliberately opposing the majority and refusing to behave like them. This behaviour is still affected by society, however.

Reasons for resisting social influence

There are many reasons why people go against social pressure.
- *Group identity* – Different social groups have different goals and so may not want to follow other majority group norms. This relates to referent social influence theory.
- *Psychological reactance* – Brehm (1966) argued that perceived constraints on freedom lead some to resist in order to assert their freedom – telling people they are not allowed to do something is often a good way of getting them to do it!
- *Socialisation* – Individual experience and the society that one is raised in can affect the level of independence. Berry (1966, 1967) discovered that Inuit, who live in an individualistic hunting society where self-reliance is highly valued, showed more independent behaviour than members of the Temmi of Africa whose collectivist agricultural society is more dependent upon co-operation, agreement and conformity.

Minority influence

At times, minority groups may not only resist but actually influence majority groups in society.

Moscovici et al. (1969) tested subjects in groups of 6 on their ability to judge the colour of 36 blue slides of varying brightness. Unknown to the other subjects, 2 in each group were confederates who acted as a minority group. They found that when the minority
- *consistently* judged the slides to be green rather than blue, the majority followed them on 8.42% of trials
- *inconsistently* judged the slides to be green rather than blue (on 2 in 3 trials), the majority followed on only 1.25% of trials.
In later individual tests, the subjects exposed to the minority were more likely (than control groups with no minority) to report ambiguous slides as green, especially if they had previously resisted the minority view, indicating a longer term influence.

Nemeth et al. (1974) replicated Moscovici et al.'s study but had their 2 confederates
- *randomly* say green on half the trials and green/blue on the other half. This inconsistency caused no minority influence.
- *consistently* say green or green/blue depending on the brightness of the slides. This led to 21% minority influence.
- say green on every trial. This consistency caused no minority influence, perhaps it was seen as being rigid and unrealistic.

Maass and Clark (1983) studied majority and minority influence on attitudes to gay rights and found that their subjects' publicly expressed views followed the majority but their privately expressed views shifted towards the minority viewpoint. This indicates minorities cause a change in private opinions/attitudes *before* a change in public behaviour.

Dual Process theory of minority influence

Moscovici (1980) argued that since minorities do not have the informational and normative influence of the majority (in fact they are often ridiculed by them), they must exert their influence through their *behavioural style – how* they express their views. *Consistency* of viewpoint, both over time and between members of the minority group, is the most important aspect of this style since this not only draws attention to the minority view and gives the impression of certainty and coherence, but also causes doubt about majority norms. Other important features of behavioural style are *investment* (the minority has made sacrifices for the view), *autonomy* (the view is made on principle without ulterior motives) and *flexibility* (the consistent viewpoint must not be seen as too rigid and dogmatic). This behavioural style means that minorities and majorities exert their influence through 2 different processes (thus *dual* process theory).
- Majorities influence minorities quickly through *compliance*.
- Minorities influence majorities more slowly through *conversion* because minority views encourage *cognitive conflict*.

44 Social theories of prejudice

Stereotyping

As Pennington (1986) notes, stereotyping involves

- categorising people into groups based on visible cues such as gender, nationality, race, religion, bodily appearance, etc.
- assuming all members of a group share the same characteristics
- assigning individuals to these groups and presuming they possess the same characteristics based on little information other than their possession of the noticeable trait or cue.

Intra-group similarities in characteristics are exaggerated

Intra-group similarities in characteristics are exaggerated

Inter-group differences are exaggerated

Individual allocated to group based on visible cues

While stereotyping is an *in-built* cognitive process, the cues seen as important to categorise (e.g. gender, skin colour, religion, etc.) and the content of the stereotype (e.g. personality traits) are historically determined and change over time.

Stereotyping, therefore, literally involves *pre-judging* an individual and, although it serves the important functions of categorising and generalising knowledge, it can lead to unrealistic perceptions, and inter-group hostility. Stereotypes serve to exaggerate the similarities within groups ('those people are all the same') and exaggerate the differences between groups ('they are not like us'), and many studies have shown how stereotyping can lead to prejudice, e.g. Buckhout (1974) and Duncan (1976).

McCauley & Stitt (1978) suggest stereotypes are best regarded as probabilistic beliefs (people estimate what percentage of a group possess certain traits compared to people in general to get a diagnostic ratio). Although the contents of stereotypes are often derogatory, and stereotyping accounts for the *thinking* in prejudice, it does *not* explain the *emotions* or all the discrimination.

Inter-group conflict theory

According to Sherif, the prejudice in society is caused by

- the existence of groups.
- *competition* between those groups.

Conflict exists between groups because each group will struggle to obtain limited resources (the basis of many wars has been resource competition). Sherif argued that competition will always provoke prejudice and conducted a field study to investigate this idea.

However, Tyerman and Spencer's (1983) study on groups of boy scouts showed that competition is not always sufficient to cause conflict and discrimination. In addition, minimal group theory suggests that competition is not even required for inter-group conflict and discrimination to occur.

Minimal group theory

Minimal group theory suggests that merely dividing people into groups is sufficient to cause prejudice to occur between them. According to this theory, competition is a *result* of group formation rather than a cause of discrimination between groups. Tajfel and Turner (1979) explain this phenomena in terms of their social identity theory (SIT), which proposes that

- people allocate themselves to groups and gain their identity from those groups

- people need to feel good about themselves and, therefore, seek positive self-esteem
- people want to feel they are in the best group and will act to make it so, even if that means putting other groups down.

Many cross-cultural studies have provided confirmation of the minimal group effect, but some of the experiments have been accused of artificiality and demand characteristics. In addition, some researchers argue that the effect only reflects the norms of competition found in certain societies – co-operative societies may not show the minimal group effect (Wetherall, 1982).

Scapegoating theory

Scapegoating theory has its roots in Dollard et al.'s frustration–aggression theory, which argues that socially frustrating conditions such as economic depression and unemployment lead to aggression. According to the theory, this aggression needs to be displaced and blame allocated, so a *scapegoat* is found – usually a minority 'out-group' which is in a less powerful position to defend itself.

The scapegoating of minorities in times of economic hardship has been historically documented world-wide, and this theory links well with inter-group conflict theory by elaborating on another effect of competition, namely the frustration it can provoke. The theory also accounts for the fluctuations of prejudice and discrimination found in societies over time, reflecting changing economic conditions.

Studies of prejudice and discrimination

A study on prejudice was conducted at a summer camp in Robbers' Cave State Park in America. A tournament was set up between two groups of 11 boys (the 'Eagles' and the 'Rattlers') that was sufficient to produce fighting and name calling.	Weatherley's (1961) experiment found that anti-Semitic subjects (those prejudiced against Jews) who were frustrated by being insulted were later more aggressive in their descriptions of people with Jewish-sounding names.
A study was conducted on Bristol schoolboys, who were randomly assigned to meaningless groups. It was found that individuals allocated more points to their own group members and would often maximise the difference between the groups – even if it meant their own group receiving fewer points overall.	Karlins et al. (1969) showed how ideas concerning the typical characteristics of 'Americans' and 'Jews' changed over a 40-year period, the former seeming to become more 'materialistic' and the latter appearing to become less 'mercenary' for example.

Conformity theory

The theories above all account for the origin of prejudice and discrimination. However, once norms of prejudice and discrimination have been established in a society, conformity theory suggests that they will be perpetuated and reinforced by conformity. When prejudice is so accepted in communities that it becomes an unquestioned norm, a 'non-conscious ideology' is said to have been formed.

Exercise 44

1 Which theories are supported by which studies above?

2 From considering the theories, how do you think prejudice and discrimination could be reduced?

1   Which theories are supported by which studies above?

- The field study in Robbers' Cave State Park in America was conducted by Sherif et al. (1961) to support *intergroup conflict theory*. Sherif believed that the competition of the tournament created the prejudice and discrimination of fighting and name-calling (this study was ethically dubious given that its goal was to deliberately create prejudice, and fighting over penknives was involved). Others have argued that the hostility between the two groups began soon after their creation, *before* the tournament, which supports minimal group theory.
- Weatherley's (1961) experiment supports the idea that the frustrated anti-Semitic subjects *scapegoated* the people with Jewish-sounding names with their aggressive behaviour.
- Tajfel et al. (1971) conducted the study on the Bristol schoolboys, whose discrimination as a mere result of being randomly assigned to meaningless groups supports minimal group theory and social identity theory.
- Karlins et al. (1969) showed how the content of *stereotypes* concerning 'Americans' and 'Jews' changed over a 40-year period, the former seeming to become more 'materialistic' and the latter appearing to be less 'mercenary' for example.

2   From considering the theories above, how do you think prejudice and discrimination could be reduced?

Education

Educating children with notions of tolerance and providing them with an insight into the causes and effects of prejudice can help reduce prejudice and discrimination. Conformity to norms theory would argue that education is necessary to prevent a 'non-conscious ideology' forming in communities where prejudice is so accepted it becomes an unquestioned norm.

The teacher Jane Elliot conducted the 'blue eyes – brown eyes' study on her classes (treating them differently just based on their eye colour) to teach them what it felt like to be the victim of prejudice. Interviews with the children as adults revealed that the study had inoculated them against discriminatory behaviour. Public campaigns by minority groups, such as the 'Black is Beautiful' movement had lasting effects on public awareness of racial issues in the USA.

Education can reduce prejudice if it is seen to be unacceptable by the majority in society. Anti-prejudice education has most effect on the young. If adults 'are compelled to listen to information uncongenial to their deep-seated attitudes, they will reject it, distort it, or ignore it' (Aronson, 1992).

Social policy

According to many theories, political and social measures can act to reduce institutionalised discrimination through

- ensuring political power sharing. Power sharing in South Africa ended Apartheid policies there.
- providing equal opportunities legislation. The Supreme Court case of Brown vs. Board of Education in 1954 started the desegregation of public schools in the USA.
- affecting the media (which perpetuates unequal stereotypes). Bogatz & Ball (1971) found white children in the USA who watched mixed race TV programmes like 'Sesame Street' developed more positive attitudes towards blacks and Hispanics.
- encouraging 'one-nation' in-group perception (to reduce inter-group discrimination according to social identity theory).
- targeting areas of economic frustration (to prevent competition and scapegoating effects).

However, policies like desegregation must be equally applied and regarded as inevitable and socially supported – half-hearted measures often cause more disruption.

Equal status contact

Meeting members of other social groups can reduce prejudice by reducing the effect of stereotypes. This occurs as

- inter-group similarities are perceived (they are like us)
- out-group differences are noted (they are not all the same).

However, contact only changes group stereotypes if

- it is between individuals of equal status
- individuals are seen as representative of their group.

Racial desegregation studies have shown that increasing contact between groups can have some success in reducing prejudice and discrimination.

Deutsch and Collins (1951), for example, found desegregated public housing increased inter-racial 'neighbourly activities' which were shown by 39% and 72% of the white housewives in the two desegregated housing projects but only 1% and 4% of those in the two segregated projects. There was evidence that racial group perceptions changed dramatically for some, as one white housewife commented 'I started to cry when my husband told me we were coming to live here. I cried for three weeks…Well all that's changed…I see that they're just as human as we are…I've come to like them a great deal.'

Star et al. (in Stouffer et al., 1949) found that 93% of white officers and 60% of enlisted men reported getting along 'very well' with the black troops they were fighting with in World War Two (everyone else said 'fairly well').

However, Sherif, in the Robber's Cave study, found inter-group contact alone was insufficient to reduce prejudice between competing groups. Equal status contact only acts to reduce prejudice at an interpersonal level and does not counter the prejudice of group stereotypes (individuals are seen as 'exceptions to the rule'), if inequality at a social level makes true equal status contact impossible.

Stephan (1978) reviewed desegregation studies and found no significant reduction in prejudice or increase in black children's self-esteem. Star et al.'s study revealed that improved racial relationships in desegregated troops were not always generalised to interactions outside of fighting conditions, for example one white soldier commented 'they fought and I think more of them for it, but I still don't want to soldier with them in garrison'.

Superordinate goals

Star et al. concluded that 'efforts at integration of white and coloured troops into the same units may well be more successful when attention is focused on concrete tasks or goals requiring common effort'. Making groups work together to achieve 'superordinate goals' (goals that cannot be achieved by groups working separately) is likely to reduce prejudice according to:

- Inter-group conflict theory – superordinate goals reduce the competition that causes prejudice.
- Social identity theory – working together may merge 'in' and 'out' groups to one whole in-group identity.

For example, Sherif et al. (1961) significantly reduced inter-group hostility between two groups of children, the 'Eagles' and the 'Rattlers', by providing 'superordinate goals' in the last phase of their 'Robbers' Cave' experiment. The children had to pool their money to afford to see a movie and had to pull together on a rope to move a supply truck that had become stuck.

Aronson et al. (1978) used the 'Jigsaw technique' with mixed-race classroom groups. Each child received a part of the whole assignment and was dependent on the other children in the group to perform well in it. Inter-racial liking and the performance of ethnic minorities were increased.

However, the inter-personal liking in these studies is not always generalised to social groups as a whole. When children leave their Jigsaw classrooms they may return to a prejudiced family or society. Superordinate goals cannot always be set up between all groups and failure to achieve them may result in worse prejudice.

45 Tajfel (1970) – 'Experiments in inter-group discrimination'

Tajfel's study illustrates a fundamental cause of inter-group discrimination – the mere categorisation of people into groups. Tajfel proposes that because of the frequent competitive behaviour shown by groups in our society, individuals do not just learn to conform to specific prejudices but learn a general tendency (a '*generic norm*') to categorise people into in-groups and out-groups ('us' versus 'them') and to act in favour of their own in-groups.

This generic norm of discriminating against the out-group soon comes to operate automatically in any group situation, without
1 any individual interest reasons for the discrimination
2 any previous attitudes of hostility or dislike towards the out-group
3 any need for negative attitudes to develop before the discrimination occurs.

Tajfel aimed to support the above theory, that people will automatically discriminate without any prior prejudice merely by being put into groups, by testing the effect of categorisation on children's behaviour without the influence of any pre-existing attitudes or self-interest.

Experiment one
Method
Sixty-four, 14 and 15-year-old schoolboys, previously acquainted with each other, were tested in groups of 8 at a time.

All subjects took part in a study that they were told tested visual judgement, involving estimating the number of dots on a screen. The boys were then informed that they would be divided into groups of 'over-estimators' or 'under-estimators' (supposedly based on their performance, but in fact at random) and were asked to participate in a task where they had to allocate reward and penalty points (that would later be translated into real money at a rate of 1 tenth of a penny per point) to other boys.

Each boy was then individually told which group they were in and tested in isolation from the others. Each received a booklet of matrices that showed how they could allocate different combinations of rewards and penalties to boys from the groups, but it was made clear that
■ they would not know the identities of the boys they were allocating points to, only whether they were members of the *same group* as themselves (in-group) or of the *other group* (out-group)
■ they would *never* be allocating points *to themselves* – their points would be determined by the actions of every other boy in the same way.

Each matrix consisted of 14 combinations of rewards or penalties, with the top and bottom row points always going to the member of one of the groups. Six types of matrix, with differing combinations of rewards and penalties, were each presented with three different group choices, e.g.

1 Between **two in-group** members:

Rewards for member 36 of 'over-estimators'	1	2	3	4	5	6	7	8	9	10	11	12	13	14
Rewards for member 23 of 'over-estimators'	14	13	12	11	10	9	8	7	6	5	4	3	2	1

2 Between **two out-group** members:

Rewards for member 42 of 'under-estimators'	1	2	3	4	5	6	7	8	9	10	11	12	13	14
Rewards for member 15 of 'under-estimators'	14	13	12	11	10	9	8	7	6	5	4	3	2	1

3 Between an **in-group** and **out-group** member:

Rewards for member 36 of 'over-estimators'	1	2	3	4	5	6	7	8	9	10	11	12	13	14
Rewards for member 42 of 'under-estimators'	14	13	12	11	10	9	8	7	6	5	4	3	2	1

In each matrix, subjects had to choose just one of the two-point combinations for the group members.

Results
Subjects could adopt one of three strategies: maximum in-group profit, maximum fairness, or maximum generosity to the out-group. It was found that
1 in choices between two in-group members or two out-group members, the strategy of maximum fairness was usually adopted (see example opposite).
2 in choices between a member of the in-group and out-group a strategy nearer maximum in-group profit was significantly shown (e.g. if the chooser's in-group was 'over-estimator' in the example grid above, the combination chosen would often be the one opposite).

Experiment two
Method
Forty-eight 14 and 15-year-old schoolboys, previously acquainted with each other, were tested in 3 groups of 16 at a time.

Subjects were again randomly divided into 2 groups supposedly based upon their preferences for the paintings of Klee and Kandinsky and were given new matrices consisting of 13 combinations of rewards or penalties to further test in-group favouritism choices. For example:
Between an **in-group** and **out-group** member:

Rewards for member 17 of 'Klee group'	7	8	9	10	11	12	13	14	15	16	17	18	19
Rewards for member 25 of 'Kandinsky group'	1	3	5	7	9	11	13	15	17	19	21	23	25

Results
Subjects could adopt one of three inter-group strategies:

Maximum in-group profit e.g. [19 / 25]   Maximum joint profit e.g. [19 / 25]   Maximum difference e.g. in favour of in-group [7 / 1]

Subjects significantly tended to adopt the strategy of maximum difference in favour of the in-group at the expense of maximum in-group profit. For example, if the chooser's in-group was 'Klee' in the example grid above, then the combination chosen would often be [7 / 1] rather than [19 / 25]

Exercise 45 (the answers are on page 111)
1 Do the results support Tajfel's theory. Why/why not?
2 How were the groups set up in the experiments different from the kinds of group people find themselves in every day?
3 How ethical was this study?

Hraba & Grant (1970) – 'Black is beautiful: a re-examination of racial preference and identification'

A study by Clark & Clark (1947) conducted in 1939 reported that black children preferred white dolls and rejected black dolls when asked to choose which were nice, which looked bad, which they would like to play with, and which were a nice colour. This implied that they thought black is not beautiful and was interpreted as meaning they would rather be white. Later research tended to support the idea that for black children inter-racial contact with white children resulted in white preference, although some research indicated the opposite or no effect. Conclusions are difficult to draw, however, because the studies were not only conducted at different times, but also used different techniques, samples and settings. Hraba & Grant aimed to closely replicate the original Clark & Clark study to test their findings.

Method

The sample of children was drawn from 5 public schools in Lincoln, Nebraska in May 1969 (where 1.4% of the population were black) that between them accounted for 73% of the black population of the correct age group of 4–8 year olds. The sample was 160 children, 89 were black (of whom 70% had white friends) and 71 were white (drawn randomly from the same classrooms). Clark &

Clark's procedure was followed closely. Four dolls were used – 2 black, 2 white (identical in all other respects). Children were individually interviewed with the dolls to investigate the effect of

- *race* – operationalised by skin colour in 2 main conditions – black (later divided into light, medium and dark) and white.
- *time* – the 1969 Hraba & Grant results were compared with the 1939 Clark & Clark results for black children.

The effect of the children's *age* was also investigated and the race of the interviewer was controlled for.

The children's *racial preference* and *racial identification* were recorded (operationalised by the children's answers to Clark & Clark's original 8 questions – see below) plus the *behavioural consequences* of racial preference and identification (operationalised by an additional question on the race of the children's best friend given to the children and their teachers).

Results

Hraba & Grant found differences in the doll choices of the black and white children and many significant differences at the P< .02 level or better between their results and those of Clark & Clark. Children mostly preferred same-race dolls.

	Clark & Clark (1939) Black children		Hraba & Grant (1969) Black children		Hraba & Grant (1969) White children	
Racial preference Give me the doll that…	**white doll / black doll**		**white doll / black doll**		**white doll / black doll**	
1 you want to play with	67%	32%	30%	70%	83%	16%
2 is a nice doll	59%	38%	46%	54%	70%	30%
3 looks bad	17%	59%	61%	36%	34%	63%
4 is a nice colour	60%	38%	31%	69%	48%	49%
Where percentages do not add up to 100% children failed to make a choice.	The black children's preference for the white doll occurred at all ages, and this *increased* with their *skin lightness* but *decreased* with *age*.		Black children preferred the black doll at all ages (*regardless of skin lightness* this tendency *increased* with *age*) and were more ethnocentric on question 4 than white children.		White children preferred the white doll and this trend also *increased* with *age* (except on question 4). They were more ethnocentric on questions 1 & 2 than black children.	
Racial identification Give me the doll that… 5 looks like a white child 6 looks like a coloured child 7 looks like a Negro child **Racial self-identification** Give me the doll that… 8 Looks like you	Correct identification for white dolls was 94%, coloured dolls 93% and Negro dolls 72%. Misidentification was more likely with younger and lighter skinned black children (80% of whom misidentified themselves as white)		Correct identification for white dolls was similar to Clark & Clark's – 90% for white dolls, 94% for coloured dolls and 86% for Negro dolls. Younger children misidentified themselves more but only 15% of lighter-skinned children did.		White children were also more likely to misidentify themselves at younger ages.	
Behavioural consequences What race is your best friend?			There was no relationship between doll preference and race of best friend by black or white children, even in those who always preferred same race dolls.			

Discussion

Doll preference – there are 4 possible interpretations for the black children not being white orientated in their inter-racial setting:

- 'Negroes are becoming blacks proud of their race' – times may be changing, although not at the same rate across the country.
- Black children in Lincoln, unlike in other cities, would have chosen black dolls 30 years ago. This cannot be tested now.
- The black pride campaign of the 'Black Movement' in Lincoln may have modelled positive attitudes towards being black.
- Inter-racial contact may increase black pride by interracial acceptance – 70% of black and 59% of white children had opposite-colour friends.

Doll preference and friendship – three reasons are given for why doll preference did not always reflect the friendship choices:

- If 'Black is beautiful' means rejection of white, the black children should all have had black friends, but this may have been impractical because they were in mainly white schools.
- The 'Black is beautiful' pride that caused the black children to choose black dolls may have been caused by contact with white

friends. This was supported by the finding that more black children who had friends of both races preferred black dolls on all questions (except question 4).

- Doll choice may not be a valid measure of friendship choice since factors other than colour may be more important.

Exercise 46

1 What kind of experiment was this and why?

2 What were the independent and dependent variables?

3 What problems might there be with the two-doll forced choice method of measuring preference?

4 Which theories of discrimination and methods of discrimination reduction do the results of the study support?

5 What particular problems might there be using children as participants in a psychological study?

Answers 45.1 – 45.3

1 Do the results support Tajfel's theory. Why/why not?

Yes they do. The children identified themselves with the groups and made choices in a discriminatory way in favour of their own group, even though they would not directly benefit from them. Not only did they allocate more points to their in-group than the out-group in experiment one, but in experiment two they were willing to choose less points for the in-group overall (7 rather than 19 points in the example) as long as they had *more than* the out-group (7 points compared to the 1 point of the out-group).

The experiments also support the theory's prediction that no previous attitudes of hostility or dislike towards the out-group are needed before discrimination can occur.

2 How were the groups set up in the experiments different from the kinds of group people find themselves in every day?

The groups in the experiment were deliberately meaningless, whereas in everyday life groups rarely are, and thus people invest more importance in them. One would, therefore, expect discrimination to be even more pronounced between real life groups.

3 How ethical was this study?

The study involved minimal deception and no real harm to the participants, so the study could be described as ethical.

Answers 46.1 – 46.5

1 What kind of experiment was this and why?

This was a natural or quasi experiment due to the lack of experimenter control over the independent variables.

2 What were the independent and dependent variables?

The main independent variables were
- *race* – operationalised by skin colour in 2 main conditions – black (later divided into light, medium and dark black) and white.
- *time* – the 1969 Hraba & Grant results were compared with the 1939 Clark & Clark results for black children.

The effect of the children's *age* was also investigated.
The dependent variables were
- *racial preference and racial identification* (operationalised by the children's answers to Clark & Clark's original 8 questions)
- the *behavioural consequences* of racial preference and identification (operationalised by an additional question on the race of the children's best friend given to the children and their teachers).

3 What problems might there be with the two-doll forced choice method of measuring preference?

The forced 2-doll preference method ignores the intensity of preference (it produces only nominal data) so it does not tell us how much more one doll was preferred to the other. Using dolls rather than people, while controlling for all variables apart from colour, may *lack validity* as a measure of race and self-liking.

4 Which theories of discrimination and methods of discrimination reduction do the results of the study support?

Social identity theory is supported (the perception of groups we identify with affects our self-perception). Also the reduction of discrimination through contact and changing norms through education may be supported by this study.

5 What particular problems might there be using children as participants in a psychological study?

There are particular ethical (in terms of consent and vulnerability to upset) and practical difficulties (such as understanding of questions, concentration levels and vulnerability to demand characteristics from adult experimenters) involved in testing children.

PREJUDICE CROSSWORD

1 According to inter-group conflict theory this causes prejudice and discrimination between groups (11)
2 The effects of this kind of contact on children's identity, preferences and choice of friends were investigated by Hraba & Grant (1970) (5-6)
3 The kind of goals that require co-operation between groups to succeed (13)
4 The kind of group theory that suggests merely dividing people into groups is sufficient to cause prejudice (7)
5 The term for an individual or group that receives the blame and displaced frustration of others (9)
6 The US state park where a famous field study of inter-group discrimination was conducted (7/4)
7 The allocation of individuals to over-generalised categories based on perceivable cues (12)
8 Tajfel proposes that people learn this general tendency to categorise people into in-groups and out-groups and to act in favour of their own in-groups, rather than just conforming to specific prejudices (7/4)
9 The kind of contact that may reduce prejudice (5/6)
10 The theory which proposes that people allocate themselves to groups, gain their identity from them and want to feel they are in the best group (6/8)
11 The equipment Hraba & Grant (1970) used to assess racial identification and preference (5)
12 The group favoured by the schoolboys in Tajfel's (1970) experiments (7)

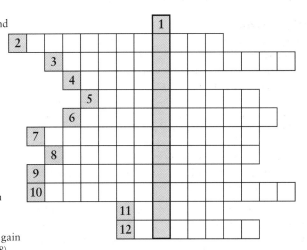

47 | The physiological approach to psychology

Sometimes known as the biological, biopsychological, neurophysiological, nativist (considering nature rather than nurture) or innate approach, physiologically orientated psychologists assume that all that is psychological (i.e. the mind, thoughts, feelings and behaviour) is first physiological (i.e. has a physical basis in the brain/body).

Assumptions

The important influence of the nervous system
If all thoughts, feelings and behaviour ultimately have a physical/biological basis, it follows that it is important to study how the nervous system, including the brain and its neurochemistry, function. Psychologists have, therefore, found it valuable to refer to findings relating to the anatomical structure, neurochemistry and action of neurones, the sympathetic and parasympathetic nervous system, and the brain. For example, much has been learnt about perception from studying how different areas of the brain are involved in different aspects of visual processing, from colour and movement analysis to the identification of shapes and objects.

The importance of genetic influences
If we accept the assumption that our physical body and brain affect our thoughts, feelings and behaviour in important ways, then one might also assume that our DNA, which contains the instructions for building our bodies and brains, also has an important influence.

Biologically orientated psychologists have argued that human genes have evolved over millions of years to adapt behaviour to the environment, therefore much behaviour will have a genetic basis. For example, aggressive behaviour could have evolved in humans, as in other species, due to the evolutionary advantage it gives in competing for resources and defending oneself against others.

In addition to humans possessing similar inherited behavioural tendencies, however, it must be remembered that genetic variation occurs between members of the same species which will create differences in the type and degree of behaviour shown by different individuals. Some of these differences in behaviour, e.g. in levels of aggression, may be inherited from the combination of genes received from each parent. Studying genetic inheritance, therefore, has important implications for explaining, predicting and even changing future behaviour.

Methods

Brain measurement and manipulation
Both observational and experimental techniques have been used in the study of brain anatomy and function.

Observational techniques usually involve measuring the activity or recording the structure of the brain from outside the skull.

- *Electroencephalograms* (EEGs) involve the attachment of electrodes to the scalp which detect the activity of the brain area beneath and amplify it to reveal the frequency of the 'brain wave'. The frequency is the number of oscillations that the wave makes in a second, and ranges from 1 to 3 hertz (delta waves – very little brain activity) to 13 hertz or over (beta waves – the sign of an active brain). EEGs have been used to distinguish between different levels of sleep and different types of subject, e.g. brain damaged, epileptic, those with Alzheimer's disease, etc.

More detailed and comprehensive information on brain activity can be gained using a variety of dynamic brain-scanning methods which can provide moving coloured images of activity levels in different parts of the brain over time.

- *Positron emission tomography* (PET scan) detects the metabolism level of injected substances (e.g. glucose) made mildly radioactive to show which parts of the brain are most active (using up energy) over a period of time. Newer techniques, however, do not require injected tracer substances.

- *Functional magnetic resonance imaging* (F-MRI scan) shows metabolic activity on a second by second basis.

- *Magnetoencephalography* (MEG scan) actually detects nerve cells firing over thousandths of a second.

These methods have revealed the brain areas that are used while people are performing psychological tasks such as imagining objects and remembering information, or while in certain states such as hypnosis.

An alternative to observing the mass activity of many thousands or even millions of brain cells is

- *direct neuronal activity recording* – where microelectrodes are directly inserted into single neuronal cells to record their electrochemical activity. This is an invasive technique – requiring surgery to access the brain itself. For example, Hubel and Wiesel inserted microelectrodes into single neuronal cells in the visual cortex of monkeys and presented various visual stimuli to different areas of the retina to discover both the area the cells represented and the stimuli they most responded to. They discovered, for instance, that some cells would only respond strongly to lines of certain orientations that were moving in certain directions.

Recording *still image structural brain scans* is an observational technique that has been used as the basis for natural or quasi-experimental investigations. Detailed three-dimensional or cross-sectional images of the brain's anatomy can be gained by

- *computerised axial tomography* (CAT scan), produced by X-ray rotation, or

- *magnetic resonance imaging* (MRI scan), where magnetic fields are rotated around the head, for example.

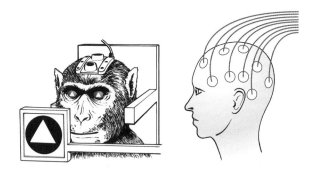

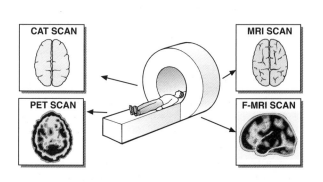

Such scans are able to reveal the location of brain damage in people who have suffered an illness or accident that has caused psychological symptoms.

A *Accidental brain damage studies* – by comparing behaviour and abilities before and after the damage, these unfortunate natural experiments can allow cautious inferences to be drawn about the normal functions of the damaged brain areas. In the past, the location of brain damage could only be discovered by signs of external damage or after an autopsy. For example, when an accident blew a 3-foot long metal rod through the frontal lobe of a railroad construction worker, Phineas Gage, in 1848, it changed his personality – making him impulsive and irritable (it was a miracle he survived at all!). This led investigators to infer that the frontal lobes might be involved in the planning and control of behaviour. Today, structural brain scans can reveal the exact location of suspected damage in living patients who have no signs of skull trauma. For example, much has been learnt about the brain's language functioning by observing the location of damage caused by strokes and tumours which have led to particular problems, such as loss of speech production, speech comprehension or reading comprehension.

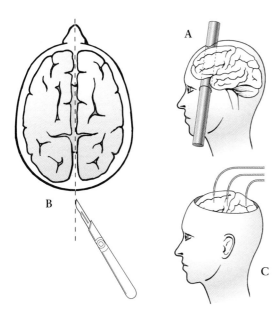

Controlled experimental techniques – a number of methods of studying brain function involve deliberately altering the brain's structure or activity under more standardised conditions.

B *Ablation or lesion studies* aim to investigate brain function by removing or destroying parts of the brain (ablation) or severing the connections between brain areas (lesion). For example, surgically removing the ventromedial hypothalamus of rats has caused them to overeat to the point of hyper-obesity, indicating a role for this structure in regulating appetite. In humans, Roger Sperry cut the corpus callosum of epileptic patients to reduce their symptoms, splitting their brain nearly in two and producing a 'split mind'. Prefrontal lobotomy was performed on mental inmates to control their behaviour, often with a number of serious side-effects (including loss of initiative and even death).

C *Electrical or neurochemical stimulation* is another experimental technique that aims to stimulate brain areas (e.g. using microelectrodes) to reveal their function through producing changes in behaviour.

Delgado, for example, stimulated areas of the limbic system to provoke aggression in monkeys and inhibit aggression in a charging bull (while standing in front of it!) by remote control.

In human studies Penfield stimulated areas of the cortex in conscious patients undergoing brain surgery and found locations that would produce body movement (primary motor cortex), body sensations (primary sensory cortex), memories of sound (temporal lobe) and visual sensations (visual cortex).

Genetic research methods

Two techniques used to investigate genetic influences and the inheritance of individual differences include family resemblance correlations and molecular genetics.

■ *Family resemblance correlations* – measure the degree of similarity in characteristics, such as intelligence or schizophrenia, between genetically related (e.g. parents and offspring, siblings and cousins, etc.) and unrelated individuals on the assumption that the closer the genetic relationship the greater the similarity. Genetically identical (monozygotic) twins, in particular, have been compared with non-identical (dizygotic) twins, while adoption studies have also been conducted to compare the similarity of genetically related people who have been reared in different families.

Bouchard and McGue (1981) conducted a review of 111 worldwide studies which compared the IQ of family members. The correlation figures below represent the average degree of similarity between the two people (the higher the correlation, the more similar their IQ scores).

	Average correlation
Identical twins raised together	.86
Identical twins reared apart	.72
Non-identical twins reared together	.60
Siblings reared together	.47
Siblings reared apart	.24
Cousins	.15

■ *Molecular genetics* – modern technology now allows researchers to extract genetic material from individuals with a certain characteristic to see how it differs from that of people without the characteristic. This can reveal the coding of the genes correlated with the characteristics and their location amongst the 23 pairs of human chromosomes. Plomin (1997), for example, found a gene called IGF2R which he believed accounted for 2% of the variation in IQ test results.

Exercise 47

1 What is the main difference between
 a dynamic brain scans and still image structural ones?
 b natural brain damage experiments and controlled ones?
 c direct recording and electrical stimulation of neurones?

2 What are the advantages and disadvantages of
 a direct recording of neurones compared to EEG recording?
 b accidental compared to deliberate brain damage studies?
 c electrical stimulation of neurones compared to dynamic brain scanning?

3 What major problem with the family and twin studies do you think led to the use of adoption studies?

4 What do Bouchard and McGue's results indicate about the strength of genetic influences on IQ?

5 What does Plomin's finding indicate about intelligence?

6 If it was revealed that IQ was highly determined by our genes, what social implications might follow?

1 What is the main difference between

a dynamic brain scans and still image structural ones?

Dynamic brain scans can directly reveal the activity of different areas of the brain in action, whereas still-image scans only provide a picture of their physical structure.

b natural brain damage experiments and controlled ones?

Natural brain damage experiments involve studying the effects of *accidental changes* on the brain's structure, whereas controlled brain damage experiments involve the *deliberate* damage of the brain (and thus manipulation of the independent variable) by the researcher.

c direct recording and electrical stimulation of neurones?

In direct recording of neuronal activity, the microelectrode is not designed to cause changes in the brain and is used for observational/measurement purposes. In electrical stimulation, however, the microelectrode is designed to trigger changes in the brain and is, therefore, used for experimental purposes (the effect is measured by recording some change in experience or behaviour).

2 What are the advantages and disadvantages of

a direct recording of neurones compared to EEG recording?

The direct recording of neuronal activity is a very precise and accurate way of investigating the living function of brain areas. However, it is very time-consuming (an extremely large number of neurones occupy even a tiny area of brain) and may be a little too focused (it neglects the interactions *between* nerve cells that are responsible for brain functions). It is also an invasive method and so produces ethical problems, especially if applied to humans.

In contrast, EEG measurements are often rather crude – the activity level of millions of neurones is measured and averaged, but the precise function of the neurones involved is not known. However, EEG measurement is a non-invasive technique that involves minimal interference with the brain's functioning so the brain activity data is more natural and valid.

b accidental compared to deliberate brain damage studies?

With accidental brain damage studies the altering damage occurs 'naturally' so there are less ethical problems compared to other methods. Unfortunately, these natural experiments suffer from the disadvantages of

- lack of precision – the exact extent of damage is not controllable and may be difficult to assess
- comparison problems – comparison of the functioning in the individual before and after the damage is less objective since it is often based on retrospective accounts of previous behaviour and abilities
- confounding variables – other non-physical effects of the damage may be responsible for behavioural differences. For example, social reactions to Phineas Gage's physical deformity may have affected his personality.

By contrast, the laboratory experimental method of deliberately damaging the brain leads to greater control – the greater precision in the location of damage and the ability to compare behaviour before and after alteration leads to higher certainty over the effects of the damage. On the negative side, there are ethical problems with this method – the deliberate changes are irreversible and need to be carefully considered. Practically, findings from brain surgery studies on non-humans may not be legitimately generalised to humans due to qualitative differences in brain structure. Also the brain is a very flexible system which can compensate for damage; removing one part of it will only show the performance of the rest of the system, not necessarily the missing part.

c electrical stimulation of neurones compared to dynamic brain scanning?

Both methods have the advantage of being able to gain information about the brain's structure and function using *conscious* patients in a *controlled experimental context* (to reveal cause and effect more reliably). The electrical stimulation acts as the independent variable, with the dependent variable being the effect on the participant's experience or behaviour. The dynamic brain scanning acts as the dependent variable to measure the changes in the brain produced by performing different mental tasks (the independent variable). Both methods seem a better way of investigating the 'living' function of brain areas.

The electrical stimulation of neurones involves altering the brain's functioning, but does so temporarily by stimulating the brain rather than damaging it (therefore it is more ethical). However, the technique still involves a surgical operation, which can be risky. Also, because of the great interconnectedness of the brain's neurones, it is not easy to know exactly how far the stimulation has spread to other areas and the behaviour produced may not be natural, indeed it is often more stereotyped.

By contrast, the only ethical problem of some dynamic scanning methods is that they require the injection of mildly radioactive tracer substances, and dynamic scans are good at identifying the interconnectivity of brain functions. Practically, though, dynamic scanning methods are expensive, and the scans themselves can be difficult to interpret and are sensitive to disruption, e.g. by small head movements.

3 What major problem with the family and twin studies do you think led to the use of adoption studies?

Adoption studies have helped *control for the similar environments* that related individuals are more likely to share. With intelligence, for example, family members who live together are more likely to share similar environmental influences (e.g. go to similar schools, read the same books, watch the same television, receive the same stimulation from parents, etc.) *as well as* genes, compared to cousins or unrelated people. Identical twins, because they look more alike, are even more likely to be treated in a similar way by others compared to non-identical twins, as well as being more genetically similar.

Adoption studies hope to provide a better control for environmental influences since those tested share their genes with biological relatives but their environment with their adoptive family.

4 What do Bouchard and McGue's results indicate about the strength of genetic influences on IQ?

The results seem to indicate a role for both genetic and environmental influences on IQ.

For genetic influence look, for example, at how identical twins raised apart (same genes, different environments) have more similar IQs than non-identical twins raised together (different genes, similar environment).

For environmental influence look, for example, at how siblings reared together have much more similar IQs than siblings raised apart (siblings share similar proportions of genes but the siblings reared apart are less likely to share similar environments).

There is much debate over the proportion of IQ that is due to genetic influences and that which is due to environmental ones, even whether the debate itself is meaningful at all. Current estimates on the variance in IQ scores that are due to genetic influences seem to vary between 50% and 80%.

5 What does Plomin's finding indicate about intelligence?

Plomin's finding seems to indicate that intelligence (as measured by IQ) may be polygenic – determined by the action of many different genes. It may also imply that intelligence is not a unitary phenomenon – there may be different kinds or types of intelligence (e.g. verbal, mathematical, visual, etc.), some of which may be under more genetic control than others.

6 If it was revealed that IQ was highly determined by our genes, what social implications might follow?

In the past, genetic research on IQ has been used for selection purposes, for example, those thought to be inherently more intelligent were sent to better schools or given better jobs. Some have also tried to apply genetic research to promote the selection of 'desirable' characteristics (an enterprise known as 'eugenics') by controlling human breeding. Such attempts have ranged from encouraging marriage between 'intelligent' people to eliminating 'unintelligent' people from the gene pool or restricting their access to it, e.g. through immigration control, sterilisation of the mentally retarded, or even gas chambers.

With improving technology, such as genetic screening and gene therapy, further ethical implications regarding the use of genetic knowledge for selection and control purposes will have to be considered. Employers may want to select their employees, insurance companies their customers, and parents their children (through abortion or gene therapy) based on the results of genetic screening. Some argue that just because the choice to genetically screen and control is placed in the hands of individuals rather than society does not make it any less 'eugenic'.

Unfortunately, however, much of the research into the genetic basis of intelligence has been based on faulty methodology and assumptions. Often, early research on the inheritance of intelligence was
- politically motivated by eugenic beliefs, often carried out by researchers biased towards discovering innate causes
- conducted using poorly controlled family resemblance studies and culturally biased IQ tests on different 'races'.

Unsurprisingly, it revealed that IQ was largely inherited (around 80%), and was used to justify, for instance, the selection of naturally bright individuals for jobs, special education at an early age and the right of immigration into the USA.

Later research indicated that around 50% of IQ is inherited, the rest is influenced by conditions in the womb and the social and family environment.

Some researchers have also leapt to conclusions based on a faulty understanding of how genes express their influence – suggesting, for instance, that genetic influences mean we are inevitably doomed to certain fates. These conclusions have important implications and have caused strong disagreements between psychologists who favour the importance of nature and those who champion nurture. A more variable influence of inherited factors in combination with environmental ones has gradually become accepted as research revealed that
- genes can only build bodies based on the environmental resources available, and environmental factors can influence the genes themselves
- human characteristics may be influenced by many genes (pleiotropy), not all of which will necessarily be inherited
- some genes, e.g. those involved in Huntingdon's disease, have more direct and inevitable effects than others, e.g. those involved in Alzheimer's disease
- genes express their effects in many different and often subtle ways.

Genetic research now implicitly investigates how genes interact with environmental factors to create behaviour and tries to determine the balance of influences for specific characteristics.

Molecular genetic research has found that individuals can possess the genes associated with a characteristic, without necessarily developing it themselves. At the moment, the possession of most human psychological traits and abilities cannot be predicted with 100% certainty using current methods.

The way genes influence intelligence is still a mystery. Genes associated with intelligence may directly affect aspects of cognitive ability, such as processing speed, or indirectly evoke environmental influences on IQ by creating characteristics such as the ability to concentrate or motivation to learn. Alternatively, perhaps the genes promote resistance to disease and the healthy development of the brain – lacking such genes might prevent the genius that a fully healthy brain would give us all!

Given the variable effects of genes upon behaviour and the methodological problems involved in assessing them, particular care needs to be taken in how knowledge of genetic influences is used and interpreted.

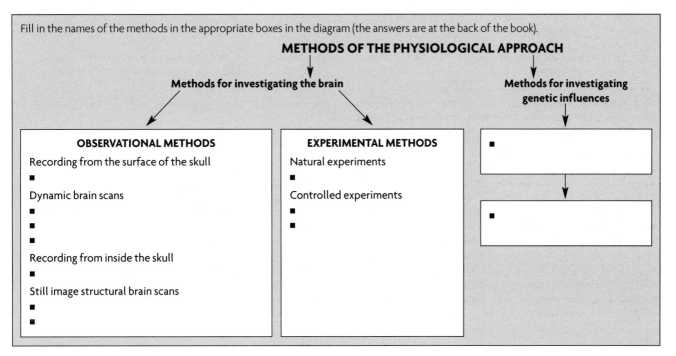

Fill in the names of the methods in the appropriate boxes in the diagram (the answers are at the back of the book).

METHODS OF THE PHYSIOLOGICAL APPROACH

Methods for investigating the brain

Methods for investigating genetic influences

OBSERVATIONAL METHODS

Recording from the surface of the skull
-

Dynamic brain scans
-
-
-

Recording from inside the skull
-

Still image structural brain scans
-
-

EXPERIMENTAL METHODS

Natural experiments
-

Controlled experiments
-
-

-

-

Previous research using a variety of techniques (e.g. brain damage effects and EEG measurements) on both humans and other animals has indicated that dysfunction in certain localised brain areas may predispose individuals to violent behaviour. Such brain structures include the prefrontal cortex, corpus callosum, left angular gyrus, amygdala, hippocampus and thalamus.

The authors of this study, by using recent brain-imaging techniques on a large group of violent offenders who have committed murder and a control group of non-murderers, hypothesised that dysfunction in the above brain structures should be found more often in the murderers than

- dysfunction of the same areas in non-murderers
- dysfunction in other areas of the murderers' brains that have been implicated in non-violent psychiatric disorders (e.g. the caudate, putamen, globus pallidus, midbrain and cerebellum).

Method

The 'murderers' were 41 prisoners (39 male, 2 female) with a mean age of 34.3 years (standard deviation of 10.1), charged with murder or manslaughter in California. They were referred for brain-imaging scans to obtain evidence or information relating to a defence of not guilty by reason of insanity, incompetence to stand trial, or diminished capacity to reduce sentencing having been found guilty. The reasons for scanning referral were very diverse, ranging from schizophrenia (6 cases) to head injury or organic brain damage (23 cases). No murderer had psychoactive medication for 2 weeks before scanning (each was urine screened).

Each murderer was matched with a 'normal' subject for age, sex and schizophrenia where necessary. Each 'normal' control subject was screened to exclude physical and mental illness, drug taking and, of course, a history of murder.

After practice trials, all participants were injected with a tracer substance (fluorodeoxyglucose) that was taken up by the brain to show the location of brain metabolism (activity) while they conducted a continuous performance task (CPT) requiring them to detect target signals for 32 minutes. A positron emission tomography (PET) scan was then immediately given to show the relative brain activity (glucose metabolised) for 6 main cortical areas (the outside of the brain) and 8 subcortical areas (inside the brain).

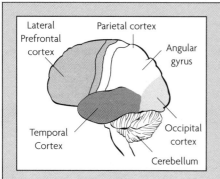
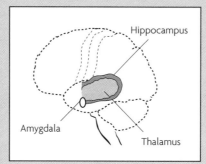
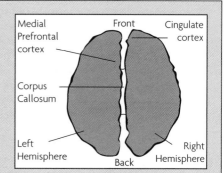

RESULTS

	Brain structure	Murderers' metabolic activity level	Interpretation
Cortex	Prefrontal cortex	Lower activity than controls	Linked to loss of self-control and altered emotion.
	Parietal cortex	Lower activity than controls especially in the left angular and bilateral superior gyrus	Lower left angular gyrus activity linked to lower verbal ability, educational failure and thus crime.
	Temporal cortex	No difference compared to controls	No difference was expected.
	Occipital cortex	Higher activity than controls (unexpected)	May compensate on CPT for lower frontal activity.
Subcortex	Corpus callosum	Lower activity than controls	May stop left brain inhibiting the right's violence.
	Amygdala	Lower activity in left than right side of the brain in murderers than controls	These structures form part of the limbic system (thought to control emotional expression). Problems with these structures may cause a lack of inhibition for violent behaviour, fearlessness and a failure to learn the negative effects of violence.
	Medial (inner) temporal including hippocampus	Lower activity in left than right side of the brain in murderers than controls	
	Thalamus	Higher activity on right side in murderers	
	Cingulate, caudate, putamen Globus pallidus, midbrain and cerebellum	No significant differences were found in these structures between murderers and controls.	No differences were expected in these structures (which are involved in other disorders), supporting the specificity of brain areas involved in violence.

No significant differences were found for performance on the CPT, handedness (except that left-handed murderers had significantly less abnormal amygdala asymmetry than right-handed murderers), head injury or ethnicity.

Discussion

A large sample was used with many controls to rule out alternative effects on brain activity. However, the PET scan method can lack precision and the findings need to be replicated and interpreted cautiously. The findings do *not*

- mean violence is caused by biology alone (other social, psychological and situational factors are involved)
- show the murderers are not responsible for their actions
- mean PET scans can diagnose murderers
- say if the abnormalities are a cause or effect of behaviour.

Exercise 48

1 What variable do you think was operationalised by testing murderers?

2 How far do you think you could generalise the results of this study from this sample?

3 Why do the authors specify what the findings do *not* show?

1 What variable do you think was operationalised by testing murderers?

The researchers seem to regard the murderers as operationalising the variable of 'aggression' or 'violence', rather than 'criminal behaviour', since they argue that previous findings on the brain structures involved in violence are supported and new findings have been revealed. While murderers do seem to be good candidates for such a variable, no information is given regarding the type or level of violence used in their offence. In addition, the task performed during scanning (the CPT) did not involve aggression and thus may not have produced the same activity, so the activity of all the brain areas involved in violence may not have been revealed.

2 How far do you think you could generalise the results of this study from this sample?

The findings apply only to a subgroup of violent offenders, not to other types of violence or crime.

3 Why do the authors specify what the findings do *not* show?

This study particularly raises the ethics of socially sensitive research. Given the possible implications of the results, the limitations of the methodology (brain scans can lack precision and be difficult to interpret) and the relatively new nature of the research, care needs to be taken with what conclusions are drawn and how they are understood and used by others. The research has many important implications and its findings need careful interpretation by scientists and the general public.

Researchers such as Gould (1981) in *The Mismeasure of Man* have pointed out that history is full of examples of failed attempts to find physical differences between criminals and non-criminals, such as cranial measurement and phrenology (interpreting skull shape), that have sometimes resulted in unfounded prejudice and discrimination.

RAINE et al. CROSSWORD

1. The scanning method used was _____ / _____ tomography (8/8)
2. The area of cortex at the back of the brain that had higher activity than expected in the murderers (9)
3. The area of cortex that had lower activity in the murderers than controls, which may be linked to loss of self-control and altered emotion (10)
4. Brain activity was measured by how much of this was used (7)
5. The term for areas inside the brain rather than on its surface (the cortex) (11)
6. The term for a substance taken up by the brain to show the location of activity (6)
7. An area of the left parietal cortex linked with lower verbal ability and thus educational failure and crime in the murderers (7/5)
8. The area of cortex at the sides of the brain where no difference was found or expected between murderers and controls (8)
9. The number of murderers tested (5-3)
10. Thirty-nine of the murderers were this (4)
11. The term for differences between hemispheres (9)
12. This was screened to exclude the influence of psychoactive medication on the scans (5)
13. The term for 'not working properly' (11)
14. The scanning method can sometimes lack this (9)
15. The results should be treated with this due to the preliminary nature of the findings and their possible implications (7)
16. Six of the murderers had been diagnosed with this mental disorder (13)
17. The kind of performance task performed before the scan (10)

49 | Schachter & Singer (1962) – 'Cognitive, social and physiological determinants of emotional state'

This study was conducted to provide support for Schachter's (1959) theory of the interaction between physiology, cognition and behaviour in emotional experience. Schachter believes that cognitive factors (thought processes) are very important in determining which emotion is felt. He argues that emotion-provoking stimuli, such as a gun being pointed at you, will automatically cause a general physiological level of arousal (the activation of the sympathetic nervous system) which is interpreted (cognitively) as fear (the emotion) in the light of our knowledge about the dangerous nature of guns.

Cognitive labelling theory

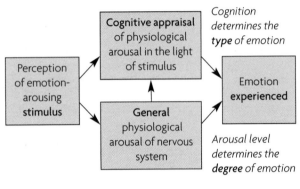

Schachter and Singer, therefore, propose the 3 following predictions from this theory:

A Given an unexplained state of general physiological arousal, the individual experiencing it will attempt to describe or label it as a particular emotion in terms of his cognitive explanations of its causes. Thus the same state of arousal could be described or labelled as joy or fury depending upon the situation they are in.

B Given a state of general physiological arousal for which an individual already has an appropriate explanation (e.g. I feel this way because I have been injected with adrenaline) there will be no need to use external situational cues to label the arousal as an emotion.

C Given no state of general physiological arousal, despite situational cues to label emotions with, an individual will experience no emotion.

Method

The subjects were 184 male college students, 90% of whom volunteered to get extra marks on their exams. They were told that the experiment was a study of the effect of Suproxin (supposedly a vitamin supplement) upon vision.

All subjects were tested individually, asked whether they would mind receiving a Suproxin injection (in fact either epinephrine or a placebo) and assigned to one of the following conditions:

1 *Epinephrine informed* – given a Suproxin injection that was *really epinephrine* and told of its *real side-effects* (general physiological arousal of the sympathetic nervous system causing accelerated heartbeat/breathing, palpitations, etc.).

2 *Epinephrine misinformed* – given a Suproxin injection that was *really epinephrine* and told *false side-effects* (e.g. itching, numbness, etc.).

3 *Epinephrine ignorant* – given a Suproxin injection that was *really epinephrine* and told there would be *no side-effects*.

4 *Control ignorant* – given a Suproxin injection that was *really a placebo* (a saline solution which had no direct effect on arousal of the sympathetic nervous system) and told there would be *no side effect*s at all.

All subjects (with the exception of the epinephrine misinformed group who were not exposed to the angry stooge) were then left alone with either

- the euphoric stooge (subjects saw a confederate of the experimenter behaving happily – throwing paper and playing with a hula-hoop)
- the angry stooge (subjects saw a confederate of the experimenter complain and behave in a outraged way, ripping up a questionnaire).

The subjects were observed through a one-way mirror to rate their behaviour for how similar it was to the stooge's behaviour (implying that they were in the same emotional state). Self-report scales were also used to assess how good or angry they felt.

Results

For subjects observing euphoric stooges

- Self-reports of emotions and behaviour were mostly significantly happier in epinephrine ignorant and misinformed subjects (who did not have a relevant explanation for their arousal) than the epinephrine informed group (who did not need to use the external cues to explain their arousal). This supports predictions A and B above.
- There was no significant difference in mood between the epinephrine ignorant or misinformed subjects and the placebo control subjects. This indicates that prediction C above is not supported.

For subjects observing angry stooges

Only behavioural observations were used since subjects feared self-reports of anger at the experimenter would endanger their extra exam marks.

- Epinephrine ignorant subjects behaved significantly more angrily than epinephrine informed or placebo subjects. This supports predictions A, B and C, however placebo subjects still followed the angry behaviour more than the epinephrine informed subjects. The results support the predictions more strongly if a) adrenaline misinformed and ignorant subjects who attributed arousal to their injection and b) the placebo subjects who showed physiological arousal in response to just having an injection, are removed from the data.

Exercise 49

1 What were the three independent variables and the dependent variable and how were they operationalised?

2 How well do you think the results support the predictions of Schachter's theory?

3 How could this laboratory experiment on emotion be accused of being artificial?

4 How representative was the sample used?

5 Do you think the study was ethical?

---

1 What were the three independent variables and the dependent variable and how were they operationalised?

The three independent variables manipulated (in an independent measures design) were:

- Physiological arousal – manipulated by giving either an
  a injection of epinephrine (adrenaline)
  b injection of a placebo (saline solution).
- Explanation of arousal – manipulated according to whether the participants were
  a informed (told the correct symptoms)
  b misinformed (told the wrong symptoms)
  c ignorant (told no symptoms).
- Situational emotion cues – manipulated by providing exposure to either the
  a euphoric stooge
  b angry stooge.

The dependent variable of experienced emotional state was measured by behavioural observation and self-report.

2 How well do you think the results support the predictions of Schachter's theory?

The study provided *some* support for Schachter's theory that physiological arousal and cognitive interpretation are both necessary but not sufficient on their own to cause emotions.

However, significant results were only found for the behaviour changes rated by the observers – no significant differences were found in the subjects' self-report of their emotions. Also, the results were not highly significant and other researchers, such as Marshall and Zimbardo (1979), have not replicated Schachter and Singer's findings.

3 How could this laboratory experiment on emotion be accused of being artificial?

Injection is an artificial way of generating physiological arousal (and can cause fear arousal in itself). The laboratory surroundings lack ecological validity and the situation of experiencing unexplained physiological arousal is rare.

4 How representative was the sample used?

Only male students were used and most of those had volunteered to get extra marks on their exams (they may, therefore, have been more motivated to behave in exaggerated ways to please the researchers).

5 Do you think the study was ethical?

Participants were deceived over the purpose of the study and content of the injection.

SCHACHTER AND SINGER CROSSWORD

1 Environmental sources of information which provide explanations for our feelings (11/4)
2 Another term for a researcher's confederate (6)
3 The percentage of students who volunteered for the study to get extra marks on their exams (6)
4 Physiological arousal results from the activation of the _____ nervous system (11)
5 The name of the vitamin supplement participants thought they were being injected with (8)
6 All the participants were this (4)
7 The condition where subjects received saline solution but were told they were injected with the vitamin and there would be no side-effects (7)
8 The condition where subjects received epinephrine but were told they were injected with the vitamin and were given false side-effects (11)
9 The kind of experiment conducted (10)
10 The confederate who complained and acted in an outraged way, ripping up the questionnaire (5)
11 The kind of mirror used to observe the participants' behaviour without being seen (3-3)
12 The term for giving a name to one's arousal (9)
13 This occurred relating to the purpose of the study and the content of the injection, raising ethical problems (9)
14 The confederate who behaved happily, throwing paper and playing with a hula-hoop (8)
15 The term for the saline injection with no active ingredients (7)
16 The kind of report scales the participants used to rate their feelings (4)

Sperry (1968) – 'Hemisphere deconnection and unity in conscious awareness'

Sperry's report presents studies investigating the behavioural, neurological and psychological consequences of surgery in which the two cerebral hemispheres are deconnected from each other by severing the corpus callosum.

Sperry uses these studies to argue that the 'split brain' shows characteristics during testing that suggest each hemisphere

- has slightly different functions
- possesses an independent stream of conscious awareness
- has its own set of memories that are inaccessible to the other.

Method

The participants were a handful of patients who underwent hemispheric deconnection to reduce crippling epilepsy.

Severing the corpus callosum prevents communication between the left and right hemispheres. Since each hemisphere receives information from, and controls the functioning of, the opposite side of the body, the capabilities of each can be tested by

- presenting visual information to either the left or right visual field when the subject is focusing straight ahead. If this is done at fast speeds (about 1 tenth of a second) the eye does not have time to move and re-focus. Thus, information presented to the left visual field will be received by the right hemisphere of the brain.
- presenting tactile information to either the left or right hand behind a screen (to remove visual identification). Thus tactile information from objects felt by the right hand will be received by the left hemisphere.

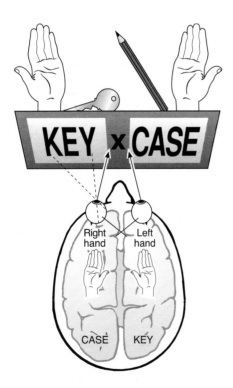

Results

For visual stimuli presented in one visual field at a time:

- Objects shown once to a visual field are only recognised if presented again in the same visual field, not the other – implying different visual perception and memory storage for each hemisphere.

- Objects presented in the right visual field and, therefore, received in the left hemisphere can be named verbally and in writing on request, indicating the presence of speech comprehension and production as well as writing ability.
- Objects presented in the left visual field and, therefore, received in the right hemisphere can not be named verbally nor in writing when requested, but can be identified through pointing, indicating that the right hemisphere has language comprehension but not speech or writing.

These tests imply that the two hemispheres of the brain have different abilities and functions.

For different visual stimuli presented simultaneously to different visual fields:

- If different visual stimuli are presented simultaneously to different visual fields, e.g. a dollar sign to the left, a question mark to the right, and the subject is asked to draw with the left hand (out of sight) what was seen, the subject draws the stimuli from the left visual field (the dollar sign). If asked what the *left hand has just drawn*, the subject's verbal, left hemisphere replies with what was seen in the right visual field (the question mark).
- If two related words are simultaneously presented to the different visual fields, e.g. 'key' to the left and 'case' to the right, the left hand will select a key from amongst a variety of objects, whereas the right hand will write what it saw in the right visual field (a case) without being influenced by the meaning of the word in the left visual field.

For tactile stimuli presented to different hands:

- If an object has been felt by the left hand only, it can be recognised by the left hand again but cannot be named by the subject or recognised by the right hand from amongst other objects.

These tests imply that one side of the brain does not know what the other side has seen or felt.

For tests of the non-dominant right hemisphere:

- The left hand can pick out semantically similar objects in a search for an object presented to the left visual field but not present in the search array of objects, e.g. a watch will be selected in response to a picture of a wall clock. The left hand can sort objects into meaningful categories.
- The right brain can solve simple arithmetical problems (pointing out the correct answer) and is superior in drawing spatial relationships.
- The right brain appears to experience its own emotional reactions (giggling and blushing in embarrassment at a nude pin-up presented to the left visual field) and can show frustration at the actions of the left hemisphere.

Sperry suggests that these tests imply that the right hemisphere is a second conscious entity that exists in parallel with the major (left) hemisphere's dominant stream of consciousness.

Exercise 50 (the answers are on page 122)

1 In the subjects which hemisphere (left, right or both) can
   a identify visual images? b identify tactile sensations?
   c store memories? d understand language? e speak?
   f write? g experience emotional reactions? h calculate?
   i draw spatial relationships? j move the left hand?

2 What method is used in this study and what advantage and disadvantage does it have?

3 What problem might be raised by the sample?

Dement & Kleitman (1957) – 'The relation of eye movements during sleep to dream activity: an objective method for the study of dreams'

Previous research by Aserinsky and Kleitman had found a relationship between rapid eye movement (REM) during sleep and reports of dreaming. In this study, Dement and Kleitman aimed to provide a more detailed investigation of how *objective*, physiological aspects of rapid eye movement relate to the *subjective*, psychological experience of dreaming, reported by subjects, by testing

1 whether significantly more dreaming occurs during REM sleep than non-REM sleep under controlled conditions.
2 whether there is a significant positive correlation between the objective length of time spent in REM and the subjective duration of dreaming reported upon waking.
3 whether there is a significant relationship between the pattern of rapid eye movements observed during sleep and the content of the dream reported upon waking.

Method

Seven adult males and two adult females were the participants, five of whom were intensively studied, while four were used to confirm results.

All the participants slept individually in a quiet, dark, laboratory room after a normal day's activity (except that alcohol and caffeine were avoided during the days before testing). Electrodes were connected near the eyes to register eye movement and on the scalp to measure brain waves during sleep (amplified and recorded using an electroencephalograph) – these were the objective measures of REM sleep.

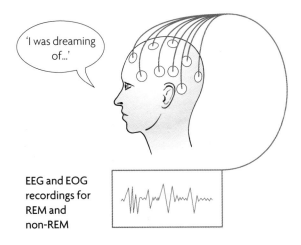

'I was dreaming of...'

EEG and EOG recordings for REM and non-REM

The participants were awoken at various times during the night (fairly evenly distributed across the average sleeping time of the subjects) by a loud doorbell noise, and immediately reported into a recording device whether they had been dreaming and the content of the dream (before any contact with the experimenter). Subjects were never usually told whether their eyes had been moving before being awoken.

Dreaming was only counted if a fairly detailed and coherent dream was reported – vague impressions or assertions of dreaming without recall of content were not counted.

Study one – Subjects were awoken in one of four different ways during either REM or non-REM sleep to see if they had been dreaming.

- Two subjects were awoken randomly.
- One subject was awoken during 3 REM sleep periods followed by 3 non-REM periods, and so on.
- One subject was awoken randomly but was told he would only be awoken during periods of REM sleep.
- One subject was awoken at the whim of the experimenter.

Study two – Subjects were awoken either 5 or 15 minutes after REM sleep began and were asked to decide whether the duration of their dream was closer to 5 or 15 minutes.

The length of the dream (measured in terms of the number of words in their dream narratives) was also correlated to the duration of REM sleep before awakening.

Study three – Subjects were awoken as soon as one of four patterns of eye movement had occurred for 1 minute, and were asked exactly what they had just dreamt.

- Mainly vertical eye movements.
- Mainly horizontal eye movements.
- Both vertical and horizontal eye movements.
- Very little or no eye movement.

Results

Generally, REM periods were clearly observed in all subjects and distinguished from non-REM sleep periods. REM sleep periods occurred at regular intervals specific to each subject (although on average occurring every 92 minutes) and tended to last longer later in the night.

- *Study one* – Regardless of how subjects were awoken, significantly more dreams were reported in REM than non-REM sleep. When subjects failed to recall dreams from REM sleep this was usually early in the night. When subjects recalled dreams from non-REM sleep it was most often within 8 minutes after the end of a REM period.

- *Study two* – Subjects were significantly correct in matching the duration of their dream to the length of time they had shown REM sleep, for both the 5 minute periods (45 out of 51 estimates correct) and 15 minute periods (47 out of 60 estimates correct). All subjects showed a significant positive correlation at the P< 0.05 level or better between the length of their dream narratives and the duration of their REM sleep before awakening.

- *Study three* – There was a very strong association between the pattern of REMs and the content of dream reports.
  - Three vertical REM periods were associated with dreams of looking up and down at cliff faces, ladders and basketball nets.
  - The only mainly horizontal REM period involved a dream of people throwing tomatoes at each other.
  - Twenty-one periods of vertical and horizontal REMs were associated with dreams of looking at close objects.
  - Ten periods of very little or no REMs were associated with dreams of looking at fixed or distant objects.

The authors conclude that this research provides support for the idea that dreams can be studied in an objective way. This then opens up other areas of research, e.g. investigating the effects of environmental stimuli, stress and drugs on dreaming.

Exercise 51

1 What are the advantages and disadvantages of using laboratory environments to study sleep?
2 Evaluate the sample used in the study.
3 Why were alcohol and caffeine avoided beforehand?
4 Why did subjects report into the recording device before any contact with the experimenter?

Answers 50.1 – 50.3

1 Which hemisphere (left, right or both) can:

a identify visual images? both
b identify tactile sensations? both
c store memories? both
d understand language? both
a speak? left
e write? left
f experience emotional reactions? both
g calculate? both, but the left better than the right
h draw spatial relationships? both, but the right better than the left
i move the left hand? right

2 What method is used in this study and what advantage and disadvantage does it have?

A natural experiment because there is a lack of control over the participants – the procedure can only be ethically conducted using certain people (who need the operation). However, their mental abilities may have been atypical before the operation.

3 What problem might be raised by the sample?

From the limited sample there may be problems generalising the results to a larger population. In fact Sperry noted that the more patients he examined who had undergone the hemispheric deconnection the more he was impressed with the individual differences they showed in symptoms.

Later research has found that there do seem to be functional asymmetries between the hemispheres, however there are many individual differences – the 1968 findings appear most typical of right-handed men. It should not be forgotten that the left and right hemispheres share many functions and are highly integrated.

SPERRY ANAGRAMS

1 I S P Y P E E L
2 N O E N D N O T I C E C
3 S P R U C O   S M A L L C O U
4 M I N T O A N D   P R I M E H E E S H

Answers 51.1 – 51.4

1 What are the advantages and disadvantages of using laboratory environments to study sleep?

Laboratory environments are useful for studying sleep because they allow greater standardisation of conditions and recording precision – with identical sleeping conditions for each participant and specialised equipment to record electroencephalograms and electrooculargrams.

However, under such unfamiliar and artificial conditions (e.g. having electrodes stuck to one's head and the knowledge of being observed) the participants' sleep patterns may not be as natural as usual.

2 Evaluate the sample used in the study.

The study used a limited sample, mostly men, therefore there may be problems generalising the results to a wider population.

3 Why were alcohol and caffeine avoided beforehand?

These two substances are known to affect sleep so if all the participants avoided them a better picture of 'natural' sleep patterns would be gained and better comparisons between participants could be made.

4 Why did subjects report into the recording device before any contact with the experimenter?

The participants immediately reported into a recording device whether they had been dreaming and the content of the dream before any contact with the experimenter to avoid any biasing information or prompts from the researchers. For example, knowledge of whether their eyes had been moving before being awoken might have led them to think they must have been dreaming (if they were aware of the hypothesis) and might have biased their recall of their dream state.

DEMENT AND KLEITMAN CROSSWORD

1 The kind of eye movements associated with vivid dreaming (5)
2 A recording of eye movements is known as an electro_____ (10)
3 All subjects showed a significant positive correlation between the length of their dream narratives and the _____ of their REM sleep (8)
4 The apparatus for recording brain wave activity is known as an electro_____ (14)
5 Dreams of looking up and down at cliff faces, ladders and basketball nets were associated with _____ eye movements (8)
6 Little or no eye movements were associated with dreams of looking at fixed or _____ objects (7)

52 | Body rhythms

Body rhythms are biological processes that show cyclical variation over time. Many processes show such cyclical variation in both plants and animals over a variety of time periods, ranging from hours or days to years, and reflect the influence of the earth's rotation upon its living inhabitants through the physical changes in the environment it produces. Body rhythms seem governed by internal, inbuilt mechanisms (termed 'endogenous pacemakers' or 'body clocks') as well as external environmental stimuli (termed 'zeitgebers' or 'time-givers').

Circadian rhythms

Circadian rhythms cycle over 24 hours ('circa' = approximately, 'diem' = day). Humans show physiological changes over a 24-hour cycle in hormone levels, body temperature and heart, respiration and metabolic rate. Of most interest to psychologists, however, has been the circadian sleep–waking cycle because of the dramatic changes in behaviour it produces.

The sleep–waking cycle

The circadian sleep–waking rhythm determines our alertness and activity levels during the day and night.

The psychological and physiological changes of the sleep–waking circadian rhythm

Psychological experience	Physiological changes	
Alertness open-eyed active consciousness with full task concentration	EEG Beta waves (13 hertz +)	EOG/EMG Eye and muscle movements reflect task.
Relaxation passive but awake conscious experience though eyes may be shut	Alpha waves (8 – 12 hertz)	Eye movement reflects thought, muscle activity shows relaxation.
Non-REM sleep involves a series of stages:		
Stage 1: Lightest stage of sleep. Easily awakened.	Theta waves (4 – 7 hertz).	Slow rolling eye movements. Muscles relaxed but active.
Stage 2: Light sleep. Fairly easily awakened. Some responsiveness to external and internal stimuli.	Theta waves Sleep spindles K-complex activity when name called.	Minimal eye movements. Little muscle movement.
Stage 3: Deep sleep. Difficult to awaken. Very unresponsive to external stimuli.	Delta waves (1 – 3 hertz) 20 to 50% of the time.	Virtually no eye or muscle movement
Stage 4: Very deep sleep. Very difficult to awaken. Very unresponsive to external stimuli.	Delta waves (1 – 3 hertz) over 50% of the time.	Virtually no eye or muscle movement
REM sleep Difficult to awaken. Vivid dreaming reported far more often when woken than from non-REM sleep.	High levels of mixed brain wave activity.	Eye movement may reflect dream content. Most muscles paralysed.

EEG = Electroencephalogram. EOG = Electrooculargram.
EMG = Electromyogram. REM = rapid eye movement sleep

In humans the circadian sleep–waking rhythm is regulated by:

■ The endogenous pacemakers or internal body clock of the *suprachiasmatic nucleus* (SCN) and the *pineal gland*. The SCN is part of the hypothalamus that regulates sleep–waking patterns by sending messages to the pineal gland to release melatonin – which is thought to stimulate the production of serotonin in the raphe nucleus to initiate sleep.

The sleep–waking body clock seems to be the product of evolution and is largely inherited, SCN cells will fire in a rhythmic way even if removed and placed in culture. Removal of the SCN in hamsters randomises their sleep–waking patterns. In humans it seems to naturally run on a cycle slightly longer than a day (around 25 hours) but there seem to be inherited individual differences between people. If the SCN of mutant hamsters which causes different sleep–waking patterns is transplanted into normal hamsters who have had their SCN removed, they adopt the mutant's circadian patterns. The sleep–waking circadian rhythm can be adjusted to a certain degree by zeitgebers, but seems mostly regulated by the internal body clock.

■ The major *external re-setter (zeitgeber)* of the circadian body clock in humans is light, which is detected at the retina and can influence (via interconnecting nerve fibres) the SCN to synchronise our rhythms to the 24 hour cycle of the day.

This has been demonstrated by studies that have removed the zeitgeber of light such as *Siffre's cave study*. Siffre, a French cave explorer, spent 6 months in a cave underground which effectively removed the external zeitgebers of the world above such as light levels and human activity patterns. No time cues were given via his telephone contact with the outside world and artificial lights were switched on when he woke up and off when he fell asleep. Under these conditions his natural body rhythms lengthened to around 25 hours, so by the time he left the cave he had experienced fewer 'days' than everyone else. This means that adjustment to new zeitgebers is easier if they involve a *lengthening* of the day, since the *circadian cycle* itself seems to have a natural tendency to lengthen.

However, while the cycle/rhythm can slowly adjust to new starting points (as happens when zeitgebers change due to human activities such as shift work or travel over time zones) and can be resisted with a struggle (e.g. in sleep deprivation studies), the basic pattern or ratio of sleep–waking activity is remarkably consistent due to its biological basis. Similar sleep–waking patterns are found cross-culturally, despite cultural zeitgebers such as siestas and environmental zeitgebers in countries who experience whole summers or winters of lightness and darkness (such as those in the arctic circle). The inflexibility of the rhythm has also been demonstrated under controlled laboratory conditions, where exposure to different ratios of light and dark hours do not affect the sleeping patterns of subjects beyond certain limits.

Exercise 52

1 What are the strengths and weaknesses of the evidence for human circadian rhythms gained from
   a non-human animal studies?
   b Siffre's cave study?

2 Why do human activities such as shift work (especially involving three 8-hour working periods rotating from night shift to evening shift to day shift on a weekly basis or less) and rapid travel over time zones cause negative symptoms (e.g. jet lag in the latter case)?

1 What are the strengths and weaknesses of the evidence for human circadian rhythms gained from

a non-human animal studies?

Studies on non-human animals allow us to conduct more controlled drug and surgical experimental techniques to investigate the brain structures and neurochemicals involved in circadian rhythms. Such techniques allow us to infer the function of brain areas and neurochemicals with greater certainty, but are deemed unethical for human participants.

On the negative side, there may be qualitative differences in brain structure and function between animals like hamsters and humans, which may make the results from non-human studies difficult to generalise to us.

b Siffre's cave study?

Siffre's cave study as a longitudinal case study had the advantage of providing a good deal of detailed information and was a rare and valuable study (not many people are willing to participate in studies of this length and nature, although these are the kind of conditions needed to properly investigate circadian rhythms in the long term).

Unfortunately, being a case study of a single person, there is a problem generalising the results to other humans. Siffre's body rhythms may be different in some ways from other people's.

2 Why do human activities such as shift work (especially involving three 8-hour working periods rotating from night shift to evening shift to day shift on a weekly basis or less) and rapid travel over time zones cause negative symptoms (e.g. jet lag in the latter case)?

Physiological research into body rhythms such as the human sleep–waking circadian rhythm has revealed that both inner biological factors (*endogenous pacemakers* or body clocks) and external environmental factors (*zeitgebers*) can influence our pattern of sleeping and waking activity.

However, research has also shown that the sleep–waking body clock is fairly consistent and slow to adjust, while zeitgebers such as work patterns and travel across time zones can change very quickly. Such a mismatch between our natural body rhythms and activity patterns can produce negative effects, which have been investigated by physiologically orientated psychologists.

Shift work

Much shift work has involved three 8-hour working periods rotating anti-clockwise, e.g. from night shift to evening shift to day shift (a 'phase advance' rather than 'phase delay' schedule), frequently on a weekly basis or less. Physiological research on body rhythms informs us this can produce long-term disorientation, stress, insomnia, exhaustion and negative effects on reaction speed, co-ordination skill, attention and problem solving, since such work schedules

- ☞ create a mismatch or desynchronisation between the body rhythms of arousal and the zeitgebers of activity levels
- ☞ do not allow enough adjustment time for body rhythms to catch up with (become 'entrained' by) new activity levels
- ☞ delay the catching up (entrainment) of body rhythms by shortening rather than lengthening the day.

This increases the chances of accidents occurring due to human error, even when other factors such as reduced hours of sleep, night-time supervision levels, etc. are taken into account.

Czeisler et al. (1982) studied a group of industrial workers who were following such a shift pattern and their suggestion that they moved clockwise in shifts (a phase delay schedule) on a three-week rather than one-week basis led to better worker health and morale, as well as higher productivity levels.

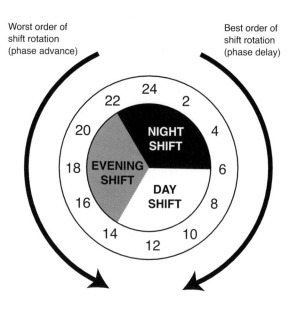

Worst order of shift rotation (phase advance)   Best order of shift rotation (phase delay)

Jet lag

Rapid air travel across time zones can produce jet lag – general disorientation and symptoms similar to those described for shift work, though not always as severe. This also

- ☞ results from a mismatch or desynchronisation between the body rhythms of the old time zone, stored in the body clock you take with you, and the zeitgebers of the new time zone, such as human activity levels (e.g. mealtimes) and light levels.
- ☞ is harder to adjust to if the zeitgebers shorten the day and the circadian cycle – causing a phase advance. This explains why rapid travel from the west to the east across many time zones tends to produce worse jet lag than travelling from east to west (which lengthens the day and causes phase delay).

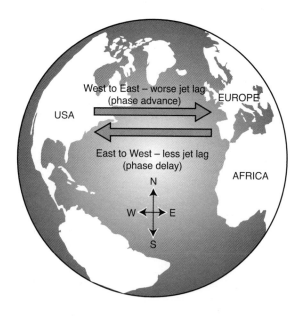

The influence of zeitgebers and endogenous pacemakers on jet lag are harder to identify since many other variables involved in travelling could cause the symptoms, such as stress, excitement, unfamiliarity and restricted posture.

Slower travel over fewer time zones as well as taking drugs that affect melatonin activity at appropriate times may reduce the severity of jet lag symptoms.

53 | Sleep and dreams

Why do we spend around a third of our lives in an unconscious state and why do we dream? Researchers from physiological, cognitive and psychodynamic approaches have all attempted to answer these questions.

Theories of the function of sleep

- **Restoration theory** – Oswald (1966) proposes that the function of sleep is simply to restore bodily energy reserves, repair the condition of muscles and cells and to allow growth to occur. Sleep could also allow the brain's neurotransmitters to replenish and aid psychological recovery, improving mood and sharpening fatigued mental faculties.

- **Evolutionary theory** – If a behaviour like sleep is found in many species, it probably has an important evolutionary survival function, possibly to conserve energy when food gathering has been completed or is more difficult (e.g. at night), and/or to avoid damage from nocturnal predators or accidents by remaining motionless. Meddis (1975) suggests the duration of sleep a species shows depends upon its food requirements and predator-avoidance needs.

Theories of the function of dreaming

- **Reverse learning theory** – Crick and Mitchison (1983) argue that dreaming can be regarded as the random and meaningless by-product of the bombardment of the cortex with random stimulation from the brain stem during REM sleep. This bombardment allows us to make the best use of our limited cortex by clearing the brain of useless or maladaptive information/neural interconnections. It is, therefore, best not to remember our dreams.

- **Activation synthesis theory** – Hobson and McCarley (1977) suggest dreams are the meaningless result of random brain activity. The activation part of the theory involves the random firing of giant cells in the reticular activating system (triggered by the presence of acetylcholine) which activates the sensory and motor areas of the brain during REM sleep. The synthesis part of the theory involves the attempt of higher parts of the brain to organise and make sense of the random activity – producing the semi-coherent dreams we experience.

- **Memory consolidation/reprogramming theory** – A number of researchers suggest this function of dreaming. Empson and Clarke (1970) propose that sleep, especially REM sleep, facilitates the reinforcement of information in memory. Evans (1984) proposed that REM sleep is required by the brain to update itself in the light of new information received during the day and that dreams are the interpretation of this assimilation. Stickgold (1998) thinks that the alternating periods of REM and non-REM sleep reflect 'conversations' between the hippocampus and cortex during which information acquired during the day is transferred and integrated with long-term memory.

- **Wish fulfilment** – Freud suggested that dreams are the disguised expressions of unconscious desires and impulses. The recalled manifest content of the dream has been disguised by the dream censor through methods like symbolism to protect our conscious self from the anxiety provoking latent (hidden) meaning of the dream.

- **Problem solving** – Cartwright proposes that dreams are a meaningful way of considering worries or problems from conscious everyday life. Dreams may provide solutions for problems using symbols or metaphors, but the meanings are not hidden and we can often interpret them ourselves.

Sleep and dream facts and findings

- *Sleep deprivation studies* – Jouvet (1967) deprived cats of sleep by putting them on a floating island in a pool of water so that when they fell asleep they fell in and woke up. The cats developed abnormal behaviours and eventually died. Rechtschaffen et al. deprived rats of sleep and they all died after 33 days.

  Human sleep deprivation studies have found mainly psychological effects, such as the increased desire to sleep, difficulty sustaining attention (although problem solving is less impaired), delusions and depersonalisation. The physiological effects seem relatively minor, e.g. problems with eye focusing. Sleep after deprivation is not cumulative (not equal to the amount lost), in fact it is not much longer than usual though more time is spent in REM sleep (a REM rebound effect). However, unlike the animal studies, human sleep deprivation studies have not been carried out indefinitely.

- *Cognitive tests* – Subjects given problems before sleep are more likely to solve them realistically if REM sleep is uninterrupted. Subjects given unusual tasks before sleep spend longer in REM sleep. Some studies have found subjects learning completely new skills perform worse if their REM sleep is interrupted but not if their non-REM is. The opposite seems true for tasks that only involve small refinements of previously learned skills.

- *Dream content* – External stimulation while asleep, e.g. water lightly sprayed on a sleeper's face, can be incorporated into dreams. Lee (1958) in a study of 120 rural Zulu women found that those who had records of infertility or had lost more than half their children were more likely to dream of babies. Dreams have provided inspiration for poets and scientists – Coleridge claimed to have composed the poem Kubla Kahn, Mendeleyev saw the periodic table of elements, and Kekule solved the structure of benzene (after seeing snakes holding their tails) in dreams.

- *Animal sleep* – All mammals sleep (the porpoise even shuts down one side of its brain at a time to do so), although the length of time varies according to the species. Lions and squirrels sleep longer. Cattle, giraffes, antelope and shrews sleep very little. The two mammals that do not show REM sleep (the dolphin and spiny anteater) have abnormally large cortexes.

- *Sleep duration* – longer sleep (particularly stage 4) occurs after large amounts of physical exercise (but is not reduced with lack of exercise) and in growing children. Fetuses spend over half the day showing REM-like brain activity, whereas REM occupies 50% of sleep in babies and 20% in adults. Sleep is greater after brain damage and periods of stress and improves mood. Those with mental disorders often have sleeping problems.

Exercise 53

1 Compare or contrast the following theories of sleep or dreams:
   a Restoration and evolutionary
   b Reverse learning and memory consolidation/reprogramming
   c Activation synthesis and wish fulfilment
   d Wish fulfilment and problem solving

2 Find facts or findings that support or do not support each theory of sleep and dreaming.

1 Compare or contrast the following theories of sleep or dreams:

a Restoration and evolutionary

Both are biological theories concerned with energy, but evolutionary theory suggests we have an evolved tendency to sleep to conserve energy (and risk) rather than restore energy.

b Reverse learning and memory consolidation/reprogramming

Both concern information but reverse learning focuses on the elimination of useless/maladaptive information, whereas memory consolidation and reprogramming theories concentrate more on the storage and integration of useful information.

c Activation synthesis and wish fulfilment

Activation synthesis theory is a biological theory which suggests dreams are random and meaningless, whereas wish fulfilment is a psychological theory that argues just the opposite. However, Foulkes (1985) proposes that dreams are meaningful interpretations of REM random brain activity in the light of our cognitive systems' organisational abilities. Dreams reflect the way we interpret information and Hobson and McCarley have come to agree with this view that dreams can be meaningful.

d Wish fulfilment and problem solving

Both see dreams as serving a psychological function but, while Cartwright agrees that they use metaphors and symbolism, she does not think they are deliberately disguised as Freud thought, or that only a psychoanalyst can interpret them correctly.

2 Find facts or findings that support or do not support each theory of sleep and dreaming.

- **Restoration theory** – seems mostly supported by the sleep duration findings and the sleep deprivation studies on animals. Longer sleep for more restoration would be required after large amounts of physical exercise, in growing children and fetuses, and after brain damage. Sleep deprivation that prevented vital restoration could have accounted for the death of Jouvet's and Rechtschaffen et al.'s animals (although the stress of the procedure could have also played a part). The restoration of important neurotransmitters could account for the improved mood after sleep and the behavioural and mood problems seen in Jouvet's cats, sleep-deprived humans and those with mental disorders.

  However, the fact that sleep is not reduced with lack of exercise, which would imply less restoration, seems at odds with the theory. In addition, if the restoration of sleep was so vital for humans, one might have expected to see more serious physical effects in the human sleep-deprivation experiments (but again, remember that these have only been carried out for limited time periods) and more time spent sleeping afterwards.

- **Evolutionary theory** – Given its universal presence amongst higher animals (all mammals sleep – the porpoise even shuts down one side of its brain at a time to do so), sleep probably does have an important evolutionary survival function. The length of time that different species sleep supports Meddis's (1975) suggestion that the duration of sleep which a species shows depends upon its food requirements and predator avoidance needs. Lions (which have few predators and meet their food needs in short bursts) and squirrels (who have safe burrows) sleep longer. Cattle, giraffes and antelope (which have many natural predators) and shrews (which also have high metabolic rates) sleep very little.

- **Reverse learning theory** – Crick and Mitchison (1983) point out that the two mammals that do not show REM sleep (the dolphin and spiny anteater) have abnormally large cortexes, perhaps to contain the useless memories they are not able to unlearn. The theory neglects the findings relating to the apparent usefulness and meaningfulness of many dreams and lacks detail over exactly how 'useless' information is identified and 'unlearned'.

- **Activation synthesis theory** – Hobson and McCarley (1977) suggest that dreams are the meaningless result of random brain activity and so neglect the findings relating to the apparent usefulness and meaningfulness of many dreams. They focus more on how dreams occur rather than why. However, the activation part of the theory has lots of biological support and the synthesis part accounts for the finding that external stimulation while asleep, e.g. water lightly sprayed on a sleeper's face, can be incorporated into dreams and explains how the content of dreams could be influenced by particular areas of brain activation (balance areas may produce dreams of flying).

- **Memory consolidation/reprogramming theory** – These theories explain why subjects given unusual tasks before sleep spend longer in REM sleep. They also explain the results of the studies that have found subjects learning completely new skills perform worse if their REM sleep is interrupted but not if their non-REM is, and the opposite finding for tasks that only involve small refinements of previously learned skills. Memory consolidation or reprogramming may also account for the longer sleep in growing children (though not fetuses), who have more to learn than adults, and the universality of sleep in higher mammals who show more learning ability than fish and reptiles.

- **Wish fulfilment** – Freud's suggestion that dreams were the disguised expressions of unconscious desires and impulses seems to be supported by Lee's (1958) study of Zulu women, who presumably dreamt of babies because of their wish to have them. However, dreaming directly of a baby (the manifest content) does not support Freud's belief in *disguised* (latent content) wishes in dreams. As Kline (1984) points out, though, Freud did suggest that wishes could directly appear in the manifest content of children's dreams or when the need is imperative, and given the importance of bearing children in Zulu culture this may have been the case. Wish fulfilment has problems with explaining many of the other facts and findings relating to sleep and dreams.

- **Problem solving** – Cartwright's proposal that dreams are a meaningful way of considering worries or problems from conscious everyday life seems a better explanation of Lee's finding above and accounts for the positive anecdotes regarding the inspiration dreams have provided for poets and scientists. The theory also explains the finding that subjects given problems before sleep are more likely to solve them realistically if REM sleep is uninterrupted. However, there is little other evidence for the theory and most problems can be more quickly solved while awake. Also, if dreams are so useful, why are they so difficult to remember?

SLEEP AND DREAMS CROSSWORD

1 An animal that does not show REM sleep (5/8)
2 Freud argued that unconscious wishes were this in our dreams (9)
3 These may affect the length of time an animal sleeps for, according to evolutionary theory (9)
4 Dreams may aid this in memory (13)
5 Reverse learning and (originally) activation synthesis theory suggest dreams are this (11)
6 The part of Hobson and McCarley's theory that involves the interpretation of random brain activity into a semi-coherent story (9)
7 The part of Hobson and McCarley's theory involving the random stimulation of sensory and motor brain areas during REM sleep (10)
8 The consciously remembered content of a dream according to Freud (8)
9 Dreams may offer these for problems according to Cartwright's theory (9)
10 This occurs most vividly in REM sleep (8)
11 The theory that sleep aids recovery (11)
12 These show REM-like activity for over half their day (7)
13 According to reverse learning theory random stimulation from the brain stem bombards this to remove unwanted neural connections (6)
14 Evolutionary theory argues that sleep aids this (8)

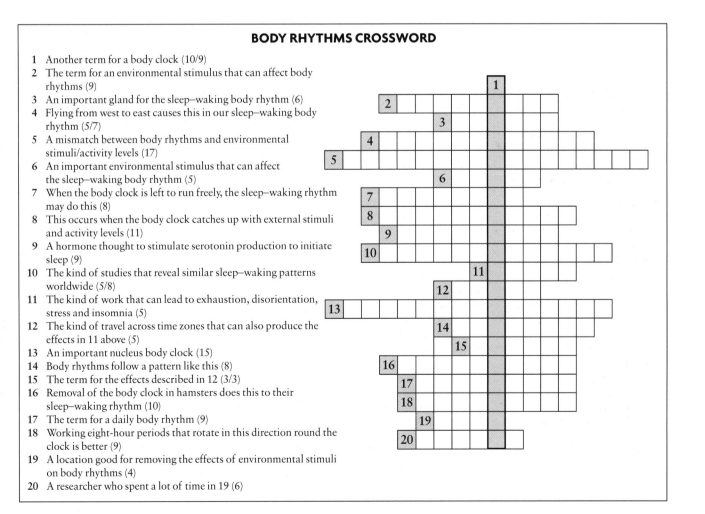

BODY RHYTHMS CROSSWORD

1 Another term for a body clock (10/9)
2 The term for an environmental stimulus that can affect body rhythms (9)
3 An important gland for the sleep–waking body rhythm (6)
4 Flying from west to east causes this in our sleep–waking body rhythm (5/7)
5 A mismatch between body rhythms and environmental stimuli/activity levels (17)
6 An important environmental stimulus that can affect the sleep–waking body rhythm (5)
7 When the body clock is left to run freely, the sleep–waking rhythm may do this (8)
8 This occurs when the body clock catches up with external stimuli and activity levels (11)
9 A hormone thought to stimulate serotonin production to initiate sleep (9)
10 The kind of studies that reveal similar sleep–waking patterns worldwide (5/8)
11 The kind of work that can lead to exhaustion, disorientation, stress and insomnia (5)
12 The kind of travel across time zones that can also produce the effects in 11 above (5)
13 An important nucleus body clock (15)
14 Body rhythms follow a pattern like this (8)
15 The term for the effects described in 12 (3/3)
16 Removal of the body clock in hamsters does this to their sleep–waking rhythm (10)
17 The term for a daily body rhythm (9)
18 Working eight-hour periods that rotate in this direction round the clock is better (9)
19 A location good for removing the effects of environmental stimuli on body rhythms (4)
20 A researcher who spent a lot of time in 19 (6)

54 Stress – concepts, sources and responses

The concept of stress

The concept of stress has been viewed in different ways. Stress has been regarded as

- an *internal bodily response* – an essentially automatic biological *reaction* to external stimuli. This neglects the type of stimuli that causes the reaction.
- an *external stimuli* that exerts a destructive force upon the organism. This neglects the fact that the same external stimuli will not always produce the same reaction.
- an *interaction or transaction* between stimulus and response that depends upon a *cognitive appraisal* of the situation – the stress reaction will only result if individuals *perceive* a mismatch between the demands of the situation and their ability to cope with it (regardless of actual demands and coping ability). This is currently the most common view and, thus, a widely used definition of stress is: 'A pattern of negative physiological states and psychological responses occurring in situations where people perceive threats to their well being which they may be unable to meet' Lazarus and Folkman (1984).

Sources of stress

Stress can result from:

- changeable or continuous causes (e.g. life-events or steady occupational demands)
- predictable or unpredictable causes (e.g. depending on the experience of control)
- biological sources (e.g. disruption of bodily rhythms, illness, fatigue), social sources (e.g. interpersonal and work related) or psychological causes (e.g. locus of control and personality type).

Life changes as a cause of stress

Stressful life events – Holmes and Rahe (1967) suggested that stress is caused by *change* and may lead to greater susceptibility to physical and mental health disorders. They compiled the 'social readjustment rating scale' (SRRS) – a list of 47 life events involving stressful change and rated them for their severity out of one hundred (e.g. death of a spouse = 100, marriage = 50, change in school = 20, etc.). Scores of over 300 life change units in a year would represent a high risk for stress-related health problems.

The SRRS has been criticised for its over-generalised approach, however. There are many individual differences in what events people find most stressful and how they react to them. Positive and predictable changes may be less stressful than negative and unpredictable ones. The evidence for the scale relating to health is mostly correlational, illness may have contributed towards the development of stressful life events such as losing employment, rather than vice versa.

Hassles & uplifts – Researchers such as Lazarus and Kanner have proposed that more *everyday* problems or pleasant occurrences are more likely to affect stress levels and health. To measure these incidents and their effects they designed the 'Hassles and Uplifts Scale', which has been found to be a better predictor of health than the SRRS since continuous diary monitoring of everyday stresses has enabled a causal link to be made with later illness (Stone et al., 1987).

Catastrophic stress – single traumatic events such as natural disasters, warfare or violent assault can provoke long-lasting stress and health problems. Mental disorder classification systems term this post-traumatic stress disorder.

Biological causes – SRRS items relating to changing work and sleep patterns could cause stress through biological changes like the desynchronisation of body rhythms with new zeitgebers, e.g. activity and light levels (see shift work and jet lag research).

The workplace as a source of stress

Workplace stressors – Occupational stress can result from factors relating to the nature of the job (e.g. its security, clarity of purpose, workload and intensity of skill use) and the social and environmental conditions in which it takes place (e.g. the co-worker relationships, organisational management, control of workload, career progression, physical workspace and noise). Workplace stressors, therefore, tend to result from stable characteristics rather than change (although changes in job and working conditions can also causes stress).

A common example is *work overload/under-load* which involves stress resulting from a perceived mismatch between the time and skills the job requires and the time and skills available to complete it. Such a mismatch may cause feelings of unfairness, resentment and lack of control – especially in overload circumstances where the deadlines are important, there is external pressure to meet them and they are set by external sources. Relief from work-overload stress is reduced by the lack of time left for other activities and the fatigue felt during such time.

Occupational burnout results from continual levels of stress due to highly demanding work requiring consistently high levels of concentration, responsibility, frustration or exposure to suffering, e.g. air traffic controllers or nurses.

Control and stress

The inability to control life event changes, everyday hassles, work schedules/deadlines and unexpected traumatic events, etc. is a major cause of stress and consequent ill health. Weiss (1972) found rats that could *control* electric shocks were less likely to develop gastric ulceration than those who could not, despite receiving an identical number of shocks. Workers with little control at the bottom of organisational hierarchies are often found to suffer the most ill health from stress. Rotter (1966) suggested that an 'external locus of control' leads people to think they have a lack of control over their lives and can result in less active coping strategies and greater stress-related illness. Even the illusion or possibility of control in humans can reduce the effects of stress. Feelings of control are thus important in increasing the perception that one has an ability to cope that is sufficient to match the demands of the situation (see definition of stress above). Very high levels of control, however, can also be stressful, especially when one is responsible for decisions and many choices are available – which may account for the executive stress of some managers.

Responses to stress

Stress as a bodily response

Selye (1976) identified the general adaptation syndrome (GAS) – a non-specific physiological response that occurs to a variety of stressful stimuli. Much research has investigated the 3 phases of the GAS.

Phase one – the alarm reaction

The alarm reaction is the physiological response triggered by stressful stimuli, thought to involve the hypothalamus and pituitary gland in the brain, the autonomic nervous system and the adrenal gland.

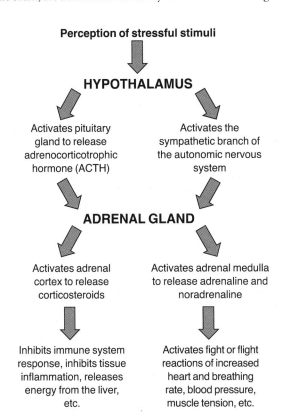

Phase two – the stage of resistance

If the stressor persists or is not dealt with, the body seeks to maintain arousal at a constant, if lower, level. However, there are many factors that could *mediate* in the resolving or continuation of this stress arousal or even modify its effects, including

- behavioural coping style – stress arousal will often not persist if fight or flight behaviours *deal with* the stressful stimuli. Optimal arousal theory states that, up to a certain level, stress can provide a beneficial motivating effect on behaviour (Selye called this 'eustress') that helps deal with the source of stress. However, not all modern-day problems can be solved through physical means and different people use different coping strategies.
- personality factors and cognitive style – Friedman and Rosenman (1974) argued that some people have '*Type A*' *personalities* which create and maintain high levels of stress in their lifestyles. These people are often aggressive, competitive and highly driven perfectionists who will not delegate and are impatient towards others.

Kobasa (1979) suggests people with '*hardy personalities*' are less vulnerable to the effects of stress because they have a greater sense of control over, and a more positive attitude towards, stressful events and a stronger sense of purpose.

Rotter agrees that cognitive style, like a sense of control over stressful events (i.e. an *internal* rather than external *locus of control*), will moderate the effects of stress.

- Gender and cultural factors – Genders and cultures may differ in the amount and type of stress experienced (e.g. discrimination in society and the workplace) or even physiological susceptibility. Men and those from capitalist/individualistic cultures may be more socialised into aggressive and competitive Type A behaviour towards stressful situations, and have different coping styles and levels of social support.

Phase three – the stage of exhaustion

Eventually, continually high, long-term, arousal levels exhaust the body's resources producing negative physiological and psychological effects.
Physiological effects include:

- *Reduced resistance to infection* – Studies on both animals and humans have shown that stress, especially in the long-term, can adversely affect the immune system as corticosteroids suppress its activity and thus increase vulnerability to infection. Stress has been associated with many illnesses, ranging from headaches (Gannon et al., 1987) and asthma (Miller and Strunk, 1979), to colds (Stone et al., 1987), stomach ulcers (Brady, 1958) and cancer (Jacobs and Charles, 1980).
- *Heart and circulatory disorders* – Stress-triggered increases in heart rate and blood pressure, as well as levels of glucose/fatty acids released into the blood stream, may result in the deterioration and blocking of blood vessels and thus increased cardiovascular disorder. Rosenman et al. (1975) found in a 9-year study involving over 3000 men that Type A personalities were more prone to suffer heart disease. However, there is debate over whether the personality traits are a cause or result of stress, and which traits are the most important since some studies have not replicated Rosenman et al.'s results.
- Stress may also indirectly cause physiological effects since it leads to *unhealthy behaviour*, e.g. lack of exercise, drinking and smoking.

Psychological effects include:

- *Anger and frustration* – Can cause a vicious circle of stress production as they contribute to a more stressful environment. Hostility may be a key stress-provoking factor in Type A behaviour.
- *Depression and helplessness* – Seligman (1975) found continual and unavoidable stress caused learned helplessness and depression, which would be inappropriately generalised to different situations.
- *Anxiety* – Different types of stressful situation can produce different types of anxiety disorder, e.g. persistent, unresolvable stress could lead to generalised anxiety disorder, whereas 'one-off' traumatic events could cause post-traumatic stress disorder.

Exercise 54

1 Why is it difficult to determine the cause and effect relationship between personality characteristics and stress levels?

2 By considering the research on the social, psychological and biological sources or causes of stress and the responses to and effects of it, how do you think stress could be reduced or managed?

1 Why is it difficult to determine the cause and effect relationship between personality characteristics and stress levels?

Cause and effect is difficult to determine because personality characteristics could be created by stress or contribute towards creating stress (or a mixture of the two). Studies that reveal which came first, stress or personality characteristics, are needed to disentangle cause and effect.

2 By considering the research on the social, psychological and biological sources or causes of stress and the responses to and effects of it, how do you think stress could be reduced or managed?

There are really only two ways that stress can be reduced or managed:

Deal with the causes of stress

Those strategies that focus on removing or coping with stressful *stimuli* or *situations* before they produce a stress reaction are known as '*problem-focused strategies*'. This is obviously the best way to deal with potential stress, but may not be possible since

- there is a huge variety of sources for stress, and it may, therefore, be impossible to deal with them all
- the individual may be unaware of the source of stress or may only realise after the stress reaction has occurred
- not all sources of stress can be avoided, some may be an inevitable part of living and working life, others may be mental worries that physical action cannot deal with.

Deal with the effects of stress

Those strategies that focus on removing or coping with stress reactions once they have occurred are known as '*emotion-focused strategies*'. This is the approach that most methods employ.

People use a variety of coping strategies in everyday life. However, specific physiological and psychological techniques have also been developed to help manage stress which individuals feel unable to deal with sufficiently on their own. Most of these techniques are emotion-focused strategies, but some aim to incorporate elements of problem-focused strategy as well.

Natural coping strategies for stress

- *Appropriate behaviour* – These range from dealing with the source of stress, e.g. time-management planning and avoiding stressful situations, to natural behavioural reactions that combat its effects, e.g. rest and relaxation (holidays), laughter, arguments, exercise and sport.
- *Defence mechanisms* – Freud would argue that many of the above natural stress reduction methods are, in fact, the products of ego defence mechanisms. Stress-related psychic energy can be given cathartic expression through displacement and sublimation, e.g. aggression towards scapegoats, laughter and physical exercise, or alternatively repressed into the unconscious and/or dissociated from consciousness through denial (which could lead to anxiety or even dissociative disorders if long-term stress was experienced).
- *Social support* – individuals who perceive they have social support (e.g. reassurance, advice and practical aid) suffer less physiological stress effects than those without such support, e.g. those with no intimate friends (Brown and Harris, 1978) or partners (Tache et al., 1979).

Natural coping strategies are not always sufficient on their own and some, e.g. arguments and aggression, may actually contribute towards further stress.

Freudian defence mechanisms have not always been supported by empirical evidence and may be counter productive – only providing short-term solutions while creating long-term problems.

Social support is significantly correlated with lower mortality rates, but causation is difficult to determine.

Biological techniques for stress management

A variety of anti-stress drugs (medically prescribed or otherwise) have been used to tackle the biological effects of the body's stress reaction.

- *Beta-blockers* – act on the autonomic nervous system to reduce physiological stress arousal.
- *Anxiolytic drugs* – minor tranquillisers, e.g. valium, combat anxiety without causing sleepiness.
- *Anti-depressant drugs* – less often used, but can be appropriate for severe anxiety.
- *Other drugs* – alcohol is an often sought remedy for stress, its sedative effects slow down neural and bodily functions and its effect on loosening inhibitions can lead to cathartic behaviour.

Biofeedback has also been used to help train people to control the adverse physiological effects of stress, such as increased heart rate and blood pressure, by providing feedback signals on these body processes.

Unfortunately, anti-anxiety drugs can cause psychological and physical dependence and a range of unpleasant side-effects. Drugs are only short-term remedies for stress that temporarily reduce its effects but may make dealing with its causes more difficult or even create further sources (especially alcohol).

Although there is debate over how it works, biofeedback can lower heart rate and blood pressure, but again it only treats the symptoms not the causes of stress.

Psychological techniques for stress management

- *Therapy – Stress inoculation training* (Meichenbaum, 1977) and *Hardiness training* (Kobasa, 1986) are both cognitive behavioural techniques designed to increase stress resistance or 'hardiness' by:
  - analysing – getting clients to learn to analyse sources and physical signs of stress
  - teaching coping strategies and techniques to combat stressful situations – e.g. relaxation, positive self-instructional statements and specific skills with stress inoculation therapy, or the re-living and reconstruction of stressful situations in hardiness training
  - changing behaviour – e.g. practising skills in simulated and real situations so a successful change is produced (with stress inoculation) or reinforcing a sense of control through performing manageable tasks (with hardiness training).
- *Mental state relaxation* – Meditation and hypnosis (including self-hypnosis) reduce stress effects through mentally inducing relaxation.

Cognitive behavioural therapies are effective, although it is uncertain whether the behavioural aspects (successfully dealing with a stressful situation) are more important than the cognitive ones (stress-reducing statements and a sense of control). The techniques aim to deal with the source as well as the effects of stress and so are potentially more effective in the long term.

Meditation and hypnosis do not have the side-effects and equipment needs of physiological methods but also tend to focus on the effects and ignore the causes.

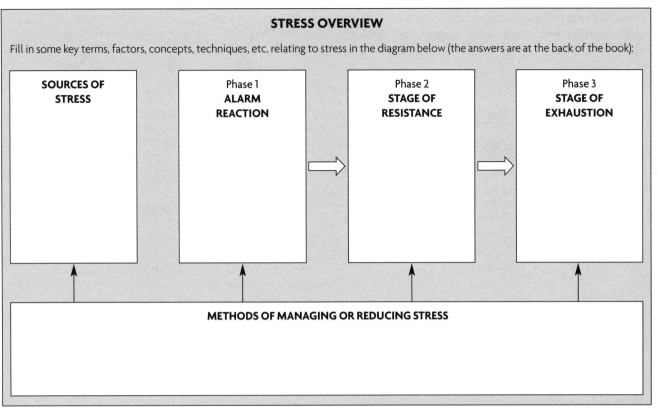

STRESS OVERVIEW

Fill in some key terms, factors, concepts, techniques, etc. relating to stress in the diagram below (the answers are at the back of the book):

SOURCES OF STRESS	Phase 1 ALARM REACTION	Phase 2 STAGE OF RESISTANCE	Phase 3 STAGE OF EXHAUSTION

METHODS OF MANAGING OR REDUCING STRESS

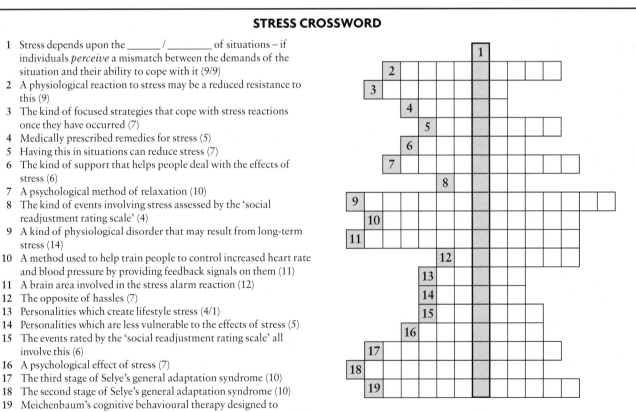

STRESS CROSSWORD

1 Stress depends upon the _____ / _____ of situations – if individuals *perceive* a mismatch between the demands of the situation and their ability to cope with it (9/9)
2 A physiological reaction to stress may be a reduced resistance to this (9)
3 The kind of focused strategies that cope with stress reactions once they have occurred (7)
4 Medically prescribed remedies for stress (5)
5 Having this in situations can reduce stress (7)
6 The kind of support that helps people deal with the effects of stress (6)
7 A psychological method of relaxation (10)
8 The kind of events involving stress assessed by the 'social readjustment rating scale' (4)
9 A kind of physiological disorder that may result from long-term stress (14)
10 A method used to help train people to control increased heart rate and blood pressure by providing feedback signals on them (11)
11 A brain area involved in the stress alarm reaction (12)
12 The opposite of hassles (7)
13 Personalities which create lifestyle stress (4/1)
14 Personalities which are less vulnerable to the effects of stress (5)
15 The events rated by the 'social readjustment rating scale' all involve this (6)
16 A psychological effect of stress (7)
17 The third stage of Selye's general adaptation syndrome (10)
18 The second stage of Selye's general adaptation syndrome (10)
19 Meichenbaum's cognitive behavioural therapy designed to increase stress resistance is known as stress _____ training (11)

55 Attachment in infancy

What is meant by attachment?

An attachment is a strong, long lasting and close emotional bond between two people, which causes distress on separation from the attached individual.

Psychologists have been particularly interested in the development of first attachments in infancy since they appear to have important consequences for later healthy development, especially concerning later relationships.

How does attachment develop?

Attachment in infancy occurs gradually over a sequence of phases:

- *Pre-attachment phase* (0 to 3 months) – Infants show preference for humans over other objects by preferential looking and social smiling (before 6 weeks the infant is said to be asocial).

- *Indiscriminate attachment phase* (3 to 7 months) – Infants can distinguish between people and allow strangers to handle them.

- *Discriminate attachment phase* (7 to 9 months) – Infants develop specific attachments to certain people and show distress on separation from them. Avoidance or fear of strangers may be shown.

- *Multiple attachment phase* (9 months onward) – Infants become increasingly independent and form other bonds despite the stronger prior attachments.

How do we know an attachment has formed?

Attachment can be tested via the 'strange situation' method developed by Ainsworth et al. (1971), where the mother and child are taken to an unfamiliar room and subjected to a range of timed, increasingly stressful (for an attached child) set of scenarios, such as

- a stranger is introduced to the child in the presence of the mother

- the mother leaves the infant with the stranger

- after the mother returns and re-settles the infant, it is left alone

- a stranger enters and interacts with the lone infant

- the mother returns again and picks up the infant.

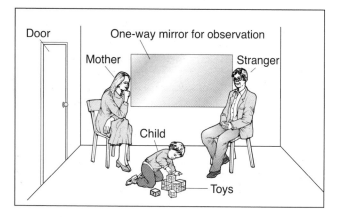

What different kinds of attachment are there?

Ainsworth et al. (1978) discovered three main types of infant attachment using the strange situation, which occurred in various proportions:

- *Type A – Anxious-avoidant* or *detached* (approximately 20% of the sample). The infant ignores the mother, is not affected by her parting or return and, although distressed when alone, is easily comforted by strangers.

- *Type B – Securely attached* (approximately 70% of the sample). The infant plays contentedly while the mother is there, is distressed by her parting, is relieved on her return and, although not adverse to stranger contact, treats them differently from the mother.

- *Type C – Anxious-resistant* or *ambivalent* (approximately 10% of the sample). The infant is discontented while with the mother, playing less, is distressed by her parting, is not easily comforted on her return and may resist contact by the mother and stranger.

Replicating studies have revealed slightly different proportions.

What causes differences in attachment?

Parental sensitivity – Ainsworth et al. (1978) suggested that secure attachment is dependent upon emotionally close and responsive mothering, whereas insecure attachments result from insensitive mothers. Although other factors are involved, the effects of maternal sensitivity have been supported.

Infant temperament – Researchers such as Kagan (1982) suggest innate differences in infant temperament and anxiety may cause certain kinds of parental reaction and attachment.

Family circumstances – Attachment type may vary over time and setting with social and cultural environmental conditions, e.g. if a family undergoes stress (Vaughn et al., 1979).

Reliability of classification – Strange situation methodology has been criticised and other attachment types proposed, e.g. D (insecure-disorganised/disorientated).

Cross-cultural differences in attachment

Using the strange situation method (Ainsworth et al., 1978), studies of cross-cultural differences in attachment types have been conducted. Van Ijzendoorn and Kroonenberg (1988) compared the results of 32 cross-cultural studies and found that there was often more consistency across cultures than within them in terms of variation in attachment. However, while the majority of children in each culture are securely attached, there do seem to be variations in the proportion of avoidant and resistant attachments in certain countries. German infants appear to have a slightly higher proportion of avoidant attachments which Grossman et al. (1985) have suggested might result from a cultural tendency for German parents to maintain a large interpersonal distance and wean offspring early from close contact. Some studies of Israeli children raised on kibbutzim have revealed a higher proportion of resistant attachments, e.g. Sagi et al. (1985), which may result from the fact that the children have contact with parents but are mainly raised communally in a large group. The strange situation may be based on American cultural assumptions and, therefore, be a flawed technique for making cross-cultural comparisons.

Country (and number of studies)	Percentage of each type of attachment		
	Secure	Avoidant	Resistant
WEST GERMANY (3)	57	35	8
GREAT BRITAIN (1)	75	22	3
NETHERLANDS (4)	67	26	7
SWEDEN (1)	74	22	4
ISRAEL (2)	64	7	29
JAPAN (2)	68	5	27
CHINA (1)	50	25	25
UNITED STATES (18)	65	21	14
Overall average	65	21	14

Percentages to nearest whole number reported by Van Ijzendoorn and Kroonenberg (1988).

Theories of attachment
Why are attachments formed? A variety of theories have been proposed.

Psychoanalytic theory
Freud believed that infants become attached to people who satisfy their need for food at the oral stage. Oral gratification gained from the sucking and swallowing of feeding causes drive reduction, which is experienced as pleasant.

While Freud was right that attachment is important for later development, his drive theory and idea that attachment is due to food has not been supported.

Cognitive theory
Schaffer (1971) focuses on the perceptual and intellectual cognitive aspects of attachment, pointing out that infants usually form attachments once they can reliably distinguish one caregiver from another and with the caregivers that stimulate and interact with them the mostly intensely.

Learning theory
Learning theory suggests that attachment should occur as parents become associated with pleasant stimuli such as food via classical conditioning. The positive emotional responses produced by these pleasant stimuli are transferred to the parents by their repeated association together, until the very presence of parents without any unconditional stimuli is rewarding to the child. As parents become secondary reinforcers, capable of producing positive conditioned emotional responses in their children, the infant will seek the presence of, and show distress on separation from, the attachment figure.

Bowlby's attachment theory
Bowlby (1951) suggested that human infants were *genetically programmed* to form attachments to a *single* carer (the mother in most cases), *within a critical time period* (approximately 2 and a half years).

Bowlby argued that attachment between infant and caregiver has evolved because it is an adaptive behaviour that aids survival. In particular, for the infant attachment provides
- food
- security
- a safe base from which to explore the world
- exposure to important survival skills shown by the parent
- an internal working model of relationships with others.

The last point is particularly important if the child is to form loving attachments in later life. For the parent it ensures a greater likelihood of their offspring surviving (and thus passing on their own genes for attachment formation).

Various innate social releasers have also evolved to elicit care giving, such as crying and smiling. If attachments have not been formed by the end of the critical time period, Bowlby suggested that a number of negative effects would result (see deprivation and privation).

While Bowlby's ideas on attachment were important, research indicates that multiple attachments can be formed within a sensitive time period (Rutter, 1981). Many researchers have disputed the idea that an internal working model of relationships formed during attachment always influences later relationships and behaviour (see deprivation and privation research).

Attachment studies
- Konrad Lorenz was an ethologist who noticed the way ducklings and goslings followed their mother after birth, and found that if he allowed greylag goslings to see him rather than their mother in the first day after hatching, then they would follow him around. Lorenz demonstrated that the greylag goslings actually preferred him to their natural mother and found that they became very distressed if he was out of their sight – he even had to go swimming himself to get them to swim. Lorenz termed this attachment and following behaviour 'imprinting' and argued that it was innate, irreversible and occurred in a critical time period (or not at all). He further suggested that the imprinting served an important survival function and provided a model for future interactions – his goslings as adult geese tried to mate with humans rather than members of their own species! Later research found that imprinting occurs in a sensitive rather than critical time period and can be reversed to some extent.

- Harlow conducted a series of studies that involved raising monkeys in social isolation. He found that the monkeys seemed to show an innate preference to form attachments to a cloth 'surrogate mother' model that provided contact comfort, rather than a wire 'surrogate mother' model that provided food.
- Schaffer and Emerson (1964) conducted a two-year, longitudinal, field study of attachment involving the measurement of infant separation distress and anxiety in the presence of strangers in the home. The study revealed that multiple attachments are possible and that the infants formed attachments towards the carers who were responsive and interacted with them the most, rather than just those who fed them.

Exercise 55 (the answers are on page 136)
1 What implications do the studies on attachment in the box above have for the theories of attachment?
2 What advantages and disadvantages are there with the methods used in the attachment studies in the box above?

56 | Deprivation and privation of attachment in infancy

Deprivation of attachment in infancy

Bowlby's (1951) maternal deprivation hypothesis proposed that if infants were deprived of their mother (whom he regarded as their major attachment figure), during the critical period of attachment of the first few years of life, then a range of serious and permanent consequences for later development would follow. These included mental subnormality, delinquency, depression, affectionless psychopathy and even dwarfism.

Rutter (1981), however, in 'Maternal Deprivation Reassessed', a thorough review of research in the area, concluded that Bowlby:
- Was not correct in his ideas about monotropy (attachment to one figure only) or strict critical periods for attachment.
- Failed to distinguish between the effects of deprivation (losing an attachment figure) and privation (never having formed an attachment).

Research has indicated a variety of possible short- and long-term effects that may result from deprivation of an attachment figure.

Possible effects of deprivation

The short-term effects of deprivation include a temporary delay in intellectual development and symptoms of the 'syndrome of distress':
- *Protest* – the infant expresses their feelings of anger, fear, frustration, etc.
- *Despair* – the infant then shows apathy and signs of depression, avoiding others.
- *Detachment* – interaction with others resumes, but is superficial and shows no preferences between other people. Re-attachment is resisted.

The long-term effects of deprivation include symptoms of 'separation anxiety':
- Increased aggression.
- Increased clinging behaviour, possibly developing to the point of refusal to go to school.
- Increased detachment
- Psychosomatic disorders (e.g. skin and stomach reactions).

An increased risk of depression as an adult (usually in reaction to the death of an attachment figure) may also occur.

Mediating factors in deprivation effects

According to Rutter (1981), there are many sources of individual differences in vulnerability to the short- and long-term effects of deprivation, including:

- *Characteristics of the child*, e.g.
  Age – children are especially vulnerable between 7 months and 3 years (Maccoby, 1981).
  Gender – boys, on average, respond worse to separation than girls.
  Temperament – differences in temperament, like aggressiveness, may become exaggerated.

- *Previous mother–child relationship* – The infant's reaction to separation may depend upon the type of attachment, e.g. secure, resistant or avoidant (Ainsworth et al., 1978).

- *Previous separation experience* – Infants experienced in short-term stays with (for example) relatives are more resistant to the effects of deprivation (Stacey et al., 1970).

- *Attachments to others* – Since Schaffer and Emerson (1964) revealed that multiple attachments are possible (in opposition to Bowlby's (1951) ideas), infants who are not deprived of all attachment figures manage the effects better.

- *Quality of care* – Research has revealed that both the short- and long-term effects of deprivation can be dramatically reduced by high-quality care in crèches and institutions respectively.

- *Type of separation* – Some research has indicated that long-term separation due to death or illness, if accompanied by harmonious social support, has less of a long-term effect than separation due to divorce.

Privation of attachment in infancy

According to Rutter (1981), the most serious long-term consequences for healthy infant development appear to be due to privation – a lack of some kind – rather than to any type of deprivation/loss. However, in his review of the research, Rutter found that the many proposed adverse effects of privation were not always directly due to a lack of an emotional attachment bond. Often a deficiency of other important things that an attachment figure may provide (e.g. food, stimulation or even family unity), but an orphanage or dysfunctional family may not, was responsible.

Major consequences of privation and their precise likely causes (Rutter, 1981)

- *Intellectual retardation* – due to a deficiency of stimulation and necessary life experiences
- *Affectionless psychopathy* – due to a failure to develop attachments in infancy.
- *Anti-social behaviour/delinquency* – due to distorted intra-familial relationships, hostility, discord or lack of affection.
- *Enuresis* – bed-wetting is mainly associated with stress during the first six years.
- *Developmental dwarfism* – due mainly to nutritional deficiencies in early childhood.

Mediating factors in privation effects

Research has revealed that there are a variety of factors which are likely to affect the severity of privation effects, including:

- *The type of child care available* – orphanages, for example, that provide a high standard of care may reduce the effects of lack of stimulation or stress, but may still have a high turnover of staff which prevents attachments forming with the orphans.

- *The duration of the privation* – the longer the time delay before making an attachment, the greater the chance of failure to form an attachment and thus developing affectionless psychopathy. Although research unequivocally says that experiences at all ages have an impact, it seems likely that the first few years do have a special importance for bond formation and social development.

- *Temperament and resilience of the child* – perhaps most importantly, there has been the repeated finding that many children are not excessively damaged by early privation, and that the effects of it can be reversed.

Studies of deprivation and privation effects

Early studies of deprivation

- Goldfarb (1943) studied children raised in institutions for most of the first three years of their lives and found they later showed reduced IQ compared to a fostered control group.

- Bowlby (1946) studied 44 juvenile thieves and argued that their affectionless psychopathy was the result of maternal deprivation.

- Spitz and Wolf (1946) investigated infants in South American orphanages and found evidence for severe anaclitic depression in them.

- Harlow and Harlow (1962) researched the effects of social deprivation on rhesus monkeys. Deprived of an attachment figure, they interacted abnormally with other monkeys when they were eventually allowed to mix with them and were unable to form attachments to their own offspring after being artificially inseminated.

- Robertson and Bowlby (1952) based their conclusions regarding the short-term effects of deprivation on observations of the behaviour of children aged between one and four, being hospitalised or placed in residential nurseries.

- Cockett and Tripp (1994) found more long-term attachment deprivation effects in children from re-ordered families (where parents had divorced and the child now lived away from a parental attachment figure) than those children who lived in intact but discordant (arguing parent) families.

Many of the above studies had their methodological flaws, from failing to take into account the amount of environmental stimulation available in institutions, to generalising from animal studies.

Case studies of extreme privation

Freud and Dann (1951) studied six 3-year-old orphans from a concentration camp who had not been able to form attachments to their parents. These children did not develop affectionless psychopathy, probably because they formed close attachments with each other (rather like the two twins raised in extreme privation studied by Koluchova, 1972), and despite developing a number of emotional problems their intellectual recovery was unimpaired.

Such extreme case studies clearly involve many sources of privation, not just of attachment figures, but also indicate the strong resilience that children's development can show.

The case of Genie (Curtiss, 1977) illustrates another problem with case studies which are conducted retrospectively – the access to accurate data. Genie had been locked away in her room with little interaction until the age of 13, and had many difficulties recovering cognitively, linguistically and socially. However, this may have been due to the length of privation or pre-existing mental retardation (the reason the father gave for locking her away in the first place).

Adoption studies

Hodges and Tizard (1989) found that institutionalised children (who had not formed a stable attachment), adopted between the ages of two and seven, could form close attachments to their adoptive parents.

However, the children returned to their own families had more problems forming attachments and all the institutionalised children had problems with relationships outside their family.

Kadushin (1976) studied over 90 cases of late adoption, where the children were over five years old, and found highly successful outcomes, indicating that early privation does not necessarily prevent later attachment.

Isolated rhesus monkey 'therapy'

Novak and Harlow (1975) found that rhesus monkeys kept in social isolation from birth could develop reasonably normally if they were given 'therapy' by later being allowed to occasionally play with monkeys of their own age.

However, despite indicating the possibility of recovery from total social isolation, generalising the results from rhesus privation studies to human privation ignores the large differences between the two species.

Exercise 56

1 Which studies above support
   a Bowlby's original claims?
   b the idea that privation effects are not inevitable?

2 Why are the effects of attachment separation difficult to assess when the children move to a new environment, such as a hospital or new home?

3 Day care refers to the minding of children by people other than the family they live with, either in their home or outside it, when the family is away during the day. By considering the research above:
   a Why do you think people are concerned about the day care of young infants?
   b What factors do you think might be involved in determining the effects of day care upon infants?

Answers 55.1 – 55.2

1 What implications do the studies on attachment in the box above have for the theories of attachment?

- Bowlby was influenced by the ideas of both Freud and Konrad Lorenz. One can see that Bowlby's ideas on irreversible attachment to a single figure (who formed a model for later relationships) within a critical time period were strongly influenced by findings on imprinting
- Harlow's finding that the monkeys seem to show an innate preference to form attachments to a cloth 'surrogate mother' model which provided contact comfort, rather than a wire 'surrogate mother' model that provided food, goes against the emphasis on food advocated by the psychoanalytic and learning theories of attachment.
- Schaffer and Emerson's (1964) study revealed that multiple attachments are possible (in opposition to Bowlby's 1951 ideas), and that the infants formed attachments towards the carers who were responsive and interacted with them the most, rather than just those who fed them.

This supports the cognitive theory of attachment in preference to the psychoanalytic and (to some extent) learning theories.

2 What advantages and disadvantages are there with the methods used in the attachment studies in the box above?

The animal studies have the advantage of being able to experimentally investigate attachment under controlled conditions, something that is deemed ethically impossible with human participants. Unfortunately, there is the problem of generalising from animal studies to humans. The two-year, longitudinal, field study of attachment involving the measurement of infant separation distress and anxiety in the presence of strangers in the home provided very detailed and ecologically valid data (compared to the strange situation method) but was heavily reliant on assessments from family members who are not necessarily as objective and precise in their recording of data.

Answers 56.1 – 56.3

1 Which studies above support
   a Bowlby's original claims?

The early studies of deprivation mostly support Bowlby's original claims, although as mentioned there were methodological problems with many of the studies.

   b the idea that privation effects are not inevitable?

The adoption studies show that Bowlby's ideas on the irreversibility of deprivation effects were not completely correct, while the 'monkey therapy' and case studies of extreme privation frequently show both the resilience of infants to the effects of privation and their ability to form attachments to figures other than the mother.

2 Why are the effects of attachment separation difficult to assess when the children move to a new environment, such as a hospital or new home?

The emotional and behavioural effects of the attachment separation may be difficult to distinguish from effects relating to their new environment and situation, e.g. fear of hospitals or unhappiness with the changes involved in moving house.

3 Day care refers to the minding of children by people other than the family they live with, either in their home or outside it, when the family is away during the day. By considering the research above:
   a Why do you think people are concerned about the day care of young infants?

Day care became an issue of concern as increasing levels of external female employment and the reduction of the extended home family in industrialised societies, led to a greater need for outside carers. These factors, combined with Bowlby's research on maternal deprivation and various social/political agendas, have created concern that day care will have

- negative effects on children – although it is now clear that children can form multiple attachments, and to carers other than the mother, the concern was that, once the mother went to work, there would be no consistent carer left to provide for the child's attachment and stimulation needs, and that outside carers would not meet these needs in the same way.

- negative effects on parents – in particular the sexist pressure of society on women to either stay at home to provide the care and feel frustrated (and possibly resent, and thus negatively affect, their child care) or go to work and feel guilty about the effects it may have.

Social-emotional effects

It has been suggested that day care could result in either

- the child being unable to form an attachment (causing privation effects) or disruption to the bond if attachment had been already made (causing deprivation effects) or
- increased sociability and social skills due to greater exposure to the outside world.

Belsky and Rovine (1988) found infants were more likely to develop insecure attachments if they received day care for over 20 hours per week before they were a year old, while other research in America has linked greater child care with worse peer relationships and emotional health.

However, these effects are not inevitable and may ignore the pre-existing attachments and quality of day care.

Kagan et al. (1980) set up their own nursery with consistent and high-quality day care, and compared 33 infants from a variety of backgrounds who attended it from 3.5 months of age with a matched home care control group. They found no significantly consistent differences between the two groups in attachment and sociability.

Clarke-Stewart et al. (1994) found peer relationships were more advanced in children who had experienced day care.

Other research indicates that the length of time in day care in itself does not significantly affect attachment and that the individual differences children show to it are more related to the quality and consistency of the day care, maternal sensitivity and the child's pre-existing characteristics.

Cognitive effects

It has also been suggested that day care could result in

- less verbal interaction, stimulation and exploration by the child due to a lack of a secure attachment figure as a base, if the day carers encourage quietness and passivity, do not want to form emotional attachments and are often changed, or
- more stimulation, interaction and educational activities for children who would not otherwise receive them.

Operation Headstart in the USA in the mid-1960s involved several hundred thousand socially disadvantaged pre-school children receiving intensive day care education. Initial short-term gains in school and cognitive performance were found, as well as longer-term academic and social benefits.

While the limited duration of the school performance gains in the Headstart programme and those studies that find worse cognitive development if day care takes place before one year of age should not be ignored, it should be noted that the cognitive effects depend upon the quality of day care *relative to that the child would otherwise have received*.

Andersson (1992) conducted a longitudinal study on 100 Swedish children and found those who entered day care before the age of one had better school performance at age 8 and 13 than those who did not have any day care (who performed the worst). However, the former did have richer parents. Sweden has very high standards of day care and its greater parental leave allowance probably enables stronger attachments to be made before the child enters day care.

b What factors do you think might be involved in determining the effects of day care upon infants?

Overall, research has tended to reveal no significant negative effects of high-quality day care. Early studies were a little too simplistic in their approach and the current opinion is that the effects of day care depend upon an interaction of influences.

Parental influences
Parents can affect
- the level of stimulation they provide outside of day care
- the security of their children's attachment bond through their sensitivity/responsiveness
- the quality of day care through their economic status and concern over choices available
- the amount of time away.

Child influences
There are individual differences in how children respond to day care based upon, for example:
- their prior temperament and sociability, e.g. shyness
- their prior security of attachment
- the age at which they experience day care.

Quality of day care
Good quality day care involves
- consistency of care – in terms of prolonged contact with the same carers who are able to devote sufficient time
- quality of stimulation – in terms of the degree of verbal interaction, emotional responsiveness and activity resources.

Research methodology
Assessment of the emotional, social and cognitive effects of day care depends upon the validity of the tests used to measure them. The strange situation method may not be a valid test of emotional effects in some studies since the child could have other (or more important) attachment figures than the mother who are not involved in the test. Also, the reactions which day care children show on their mother's return may reflect their increasing independence or enjoyment of day care rather than just their emotional reaction to her. Different studies may use different cognitive and IQ tests of varying reliability and validity.

Fill in the table

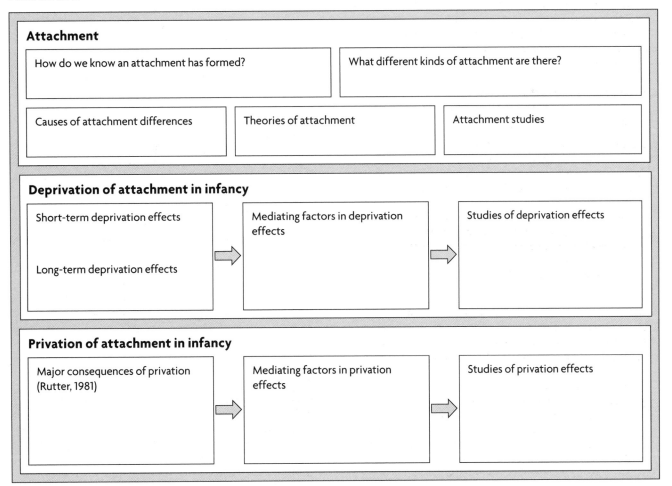

Attachment

| How do we know an attachment has formed? | What different kinds of attachment are there? |

| Causes of attachment differences | Theories of attachment | Attachment studies |

Deprivation of attachment in infancy

| Short-term deprivation effects

Long-term deprivation effects | Mediating factors in deprivation effects | Studies of deprivation effects |

Privation of attachment in infancy

| Major consequences of privation (Rutter, 1981) | Mediating factors in privation effects | Studies of privation effects |

Attachment

How do we know an attachment has formed?
An attachment is a strong, long-lasting and close emotional bond between two people, which causes distress on separation from the attached individual. It can be tested via the 'strange situation'.

What different kinds of attachment are there
- Type A – Anxious-avoidant or detached
- Type B – Securely attached
- Type C – Anxious-resistant or ambivalent

Causes of attachment differences
- Parental sensitivity
- Infant temperament
- Family circumstances
- Reliability of classification
- Cultural differences

Theories of attachment
- Psychoanalytic theory – food at the oral stage.
- Cognitive theory – perceptual and intellectual aspects
- Learning theory – parents become associated with food
- Bowlby's attachment theory – human infants are genetically programmed to form attachments to a single carer (the mother in most cases), within a critical time period

Attachment studies
- Lorenz's imprinting studies with goslings
- Harlow raising monkeys in social isolation
- Schaffer and Emerson's (1964) two-year, longitudinal, field study of attachment in the home

Deprivation of attachment in infancy

Bowlby's (1951) maternal deprivation hypothesis – if infants are deprived of their mother during the critical period of attachment of the first few years of life, then a range of serious and permanent consequences, including mental subnormality, delinquency, depression, affectionless psychopathy and even dwarfism will occur.

Rutter (1981) concluded that Bowlby was not correct in his ideas about monotropy (attachment to one figure only), or strict critical periods for attachment, and failed to distinguish between the effects of deprivation (losing an attachment figure) and privation (never having formed an attachment).

Short-term deprivation effects
- 'Syndrome of distress' – protest, despair, detachment

Long-term deprivation effects
- 'Separation anxiety' – increased aggression, clinging behaviour, detachment, psychosomatic disorders, risk of depression as an adult

Mediating factors in deprivation effects
- Characteristics of the child, e.g. age, gender, temperament
- Previous mother–child relationship
- Previous separation experience
- Attachments to others
- Quality of care
- Type of separation

Studies of deprivation effects
Early studies of deprivation
- Goldfarb (1943)
- Bowlby (1946)
- Spitz and Wolf (1946)
- Harlow and Harlow (1962)
- Robertson and Bowlby (1952)
- Cockett and Tripp (1994)

Privation of attachment in infancy

The most serious long-term consequences are due to privation – a lack of some kind – rather than to any type of deprivation / loss. However, privation effects are *not* always *directly* due to a lack of an emotional attachment bond, often a deficiency of other important things (e.g. food, stimulation or even family unity) causes them.

Major consequences of privation (Rutter, 1981)
- Intellectual retardation
- Affectionless psychopathy
- Anti-social behaviour/delinquency
- Enuresis
- Developmental dwarfism

Mediating factors in privation effects
- The type of child care available
- The duration of the privation
- Temperament and resilience of the child

Studies of privation effects
Adoption studies
- Hodges and Tizard (1989)
- Kadushin (1976)

Isolated rhesus monkey therapy
- Novak and Harlow (1975)

Case studies of extreme privation
- Freud and Dann (1951)
- The case of Genie (Curtiss, 1977)

Hodges & Tizard (1989) – 'Social and family relationships of ex-institutional adolescents'

Hodges and Tizard aimed to investigate (longitudinally and with a matched comparison group of control children) whether experiencing early institutionalisation with ever-changing care-givers until at least two years of age will lead to long-term problems in adolescence for adopted and restored children.

Early studies by Bowlby (1951) and Goldfarb (1943a) found that there were many short- and long-term effects of the early institutionalisation of children, which were attributed to maternal deprivation or privation and which were regarded as largely irreversible.

However, later studies by Tizard and others on a group of adopted, fostered and restored children with early institutional experience showed that there were markedly *less-dramatic effects* on intellectual and emotional development (probably due to improved conditions) but still *difficulties in interpersonal relationships*. The children were studied at age 4 and again at age 8, by which time the majority had formed *close attachments* to their parents, but showed, according to their teachers, more problems of attention-seeking behaviour, disobedience, poor peer relationships and over-friendliness.

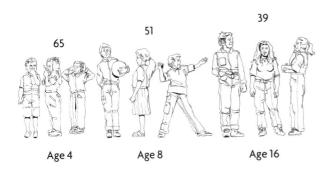

Age 4   Age 8   Age 16

The present study was conducted as a follow-up study to see

- if these children would continue to 'normalise' and lose further effects of early institutionalisation at age 16 or worsen with the stresses of adolescence

- if adopted children would continue to do better than restored children by age 16, as earlier studies had indicated.

Method

All 51 children who had been studied at age 8 were located, of whom 42 were available to study at age 16. From these, 39 were interviewed, of whom

- 23 were adopted (17 boys, 6 girls)
- 11 were restored (6 boys, 5 girls)
- 5 were in institutional care (3 boys, 2 girls).

A *matched* comparison group of children who had not experienced institutionalisation was gathered for the family relationship study.

Another comparison group of children who had not experienced institutionalisation was formed for the school relationship study from the classmates nearest in age of the same sex.

The adolescents were interviewed on tape and completed the 'Questionnaire of social difficulty' (Lindsay and Lindsay, 1982). Mothers or careworkers were interviewed on tape and completed the 'A' scale questionnaire (Rutter et al., 1970). Teachers were asked to complete the 'B' scale questionnaire (Rutter et al., 1970) on the adolescent's behaviour.

Results

- Institutionalised children differed in their degree of attachment to their parents in that:
  a adopted children were *just as attached* to their parents as the comparison group
  b restored children were *less attached* to their parents than the comparison group and adopted children.

- Adopted children were *more affectionate* with parents than restored children (who were less affectionate than the comparison group).

- No difference was found in confiding in, and support from, parents between institutionalised children and comparisons, although the former were less likely to turn to peers.

- Institutionalised children had *more problems* with siblings than the comparison group, especially the restored children.

- Institutionalised children showed significantly worse peer relationships, were less likely to have a particular special friend and were noted by teachers to be more quarrelsome and less liked by, with more bullying of other children.

Discussion

Hodges and Tizard outlined a number of explanations for the general trend that the *adopted* adolescents seemed j*ust as attached* to their *parents* as the comparison group but the *ex-institutional group* as a whole *differed* from their comparison groups in their *relationships with peers and adults* outside the family.

In particular, they noted that the adoptive parents as a group tended to be different from the restored parents. The adoptive parents very much wanted the children and put more effort into building a relationship with the child and tolerating their dependency. However, unlike the highly motivated parents, the adolescents' peers, teachers and other non-family adults were less likely to tolerate or make special efforts towards children who could not already relate well to others or who were attention-seeking.

Another explanation is that, compared to children who could form attachments at a normal (younger) age, the institutionalised children were showing a developmental delay on Anna Freud's (1966) 'developmental line'. This suggests that children have to form an adequate relationship with their parents before they can relate normally to peers and those outside the family. There is some evidence for this – close attachment to a parent at age eight was related to good peer relationships at age 16, for example.

1 What are the advantages and disadvantages of the longitudinal compared to the cross-sectional method in this study?

The advantage of the longitudinal method in this study was that the same children could be studied at different ages, so the changes in their relationship behaviour could be better compared than if different age groups of different children had been tested at the same time.

The disadvantage is that some of the participants dropped out of the study over time and these children may have been different in some respects from the others, thus affecting the overall results of the study.

2 Matched control groups were set up. What criteria would you have used to match the children for the family study?

Hodges and Tizard matched the children in terms of, for example, age, gender, parental occupation and position in the family.

3 What type of experiment does this study represent and how might this affect the conclusions drawn?

A natural or quasi experiment – the experimenters lacked control over the independent variable since the children were not randomly assigned to the adoptive, restored and control groups. There always remains some doubt, therefore, over the effect of the children's personality characteristics on the results.

4 What are the advantages and disadvantages of the interviews and questionnaires in this study?

The questionnaires and interviews would have provided data and insights (e.g. relating to personal feelings) which would not have been so easily gained by any other method.

As self-report measures, however, socially desirable answers or deception may have distorted the data on the subjects' part and experimenter expectation on the interviewer's part.

5 What are the problems with asking mothers if they love all their children equally?

Asking mothers if they love all their children equally might disrupt their interpersonal relationships and cause distress, raising ethical problems.

6 Does the study support Bowlby?

The results imply that while Bowlby was wrong about many of the more dramatic effects of early institutionalisation, some long-lasting effects on interpersonal relations do persist into adolescence, particularly with relationships outside the family. Further follow-up study needs to be conducted to see if adolescent behaviours and feelings persist into adulthood, however.

7 What are the implications of the study for adoption?

There are some important practical implications for adoption practices from this study. In general, adoption with the right family can be more successful for ex-institutionalised children than restoring them to their own families if there is a lack of full commitment. However, there are many individual differences between ex-institutional children that need to be considered and families should be made aware that help may be required with relationships with peers and people outside the family. There should also be further replications of the study to confirm these results before firm conclusions are drawn and the findings practically applied.

HODGES AND TIZARD CROSSWORD

1 The type of study conducted on the children (12)
2 A researcher who found many short- and long-term effects of early institutionalisation and regarded them as largely irreversible (6)
3 The group of children who were just as attached to their parents as the comparison group (7)
4 The age the children were in this report (7)
5 The age the children were last time they were tested (5)
6 All the children in the experimental groups had originally been this (17)
7 The group of children who were less attached to, and affectionate towards, their parents than the comparison group (8)
8 The type of experiment that this study represented (7)
9 The answers to the interview and questionnaire questions may have been this (8/9)
10 The adolescents were interviewed and completed the 'Questionnaire of _____ / _____' (6/10)
11 The number of children interviewed (6/4)
12 The questionnaire completed by the mothers or care workers (1/5)
13 Comparison groups of children were gathered for the family relationship study and the _____ relationship study (6)

58 Defining abnormality

How can we determine the difference between normal and abnormal behaviour, apart from merely saying they are the opposite of one another? Attempts have been made to define abnormality in a more precise fashion.

Statistical infrequency

Abnormality can be defined as deviation from the average, where statistically common behaviour is defined as 'normal' *while statistically rare behaviour* is 'abnormal'. Thus, autism is sufficiently statistically rare (it occurs in 2 to 4 children per 10,000) to be 'abnormal', as is multiple-personality disorder.

This does not necessarily mean the behaviour concerned is qualitatively different from 'normal' – many human characteristics are shown by everyone in the population to a certain degree, and if they can be measured every individual can be placed upon a dimensional scale or continuum that will reveal how common their score is in comparison to everybody else's. These comparisons can be standardised by the use of *normal distribution curves*, the mathematical properties of which enable us to determine the statistical rarity or commonness of a characteristic if we know the mean and standard deviation of our sample's measurements of that characteristic. Many characteristics could be placed upon normal distribution curves as dimensions, such as intelligence, neuroticism, mood or fearfulness. Most people fall somewhere in the middle of these continuums, but if an individual shows an extreme deviation from this average then they may be regarded as abnormal.

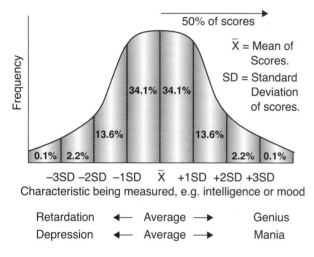

Deviation from social norms

Norms are expected ways of behaving in a society according to the majority. Those members of a society who do not think and behave like everyone else break these norms and so are often defined as abnormal. The definition is based on the facts that

- abnormal behaviour is seen as vivid and unpredictable, causes observer discomfort and violates moral or ideal standards (Rosenhan and Seligman, 1989) because it differs from most other people's behaviour and standards

- abnormal thinking is delusional, irrational or incomprehensible because it differs from commonly accepted or usual beliefs and ways of thinking.

The deviation from social norm definition of abnormal behaviour is thus a *socially based definition* and is explained by social constructionism and social identity theories.

Researchers such as Szasz (1960) have argued that 'abnormality', especially relating to certain mental disorders, is a socially constructed concept that allows people who show different, unusual or disturbing (to the rest of society) behaviour to be labelled and thus treated differently from others – often confined, controlled and persecuted. Social identity theory would argue that people who do not share similar behaviour and beliefs are not included in the 'in-group' (in this case the majority in a society) and are therefore categorised as 'other' (abnormal) and discriminated against.

Failure to function adequately

Maladaptive behaviour, which causes a failure to function adequately in the social and physical environment, seems a more objective way of defining abnormality. Everyone experiences difficulties coping with the world sometimes but if an individual's abnormal behaviour, mood or thinking adversely affects their well being (e.g. ability to maintain employment, a bearable quality of life, normal social relations, etc.) then the definition will draw attention to the fact that help is needed. On a more extreme level, if an individual's abnormal behaviour becomes a danger to their own safety (e.g. neglecting self care, self mutilation, suicidal, etc.) or the safety of others (e.g. dangerous behaviour) then they may be defined as abnormal and institutionalised ('sectioned' under the Mental Health Act, 1983, for example).

Deviation from ideal mental health

The idea that a single characteristic can be used as the basis of a general definition of abnormality has been rejected by some in favour of a set of criterion characteristics of abnormality or normality. Jahoda (1958), for example, has described several characteristics that mentally healthy people should possess, such as:

- the ability to introspect
- integration and balance of personality
- self-actualisation
- autonomy
- the ability to cope with stress
- the ability to see the world as it really is
- environmental mastery.

It should be noted that many psychologists object to the general term 'abnormality' and prefer the more constructive approach of describing the precise behavioural symptoms for particular mental disorders.

Exercise 58

1 In comparison to autism, there is thought to be a 1% lifetime risk of developing schizophrenia and a 9% risk of developing some kind of mood disorder. What problems does this pose for the 'statistical infrequency' definition of abnormality?

2 From looking at the definitions of the extremes of intelligence (at + 3 standard deviations) and mood on the normal distribution curve, would you define them as equally 'abnormal'?

3 According to social norm theory, different cultures may have different norms (expected or appropriate ways of behaving in certain situations). What problems does this pose for the 'statistical infrequency' and 'deviation from social norms' definitions of abnormality?

4 Who do you think should decide when a person is failing to function adequately, the individual concerned, the individual's family, or others in society?

5 According to Jahoda's criteria, do you think that you are completely 'normal'?

1 In comparison to autism, there is thought to be a 1% lifetime risk of developing schizophrenia and a 9% risk of developing some kind of mood disorder. What problems does this pose for the 'statistical infrequency' definition of abnormality?

Practically, there are problems deciding how statistically rare (2 or 3 standard deviations?) behaviour has to be to be considered as abnormal. Some currently accepted mental disorders, such as mood disorders, are probably not statistically rare enough to be defined as 'abnormal'.

2 From looking at the definitions of the extremes of intelligence (at + 3 standard deviations) and mood on the normal distribution curve, would you define them as equally 'abnormal'?

Statistical deviation from the average does not tell us about the desirability of the deviation. Depression and mania are thought of as abnormal since they occupy the opposite extremes on a continuum of 'mood', however not all statistically rare extremes are regarded as undesirable. Both mental retardation and genius are statistically rare (at + 3 standard deviations) but only the former tends to be regarded as 'abnormal'.

3 According to social norm theory, different cultures may have different norms (expected or appropriate ways of behaving in certain situations). What problems does this pose for the 'statistical infrequency' and 'deviation from social norms' definitions of abnormality?

According to the statistical infrequency definition different subcultures may show behaviour that is statistically rare in the majority culture and thus be defined as abnormal.

Since deviation from social norms is a socially based definition, it implies that different societies or cultures with different norms will define different behaviours as abnormal and may even disagree over whether the same behaviour is abnormal. This *cultural relativism* means that an objective definition of abnormal behaviour that is fixed and stable across cultures and time is difficult if not impossible to achieve, which may lead to unfair and discriminatory treatment of minorities by majorities. Indeed, concepts of abnormal behaviour have been shown to differ cross-culturally (a belief in voodoo in one culture may be thought to be paranoia in another) and in the same culture over time (unmarried mothers in Britain and political dissidents in the Soviet Union have been confined to institutions for their 'abnormal' behaviour).

Thus it has been argued that in some cultures the symptoms of schizophrenia such as strange visions, speech and behaviour might be regarded as special or sacred rather than abnormal and undesirable. However, research by Murphy (1976) on non-western cultures (such as Inuit tribes) has indicated that linguistic distinctions are made between the 'shaman' and 'crazy people' in their society.

In the same way, other cultures may regard those defined as suffering from anti-social personality disorder (psychopaths) by western diagnostic systems as just plain evil or bad. Western societies have medicalised disorder to a greater degree than non-western societies in Africa and India, for example, where mental well-being is far more tied up with religious and social well-being. Even in different western cultures, different diagnostic classification systems and expectations have been shown to influence the determination of abnormality.

4 Who do you think should decide when a person is failing to function adequately, the individual concerned, the individual's family, or others in society?

Some individuals who show a failure to function adequately may not *realise* they are (e.g. those who are in a psychotic state and lack insight) or care about it (e.g. those with anti-social personality disorder who lack a conscience). The definition may, therefore, have to be applied by others in society. However, how 'inadequate' functioning has to be before the definition of abnormality is applied is, to some extent, a social judgement, which may not be made impartially.

Given the negative consequences of being 'defined as abnormal' (e.g. stigmatisation, rejection or loss of self-responsibility if 'sectioned' under the Mental Health Act), family members may be unwilling to admit that their relative has problems.

'Sectioning' under the Mental Health Act (1983)

'Sectioning' involves the compulsory detention and even treatment of those regarded as mentally ill, if they represent a danger to their own or other's safety. This is based on the assumption that mental illness leads to a loss of self-control and responsibility. A social worker is required to section somebody in addition to a GP and a psychiatrist, implying that social as well as physical factors need to be taken into account.

- Section 2 of the act can be used to detain people for up to 28 days for observation and assessment of mental illness.
- Section 3 of the act involves the enforced application of treatment and loss of rights.

Power is firmly in the hands of society since

- Section 5 of the act can prevent the right of even the nearest relative to withdraw the sectioned individual from care.
- Section 136 gives the police the right to arrest in a public place anybody deemed to show mental illness to maintain security.
- Section 139 removes all responsibility of mistaken diagnosis from those involved in sectioning providing the diagnosis was made in good faith and the legal procedures were carried out correctly.

As for others in society, because people often feel threatened by unusual behaviour, the label of abnormality may be applied based more on threats *perceived* by the majority in society than actual threats or a genuine concern to help the individual with problems. In addition, difficulties in functioning adequately may be partly the result of the social rejection people defined as abnormal face.

5 According to Jahoda's criteria, do you think that you are completely 'normal'?

Unfortunately, this criterion approach has also had its problems as a definition, since just how many of these characteristics do you have to lack or possess, and to what degree, to be regarded as normal or abnormal? Jahoda's characteristics of mental health have been regarded as too idealistic, in fact it is 'normal' to fall short of such perfect standards, and humanistic psychologists such as Maslow would argue that very few people actually reach self-actualisation. Not everyone agrees with the ideal characteristics or that all are necessary for mental health, for example, other cultures may disagree with the ideals of autonomy and independence, and view other characteristics as more important.

59 | Models of abnormality

There are many models of abnormality, and each not only has different assumptions about the cause of normality and abnormality, but also has practical implications for the treatment of those defined as 'abnormal'.

The medical model

Assumptions about the causes of 'abnormality'
The medical model, based on the biological, physiological or somatic approach, suggests that 'normality' depends upon a properly functioning physiology and nervous system and no genetic pre-dispositions to inherit mental disorder.

By implication, therefore, the medical model assumes that, like physical illness, 'abnormality' results from *mental illness* which has an *underlying physical / bodily cause*. *Genetic, organic* or *chemical disorders* cause mental illness which gives rise to psychological (behavioural and mental) symptoms. These symptoms can be classified to *diagnose* the *psychopathology*, which can then be treated through *therapy* in psychiatric *hospitals* to *cure* the *patient*. Note the use of medical terminology this approach has borrowed.

Practical implications for the treatment of the 'abnormal'
The idea that the 'abnormal' individual is mentally 'ill' means that the individual is not to be held responsible for their predicament. As with physical illness, they are more likely to be seen as a victim of a disorder that is beyond their control and, therefore, in need of care and treatment. The medical model is, therefore, intended to be a more caring and humane approach to abnormality – especially given the blame, stigmatisation and lack of care for abnormality that had been the norm before the approach. The use of the medical model to define abnormality as mental illness can lead to

- *institutionalisation* – hospitalisation allows the removal to a controlled environment of individuals who may represent a danger to themselves or others. The controlled environment allows the close monitoring, support and treatment of those suffering from mental illness.
- *biological treatments* – including drug treatment, electro-convulsive therapy or even psychosurgery to correct the current underlying physical cause of the mental illness or at least alleviate the symptoms.

The psychodynamic model

Assumptions about the causes of 'abnormality'
The psychodynamic model, according to Freud, assumes that 'normality' results from a balance between id, ego and superego, sufficient ego control to allow the acceptable gratification of id impulses, and no inconvenient fixations or repression of traumatic events.

'Abnormality' results from emotional disturbance or neurosis caused by thwarted id impulses, unresolved unconscious conflicts (e.g. Oedipus complex) or repressed traumatic events deriving from childhood. Both psychological and physical symptoms are thought to be expressions of unconscious psychological causes.

However, Freud argued that conflict and neurosis are always present to some extent, so the difference between the 'normal' and 'abnormal' is only quantitative (a matter of degree only).

Practical implications for the treatment of the 'abnormal'
Due to the difficulty of discovering the *unconscious causes* of psychological problems that usually originate in the *past* (especially childhood), plus the *resistance* patients put up to accepting these (often disturbing) unconscious causes

- several sessions a week for many months, even years, are usually required (shorter versions such as Mallan's brief focal therapy have been developed)

- the patient must trust and accept the therapist's interpretation and instructions.

However, because psychoanalysis is an insight-based therapy, and is not generally regarded as suitable for serious psychotic states, it does not usually involve institutionalisation and occurs under voluntary conditions. Psychoanalysts do not blame or judge the patient who is not responsible for their problems.

The behavioural model

Assumptions about the causes of 'abnormality'
The behavioural model is based upon the behaviourist or learning theory approach and suggests that a learning history that has provided an adequately large selection of adaptive responses will produce a 'normal' individual.

'Abnormality' is, thus, also a result of environmental experience – either maladaptive (unhelpful in the environment) responses have been learnt or adaptive ones have not been learnt. Observable, behavioural disorder is all abnormality consists of. Unlike other models, the behavioural model assumes that 'abnormal' behaviour is not a symptom of any underlying cause – only what you see or hear (actions and utterances) needs to be changed.

Practical implications for the treatment of the 'abnormal'
Behavioural treatments aim to rectify specific maladaptive behaviours through removing bad responses or learning good ones. No underlying causes are considered, and the focus is on current, observable behaviour only. A range of learning techniques is used – behaviour therapy uses the principles of classical conditioning, whereas behaviour modification methods use operant conditioning ideas. The therapist's instructions and procedures have to be closely followed and a laboratory environment may be required to ensure control with certain treatments, e.g. selective reinforcement for anorexia, but most techniques are relatively quick to administer.

The cognitive model

Assumptions about the causes of 'abnormality'
This model is based upon the cognitive psychological assumptions regarding mental thought processes. 'Normality' results from properly functioning and rational cognitive thought processes that can be used to accurately perceive the world and control behaviour. 'Abnormality' is, therefore, caused by

- unrealistic, distorted or irrational understanding, perceptions and thoughts about oneself, others or the environment
- difficulty in controlling thought processes or using them to control actions.

Practical implications for the treatment of the 'abnormal'
Cognitive treatments aim to cure or alleviate the underlying mental causes of disorder by restructuring the maladaptive thought processes that are causing it. Cognitive therapies focus on *current* problems in thinking and try to empower people to change their thinking by providing them with strategies designed to combat illogical or irrational thoughts and control their behaviour.

Exercise 59

1 How might medical diagnosis, a loss of responsibility and institutionalisation have negative effects?

2 Identify one way in which each model differs from the others.

1 How might medical diagnosis, a loss of responsibility and institutionalisation have negative effects?

The medical model diagnostic assumption that mentally ill people are distinctly different from mentally well people can lead to labelling and prejudice against those defined as abnormal under the medical model.

Medically 'labelling' an individual as 'mentally ill', can have many adverse effects, such as

- *self-fulfilling prophecy* – patients may begin to act as they think they are expected to act. Goffman argues that they may internalise the role of 'mentally ill patient' and this could worsen their disorder rather than improve it.
- *distortion of behaviour* – medical diagnosis tends to label the whole person and once the label of diagnosis is attached then all the individual's actions become interpreted in the light of the label. Sometimes even normal behaviour is ignored or interpreted as a sign of the individual's mental disorder. Rosenhan's (1973) study supports this.
- *discrimination* – Rosenhan talked of the 'stickiness' of diagnostic labels; when an individual returns to society their record of mental illness goes with them. This can lead to stigmatisation, stereotyping and discrimination, making reintegration back into the community difficult.

Researchers like Szasz and Scheff suggest that the majority in power in a society attach stigmatising labels to those who show different or frightening behaviour and so justify their control and treatment. Labelling people as abnormal helps society overcome its anxiety and establishes clear norms of reality and appropriate behaviour. The major ethical implication here is that the medical diagnosis serves the purposes of the majority in society only, and that it is wrong to assume it is helpful for those seen as 'abnormal'.

Some would also argue that society has merely tried to 'medicalise' disruptive behaviour, to find a cause 'within' the person for bad behaviour, rather than looking to the environment for causes. The assumption that there is always a biological underlying cause for abnormality may be incorrect and, therefore, lead to the wrong diagnosis and/or treatment being given. There is not always a clearly identifiable underlying biological cause for abnormal behaviour.

The assumption that abnormal people are mentally ill and, therefore, not responsible for their actions can lead to

- the loss of rights, such as the right to consent to treatment or institutionalisation and even the right to vote if sectioned under the Mental Health Act
- the loss of an internal locus of control, loss of self-care and an abdication of responsibility to others
- the idea that directive therapy (where the therapist has more power than the patient) is needed for the benefit of the mentally ill individual. The concept of directive therapy may be less debatable with profound psychoses where insight may be totally lacking, but becomes more controversial when we consider the rights of someone suffering from depression to withdraw from their drug therapy when that withdrawal may result in their suicide.

Institutionalisation may worsen the condition of the patient, providing them with an abnormal environment and causing the internalisation of the passive and dependent role of 'mental inmate'. Rosenhan's study 'On being sane in insane places' revealed the often negative treatment received in mental institutions in the early 1970s.

2 Identify one way in which each model differs from the others.

- The medical model is based on *biological* or physiological principles, whereas the psychodynamic, behavioural and cognitive models are based on *psychological* concepts (thoughts, feelings and behaviour).
- The psychodynamic model, according to Freud, is the one most concerned with *past* causes of abnormality, the others focus on *current* physical, behavioural or mental problems.
- The behavioural model focuses only on *observable behaviour*, whereas the others are only interested in behaviour as a symptom of *underlying* biological, unconscious or mental causes.
- The cognitive model seems less directive, by focusing more on voluntary participation, self-responsibility and self-empowerment strategies. In the other models the therapist has a greater power role, prescribing medical treatment, persuading clients into believing the analyst's interpretation of unconscious problems and enforcing behavioural procedures.

MODELS OF ABNORMALITY ANAGRAMS

1 ORACING ACUSES

2 HOPCATSPYHOLOGY

3 CHIHOLODD RATUMA

4 LINIUISTATIONSTATION

5 HISTING-BEADS YETHARP

6 DIALAMPAVET SPORSENSE

7 RATIRIONAL STONEPRCEPI

8 UNSOONCCIUS PRESSORINE

9 LEROTEC-CLOSEUVINV HEPYRAT

60 Rosenhan (1973) – 'On being sane in insane places'

Rosenhan argued in this article that there are significant problems involved in the diagnosis and classification of mental illness. At the time of writing, he described how the view had arisen that the psychological categorisation of mental illness was, at best, useless and, at worst, harmful, misleading and pejorative. In particular, many researchers were arguing that it seemed unclear whether the characteristics that led to a diagnosis of insanity resided in the patients themselves or in the environments and contexts in which observers found them.

The aim of this study was, therefore, to illustrate experimentally the

- poor reliability of the diagnostic classification system for mental disorder at the time (as well as general doubts over its validity)
- negative consequences of being diagnosed as abnormal and the effects of institutionalisation.

Method
Eight sane people (3 women and 5 men from a small variety of occupational backgrounds), using only fake names and occupations, sought admission to a range of twelve hospitals (varying in age, resources, staff/patient ratios, degree of research conducted, etc.)

Each pseudo-patient arranged an appointment at the hospital and complained that he or she had been hearing voices. The voices were unclear, unfamiliar, of the same gender, and said single words like 'empty', 'hollow' and 'thud'. Apart from the aforementioned falsifying of name and occupation and this single symptom, the pseudo-patients did not change any aspect of their behaviour, personal history or circumstances.

On admission to the hospital ward, every pseudo-patient immediately stopped simulating any symptoms and responded normally to all instructions (except they did not swallow medication) and said they were fine and experiencing no more symptoms. Their tasks were then to

1 seek release by convincing the staff that they were sane (all but one pseudo-patient were very motivated to do this)
2 observe and record the experience of the institutionalised mentally disordered patient (done covertly at first, although this was unnecessary).

Results
Experimental results
- *Admission* – Pseudo-patients were admitted to every hospital, in all cases except one, with a diagnosis of schizophrenia, and their sanity was never detected by staff – only by other patients (35 out of 118 of whom voiced their suspicions in the first three hospitalisations).

  To check the poor reliability of diagnosis and to see if the insane could be distinguished from the sane, a later study was conducted where a teaching hospital (which had been informed of Rosenhan's study) was told to expect pseudo-patients over a three-month period. During that time 193 patients were rated for how likely they were to be pseudo-patients – 41 patients were suspected of being fakes, 19 of whom were suspected by both a psychiatrist and one other staff member, even though no pseudo-patients were sent during that time.

- *Release* – Length of stay ranged from 7 to 52 days with an average of 19 days. All except one were released with a diagnosis of 'schizophrenia in remission', supporting the view that they had never been detected as sane.

Observation results
- *Lack of monitoring* – very little contact with doctors was experienced and a strong sense of segregation between staff and patients was noted.

- *Distortion of behaviour* – all (normal) behaviour became interpreted in the light of the 'label' of 'schizophrenia', for example:
  a A normal case history – became distorted to emphasise the ambivalence and emotional instability thought to be shown by schizophrenics.
  b Note taking – pseudo-patients were never asked why they were taking notes, but it was recorded by nurses as 'patient engages in writing behaviour', implying that it was a symptom of their disorder.
  c Pacing the corridors out of boredom – was seen as nervousness, again implying that it was a symptom of their disorder.
  d Waiting outside the cafeteria before lunch time – was interpreted as showing the 'oral-acquisitive nature of the syndrome' by a psychiatrist.

'hungry, bored or showing the oral acquisitive nature of his syndrome?'

- *Lack of normal interaction* – for example, pseudo-patients courteously asked a staff member 'Pardon me, Mr (or Dr or Mrs) X, could you tell me when I will be presented at the staff meeting? (or…When am I likely to be discharged?)'. They found mostly a brief, not always relevant, answer was given, on the move, without even a normal turn of the head or eye-contact (psychiatrists moved on with their head averted 71% of the time and only stopped and talked normally on 4% of occasions).

- *Powerlessness and depersonalisation* – was produced in the institution through the lack of rights, constructive activity, choice and privacy, plus frequent verbal and even physical abuse from the attendants.

> ## Exercise 60
> 1 Based on the results of the study, do you think
>   a diagnostic classification was demonstrated to be reliable and useful?
>   b institutionalisation is helpful for patients with mental disorders?
> 2 What is the alternative to institutionalising people with mental disorders, and is this any better?
> 3 Do you think the study was ethical?

1 Based on the results of the study, do you think
  a diagnostic classification was demonstrated to be reliable and useful?
  b institutionalisation is helpful for patients with mental disorders?

Despite the fact that 'schizophrenia in remission' is an unusual diagnosis according to Spitzer (1976), the study is widely held to have fulfilled its aim of showing
a the deficiencies of the classification system for mental disorder at the time (the DSM II) and
b the negative consequences of being labelled and institutionalised for mental disorder (see the medical model of abnormality for more details).

Studies like these led to pressure to revise and improve the accuracy of the classification systems and the quality of institutions for the mentally disordered.

However, it should be remembered that diagnostic classification has improved as the classification systems have developed. Rosenhan's pseudo-patients would probably not succeed in gaining admission to mental hospitals today (or would have to lie about a lot more!). Also classification aims to help those with mental disorders and, therefore, fulfils a potentially very useful function – medical diagnosis had, and still has, problems with classification, yet we would not think of rejecting it today. The classification systems have led to the development of many effective therapies and treatments which have helped to either cure, alleviate or control a wide variety of disorders.

2 What is the alternative to institutionalising people with mental disorders, and is this any better?

The alternative is care in the community, which involves providing treatment and support for those suffering from mental disorder under *more socially integrated*, naturalistic and less-controlling conditions, rather than in long-term institutions, wherever possible.

While those with very serious disorders or those who represent a danger to themselves and others (see 'sectioning' under the Mental Health Act, 1983) may require round-the-clock care, support and control, others may benefit from varying degrees of these factors. Care in the community can, therefore, take the form of
- short-term in-patient care in local hospitals or residential treatment programmes – these involve high degrees of support, control and/or therapy, but for shorter periods than in long-stay institutions
- half-way houses, 'family group' homes, night-care or sheltered housing – these involve higher degrees of support and less official therapeutic measures, but are still tied to less socially integrated residential arrangements.

  Individuals can indulge in productive and everyday activities during the day, e.g. employment, but still live with others with mental health difficulties and access to support is usually on hand from health-care staff.

- home care (ideally with respite care arrangements), day care, outpatient therapy at local hospitals or drop-in centres – these involve socially integrated, independent residence or home residence with relatives, with some access to therapy.

Community care in Britain and the USA developed as a response to
- the many problems of long-term institutionalisation for the mentally ill, e.g. as described by Rosenhan's study
- a humanistic questioning of the motives behind institutionalisation (see Szasz's argument – who does it benefit, society or the mentally disordered?)
- financial pressures to find a more efficient use of tax-payers' money (institutions are supposedly more expensive to run, but of course this depends on the quality of community care provided)

The therapeutic rationale for community care is that more normal living conditions and social integration will encourage greater independence, self-care skills, social skills, self-esteem, and 'normal' and productive interactions, activities, relationships and behaviour, compared to care in institutions.

The various methods of community care can more flexibly meet individual needs and abilities, since mental health problems differ in severity between individuals and over time. Work, friend and family relationships can be more readily maintained.
However, there are disadvantages, for example:
- problems are encountered in assessing, monitoring and financing individuals' mental health needs.
- the difficulties of diagnosing and treating mental disorders as well as insufficient government funding and local authority provision means some individuals may not receive all the support, control or therapy they need without the necessary contact with health professionals.
- practically, stigmatisation and prejudice against the mentally disordered may make social integration difficult. This is not helped by media publicity of the comparatively rare cases where released mentally disturbed individuals have attacked or murdered others.
- home care may become unbearably stressful for both relatives and the mentally disordered.

The above problems may lead to patients dropping out of care, not taking medication and becoming homeless.

3 Do you think the study was ethical?

The study involved deception, but it might be argued that the hospitals had the power not to be deceived and were in fact being tested in their jobs. In addition the study's ends (its valuable contribution) outweighed its slightly unethical means, and kept data confidentiality.

ROSENHAN ANAGRAMS

1 M O R E I S I N S	1
2 L E G A L B I L N	2
3 I N C H I P S O R H A Z E	3
4 S N O R E S L E E P S S W	4
5 D O P E U S S E T P A I N T	5
6 I D L E S T O N E S O N A R P A I	6

Thigpen & Cleckley (1954) – 'A case of multiple personality'

This article describes the case study of a 25-year-old married woman referred to two psychiatrists for severe headaches and blackouts but soon discovered to have a multiple personality. The article presents evidence for the existence of this previously rare condition in the subject in a cautious but convinced manner.

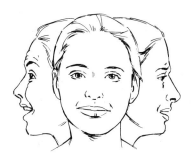

Summary of the case

The first few interviews of the woman, Eve White, only found her to have 'several important emotional difficulties' and a 'set of marital conflicts and personal frustrations'. The first indication of multiple personality came when the psychiatrists received a letter from Eve that she did not remember sending and which contained a note at the end written in a different and childish handwriting. On her next visit, after a period of unusual agitation, she reported that she occasionally had the impression that she heard a voice in her head – and then suddenly and spontaneously showed a dramatic change in her behaviour, revealing the character (and answering to the name) of Eve Black.

Over a period of 14 months and around 100 hours of interview time the two psychiatrists investigated the two Eves, first using hypnosis, but later without the need for it. Eve White was found not to have access to the awareness and memories of Eve Black (experiencing blackouts when Eve Black took over control), although the reverse was true for Eve Black (who often used the ability to disrupt Eve White's life by taking over and getting her into trouble or by giving her headaches).

Later, during the course of therapy, a third personality emerged called Jane – again suddenly and with a different set of characteristics. Jane had access to the consciousness of both Eves, but incomplete access to their memories before her emergence, and could only emerge through Eve White.

The authors admit the possibility of fakery, although they think it unlikely that someone acting over such a long period of time could avoid giving herself away even once. They argue for more research to answer some fundamental questions concerning the multiple-personality phenomena. Such questions relate to

- how different multiple-personality disorder is from ordinary hysterical conversions and dissociations or schizophrenia
- whether the personality was originally intact or had always been fragmented
- what is meant by the term 'personality'?

Evidence for the existence of multiple personality

Thigpen and Cleckley provide three different sources of evidence for the existence of a multiple personality in their patient.

Personality distinctions gained through interview

- Character – Eve White was described as self-controlled, serious, matter of fact and meticulously truthful. Eve Black, on the other hand, was childish, carefree, shallow, mischievous and a fluent liar.
- Attitudes – Eve White was distressed about her failing marriage and showed a warm love for her daughter. Eve Black, however, thought Eve White's distress and love was silly, and seemed 'immune to major affective events in human relationships'.
- Behaviour – Eve White behaved in a responsible and reserved way, while Eve Black was irresponsible, pleasure- and excitement-seeking, and sought the company of strangers to avoid discovery.
- Mannerisms – the authors stated that there were 'A thousand minute alterations in manner, gesture, expression, posture, of nuances in reflex…of glance' between the two Eves.

Personality distinctions gained through independent psychological testing

- Psychometric tests – the IQ of Eve White was 110, whereas the IQ of Eve Black was 104. Differences between the two were also found in memory function.
- Projective testing – the Rorschach projective ink-blot test was used (a trained psychologist interprets what the person being tested sees in ambiguous pictures of ink blots). It revealed that Eve Black showed regression and hysterical tendencies, but seemed to be far healthier than Eve White. Eve White showed repression, anxiety, obsessive–compulsive traits and an inability to deal with her hostility in the test. The psychologist was of the opinion that the tests revealed one personality at two stages of life – that Eve Black represented a regression to a carefree state as a way of dealing with her dislike of marriage and maternal pressures.

Personality distinctions gained through physiological EEG testing

Eve White and Jane were found to show similar Electroencephalograph readings, with Eve Black definitely distinguishable from the other two.

Exercise 61

1 What are the advantages and disadvantages of using the case-study method in this investigation?

2 How valid do you think the tests were that were used as sources of evidence for the existence of a multiple personality in the patient?

3 Overall, do you think that Eve was not faking it and multiple-personality disorder is a valid diagnosis? Why or why not?

4 'Eve White' was not the patient's real name. Why was a pseudonym used instead?

5 What do you think the legal implications would have been for Eve White if Eve Black had committed a crime?

1 What are the advantages and disadvantages of using the case-study method in this investigation?

The case-study method is used in therapeutic contexts in order to have the long-term, individual contact required to gain an in-depth understanding of the patient and, of course, to have the opportunity to help and monitor progress. However, such long-term contact may lead to a lack of objectivity on the therapist's part, especially when the aim is to try to help the patient through therapy rather than attempting rigorous experiments to test the possibility of fakery.

2 How valid do you think the tests were that were used as sources of evidence for the existence of a multiple personality in the patient?

Those tests that were conducted were of doubtful validity because they could have been affected by deliberate attempts to fake, except perhaps the EEG test although what the differences found represented is open to interpretation. Interviews and psychometric tests are self-report methods and projective tests can be of doubtful reliability due to the subjective nature of their interpretation.

3 Overall, do you think that Eve was not faking it and multiple-personality disorder is a valid diagnosis? Why or why not?

In addition to the test results, Eve's behaviour showed such remarkable consistency within characters over a long period of time that two psychiatrists were persuaded she was not deliberately faking. However, doubts about the validity are caused by Chris Sizeman (the real name of Eve) later revealing that she had other personalities before (and after) 1954, yet these were not detected or mentioned at the time.

Even if Eve was faking, multiple-personality disorder could still be a valid disorder which other people really suffer from. Further study of other cases has revealed that the diagnostic features of multiple-personality disorder (MPD) or dissociative-personality disorder (DPD) involve

- *dissociation of the self* – the self becomes divided into two or more distinct personalities, each with their separate thoughts, characteristics and memories
- *alternation of control by the personalities* – bodily control and access to consciousness switches between the personalities although some may be more dominant
- *amnesia and unconscious barriers between personalities* – there may be a mutual or one-way lack of conscious awareness and memory access between personalities. Some may experience 'blackouts' or lost time when the others take control, some can be directly aware of the other personalities' existence, thoughts and memories.

Some researchers argue that MPD is a genuine, spontaneous, pre-existing mental disorder that therapists merely discovered and classified. Theories of the origin of MPD, include

- psychodynamic theories involving defensive amnesia or the repression of traumatic childhood events
- social theories, such as self-hypnotic role-playing escapism as a coping mechanism
- cognitive theories, e.g. involving powerful state-dependent memory effects
- behavioural learning theories, e.g. selective reinforcement for different behaviours in different social contexts.

Evidence that MPD is genuine and spontaneous comes from

- numerous hours of interviews, observation and personality tests from many case studies
- physiological methods, e.g. electroencephalograms, galvanic skin responses, and brain scans

- the finding that the disorder is often developed in childhood and is associated with traumatic or disturbed family relationships (the causes far precede therapy). MPD is more common in women than men, which may reflect the higher level of childhood abuse suffered by girls than boys.
- the increased rates of MPD which may reflect increased public awareness of the disorder, that could have enabled or encouraged therapists and sufferers to more readily recognise the symptoms and seek or provide treatment for it.
- the fact that just because cases of MPD have been simulated and may have been faked to avoid responsibility for crimes, does not mean there are no genuine cases.

Alternatively, MPD may not be a spontaneous disorder but one created by therapists themselves (an iatrogenic phenomenon) through

- *treatment techniques which suggest the disorder* – the mistaken theoretical *expectation* that MPD can explain memory lapses or erratic behaviour may lead therapists to suggest its presence in the patient. Leading and suggestive interviews, selective attention and social reinforcement, and hypnotic suggestion and prompting may actually have created, maintained and legitimised MPD.
- *the construction of a mistaken diagnostic label* – this may have unconsciously led other people who heard about the disorder to think they have the problem, explain their memory lapses or troubled and poorly understood behaviour in terms of it, and thus seek treatment for it. Others may use the disorder to escape responsibility for their actions and consciously fake it.

Those who believe this view argue that

- self-report and non-experimental methods may have made it easier for therapists to have been duped or misled about the existence of MPD in the first place or to transmit their expectations to the patient.
- physiological differences could just reflect the different demands of role-playing different personalities and, of course, the therapist could still have created the personalities.
- False memories of early abuse could be invented by fakers of MPD (although some cases have been independently verified) or created by therapeutic suggestion and hypnosis (false memory syndrome).
- if MPD is due to spontaneous repression of abuse, escapism, state-dependent memory and selective reinforcement, it might be expected to occur more frequently than it does.
- cases of MPD have dramatically increased with media coverage and public awareness of it in recent times, and mostly in the USA rather than other countries (suggesting a culturally created disorder). The vast majority of MPD cases are reported by just a minority of therapists (are they specialised at diagnosing or creating MPD?).
- simulators can convincingly fake MPD (any differences could just be due to lack of practice) and if fakers recall memories they should not be able to, they can easily switch identities or create a new one.

4 'Eve White' was not the patient's real name. Why was a pseudonym used instead?

For ethical reasons – to protect the confidentiality of the data.

5 What do you think the legal implications would have been for Eve White if Eve Black had committed a crime?

Since some psychologists have testified that the switching of personalities in MPD is beyond conscious control, those suffering from it have been occasionally found not guilty of their crimes by courts in the USA.

62 | Eating disorders – symptoms, diagnosis and explanatory theories

Eating disorders like anorexia and bulimia are fairly recent arrivals to the classification manuals – appearing for the first time in the DSM III in 1980. There is debate over whether these disorders have always existed, but they do seem to have increased in prevalence in recent years and are ten times more common in women than men.

Anorexia nervosa

'Anorexia' comes from the Greek term for 'loss of appetite' and involves problems maintaining a normal body weight. It seems to affect 0.5 to 1% of females in adolescence to early adulthood. The DSM IV classification manual states that the symptoms below must be shown for the diagnosis to be made:

- Behavioural symptoms – a refusal to maintain a body weight normal for age and height (weight itself is less than 85% of that expected).
- Cognitive symptoms – distorted self-perception of body shape (over estimation of body size) and over-emphasis of its importance for self-esteem. Denial of the seriousness of the weight loss.
- Emotional symptoms – an intense fear of gaining weight even though obviously under-weight.
- Somatic symptoms – loss of body weight and absence of menstruation for 3 consecutive months.

The DSM IV also suggests two sub-types:

- The 'restricting type' maintains low body weight by refusing to eat and/or indulging in frequent exercise.
- The 'binge-eating/purging type' maintains low body weight by refusing to eat in combination with bingeing and purging (like bulimia but usually less frequently)

Bulimia nervosa

'Bulimia' is derived from the Greek for 'ox appetite' and involves binge eating followed by compensatory behaviour to rid the body of what has just been consumed. It is thought to affect around 1 to 3% of females in adolescence to early adulthood. The DSM IV states that the symptoms below must be shown for the classification to be made, and includes a 'non-purging' sub-type who binges but uses excessive physical exercise instead of purging to compensate.

Behavioural symptoms:

- Recurring binge eating – excessive quantities are consumed within a discrete period of time (e.g. 2 hours) without a sense of control over what or how much is eaten.
- Recurring inappropriate compensatory behaviour to prevent weight gain – such as self-induced vomiting, misuse of laxatives or fasting.
- Binge eating and compensatory behaviours occur on average at least twice a week for three months.

Cognitive symptoms:

- The self-image is overly influenced by body size and shape.

The main differences between the two disorders are that bulimia sufferers usually maintain their weight within the normal range (although bulimia causes much other damage to their bodies) and, despite some anorexia sufferers being obsessed with food and reporting hunger, bulimia involves an urge to overeat that often causes bingeing long before purging and other methods are used as compensations.

However, some researchers think anorexia and bulimia should be thought of as two variants of the same disorder, since they have many features in common, are often both found in the same person (anorexia can progress to bulimia with age), and have similar theories provided to explain them.

Explanatory theories of eating disorders

- *Genetics* – Family studies have shown that there is a higher risk of developing anorexia or bulimia if a first-degree relative suffers from it, while monozygotic (MZ) twin concordance studies have suggested there may be a stronger genetic link with anorexia than bulimia. Holland et al. (1984) found the likelihood of one identical (MZ) twin also getting *anorexia* if the other developed it was 55%, compared to 7% for non-identical, dizygotic (DZ) twins. Kendler et al. (1991) reported concordance rates of 23% for MZ twins and 8.7% for DZ twins with *bulimia*.

- *Physiology* – Early research indicated that disruption to the ventromedial or lateral areas of the hypothalamus could severely affect eating behaviour. Ablating the ventromedial hypothalamus in rats, for example, caused them to overeat until they became obese, while removal of the lateral hypothalamus caused them to refuse to eat. Set point theory suggests an imbalance in the relative influences of these areas of the hypothalamus may be involved in eating disorders. Eating disorders have been linked to depression and some studies have found lower levels of the neurotransmitter serotonin in sufferers of bulimia. The neurotransmitter noradrenaline and the hormone CCK-8 may also be involved.

- *Psychoanalytic theory* – has produced various explanations for eating disorders. The anorexic's refusal to eat has been interpreted as an unconscious denial of the adult role and wish to remain a child (in figure at least) provoked by the development of sexual characteristics in puberty. The timing of onset in anorexia and the loss of menstruation support this idea. Another psychoanalytic interpretation is that anorexics are unconsciously rejecting their bodies as a reaction to sexual abuse in childhood.

- *Cognitive theory* – Cognitive psychologists have suggested that irrational attitudes and beliefs, and distorted perception are involved in eating disorders. These beliefs may concern unrealistic ideals or perception of body shape, or irrational attitudes towards eating habits and dieting (e.g. the disinhibition hypothesis – once a diet has been broken, one might as well break it completely by bingeing). Cognitive researchers have also proposed that sufferers of eating disorders may be seeking control and perfection in their lives to an excessively idealistic extent.

- *Learning theory* – explains eating disorders in terms of reinforcement consequences for eating behaviour. Social praise or respect from a society that places a high value on slim female appearance may reward weight loss or control. Alternatively, the attention and concern shown towards someone with an eating disorder may be reinforcing. Social learning theory would suggest that thin or dieting role models would be imitated, while some learning theorists have proposed that a weight gain phobia is involved in eating disorders.

Exercise 62

1 What does the finding that the highest concordance rate for eating disorders in identical twins is 55% imply for the genetic theory of these disorders?

2 When positive *correlations* between physiological differences in the brain and eating disorders have been found, why is cause and effect difficult to determine?

3 If those with eating disorders are seeking perfection, what areas of their lives other than their weight might be affected and where might this drive come from?

4 What cultures and social groups might be particularly exposed to environmental learning experiences that encourage a thin appearance and thus be more likely to develop eating disorders?

Answers 62.1 – 62.4

1 What does the finding that the highest concordance rate for eating disorders in identical twins is 55% imply for the genetic theory of these disorders?

Since concordance rates are nowhere near 100% for monozygotic (identical) twins, it implies that the genetic theory on its own is an incomplete explanation and eating disorders are not completely genetically determined. This means that environmental influences or triggers do seem to be involved, one is not doomed by genes to develop an eating disorder. In fact, some twin studies have not always controlled for the effect of similar shared environments (e.g. by using adoption studies) which further weakens some of the genetic evidence, or have found more environmental than genetic influences in eating disorders.

It is also uncertain what is actually inherited to cause the eating disorder, some researchers suggest personality traits such as perfectionism, others a predisposition to inherit mental disorder in general.

2 When positive *correlations* between physiological differences in the brain and eating disorders have been found, why is cause and effect difficult to determine?

The biological cause and effect of eating disorders is difficult to determine since the physical disorders (e.g. differences in brain neurotransmitters) found in anorexia and bulimia may be an *effect* of starvation and purging rather than a cause.

Post-mortem studies have not revealed damage in the hypothalamus of those with eating disorders, however anti-depressants that increase serotonin levels have been found to be effective in treating bulimia as well.

3 If those with eating disorders are seeking perfection, what areas of their lives other than their weight might be affected and where might this drive come from?

Dura and Bornstein (1989) found this drive for perfection in hospitalised anorexics extended to academic achievements, which were much higher than their IQ scores predicted.

Some researchers have suggested that the drive for control and perfection may be caused by certain family influences, and have found that the families of children with eating disorders have the following characteristics:

- They are less emotional and nurturing – which may lead to eating disorders developing as an attention-gaining tactic.

- They are overly protective – restricting independence may force the child to assert its own control and autonomy through the eating disorder.
- They have middle class, overachieving parents – whose high expectations of success may lead their children to overly idealistic notions of success in matters of weight control.

Other researchers argue that the drive may come from broader social and cultural influences than just the family, e.g. televised images of perfection (see below).

4 What cultures and social groups might be particularly exposed to environmental learning experiences that encourage a thin appearance and thus be more likely to develop eating disorders?

The idea that cultural exposure to socially desirable conceptions of body shape is responsible for eating disorders has received much support. For example, anorexia and bulimia occur most in

- cultures where thinness is socially desirable, e.g. North America, Western Europe and Japan. Indeed evidence suggests that immigrants to these countries show higher levels of eating disorder than their native countries.
- western women – physical attractiveness is the best predictor of self-esteem in western girls.
- groups where thinness is particularly valued, e.g. ballet dancers, models and gymnasts.

While cultural and family experiences do seem correlated with eating disorders, it is difficult to always work out the cause and effect. For example, those with anorexia already may choose to become ballet dancers, models, etc. rather than develop the disorder as a result of these professions. The increased prevalence in eating disorders in recent years could be due to the media actually influencing the frequency of the disorder (with its increasing exposure of thin models, actresses, etc.) or due to increasing media publicity drawing attention to the disorder and thus making referral and diagnosis more common. There are some who argue that the latter is responsible for the rise and that eating disorders have always existed.

In addition, not all people will react in the same way to these experiences, some may under-eat, others over-eat and yet others show no change in diet. Whether individuals are susceptible to environmental triggers for eating disorders may depend on whether they have an inherited (genetic) predisposition to develop anorexia or bulimia.

EATING DISORDERS CROSSWORD

1. The term for consuming excessive quantities in a short time without a sense of control (5/6)
2. The hypothesis that once a diet has been broken, one might as well break it completely (13)
3. The type of anorexic who maintains low body weight by exercising and/or refusing to eat (11)
4. The likelihood of one twin also getting anorexia if the other has it is termed the _____ rate (11)
5. The term for twins that are identical (11)
6. Anorexics have a _____ self-perception of body shape (they over-estimate body size) (9)
7. This affects eating behaviour according to learning theory (13)
8. A brain area involved in eating behaviour (12)
9. This is absent for 3 months in anorexics (12)
10. A defence mechanism refusal to accept (6)
11. A neurotransmitter possibly involved in eating disorders (9)
12. Inappropriate compensatory behaviour to prevent weight gain (7)

Answers to review activities

SAMPLING WORDSEARCH (page 24)

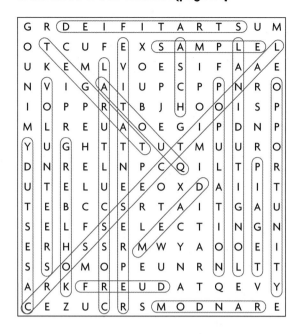

DEREGOWSKI CROSSWORD (page 26)

```
            1
            C
  2 E T H N O C E N T R I C
    3 O V E R L A P
  4 A N T H R O P O L O G I S T S
5 T W O D I M E N S I O N A L
    6 U N I V E R S A L
      7 A N E C D O T A L
        8 H U D S O N
        9 S P L I T
      10 A N T E L O P E
    11 L I N G U A F R A N C A
        12 T R I D E N T
        13 Z A M B I A N
      14 F A M I L I A R
```

RESEARCH METHODS ANAGRAMS (page 31)

```
1  M O D E
2  V A L I D I T Y
3  N O M I N A L
4  R E L I A B I L I T Y
5  H I S T O G R A M
6  C O R R E L A T I O N
7  S T A N D A R D I S A T I O N
8  O P E R A T I O N A L I S A T I O N
9  O P P O R T U N I T Y   S A M P L E
10 N O R M A L   D I S T R I B U T I O N
```

RESEARCH METHODS CROSSWORD (page 31)

```
                  1
                  D
  2 M A T C H E D P A I R S
    3 O R D E R E F F E C T S
4 R E P E A T E D M E A S U R E S
    5 O N E T A I L E D
      6 R A N D O M
  7 D E P E N D E N T
  8 P A R T I C I P A N T
    9 B A R C H A R T
   10 E X T R A N E O U S
11 S C A T T E R G R A M
   12 D E V I A T I O N
     13 P I E C H A R T
   14 Q U A L I T A T I V E
   15 D O U B L E B L I N D
   16 S E L F R E P O R T
     17 M E D I A N
   18 S E L F S E L E C T I N G
   19 L O N G I T U D I N A L
     20 O R D I N A L
 21 S I G N I F I C A N C E
   22 C A S E S T U D Y
```

FREUD CROSSWORD (page 40)

```
              1
              D
      2 I D
  3 H Y S T E R I A
  4 M A N I F E S T
      5 E G O
      6 A N A L
7 O E D I P U S C O M P L E X
      8 E R O S
  9 S U B L I M A T I O N
 10 S U P E R E G O
11 U N C O N S C I O U S
     12 P H A L L I C
   13 O R A L
   14 A N N A O
 15 F I X A T I O N
 16 R E P R E S S I O N
   17 D R E A M S
   18 P L E A S U R E
```

FREUD ANAGRAMS (page 40)

1	L	A	T	E	N	C	Y							
2	E	L	E	C	T	R	A							
3	E	G	O	-	I	D	E	A	L					
4	T	H	A	N	A	T	O	S						
5	S	Y	M	B	O	L	I	S	M					
6	C	A	S	T	R	A	T	I	O	N				
7	R	E	G	R	E	S	S	I	O	N				
8	D	I	S	P	L	A	C	E	M	E	N	T		
9	P	R	E	C	O	N	S	C	I	O	U	S		
10	R	E	A	C	T	I	O	N		F	O	R	m	A	T	I	O	N

GARDNER AND GARDNER CROSSWORD (page 56)

1 (down)
2 W A S H O E
3 I N S T R U M E N T A L
4 F I F T E E N
5 T H I R T Y
6 I M I T A T I O N
7 P R O D U C T I V I T Y
8 B A B B L I N G
9 D I F F E R E N T I A T I O N
10 T R A N S F E R
11 T I C K L I N G
12 S H A P I N G
13 R O U T I N E

BANDURA et al. CROSSWORD (page 60)

1 (down)
2 B O B O D O L L
3 T E N
4 M A T C H E D P A I R S
5 T W E N T Y
6 P A R T I A L
7 S E V E N T Y T W O
8 S A M E S E X
9 R E L I A B I L I T Y
10 N O N A G G R E S S I V E
11 V E R B A L
12 L A B O R A T O R Y
13 C O N T R O L

SAMUEL AND BRYANT CROSSWORD (page 68)

1 (down)
2 D E C A L A G E
3 E R R O R S
4 D E M A N D
5 M A S S
6 F I X E D A R R A Y
7 F O U R
8 S E V E N
9 B L A N K
10 T W O
11 L I Q U I D V O L U M E
12 O N E
13 N U M B E R

BARON-COHEN et al. CROSSWORD (page 73)

1 (down)
2 R E A L I T Y
3 E I G H T Y
4 F I F T E E N
5 M E M O R Y
6 N A T U R A L
7 S A L L Y A N N E
8 Z E R O
9 A R T I F I C I A L
10 N A M I N G
11 B E L I E F
12 D O W N S
13 S E C O N D O R D E R

MODELS OF MEMORY CROSSWORD (page 83)

1 (down)
2 P R O C E D U R A L
3 C E N T R A L E X E C U T I V E
4 V I S U O S P A T I A L
5 F R E E R E C A L L
6 C O N C U R R E N T
7 M U L T I S T O R E
8 P R I M A C Y
9 A N T E R O G R A D E
10 S E M A N T I C
11 A C O U S T I C A L L Y
12 E L A B O R A T I O N
13 S T R U C T U R A L
14 A R T I F I C I A L
15 P H O N O L O G I C A L
16 L O N G T E R M

MEMORY MODEL ANAGRAMS (page 83)

EFFORT

RECENCY EFFECT

DISTINCTIVENESS

PHONETIC PROCESSING

PHONOLOGICAL STORE

ARTICULATORY

CONTROL SYSTEM

LOFTUS AND PALMER CROSSWORD (page 91)

2. LABORATORY
3. INDEPENDENT
4. SEVEN
5. SPEED
6. DISTORTED
7. CONTROL
8. STUDENTS
9. ONE WEEK
10. BROKEN
11. LEADING
12. CONTACTED
13. SMASHED

FORGETTING AND APPLICATIONS CROSSWORD (page 92)

2. INTERFERENCE
3. CAPACITY
4. DISPLACEMENT
5. WORDS
6. LEADING
7. RECONSTRUCTIVE
8. RECOGNITION
9. REPRESSION
10. INACCESSIBLE
11. FLASHBULB
12. CONTEXT DEPENDENT
13. POST EVENT
14. SCHEMA
15. LOFTUS
16. SERIAL
17. ENGRAM
18. RETROACTIVE
19. UNPLEASANT
20. DECAY

FORGETTING AND APPLICATIONS ANAGRAMS (page 92)

1. HYPNOSIS
2. BARTLETT
3. AGE REGRESSION
4. CONFABULATION
5. RECOVERED MEMORY
6. ENCODING SPECIFICITY
7. WEAPONS FOCUS EFFECT
8. PETERSON AND PETERSON
9. PROACTIVE INTERFERENCE
10. STATE-DEPENDENT FORGETTING

SOCIAL PSYCHOLOGICAL APPROACH ANAGRAMS (page 94)

1. ROLES
2. NORMS
3. SURVEY
4. CULTURE
5. REWARD POWER
6. FIELD EXPERIMENT
7. LEGITIMATE POWER
8. SOCIAL IMPACT THEORY
9. SOCIAL CONSTRUCTIONISM
10. SOCIAL COMPARISON THEORY

HANEY, BANKS & ZIMBARDO CROSSWORD (page 96)

2. PRISONER
3. DISPOSITIONAL
4. FUNCTIONAL
5. FOURTEEN
6. GUARD
7. QUALITATIVE
8. SIX
9. RANDOMLY
10. CONSENT
11. STANFORD
12. PATHOLOGICAL

HANEY, BANKS & ZIMBARDO ANAGRAMS (page 96)

1	U	N	I	F	O	R	M					
2	E	M	A	S	C	U	L	A	T	I	O	N
3	D	E	H	U	M	A	N	I	S	A	T	I	O	N
4	M	U	N	D	A	N	E		R	E	A	L	I	S	M
5	A	R	B	I	T	R	A	R	Y		C	O	N	T	R	O	L

OBEDIENCE CROSSWORD (page 104)

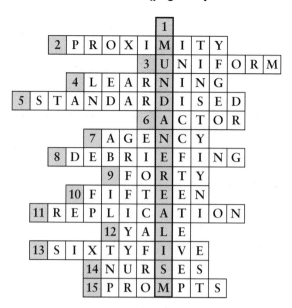

2 PROXIMITY
3 UNIFORM
4 LEARNING
5 STANDARDISED
6 ACTOR
7 AGENCY
8 DEBRIEFING
9 FORTY
10 FIFTEEN
11 REPLICATION
12 YALE
13 SIXTYFIVE
14 NURSES
15 PROMPTS

PILIAVIN et al. CROSSWORD (page 98)

2 BLACK
3 NEWYORK
4 DIFFUSION
5 COSTS
6 REWARDS
7 CANE
8 FIELD
9 SEVENTY
10 DRUNK
11 AROUSAL

PREJUDICE CROSSWORD (page 111)

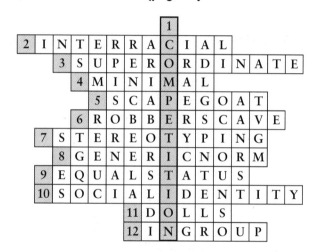

2 INTERRACIAL
3 SUPERORDINATE
4 MINIMAL
5 SCAPEGOAT
6 ROBBERSCAVE
7 STEREOTYPING
8 GENERICNORM
9 EQUALSTATUS
10 SOCIALIDENTITY
11 DOLLS
12 INGROUP

CONFORMITY WORDSEARCH (page 100)

N	U	D	L	E	I	F	H	C	T	U	R	C
O	E	W	Y	E	U	T	N	R	I	S	G	U
I	S	L	B	M	V	A	O	Z	N	H	A	K
T	L	H	A	I	J	I	I	S	F	T	M	R
A	O	D	E	C	E	P	T	I	O	N	B	E
S	S	M	E	R	T	F	A	A	R	C	I	F
I	S	H	C	S	I	U	C	R	M	A	G	E
L	E	O	N	H	O	F	I	T	A	R	U	R
A	N	P	A	X	K	E	F	I	T	L	O	E
N	N	S	I	E	K	D	I	F	I	Q	U	N
R	E	P	L	I	C	A	T	I	O	N	S	T
E	J	M	P	B	E	R	N	C	N	O	P	U
T	A	E	M	A	H	N	E	I	A	S	C	H
N	L	P	O	E	Y	I	D	A	L	M	L	K
I	C	J	C	N	U	T	I	L	F	I	G	A

RAINE et al. CROSSWORD (page 117)

2 OCCIPITAL
3 PREFRONTAL
4 GLUCOSE
5 SUBCORTICAL
6 TRACER
7 ANGULARGYRUS
8 TEMPORAL
9 FORTYONE
10 MALE
11 ASYMMETRY
12 URINE
13 DYSFUNCTION
14 PRECISION
15 CAUTION
16 SCHIZOPHRENIA
17 CONTINUOUS

METHODS OF THE PHYSIOLOGICAL APPROACH (page 115)

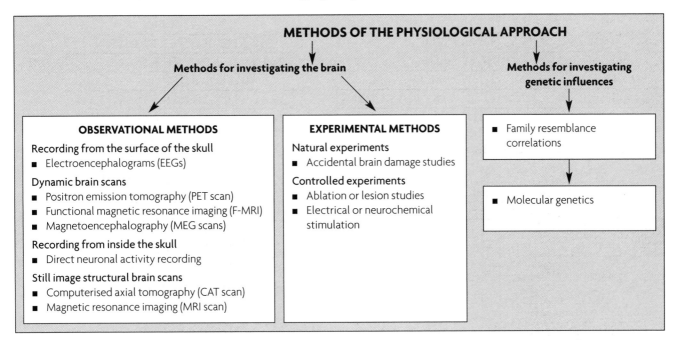

METHODS OF THE PHYSIOLOGICAL APPROACH

Methods for investigating the brain

Methods for investigating genetic influences

OBSERVATIONAL METHODS

Recording from the surface of the skull
- Electroencephalograms (EEGs)

Dynamic brain scans
- Positron emission tomography (PET scan)
- Functional magnetic resonance imaging (F-MRI)
- Magnetoencephalography (MEG scans)

Recording from inside the skull
- Direct neuronal activity recording

Still image structural brain scans
- Computerised axial tomography (CAT scan)
- Magnetic resonance imaging (MRI scan)

EXPERIMENTAL METHODS

Natural experiments
- Accidental brain damage studies

Controlled experiments
- Ablation or lesion studies
- Electrical or neurochemical stimulation

- Family resemblance correlations

- Molecular genetics

SCHACHTER AND SINGER CROSSWORD (page 119)

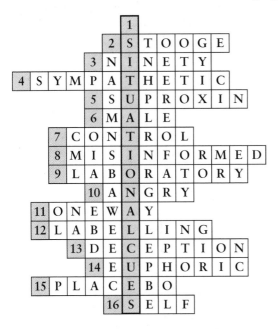

1 S
2 STOOGE
3 NINETY
4 SYMPATHETIC
5 SUPROXIN
6 MALE
7 CONTROL
8 MISINFORMED
9 LABORATORY
10 ANGRY
11 ONEWAY
12 LABELLING
13 DECEPTION
14 EUPHORIC
15 PLACEBO
16 SELF

SPERRY ANAGRAMS (page 122)

1 EPILEPSY
2 DECONNECTION
3 CORPUS CALLOSUM
4 DOMINANT HEMISPHERE

DEMENT AND KLEITMAN CROSSWORD (page 122)

1 R
2 OCULARGRAM
3 DURATION
4 ENCEPHALOGRAPH
5 VERTICAL
6 DISTANT

SLEEP AND DREAMS CROSSWORD (page 127)

1 S
2 DISGUISED
3 PREDATORS
4 CONSOLIDATION
5 MEANINGLESS
6 SYNTHESIS
7 ACTIVATION
8 MANIFEST
9 SOLUTIONS
10 DREAMING
11 RESTORATION
12 FETUSES
13 CORTEX
14 SURVIVAL

BODY RHYTHMS CROSSWORD (page 127)

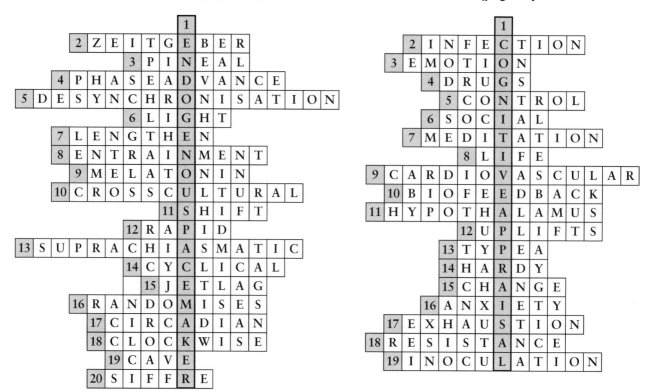

2. ZEITGEBER
3. PINEAL
4. PHASEADVANCE
5. DESYNCHRONISATION
6. LIGHT
7. LENGTHEN
8. ENTRAINMENT
9. MELATONIN
10. CROSSCULTURAL
11. SHIFT
12. RAPID
13. SUPRACHIASMATIC
14. CYCLICAL
15. JETLAG
16. RANDOMISES
17. CIRCADIAN
18. CLOCKWISE
19. CAVE
20. SIFFRE

STRESS CROSSWORD (page 131)

2. INFECTION
3. EMOTION
4. DRUGS
5. CONTROL
6. SOCIAL
7. MEDITATION
8. LIFE
9. CARDIOVASCULAR
10. BIOFEEDBACK
11. HYPOTHALAMUS
12. UPLIFTS
13. TYPEA
14. HARDY
15. CHANGE
16. ANXIETY
17. EXHAUSTION
18. RESISTANCE
19. INOCULATION

STRESS OVERVIEW (page 131)

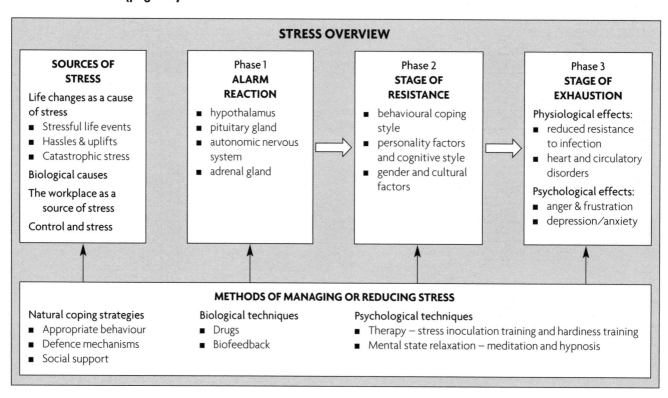

STRESS OVERVIEW

SOURCES OF STRESS

Life changes as a cause of stress
- Stressful life events
- Hassles & uplifts
- Catastrophic stress

Biological causes

The workplace as a source of stress

Control and stress

Phase 1 ALARM REACTION
- hypothalamus
- pituitary gland
- autonomic nervous system
- adrenal gland

Phase 2 STAGE OF RESISTANCE
- behavioural coping style
- personality factors and cognitive style
- gender and cultural factors

Phase 3 STAGE OF EXHAUSTION

Physiological effects:
- reduced resistance to infection
- heart and circulatory disorders

Psychological effects:
- anger & frustration
- depression/anxiety

METHODS OF MANAGING OR REDUCING STRESS

Natural coping strategies
- Appropriate behaviour
- Defence mechanisms
- Social support

Biological techniques
- Drugs
- Biofeedback

Psychological techniques
- Therapy – stress inoculation training and hardiness training
- Mental state relaxation – meditation and hypnosis

HODGES AND TIZARD CROSSWORD (page 140)

1
2 BOWLBY
3 ADOPTED
4 SIXTEEN
5 EIGHT
6 INSTITUTIONALISED
7 RESTORED
8 NATURAL
9 SOCIALLYDESIRABLE
10 SOCIALDIFFICULTY
11 THIRTYNINE
12 ASCALE
13 SCHOOL

EATING DISORDERS CROSSWORD (page 150)

1
2 DISINHIBITION
3 RESTRICTIVE
4 CONCORDANCE
5 MONOZYGOTIC
6 DISTORTED
7 REINFORCEMENT
8 HYPOTHALAMUS
9 MENSTRUATION
10 DENIAL
11 SEROTONIN
12 PURGING

MODELS OF ABNORMALITY ANAGRAMS (page 144)

1 ORGANIC CAUSES
2 PSYCHOPATHOLOGY
3 CHILDHOOD TRAUMA
4 INSTITUTIONALISATION
5 INSIGHT-BASED THERAPY
6 MALADAPTIVE RESPONSES
7 IRRATIONAL PERCEPTIONS
8 UNCONSCIOUS REPRESSION
9 ELECTRO-CONVULSIVE THERAPY

ROSENHAN ANAGRAMS (page 146)

1 REMISSION
2 LABELLING
3 SCHIZOPHRENIA
4 POWERLESSNESS
5 PSEUDO PATIENTS
6 DEPERSONALISATION

Index

*Main entries are in **bold**.*